AMERICA
COME AND GET IT

KASALOBI

STRATTON
—PRESS—
Publishing Life

AMERICA COME AND GET IT
Copyright © 2021 **Kasalobi**

Stratton Press Publishing
831 N Tatnall Street Suite M #188,
Wilmington, DE 19801
www.stratton-press.com
1-888-323-7009

ISBN (Paperback): 978-1-64895-410-8
ISBN (Ebook): 978-1-64895-411-5

Printed in the United States of America

Without any doubt, it is accepted as true that the only way to break through in life is to go to America. Once in the United States, Mr. Kasalobi found it the hard way. He stumbled on an unbreakable truth that in America, people do not gather money from trees. The only thing he gathered for sure was a huge legal fight to regain back the custody of his two daughters. Loylla, his youngest, was eight months old when Sheebah, their mother, abandoned them. Eight years later, armed with nothing but lies, she came back to kidnap both of them. The Hurst Police Department believed her. Child Protective Services decided to close their eyes to the abuses. They ignored the cruel mistreatments these two little girls were going through. And the family court doubted Mr. Kasalobi's truthfulness. Worse was the fact that the real harm was coming not from him but from the hand of their own mother. Instead of that promised honey running in the American rivers to be fetched he was made to believe in, Mr. Kasalobi realized that he was now alone in the court of the law, and that court of the law was threatening to take his daughters away. But for his daughters, he did not hesitate to move skies and to empty water in seas. Despite all that, it was a lost fight for the reason it was believed girls are better off with their mother. As days went by, the fighting became bigger and tangled itself on one side, the mother's side. Mr. Kasalobi did not get desperate. He did not give up either. He thought alone doing nothing but legal battles against everyone involved, including every established institution possible. At the end of the day, did he get both children back? This is what *America, Come and Get It* is all about.

Dedicated to you my brother Commander Kalenga Kasongo, I did not forget. I am always grateful to you.

To all my children, life has a value only in the contents and implications that it has for others.

CONTENTS

PART I

KIDNAPPING

I hope you never fear those mountains in the distance
And never settle for the path of least resistance.
—Lee Ann Womack

CHAPTER 1

STALKING

As I was trying to reach Glenn Rose apartment, driving on 183 West, I noticed again, through the retro mirror of my friend Eight, the menacing lights of the blue Nissan. I did not have a reason to worry about anything, but I felt that there was a reason that car was directly behind me. I became concerned. To verify a fact, I brutally drove across into the center lane. Not only it followed me, it also dangerously aligned itself behind me. That blue Nissan was driven by a person whose intent of doing me harm was written all over. Because of the way he recklessly changed these two lanes to reach me, my doubts got confirmed: I was followed, clearly followed. To establish my theory one more time, I slowly moved to the faster lane. Once more, the blue Nissan traversed over. The way it crossed over did not make me suspicious anymore because it aligned itself behind me.

I decided to pass the city of Irving by strictly driving on its highway's second lane. I was westbound anyway, and at that time of the day, the traffic was at its peak. It was safe that I stopped testing the driver behind me since we were already driving bumper to bumper. For a little while there, that blue Nissan hid perfectly in the rear of an eighteen-wheeler Volvo truck. They both were directly behind me. It did not bother me anyhow; I have been walking tall, with a serene conscience. I did not have anything in me to be blamed for. While driving my 1998 Ford Escort that I usually called my friend Eight, I turned my head around numerously and looked behind.

My friend Eight was a well-known car. People recognized it easily. From the first day I bought it in 1998, I used it as a taxi for five years in a row. I then turned it into a learner's driving car after that. I used it in L'Africana, my driving school. Since 1998, we had each other; we visited the all United States mainland together, excluding Florida. We went to Mexico one time and in numerous occasions in Canada. I thought it had a spirit of its own. It protected me against my own insanities. When I was drunk, it drove itself with me inside, from different places, and dropped me safely inside my apartment complex. I used its wagon as my secondary bed when I was sad, felt low in fortune, or simply when I needed to stay away from the usual routines. I utilized it also for recreation purposes, most of the time when I couldn't lay down and sleep in my bed. I never let anyone borrow it even when it was extremely needed. It had been there for me in all circumstances of four seasons since '98. This was the main reason I called it "my friend Eight." I knew at that point that in it, my children and I will be protected against the person following me behind.

I turned around and looked at my friend Eight retro visor mirror again, not because I was scared but because I was living the normal time in my life. This looking over the shoulders was one of the things I had to do, a thing that I have done frequently. It is a technique African elders copied from the nature of things. In this present case, they learnt it from looking at the feline's behavior, especially the leopard. In the African savanna, the leopard is not the strongest animal. It is not an animal that easily attains high velocity in running business either, but it continued to exist for being an explosively smart cat. It exited because it looks above its shoulders. The leopard doesn't climb a curved tree. It doesn't go up a bole of trees with lower branches or with a compromised trunk. It does so to avoid a lion going up after him and confiscates its catch. The leopard is never scared of walking night; it trusts its eyesight because they are ardent, many times greater than what any other animal ever had. The leopard's eyes help him swim in crocodile's muddy water. They can pierce through the darkness. So just like the leopard, trusting all senses I was equipped with, I was going forward and looking behind at same time. I was looking over my shoulders. Not because I was scared, but because of the pledge of survival. I had my daughters with me. I was doing what a male animal, in its good spirits, would have been doing in this case.

I have personally never seen a leopard do it, but brave and wise African elders who observed this behavior took the necessary time to transmit this knowledge, by initiation, to young bloods that we were. They did so to guarantee our survival. Since then, I exactly lived like Mr. Leo. I stayed alive. I stayed alive and lived on. I was looking in my car mirrors because of the world I am living in, a modernized jungle. I had to look because my guts were whispering to the ears of my spirit that I was in danger.

Then again, people do drive behind other people all the time. In a turn of strange moments, they even do take the same corners and same curves from the same route. That coincidence gives you the impression of being followed around. I stepped on the gas pedal, veered to the right, and disappeared on Highway 10. I peacefully entered Hurst, Texas, so I thought.

The sky was blue and clear. For hunters, it was a good day to go fishing. In fact, it was one of these nice days of June and a perfect afternoon to go out, under the sun, and just laze around. I adjusted my retro mirror one more time. The blue Nissan was not behind me, it disappeared from my sight. I composed with my conscious. That stopped me from experiencing a series of complicated feelings.

From Pipeline, I entered into Bellaire Drive relaxed. I looked behind one more time, no Nissan around. I relaxed more. I loosened my body and mind. In order to give enough driving room to the small truck that was directly behind me, I accelerated and swiftly parked my friend Eight in my usual spot, at Glen Rose Apartment. I asked my two little girls to take groceries inside. Suddenly the blue Nissan zoomed in. He blocked us in as I was opening my door to step out. The driver forced his way in; he placed himself between my friend Eight and the small truck behind me. Doing so, he also blocked us out. That confirmed what I was seeing: he was not minding his own business, he was up to no good. By the time I completely opened my driver's side door, two ladies were running toward us. I twisted my body on my left side, which was not an easy task to do. I saw a heavyset, short, and old black woman picking up Loylla from the ground. She was the driver of the Nissan. The woman was not worth to be looked at twice. At this point, my Dell Inspiron laptop was already hanging on my left shoulder. I dropped it on the ground. I stepped forward to cut that black woman's means of access to the blue Nissan. I was delayed by the computer belt that, at that given moment, chose to twist my right foot. Meanwhile, the lady from the passenger seat had Tabô already lifted from the ground. She was white. She was directing herself toward the car door she deliberately left ajar. I saw her forcing Tabô in.

She was wearing a blue jeans knee-short skirt, a red muscle shirt under which one could see a dirty white bra. That piece of clothing was holding her together. The woman was very huge. The rest of her upper body was the exact details of a person who likes to visit fast-food restaurants. Both ladies entered the blue Nissan. They closed the car doors. I untangled the computer belt from my foot, closed the opened car door that was on my way, and put myself in a position of force, a position from which I knew I would be able to reach my daughters' kidnappers. Visibly, they locked themselves in. The black lady started the engine and begun to back up. I rushed in and stood behind the moving car.

She stopped. Not because I was obstructing her but because she was not able to go much further; cars were parked behind them. She drove forward, I ran at the front of the Nissan. She stopped at one-inch distance from both my legs. Because of the way she blocked me in earlier, my friend Eight was now on her way. She moved back again. I followed that maneuver without blinking. I knew that her only way out from there was through me. I started moving all my muscles, including the one from my throat. My voice vibrated.

People started to gather around. I knew at this point she will not run me over. They were watching her, trying to maneuver the car back and forth. Suddenly, she burned her tires. To an African that I am, that was a warning. It was something closer to what a water buffalo would do before attacking. Without moving her car, she burned her front tires one more time. The air got mixed to the smoke and to the smell of the squishing rubber. That did not impress me; I stood still and held my ground. The Nissan was desperately roaring. I was sure the driver won't unleash and run me over; at least that was what I was thinking at that moment. I stood there reading the face of the black woman who was behind the steering wheel; she was serious. She burned her front tires again, and I saw in that act, her last warning. Suddenly, she released her brakes. Like a cape buffalo, the Nissan came rushing forward. I stood my ground, still. She stopped at one-hair distance from my knees. This time, I ran her last nerve out. She lowered her window and screamed a litany of unheard cursing words at me.

That rain of rudeness alarmed my neighbors more than the smoke that was coming from her exhaust pipe and her driving back and forth. It made the crowd grow bigger. Everyone began paying attention to the war that was slowly developing. Afraid of that swarm of now-friendly people gathering around her car, the driver burned her tires once again. She drove forward. I thought it was the last. She suddenly stopped. People were still screaming, some telling her to stop, others yelling at me, and the rest wanted me to step aside. I remembered when my father and I encountered a horde of five lions and he stood his ground for me.

We were moving farm products on bikes. Mine got a flat tire. We sat down to fix it. Just like that, Pa told me not to move. He said that there was a smell of a lion in the air. He slowly stood up to investigate. From where we were, I counted five lions sitting at about a hundred feet. They were there, lazing around when we stopped. Since they weren't doing a thing, the wind hid their breathing to us, and we confused their bodies' color to the grass and to the yellow stubbles. The lion with a black regal mane stood up; he started to growl, just the way the Nissan was doing, only with real menace this time. He looked very big and protective. Slowly, Pa hid me behind his back; he shielded my body against his. He did not move and did not step back.

Lions rarely attack human beings. When they do, they start with the weak. In this case, that growling lion could have started with me if it was not for my pa. I was a child, the weaker of both of us. Pa did not step aside; his body language did not show he was scared of the animal. He stood taller than the lion.

"Mr. Lion, this is my son. I have a wife and more children in the village. I am sure those are your wife and children. I will protect my son with my life. If you touch him, my village and I will hunt down your family. We will kill your children one by one. I will make sure to it that I personally kill your wife. You will be the last to die for a simple reason that it will be my desire to see you feel the pain, the same pain I would feel if your paw touches and mauls my child. Now, to avoid that tragedy, go your way and my village won't move a muscle against your family," my pa said.

The lion with a black regal mane roared, as if he agreed with my pa. Those sitting down stood up as if they were in choir. It seemed that he asked them to do so. At that point, I felt like all ten holes of my body were about to lose their natural brakes and leak. The big lion roared again; he gave some kind of order and turned around. The pack stepped after him. They all followed their leader and left.

I stood up in front of that Nissan despite the crowd yelling at me. Just the way Pa did it against lions, I challenged death by car. I was not nuts, and I did it for my children. I was not about to let my daughters go, kidnapped by these two ladies. The driver blew the horn. I was pretty sure that when she drives, she won't stop this time. I did not care. The blue Nissan vibrated. It got released forward. The front bumper hit the lower side of my right leg, instantly lifting me in the air. I landed hard on the top of the hood. My right elbow stroked the metal. I felt it getting burned by the heat from the engine. I struggled hard and barely reached the far left edge of the hood. I held myself on the base of the windshield wipers. Trying to knock me off, she brutally stopped the car. I held on. She went back and forth and stopped again. Nothing happened. She then decided to rock her car up by repeatedly stepping on brakes and releasing them. My grips stayed firm. She was not able to drop me down, on the pavement, as she wanted to. I continued lying on the top of her hood.

Shanaqua Rangel, my lady neighbor, one among the crowd, who was watching like everyone, started to hit the top roof of the Nissan without fear. Using her Michoacán Latina accent, she called upon the black lady to stop her craziness. She yelled at her and yelled more. The driver did not wake up. Like everyone who was present, Gilbert Velasquez, her boyfriend, was also saying "Stop" numerously. Because the word "Stop" was so loudly pronounced with his Mexican accent and on the top of his lungs, it seemed at a certain point that he was saying "Jopp, Jopp, Jopp." I thought he was calling Jopp to help out. Jopp was the muscular man who lived upstairs from my apartment. He was their common friend. Negrita and Amy, their other common friend, were also loudly shouting, but the driver continued to ignore them.

With my right hand extended, the driver saw me reaching my phone from my pants back pocket. I dialed 911. The dispatcher responded. She asked me what my emergency was. With a loud voice, I begged her to send the police over.

"Two ladies in a blue Nissan just kidnapped my girls. They are now trying to kill me. They hit me already, using their car as weapon. They are trying to run me over. Please send the police at 787 E. Pecan Street before they achieve this."

I described both ladies, what they were wearing, and how they looked like. The dispatcher lady heard the yellings and cursings through my phone. She also heard the mob trying to stop them. She asked me where the girls were.

"They are inside the car with them," I answered.

"Are they crying?" she asked.

"I cannot see them from where I am. The windshield is tinted."

"Where are you, sir, where are you now?"

"I am still perched on the top of the car. I am on the hood without any balance whatsoever," I answered.

"The officers are there already. Look, they are behind you."

It was 16:41 on my cellular phone when, a minute and half later, since the time I called, the black lady stopped rocking the car. I looked around; it seemed that every single thing, more or less, stopped moving, unexpectedly for a moment. It was at that exact time that I saw the emergency red, blue, and white lights flashing by reflection on the surface of the windshield on which I was still hanging on.

I turned around. I saw at the south entrance of the main parking lot the complete picture. The marine blue Hurst police cruiser car was already on the walkway near the curbside that led to the apartment laundry room. The same car was also in a plain view of the black lady. That was the reason she stopped at standing still. The police saw her trying to run me over by rocking her Nissan. Her mouth was till spitting verbal abuses. Then an officer stepped out. It was K. Broome. He shut the door after parking his cruiser at reasonable distance, directly in front of the Nissan. He closed the rest of the distance by foot and ordered me to step down since I was still on hood when he arrived. His radio was barking on his shoulder. It continued giving him volume of directives to follow. I stepped down from the Nissan and became disoriented. I saw puddles of water on the floor on the empty parking lot. Even if it was supposed to reach 117 on the index that afternoon, that was not normal. When these puddles changed to ponds, I violently moved my head, left and right, to wake myself up. It was at this moment that my eyes started to see these ponds materializing themselves to man-made little pools. I was getting crazy. I felt my head getting lousy heavy. It was hurting. I touched it. I had a bump. I realized that I must have hit something on the Nissan. I got scared when I distinctively saw these pools of water fade away right in my sight. Since no one else but me saw them, I concluded that it was not the heat from the sun. The water I was looking at, on the concrete road, was nothing but mirage puddles that were been created inside my head, due the brutal movements of my body and because of the rocking of the car.

K. Broome asked me if I was the one who was yelling. I said, "Yes, but I was not exactly yelling. I was explaining loudly what it was. I said to the dispatch lady that those two ladies were kidnapping my two children, they intentionally hit me with the blue Nissan."

"That is what I need to know for now, go and sit down on the curbside," Officer K. Broome calmly ordered.

The day was June 12, 2009. My encounter with Officer K. Broome happened just a few hours after I was advised by Officer D'Israeli Arnold of Hurst Police to always carry any received court documents with me when I am out with my children. Since Sheebah and I were fighting in court of the law and none of us had a legal custody, to avoid being charged with something in case there is a police intervention, I had to have them in my possession. I had to have them on my person, all the time, mainly in case of an emergency.

He was right; their mother was out there trying to get them per force. She spent the full day of June 11, calling both my cell and my land line phones. Every time I answered, instead of talking about her girls, she unstoppably harassed me. She accused me of sending her to jail. At the end, I called the police some minutes after midnight. Officer D'Israeli Arnold came over. As he was interviewing me and listening to her messages, she called again. Officer Arnold answered. He introduced himself as such. Sheebah hung up. That was the time he gave me that advice. He told me that because of all threats he heard out of that answer machine, I had to provide these papers, as evidence, to any officer of the law, to show that the decision was not made yet. I had to do so to show that both girls were still residing with me. Following that advice, I had both documents in my back pants pockets when Officer K. Broome asked me to sit down.

I followed Officer K. Broome's orders. Without adding another word, even if he did not let me finish my plea, I sat down on the top of the curbside he indicated to me. I looked around and listened to the noise of everyday people. It was Friday. I smelled barbeque in the air. The moment of the day was gorgeous, and I was getting doomed. People were having a good time outside, and I had my butt forced on the hot concrete instead of going fishing or doing something in that order. Officer K. Broome looked at my direction. He saw me completely seated. He felt safe. I saw him started talking to the white lady. I overheard her explain a bunch of stuff that did not make sense. It seemed to me that these stuff were even harder for the officer to swallow. Then I saw the driver, the black woman who was still behind the wheel, intervened. She handed a pile of papers to the officer. The white woman did not stop talking; she was babbling about her husband, her life, and her children. The officer took a look at these documents. He quickly read them. A second or two later, he directed himself toward me. He had a menacing attitude in every step he took.

The man was in his thirties. He visibly looked athletic and strong young dude. He was about an inch taller than the boxer Tyson even if he physically presented less body muscles. With his menacing attitude, he came near the top of the hard concrete where he sat me down earlier and asked to verify my identification. I took a good look at him; his hairdo was done as a trend people stay away from. He was almost bald from front to neck, the young skinhead-drift style. That cut was not from a known military hair style despite the fact that he was in forces. As a black man, I knew at this point, that this kind of man, even if he was in force, would mess up the remaining of my day. Given everything I saw so far, I decided to remain calm. I did not want to bless his day and be the reason he would have to take the real colors out of my June 12. I asked him if I could slowly stand up to reach my pocket and give him my documents. He shook his head as a yes. I then handed him my Texas driver's license. This time, he politely obliged me to move one foot down and sit where two curbsides met to form an angle.

"Both hands behind your back and sit tight. I want to be able to clearly see you from my cruiser," he ordered.

I sat on the burning concrete. It was here where I remembered what the weatherman did to prove how hot it could possibly be. An egg was cracked on the hood of a parked car as the camera was rolling. It did not take long; the entire transparent mushy liquid around the yellow became snow-white hard. In less than five minutes, that chicken egg was cooked. It was hot, really hot outside to sit on the concrete. My blue jeans did not help. The high temperature was going through my pants. As matter of fact, each part of my body that was touching the floor was getting burned. It was extremely hot. One could distinctively hear the furious snapping of the green grass, the same way it would have sounded if a person would have walked on it. I stayed down anyway. I sat still at exact place where the officer pointed me until I couldn't handle the heat anymore.

CHAPTER 2

THE SUMMON

"Officer, the pavement is too hot to sit on," I loudly said.

"You will speak only when spoken to," Officer K. Broome ordered.

"These two ladies are kidnapping my daughters and I am the one sitting under the heat," I said.

"Speak when spoken to, sir," he said again with a voice that was meant to be authoritarian.

He continued writing things on his police cruiser computer using only his index finger. He probably was checking my record. He then reappeared with my driver's license on his right hand. Instead of directly walking toward where I was sitting on the ground, he stopped to continue questioning these two ladies. It was at that precise moment that I heard the white lady say something like "he took my kids when I was in jail. I spent twelve days in jail. I just got off this morning." The black lady confirmed what she was saying. At this point, I did not have an idea of what they were talking about.

K. Broome approached me. He wanted me to explain what was really going on. I started by talking about the Nissan stalking us. When I arrived where these ladies kidnapped my girls, he shut me off. "This is not a kidnapping of any kind, sir. The woman in that car is your wife. She is taking her daughters where they belong, back with her."

"My wife, she is my wife? I am not married, I don't have a wife. What do you mean by not kidnapping? They are kidnapping my children, Officer. Aren't they in that car, Officer?"

"You mean you don't…who is that woman behind the wheel of that car?" he asked.

"I never ever have seen that woman in my entire life. I do not know who that woman is," I answered.

"You mean, you do not know that black woman? Her name is Sheebah. In case you forgot, she is your wife and the mother of your children."

"That is not Sheebah, that woman is not the mother of my children. Officer, I am not married."

"Sir, Hurst Police Department has lot to do. Sheebah is your wife, she is the mother and she has full custody as it is written in these court papers."

"Where is Sheebah? What kind of court papers are you talking about? What custody?" I asked.

"The black woman sitting in that car is Sheebah. You, sir, you are insulting the intelligence of Hurst PD."

"Sheebah is white, my kids are half-caste. That black woman is not Sheebah, she is not the mother of my mixed kids."

K. Broome's radio came on, crashing inaudible words. He leaned his head on the left shoulder where the microphone was hanging, smashed the button, and spoke. He said, "In the car with their mother, yes, they are safe."

It was here where it ticked me. I was K. Broome's suspect. I was the one who called for help, whose children were been taken away, and yet I was the one who was treated as a suspect. This officer did not ask to verify these two women's identities. I did not see them handing any identification or other means to prove who they were. Something in me told me there was an injustice in the air. I decided to stand up and go get my children out of the car by my own self. Just when I was deciding, I saw a black and white Chevrolet Charger, painted into police colors, coming forward. It was driven by J. Delfeld. He was a backup officer. He asked me what was going on as Officer K. Broome went to talk to the ladies, again.

This man was posed. He had grey hair on both side of his head. Age wise, he could have as well been considered as Officer Broome's father. I gave him the same answer I gave Broome. "These two are kidnapping my daughters. I was expecting help from the police, but Officer Broome here just said on his radio that they are safe. How can they be? They have been kidnapped. What is going on, Officer?"

"One of these ladies in that car is the mother. She had legal papers to get physical possession of her children," Officer J. Delfeld said.

I felt at that instant that I was no more part of anything. The only people who were supposed to protect me were separating me from my little ones. They were separating me from everything. I sat back on the curbside and said, "Not one of us has legal custody. Both girls live with me. They have been living with me for their entire lives. Their mother had been living with friends sometimes. She had been in shelter numerously. As I am talking to you right now, she spends her nights under Riverside Street and Lancaster Avenue last bridges, just out of downtown Fort Worth, around the Presbyterian shelter. You can verify with the manager of Braum's Ice Cream & Dairy on 287, she will tell you that she is on the streets. She also lives inside a school van. When she left us, Loylla was barely eight months. Tabô was a year old. Loylla is eight years old today. I have been raising them both by myself for the past eight years. Sheebah doesn't have custody. I have administration papers to prove it. There is not a legal paper that authorizes her to be my daughters' legal custodian or a possessor of any kind." I said.

He looked at me as if I just lost some screws inside my head. I stared back, ready to give him an answer. I just did not have enough polite words remaining in me to formulate it in a well-mannered way. That was at this moment that Officer Broome approached. He said, "I just read the court orders, sir, the mother is authorized to take custody of the kids."

"Officer, there is no such order. We have to go in front of a family judge again. That piece of paper you are holding doesn't qualify as an order. It is not an order."

"What it is then?" he asked. "Did you really read it, sir? What is this piece of paper? Are you saying that this document is not an order?"

"Indeed, sir. That document is a summon, a legal document from the court that was served to each one of us to appear. We both have to be there on August 17, 2009," I said meanly.

"What do you mean by a summon?" K. Broome asked again; he was very confused and irritated.

"A summon is just a…that is when an officer of the law serves a person, and that person is obliged to appear in the court and when you have been sued and when you may employ an attorney. Sir, you are a police officer, you do give citations and the court issues summons. Actually, I do have the same copy in my pocket. The office of attorney general sent it to me. If you allow me to stand up, I will reach my pocket and will be able to read mine to you," I bitterly answered.

Officer K. Broome's stern face became sincere. His question about the summon was indisputably straight. He looked at Officer J. Delfeld, seeking for a confirmation. It seemed to me, at that moment, that Delfeld agreed with me. My hesitating definition of summon was not confusing to him. He went through long college hours and tough trainings on the field. The man of the law was honestly harassment, but they were a team. It was clear he was apt to serve people and to reinforce the law. His arrest officer K. Broome had yet to learn a thing or two about everything. That was crazy he did not know. I gently whispered a couple of questions to my own ears and said, "Is it serious that this man does not know what the summon is? Is he playing injustice with the judge's court order?"

K. Broome reminded me of Sarah Palin, another official representative. She was told by a member of the Republican Party that from the moment she is a nominee to be vice president of the United States and forward on, she will never use her personal bodyguards on her security detail anymore. She will be protected by the Feds instead. She asked, "What is that? What do Feds mean?" It happened again during the presidential election process questioning, Sarah Palin did not know that there were two Koreas; she didn't even know if the Queen of England was the head of the government or the head of state. When the boxer Muhammad Ali passed away, she confirmed in her tweet that "Muhammad Ali was the greatest pro-wrestler of all time at Wrestlemania." This was after she had confused Steve Harvey to President Obama, when Steve made a mistake on Miss Columbia and Miss Philippines business. She said that "Obama sure screwed up that Miss Universe show." It was hard to comprehend how Sarah Palin could confuse things that way as it was also equally hard to understand what K. Broome was doing. They both were dealing with these things on regular basis. But Sarah was blessed with eagle eyes that were able to see Russia from Alaska, so she said. That was the only difference.

Officer K. Broome needed to sharpen his eyes like that instead of putting them in his pocket. He needed to see far from his nose. By the advice of Officer D'Israeli Arnold, I had two court documents in my pocket. I asked if it was possible for me to stand up and reach my pants. I wanted him to read them, maybe he would open his understanding. Strangely enough, he refused.

"Didn't you hear me the first time, sir? I said stay seated," he dryly ordered again.

I complied the first time he asked me to because I knew what people like him would do to people like me. I continued keeping my butt burning on hot concrete. I even put both my hands visibly on the grass and ignored him for a moment. There, I started watching the overwrought vapor that was transparently coming out from the ground. This time, I froze. Two squirrels wandered down from the pecan tree. They went toward the blue trash bin and came out at the other side of the laundry room. I questioned myself how they were able to jump around, from place to place, pick nuts up, and disappeared without been bothered by that translucent, almost opaque heat vapor as I was.

"They are animals, and that is what Broome thinks I am exactly," I answered my question myself. "I only want to reach my back pocket to let you at least read these two documents." I politely asked.

"If they are the same legal papers that your wife gave me, then there is no need to," he answered.

"Please, Officer, if she gave it to you, I also have same given right, just like her, to give it to you. There are two sides to every story," I vainly explained.

"Let me see the document," asked Officer J. Delfield.

Slowly, without standing up, my hand found its way in my back pocket. I pointed where the word *summon* was written and what was explained on it. He took the first document, read it, looked at me, and kind of smiled. It was not quite a smile, but I saw his face lighten just a bit. He took his time, walked K. Broome aside, readjusted his voice, and then explained the document with maturity.

There was a reason he explained things that way. He had enough field experience to handle family matters. That seemed not to be the answer that K. Broome was expecting for. He said to him that "It is said right here, in this document, that Mr. Kasalobi is the Non-Custodial Parent."

"Yes, I am aware of what the document says, Sir K. Broome. My lawyer knows what that document says too. The thing is, this is a lawyer motion. It is not the court decision. That letter you have and what is written inside is what Sheebah declared to her lawyer. She wrote the accusation from what she heard from her. We still have a court hearing to go to and the date is set. That is the reason why this summons is there. It is to notify me and her for that matter that a court hearing has been set in the above-referenced case, on August 17, 2009. My failure to appear will result in default order being entered against me. It may result in a warrant for my arrest. It goes the same for Sheebah," I said.

"Who is Sheebah?" Broome asked.

"The mother of my daughters," I answered.

"One of the women in that car you mean?" K. Broome asked.

"None of these two women. Sheebah is not that fat. These two, in that car, are kidnapping my children."

Officer J. Delfield who, despite all his efforts, didn't convince his partner about the document, looked at me, adjusted his voice again, and said, "The woman in that car is really their mother and your babies are already inside there. At this point and by the law, there is nothing we can do."

"They are kidnapping them and…"

"There is not kidnapping here, sir. Do you hear your babies crying? They are with their mother," intervened K. Broome.

"Which one, Officer, which woman are you talking about to being my wife?" I asked Officer J. Delfield, completely ignoring K. Broome's interruption.

Officer J. Delfield did not answer, but Officer K. Broome looked at me with an expression of plain disappointment on his face, as if I was a dense brainless. I added and said, "My kids did not get themselves in that car. They were forcefully removed from the ground, against their will, and put inside there. By definition of the law, if that is not kidnapping, what is it?" I respectfully explained.

"Stay seated, sir." K. Broome ordered me once more.

The heat from the ground was creating a transparent smoke on solid materials. That smoke was similar to the one from the evaporating gasoline fuel. The top of the grass, in which I had both my hands, was steaming. While my buttocks were in flames, the rest of my body was cooking like the weatherman's egg on the hood of the car. The only protection I had was my own sweat on my clothes. I wished I was one of these two black birds I was watching. They were out cooling themselves off in the circumstantial pool, created by the washetaria drain. Doing so, they were more or less been pounced by a cat. I watched them fearlessly challenging it by flying in and out to cool off. With Broome around, it was impossible for me to challenge the heat like them.

"I am already seated, sir, but can I please call my lawyer at least?" I said as he was looking at me with an intimidating stare.

I looked back. My eyes did not quite verbalize my thoughts and everything that was behind my mind, but my entire face told him that we were at the very end of polite dialogues. I will not hesitate to disobey him. He took my driver's license card from his shirt pocket and held it as if he was about to give it back. I asked him one more time to call my lawyer.

"At this point, police don't listen to lawyers," he replied.

"Of course they do. They even wait for them, and when they arrive, they listen to them talk to justify their cause. What do you think there is a 'you have right to an attorney' for?" I answered.

"At this point, sir, you are not under arrest, you do not need a lawyer. Your wife has a point though."

"Why are you guys calling her my wife? That woman is playing you."

"She said the same thing about you. As now, you are manipulating the system. You just said that black woman is not your wife and yet you just called her Sheebah, the mother of your kids."

"Sheebah is the mother to my kids. That is a given. But she is not my wife. The Sheebah I know is not a black woman as you keep saying it. She is a 120-pounds woman of Irish descendant with browned golden hair," I answered.

"You are lying to us again, sir," accused K. Broome.

"Why would I go and pick a flabby woman to be my wife? Sorry, I don't like fat women."

"She ran from you because of your history of family violence."

"Family violence you said? There is not family violence between Sheebah and me. How could it be? I do not live with the woman. We don't live together. No police in this United States ever arrested me for family violence, no court ever condemned me for family violence. What are you talking about?"

"You are living together, she said so. She ran from you and took you twice to court for family violence."

"You said first that she lives with me...now you are saying she ran from me. Is not that confusing? If she...of course we went to court twice, the last time was on this June 1. That day, and to prove you that we do not live together, we were obliged to communicate only per text messages, not through children, directly or indirectly. We also were ordered to refrain from inflammatory language to each other in e-mails. I will have a home social study tomorrow, June 13 with Kathryn Omarkhail. But we...let me give you the document again. You will see in it that we were already in court this June 1. Why do you think she did not give it to you, because you would have discovered that we do not live together, and she is the one who is aggressive toward me. People always accuse other people from the experience of things they themselves do or have been doing to others. She knew it would work if she based her accusations on family violence. And that is exactly what she is doing."

"You were inside that courtroom with her so many times. How dare you…"

"She never showed up even once, her lawyer represented her."

"Why is that?" K. Broome asked.

"Her lawyer said it was because she was scared to be in the same room with me."

"Was she?"

"She was not. This was just a part of their games," I confirmed.

Without saying another word, K. Broome adjusted his gun belt, one more time, handed my license back and reminded me to keep sitting on the ground. I complied and kept my incidental seat tide as I had been doing. I had, at that instant, the feeling that he had decided against me. After a short briefing with Officer J. Delfield, he directed himself to the Nissan and asked the two ladies to leave. It was decided from the time he showed up. I sat there and watched my two little birdies been taken away. He then came back, pulled up a business card from his shirt pocket, wrote sequence numbers on it, and handed it to me. I refused to take it. He said, "Judging things by your accent, you are not probably from over here. I don't know about where you are coming from, but in this country, we go by the law of the land. Up to the documents she presented and because both girls were already in her car, I let them go with her."

"I am American. In this great country, we don't judge people by their accents or because of where they are coming from. How about the black lady? She hit me with her car. I am very dizzy. She bruised my elbow and my legs are swelling. That is an assault with deadly weapon. Are you going to let her go too?"

"As I said it already, your children were inside their mother's car when I arrived. I just couldn't have told her to give them back to you. It would have been the same if they were inside your house. I wouldn't have taken them from you and handed them to her."

He handed me his business card again, I refused to take it. He began explaining more nonsense. He said he wrote my Hurst Police case, with the sequence number # 090601997 on it.

"I don't need your card, Officer," I politely said to him. I asked him the permission to stand up. He allowed me. I stood up and directed myself toward my apartment.

"You initiated that. She hit you with the car because you blocked her in," Broome answered.

"I see. It is my fault now. She initiated things, she stalked us, blocked us in with the Nissan before I even parked, kidnapped my children, and then hit me. So how I am responsible for that?"

"You shouldn't have jumped in the front of a running car," he continued accusing me.

PART II

SOCIAL STUDY

CHAPTER 3

INTRODUCTION

I asked the permission to leave and walked away. When I entered my apartment, CNN was on.

"Today, June 12, 2009, is the last day for television as we know it," said Wolff.

He was telling people that, the analogue television broadcasting will get turned off at midnight to give a way to the digital transmission. As he was explaining, Negrita, my Latina neighbor, opened my apartment front door without knocking it. She entered and handed me a piece of paper on which was written an 800 number. After words of comfort, she pulled a chair, sat next to me, and said, "That is the internal affairs number."

She wanted me to call in against Officer K. Broome. I had to report him to people who could investigate him and what was going on, people who would make a no foregone conclusion, and people who do not write a prejudicial report. I thanked her, folded the paper, and put it in my jeans pocket. A moment later, she also started to listen to CNN. Wolff was advising people with the old analogue television set to require a flat machine to buy a convertor or simply to buy a new equipment to receive a digital signal. I had a new system already. I purchased it before that announcement. So that broadcast did not concern me. Negrita continued watching TV while I was mourning with pain in my heart.

It was when Negrita, my Latina neighbor, left my apartment that I felt it. Two fat women played the system. They kidnapped my daughters. One of them was wearing a bra made out of white-colored materials that was dirty. That bra was visibly past the meaning of dirty, way past. It looked yellow brown because it was severely not cleaned for a long period. Clearly, that showed the filthiness of the person who was wearing it. Incredibly, she was smart. She planned everything and stalked me. She even organized her time to have the entire Hurst Police Department on her side. They believed that she was Sheebah.

My intuitions were right. I knew I was followed. For a moment there, I lost my leopard instinct and I paid an imaginable toll. I blamed myself for not keeping Mr. Leo's techniques as rule of survival. But it was not clear enough how whoever stole my children knew where we were. I went to buy a used engine for my Ford Taurus. On my way back, from Grand Prairie Junkyards, kids wanted to talk to their mother. Because I did not want them to talk through my cell phone, I stopped at QT gas station. I had to let them use the public phone because on June 1, 2009, Meda Bourland, their mother's attorney, accused me of harassing Sheebah. She showed up, in that last court hearing, with her phone and gave it to the judge. She told her that I was harassing her client, days and nights, using that particular phone. I was not harassing her; I never did call her either.

Her daughters used my cell phone numerously. She locked messages that selectively said "I love you, Mama" in and gave it to her lawyer. Since her phone was given to the court, insisting on how many times my number is printed in as sign of harassment, the associate judge decided. I was obliged, and per her orders, not to give that particular cell phone to my children anymore.

"If they want to talk to their mother, let them use a different phone, a public phone for instance." She ordered so because she did not believe an iota of my side of story. That was the reason I stopped at the crossroad of I-30 E and Beltline to let them call her, using the public phone. After that hearing, as she was driving home, Sheebah was stopped for driving erratically. She was arrested for outstanding tickets and spent eleven days in jail.

I never took a straight route going home or coming from somewhere anyway. To be easily followed like that was a strange event. If it was the mother who kidnapped them, then it was my daughters who unconsciously responded to her tricky questions. They may have told her my whereabouts. That justified the timing of the Nissan driver. Either way, I was not alarmed enough to the level my elders would have wanted me to be. Therefore, I failed my lessons. I stood accused. I helped her take my birdies away from me. They were kidnapped and gone, that was fact, but I knew they were somehow safe as long as the Hurst Police was involved, meanly involved that was, but involved anyway. But the clock stopped. Without the fighting they used to do among themselves, their arguments and other noises from my kids, the time stopped. My apartment became empty and cold. I refused to cry. I closed my fist and decided to get ready for a long fight.

Just like that, my phone rang. It was Tabô.

"We live now at Charlene's. My mom is not here. I am hungry, Loylla is hungry too," she said.

I woke my mind up from drifting. A female voice yelled from the back room; she asked her who she was talking to. I heard her say something like "I am not talking to nobody."

She got roughly disconnected as she was answering. The only Charlene I knew was one of her caretakers, a teacher at Hurst daycare.

Tabô's speech gave me more doubts than solutions. I called Kathy Ehmann-Clardy. I somehow hopped to get help that night. She was my second lawyer on the matter. Dorothea Laster was the first to represent me in this court custody battle. Instead of doing her job, she spent that time milking me. It was like I was working for her instead of the other way around. I know lawyers have difficult job, but since they are paid for it, they ought to be professional. Dorothea Laster was purposely making me lose my case. I did not know who she visibly was working for. For instance, she was asking me to bring legal papers in, the kind she only, as a lawyer, could find and gathered for the purpose. She could just walk inside any office of any county and get them from any guardian of records. She continued demanding me to produce evidences that were her to find, documents that did not matter to anyone else eyes and files she had already received. To me, because she was not doing the job she was hired for and yet wanted more money as if she never received any from me, Dorothea Laster was a rerun of all lawyers. Every time she asked for more, I asked her to justify the reason. Her best answer was in form of a spoken sentence. She always said that "I have bent over backward to make representation financially possible for you..."

At the end of the day, I told her she won't receive a penny more till I see the work been done, to the equivalence of the amount she had already received. She got mad at me and stopped corresponding with me. On my first trial day, February 23, 2009, Dorothea Laster alias Karambee quit on me. The woman never represented me; she never defended me either. We were inside the court room, in front of the judge for the first time when she did that to me. The judge shielded her against my verbal insanity. I saw in my mind at that very instant, a picture of William Striler. I understood why he once pulled his gun and fired six shots at Gerry Curry, his lawyer. He was upset. His dissatisfaction was over the edge. If it was not for a small tree he kept hiding behind, Gerry Curry would have been killed. I did not miss Dorothea Laster when she quit; she was a misfired woman. She spent her valuable time, trying to look like an eloquent man.

I called Kathy Ehmann-Clardy hopping to get a solution that night. She knew how to get people out of desperate situations with far lesser amount of money than Dorothea Laster. I had proves of what she was capable of already. Her office received only the initial fee of $300 to represent me. That little money climbed the mountain. She provided me tons of evidences. She also gave me Sheebah's driving record, her lease rental record, and gave me the address where my kids were first hidden in Arlington.

Kathy answered my call. She was out of town, she said. Nevertheless, even if the June 13, 2009, social study with Kathryn Omarkhail was scheduled to take place inside my apartment, at

Glen Rose, she advised me to cancel it. She asked me to go to the hospital instead.

"When you are hit by a car, even if you stand up and walk, there is always a late reaction. By the end of the day, you will feel pain. People died after that," Kathy Ehmann-Clardy said.

Kathryn Omarkhail refused to reschedule. The family law center case worker said that because the first part of the social study was done already when I went in her office for the interview, she wouldn't change dates unless ordered otherwise by the court. She also added that since the fee was not paid separately by each party as ordinarily ordered by the court and because it was entirely paid by me to ensure that my case would be quickly assigned, she legally won't be able to postpone. Everything will go as scheduled.

"It was for these two reasons that you attended the orientation. We will have the social study at your place tomorrow. Make sure I meet all your children and friends or anyone who has knowledge of this matter. I want them in your apartment before 1400 hours. Let this be an advice to you: I will call it a no-call, no-show if the home visitation is rescheduled," she concluded.

I reported my phone call meeting with Kathryn Omarkhail to Kathy Ehmann-Clardy that same very day. She warned me about her. She also cautioned me about changing anything from the way I have been living with the two little ones. Kathryn Omarkhail was setting things up to find a way to ask out-of-bound questions to my friends, Kathy Ehmann-Clardy said. Her intention is to apply her routine stupid questionnaire to older children. Her desire is to confront them with complicated issues possible to say that my place doesn't have enough leg room for my little girls. Because she knows I had limited living spaces, she wants to trick them to accept that they all live in my two-bedroom apartment. She wishes to write down all that and say that she saw them, talked to them, and interviewed each one of them.

"Based on all that, she will say both girls don't have a living place in their own home. The judge will decide, and you know who the court will believe. I worked with Kathryn Omarkhail, she hates men. If you paid attention when she was talking, you would have noticed that she was coming after you. Before the law finalizes her divorce, she had issues with her ex-husband. She still has a thing or two against him. Men in general are paying for. Lot of them lost their custody battle because she was involved in their case. She is working on getting her maiden name back, so I heard, maybe she will change then. While waiting, we need to be careful. As now, she will take side. She will see you through her ex-husband and will lie on her report, against you," Kathy Ehmann-Clardy explained.

I postponed my visit to the hospital because I was warned about the investigation Kathryn Omarkhail would have done on me. If I went anyway, doctors would have found something wrong with my body because of the car impact. It would have been days before I got released. She would have ruled against me. I knew where to stand since she threatened it to be no-call, no-show.

I received Kathryn Omarkhail in my apartment. It was exactly 1400 hours when she knocked on my door. The woman was tall, six feet I guessed. She was in light blue khaki pants on top of which was a man's long sleeves catholic blue shirt. Short hair, puffy on top, cut on each side, and forcefully combed toward the back of her head. She looked like a male Indian with a grown-up back Mohawk. After introducing herself for the record, she opened the refrigerator. She said, "I see you have enough food. Of course, you knew I was coming."

That was a smart comment I did not want to ignore. To me, it sounded as if she was telling me she was the reason people cook in their houses. With a smile on my face, I answered and said, "I am African, we do not feed our children simply because officials from the county are visiting."

"I see, you have jokes," she said.

"You started it," I replied. I did not have jokes. I was serious.

She opened each kitchen cabinet including the food storages. She entered the bathroom and visited both bedrooms. She inspected every corner of the apartment in great details. Every time she moved around, she took a blue pen between her left ear and her skull, where it was stuck, and wrote something on her green clipboard.

"Where is your son?" she asked.

"Which one? Including my adopted Latino son, I have three."

"The one who lives here with you," Kathryn suggested.

"None of them lives here with me. My Latino son lives now with his biological grandmother. My natural two are in Fort Worth, living on their own," I politely answered.

"Then whose clothes are those, in that hall closet?" she questioned with intimidation in her voice.

"Mine, they are my working gears," I said.

"Where does your son put his clothes and stuff then?" she insisted.

"They took most of their things with them when they moved out."

"So that line of clothing doesn't belong to your son, the one who lives here with you then?" she insisted again by bringing into play a strange face.

That strange face seemed to show anger. From a professional, it tickled me a bit. Why she was insisting on one son particularly, I asked myself. My mind wandered on that "why" and why she wasn't talking about others. There, I felt it; Kathryn Omarkhail's lack of ability to conduct a fair investigation was already jumping on my face. She was not an incompetent lawyer and yet that doggedness on a question, that persistence on one son who did not have anything to do with her investigation, sounded like an accordion out of tune. Since she went to school to learn how to do a good job, it was a disappointment that put doubt in my mind. She was trying to add a wrong comma on the letter of a legal matter to mess things up for me. In fact, she was demonstrating just that instead of asking investigation questions concerning my two little girls. She was already making things happen for Sheebah. She knew by then that she led a black lady, Mrs. Zora Warner, to run me over with a car. She knew that my daughters were not with me anymore. She knew it was not about my son, it was about my two daughters.

"My sons, as are my older daughters, do not reside here with me anymore. Why are insisting on that, which one of them are you talking about anyway?"

"The one whose clothes are in the hall closet: jeans, weather boots, jackets with hoods. I mean youth clothes. Those are your son's clothes. Aren't they?"

"That should be qualified as defraud in your investigation method, Kathryn. You are taking advantage of your position, as Ma would have said it, in order to 'try cutting me to the quick.' You can just assume that those clothes belong to my son," I said.

Slowly but surely, I started to feel her. That cheap confirmation that shouldn't have been brought up, in such study, was the style of hers I was warned about. Even if it was her right to ask annoying questions, a confirmation like that one, was a statement empty of substances, it matched her techniques. Only answers from my heart, not from my brain, could have stopped the razor blade of her tongue to keep on slashing my pain. I decided to impassively give these answers to her.

"We are not here to talk about my son. We met today for my daughters. They are kidnapped, which is for me a matter of life or death. As I said it before, none of my sons do live here. And no, these are not my son's clothes, they are my working clothes. Once again, which one of my sons are you still talking about?" I dryly asked because we were not around a beer where we would have been making discussions without grace. We were debating on a serious matter.

"I have never seen you in hoodies and jeans or in sandy sandals and safari shoes. Those are not working gears. Those are everyday duster clothing," she continued guessing.

"Ma'am, we are not on the table of games of circumstance and trickery where you have to bet based on the card you have or you think you have. We are not playing poker here, ma'am. Let's stop guessing. What I am saying to you is what I am saying to you. I do not wear hoodies or tennis clothing in court of the law. This is the only place you ever seen me. This meeting here is the second of the kind in which you are seeing me. This is not enough to judge me by my dresses," I said those things to make her understand that intimidating me, by asking questions like that, was not the best way to penetrate my intelligence to its molecular level. For every inquiry that would have been coming out from her mouth from that moment on, I wanted them to be straight. I wanted her to know that I had a surgical bistoury of my own to cut apart her intentions. The fact of the matter was that I had the truth on my side and I was ready to lacerate her horrific plan.

She used her clipboard and wrote something down; maybe it was my reaction toward her question or simply the response I gave her. It did not matter anyway, I knew her by then. She sat down on my living room L couch. I noticed that she had on her feet some Johnston&Murphy brown shoes, with red bottoms. Those were expensive footwear, even for a woman.

On unforgettable Sunday in Maryland, I had the privilege of been blocked in Johnston&Murphy store by the security services. This was after President Barack Obama entered. By the time he left, after shopping, his presidential hand bag had about four pairs, all of them black. I know shoes. I wear shoes, quality shoes that it is, especially expensive ones, like Johnston&Murphy. Those on Kathryn Omarkhail's feet were from the same name store where the President of United States goes shopping. The long question that etched in my mind when she sat down was "what is a $800 pair of shoes doing under the feet of Kathryn Omarkhail, a city employee, and why is she wearing khaki and a long-sleeve male shirt. These clothes are changing her image." I guessed it was because she was trying to equal herself to the man she hated so much, the man she divorced from. She was becoming him. She did not leave him behind; she just withdrew from him for a moment. She was becoming a man she will never be, to show to the world she can stand as such. In the backyard of places where I am from, looking good is an art. Looking good, wearing nice clothes, is business. Dressing a woman some nice male clothes is just wrong; it doesn't look good at all. Kathryn Omarkhail was making a real man that I am, look bad and confused, very confused.

She sat down on my L couch, opened her laptop, read a little bit, and said, "We have been ordered by the court to conduct a social study concerning your background, childcare plan, and other issues relevant to parenting. The goal of the court is to make the best possible decision for the children's welfare. State your names for the record."

"My name is Kasalobi," I answered.

She then explained things I was not interested in. I played a good student. Her speech became interesting when she said that even if she asked me lot of questions at her office, she needed "for the record" to know everything that have happened between Sheebah and me. She wanted me to start from the beginning of our relationship through children. She also wanted to know the way we lived with them.

I started with my intervention by saying to her that for the past twenty years, I exclusively lived in Hurst, Texas. I never have been convicted of any crime in this city or any family violence of any kind somewhere else on this American land, as Sheebah had been claiming. Her lawyer stated the same thing on my last appearance, inside of the court room too. I have children, grown and younger. I raised all of them by myself. They all depended on me. I did so with no help whatsoever, from anyone or from their mothers. Tabô and her little sister Loylla are among them. I had them by Sheebah. As it is stated in their respective schools, medical and lease records, as it is sealed, written, given, and received under oath by the custodian records, as it is provided by Hurst, Euless, and Bedford Police as evidences toward this matter, and as it is certified in Child Protective Services files in my possession, I have been raising them two, by myself, from the moment their mother left us. Loylla was eight months old when that happened. She is almost nine years today. By choice, I do not drink, I do not smoke, and I do not do drugs. By the force of nature, I am diabetic, but I am sound of spirit.

I reminded Kathryn Omarkhail that the last time I was in her office, I gave her copies I received from each named department, and I was ready to give her more as we were progressing with the conversation. She smiled and looked at me when I said that. She touched her head with her left hand, slid it from the top, and negligently followed her mohawk all the way to the puffy hair left on the back her neck. The women had a serious problem with her hairstyle; it was cut and arranged in defiance of female fashion rules. She then put her eyes back on her keyboard and said, "Who is Sheebah? How did you meet her? I want the truth."

"As it was declared in the court, everything I will say is true. Sheebah is the mother of my two little girls," I replied.

When we met, I explained, she told me she was abandoned in the hospital by her mother, as soon as she was born. Katy, her biological mother, was fifteen years old then. She was the baby in the family of three. She saw herself traveling with Mr. Freeman and his wife, Shehan, her parents to Europe. They were in US army corps of peace mission. They did not know that their daughter, Katy, was pregnant. When the time came, Katy delivered her baby girl in Ireland, inside the hospital that belonged to the Queen Elizabeth. That little girl is Sheebah. Katy hid her from her parents and then abandoned her inside the maternity. At the end of her parents' mission, she left her behind. There was a decree-law at that time in Ireland. That law said that if a girl is found abandoned, she will bear the name of the Queen. The hospital then named Katy's daughter after the Queen, she said to me.

CHAPTER 4

JAIL RECORD

Eight years later, Freeman and Shahan were told by the Irish government that they were indebted. They had to pay child support. Katy delivered a baby girl and abandoned her in their country. Instead of paying from a distance, they decided to go back to Ireland. They got Sheebah and brought back home in the US. She was nine years old. They did not want Katy to take care of her anymore, and because they were already old people to do it themselves, they directly put her into boarding army school. Sheebah grew in the system till she was nineteen. The first day she was released was the day I met her for the first time. We met again at DFW where we worked inside the Delta terminal. Besides juvenile stuff, she did not have any crime on her report. She was very nice then. She moved in with me when her lease expired. I bought her a 2600 Mazda truck to go to school with. That was then. Today she has a long list of crimes, I said to Kathryn Omarkhail.

"Do you have proof of that accusation?" Kathryn Omarkhail asked.

"She has a long record of crimes, felonies on her names, numerous tickets and warrants, written in CPS case # 31044591. She has been using different names to hide herself from all that. She is also flipping my name, from first to last, and changing the order of letters

44

in it to apply for government advantages. She heavily drinks and does drugs profoundly. If that is not enough, you can see what I am saying by yourself, it is all over the internet," I said to her. I then opened my e-mail. I showed her pictures of Sheebah doing drugs in her apartment.

"Where did you get these pictures?" Kathryn Omarkhail asked.

"Her own boyfriend does post them in Facebook. She has numerous boyfriends. One of them even pulled a gun on me. This story is recorded by Hurst Police Department. They are all dangerous. As matter of fact, she has been addicted herself to so many drugs to a point that her criminal record shows everything. She also has been on Prozac since she was twelve," I said.

"How do you know her...where did you get her criminal record?" she asked.

As Ma would have said it, a question like "where did you get her criminal record" is simply a turndown of civilization. I did not want to show her that she was making me mad already, which would have been against Madiba's advice in this kind of situation. "To be angry and to be bitter is like drinking poison and expecting your enemies to die," he said. I wouldn't win by getting out of line, so I carefully, deliberately ignored her question for a moment and stood firm, accusing Sheebah. I felt her pressure. I decided to show her who belonged and who was visiting.

"I named CPS first, I will cite police departments, it is on public record. As matter of fact, she just got off from jail two days ago. She was arrested just after the preliminary hearing we had on June 1, 2009. On her way back home, she was pulled over by the Fort Worth police and arrested for eleven outstanding warrants and for driving with a suspended driver's license," I answered.

After paying her due with the city of Fort Worth, she was transferred to Bedford. From there she went in Grand Prairie jail where she sat for her active warrants. Grand Prairie transported her into Irving. She was released on June 11, 2009, from Hurst jail. She sat in for her tickets. That was how she was able to pay thousands of dollars she owed.

"Now to answer your question about how I got her criminal record, let me just say this: I had to substantiate my statements by proof. I contacted criminal lawyers. That is how I got her records. This here is a copy of her old medical prescriptions and a copy of used Prozac prescription," I said.

I then said to Kathryn Omarkhail that inside Fort Worth police files, the report #0411325486 of November 10, 2004, shows one of the crimes. She was arrested for burglary. We were already living together as boyfriend and girlfriend in the same apartment at that time. She was driving that day and got pulled over by Hurst police as we were coming from Arbordaze, the carnival. We were on Ector Drive going south, just before 183. As written in the report # 04-1040946, she was identified as the burglar, shamefully handcuffed, and taken to jail. I found out that it was in Hurst where she sold stuff she had stolen in Fort Worth. I asked her when she did that since we were together all the time. She said it was after midnight, when I was deeply asleep. She wake up, drove to Fort Worth, and broke in someone's apartment. I posted bond for her release. She then promised me she won't steal again. She did not stop here. On December 18, just days after that dishonesty, she was taken in for assault with bodily injury. She used her car as weapon once more. That story is clearly described in Euless police report # 04-00766877. I was sleeping that night when she called me at two in the morning. She wanted me to go bail her out and collect her from the Euless jail.

"How can you be in jail? By the time I joined you in bed, you were snoring already. When did you end up in jail over there?" I asked.

She answered, but told me an incredible story. Not only I did not believe an iota of what she was saying, I also had a cold in my brain just for listening. Officer Ayamas Hinajosa then told me another version. At about one in the morning, he said, Sheebah found her boyfriend with another girl. They started to argue. Then the girl left and Sheebah followed her, jumped in her Mazda truck, and rammed that girl car in the back. Luckily for Sheebah, this girl refused to press charges. Then she went upstairs to watch TV with her boyfriend as if nothing happened. After making love, the boyfriend said the argument broke again. She started to break things inside the apartment. She then ripped his T-shirt and broke his nose. This man suffered pain and discomfort, Officer Ayamas Hinajosa said. Sheebah was arrested and booked in on violent behavior. And this was just two days after she had been released from Irving jail on another assault charge. So I joined her in the bed that night, made love to her, and passed profoundly asleep, very tired from working two jobs. Once again, Sheebah woke up and got out from the apartment. She went to sleep with another man, got into a violent fight, and ended up been arrested. I did not pay her bond that time. I asked her to leave when she was released. She did not. She did not have a place to go. With the time, I forgot the entire cheating story and her use of a truck as a weapon.

"This was not the first time she hit people with her vehicle," I said to Kathryn "Omarkhail. In mid-2005 at DFW airport parking lot, as it is recorded in public safety record, she was arrested on violent behavior after using her truck as a weapon. Included in the report you have is a well-documented evidence about this case," I said to Kathryn Omarkhail. We both were working for Intex security. After the shift, I stayed behind socializing with friends at the exit of the parking lot. She went for her Mazda truck. I saw her driving forward and intentionally hit this African guy from Kenya. The Texas Public Safety was called. In details, Sheebah said to them that she knew him; she approached to talk and did not realize how close she was. It was an accident, she said. As a witness, the Public Safety explained to me that these two are lovers. I needed to tell them what I saw so they can take Sheebah away for family violence. Since they did not know who I was to her, I told them that I did not see a thing. The Kenyan guy refused to press charges. He was illegally living in the United States. He said it was an accident and he was okay. The Public Safety made a report and obliged Sheebah to leave the commercial facility and to never come back. Again, I found a hard time that Sheebah stood cheating on me in plain sight, with a coworker. I let it slide.

She also was arrested on February 13, 2007. Officer Vallada Marcores says on his Euless police report # 07-01261887 that the hysterically crying Sheebah was booked in on aggravated assault, after using her truck as weapon. Because of $300 that her common-law husband owed her, she intentionally burned her Mazda P/U tires, leaving aggressively skid mark behind and rammed with aggression into the rear end of the Mazda 626 that was occupied by four children. There was evidence of tire marks in the parking lot about thirty feet behind and in direct line with the rear bumper of the 626. After testifying, Officer Althouse took her to Euless Jail. This was another case that also proved how long Sheebah stood cheating on me. She had, under my nose, the time for a common-law husband I did not know about, and I wouldn't have known anything about if it was for Vallada Marcores.

The third time Sheebah was arrested for hitting people with her car was also on violent behavior. On January 6, 2008, she was accused of hitting a man called Christopher with her Mazda pickup over a lady called Stephanie Love. Officer Garner of Hurst Police says in his report 08-142 that Sheebah did not want Christopher to leave without talking to her. She then parked her car in a way to provoke an accident. And it happened. She hit Christopher's car. Officer Garner checked the dl/warrant on Sheebah. Hurst dispatch confirmed several traffic warrants on her. She was taken to jail.

I told Kathryn Omarkhail that Sheebah always hit people with her car. She never got trouble for it, and she never hesitated to continue doing so. It happened again yesterday, June 12, 2009.

I was hit by a car driven by a heavyset black lady. In that car was a white heavyset lady who was her passenger. I did not recognize either lady. To protect them, Officer K. Broome let them go unpunished. He said that the black woman was my wife. She was not. That made me thinking. When Tabô called me from where she was been hidden, she told me that the white passenger lady was Sheebah, her mother. Zora was the black lady, she was the driver. It still was not fair to let my children go. That was a kidnapping, just the way it was the first time around when she ran with them in the Valley. Back then, by using family violence on me, just the way she was doing it today, she manipulated the Hurst Police Department and ran with them. She was using violence experience against me again. It worked with the police and with people of the court.

"What do you mean by using violent experience…is she just violent?" Kathryn Omarkhail asked.

CHAPTER 5

CHILD PROTECTIVE SERVICES

"Sheebah is a violent woman. Bunch of tickets she received from fighting turned into warrants. She let them because she couldn't pay," I said to Kathryn Omarkhail. The Hurst Police report 05-1713 of February 24, 2005 shows her been taken to jail for getting into a fight with Ruben Eduardo, one of numerous men she was sleeping with when we were living together. That is violence. As written in the report 05-3338 of April 12, 2005, she was back in jail, arrested this time by Trooper Jimmy Sanchez for fighting. She had to sit her tickets for as long as four months. January 29, 2006, she goes to jail again, arrested by Officer Mark Bruner of Hurst PD for standing eleven warrants. That story is written in Hurst Police report 06-875. Since she was released on bond and did not take care of those tickets, on March 27, 2006, it shows in report # 06-2695 of Hurst police that she went back in for outstanding warrants. November 22, 2008, Sheebah is arrested again for fighting, testified by Hurst police report 08-9786. December 20, 2008, she goes in again. February 3, 2009, she is arrested by Office Jimenez at Sutton Square. Officer Miguel confirmed that arrest in Hurst Police Report 09-957.

"You seemed to have read all her criminal history," said Kathryn Omarkhail with a joking smile on her face.

"I actually shortened them. You can go through the whole file I gave you the last time I was in your office. It will confirm any other doubt you may still have about her being violent, about her criminal record, and how many times she had been in jail. Her record speaks by itself. She had been arrested, booked, and had been jailed on average of two times every three months. The woman is a mess. She is a bad influence to my children. Since it is a well-known fact that 'you only give who you are to your own children,' and because it was confirmed by Tabô that it was her who kidnapped them, I am scared to see who my children will be," I said.

"She did not kidnap the girls. It seems that you are the one who took them from her. Explain to me what happened."

"June 1, 2009, as I said it already, was her very last time she was in for outstanding tickets and warrants. Per Tracy Burkhart, the Child Protective Services specialist, she made a phone call to her from there. She claimed that I checked both girls out from school without her consent and ran with them out of town, probably to Africa..."

"You did not..."

"I indeed stopped by Bell Elementary. It was hours after Kathy Ehmann, my lawyer, showed pictures of Tabô in court. She had bruises all over her legs. It was proven that Daven, Sheebah's boyfriend, left them there after beating her with a stick. He had been doing this every time both girls went to Fort Worth to visit with their mother. Either way, I did not need Sheebah's permission to sign them out. They were living with me, in Hurst, ever since. She abandoned them years earlier and left them behind with me. I checked them out not because I wanted to take them out of this United States, but because I had to take them for their physical at clinic," I said.

In the last court hearing on June 1, 2009, I was asked to show proof of children being vaccinated. I promised to take them at CareNow hospital. In the same hearing, after Kathy Ehmann introduced pictures of Tabô being bruised all over her little body, she also presented a motion to restrain Daven. He had a history of abusing my children, beating them with open fists and molesting them. Judge White ordered him not to be near them anymore. He had to steer clear hundred feet from them. My lawyer advised me to take the restraining order against Daven to Hurst Police to have it registered. I did just that since we got off earlier from the court hearing that day. Officer J. Ceja recorded it as incident # 090600277. I decided to take both children at CareNow hospital after that. Tabô was also suffering from rashes. She was badly itching. At CareNow hospital, both children got their physicals done. Doctor prescribed yeast infection medicines to Tabô.

Since I did not answer her phone call, Tracy Burkhart came dashing at my doorsteps. Tabô was sitting on the computer desk when she arrived. She found Loylla in her room watching television. She interviewed both girls. I explained that I did not need CPS permission to get them out of school, and it was not that easy to travel with them to Africa. She left. We did not talk anymore, which was good. The woman was a little bit off. I found that out the first time I met her inside Suzy Dale's house at 9160 E. Walter Street in Bedford. At that time, I did not know she was a CPS agent. I thought she was one of Suzy Dale's caregivers or a teacher at one of her many daycares. Tracy Burkhart is tall and very slender. It is easy to confuse her with Popeye's wife. For a woman who was in someone else's house, she was very loud. I knew right there that she was off in her mind.

She left after interviewing my girls and without saying another thing to me. This was not her first contact. The woman was not fair and was not doing a reasonable job in her investigation regarding my child care situation. She was not satisfied to see them happy where they were and how they lived with me. She wanted Sheebah to gain custody. She was homeless at that very time. Tracy Burkhart wanted to help her get out of the situation she was in. If she could have them, I would be obliged to pay child support. I also found out from Brenda, a female daycare teacher, that Tracy Burkhart was over Suzy Dale to continue setting things up about Boney's paternity test. She was there for the same reason the first time I saw her. Boney is Sheebah's third daughter. They wanted to include her as my daughter in child support payment. So much so that before it was verified through DNA test, I would have been already paying something to help Sheebah.

To confront Tracy Burkhart about that was the equivalent of fighting the entire system. I did it at the end of the day and things didn't go well. She felt exposed and started calling me from 800 numbers. When I answered, if she did not abuse me verbally, she threatened me. I got fed up and began growling back. That was a mistake. Unknown to me at that time, I was giving her ammunitions to build a case against me. She did it around my reactions and concluded that I was a violent person. She showed up three times after that, back to back, in three days, trying to catch me on some mistakes. And each time she arrived, she found both kids dandy, playing or intellectually occupied.

"Sheebah is a good mother. Why are you trying so hard to expose her criminal history?" asked Kathryn Omarkhail.

"See, that is the thing. Instead of trying to set me up, Tracy Burkhart should spend her time investigating Sheebah's criminal record. She is not a good mother. I just established that to you. I just gave you a shortened list of who she is. What kind of good mother are you talking about anyway? Of course, the kind that comes out from people like Tracy Burkhart's reports? Anyone can be fouled with that kind. Sheebah is not a good mother. As matter of fact, as we are talking at this present moment, she doesn't even have a place to lay Baby J.'s head down. She is homeless. Baby J. is her last born."

"That can't be right. You just said she lives with Daven, where your kids are beaten. Child Protective Services is placing her in her own apartment, in Bedford, Texas, together with her five children," confirmed Kathryn.

"I never said she lives with Daven. But I will tell you this: her last known address was 1002 Fuller-Wiser Road in Euless, Texas. That was my daughter's place. I know which address in Bedford you are talking about."

I went on and told her that Sheebah was pregnant at that time. She did not have a place to go. She asked my daughter if she could live with them the time for her to give birth. This was about one month before Baby J. was born. Since she was home alone all the time, she was asked to contribute to the electricity bill only. It was her who spent a chunk of electricity. She said she was not able to because she did not have a job. But using Suzy Dale's physical address, she was receiving tandiff, food stamps, and all kinds of government benefits. She refused to contribute and moved out. She went to live inside the van, the daycare van that was provided to her by Suzy Dale. She refused to contribute not because she did not have the means to, but because she liked free passes. This was the reason she was after my kids. She wanted free passes in a form of child support. At that time period, Mrs. Suzy, one of her friends and the boss lady of numerous daycares, had different apartments. She was renting them from "The Wood of Bedford" in Bedford and leasing them out. This apartment complex was located at 2502 Central Drive. Her son, who had a runout with the law, was living in one of these apartments. He was arrested and jailed. He left his place, a six-month prepaid rent efficiency apartment, unoccupied. Suzy needed someone to take over the rent and to keep her son's credit alive. She proposed it to Sheebah. She hesitated, not because she didn't have money, she was selling food stamps, but because she did not want to be a burden. She preferred to spend her nights in the school van. When Baby J came along, she was still homeless, living on the streets, in the school van. I knew this because she came in Hurst and asked for a favor. She wanted Negritta, my next-door neighbor, to give her a place to stay with her newborn, the time to find an apartment. Negritta did not refuse to help her, but she had three roommates already in her one-bedroom apartment. Sheebah went back to live in the van.

With time, CPS got involved. It was just a matter of time. Someone may have called on her. Following Tracy Burkhart's advices, Sheebah was poking them, hoping they wouldn't react. You don't poke a sleeping giant because you are told that you are cut from the same cloth. CPS got involved and went looking for her over Suzy Dale, the only address in their record. They were told by Suzy's daughter that she did not live there. They subsequently went at daycare. She was by then working there as one of caregivers. Suzy Dale panicked. She worried for the simple reason that Baby J. was now three months old. She could easily have been taken away. It was cold and windy, and the girl needed a place to stay. This was the time when Sheebah remembered Suzy's suggestion. She talked to her when CPS left. It was kind of late because the apartment that belonged to her son was already proposed to someone else. Instead, Suzy gave her a different apartment. She temporarily moved in to wait for CPS' next visit. That place was the opening for Tracy Burkhart. Since the beginning, her intention was to help Sheebah show to CPS that she was the only parent who have had taken care of all her children, at all the time. It was also the opportunity Sheebah had been waiting for. She knew that if she had a place of her own, sooner or later, investigators will come to question her. When they do, they will find all children gathered together with her. They would document everything they would see. The court will decide from what is written down. She was hoping on the system to help her achieve her lies. The system did just that and Kathryn Omarkhail was one of the officials who directed her investigation referring to these lies.

To ascertain that she had been living inside that new address given to her by Suzy, she gathered her children in. She knew what she was doing. She did this many times around before at the moment like this. She manipulated the system every time she had a physical address. To show to CPS that she had been having my daughters all along, she collected them, all of them, openly at one place.

After she installed herself in, she called CPS on herself. She wanted that apartment of circumstance documented. She had done it so many times before too. That was exactly what was about to happen. When they confirmed the appointment to visit children, she realized that the place was not well equipped and suitable to be investigated in. It was not ready for an official visit, at least at CPS standard. On Tracy's insistence, she reached Suzy Dale again. The woman accepted to borrow her son's efficiency, inside "The Wood of Bedford," at 2502 Central Drive. Sheebah temporarily occupied apartment 10.

"You said CPS is placing her in her own apartment in Bedford, Texas, together with her five children. This is not the apartment you are talking about. Let me show you that…How does a person call CPS on himself?" she asked.

"Simple, you call against you as someone else, often anonymously, accusing you of mistreating children in your house. They will come to investigate. They will write down things they will see. They will mainly write about children you have at that moment.

Then they will go visit the other party, there they will notice the absence of the said children, voila," I answered.

"You mean CPS-trained specialists wouldn't see that designed and calculated scheme?" she asked.

Sheebah was sneakier than the smartest of all Child Protective Services specialists combined. She grew up in the system; she was in the system since she was eight. She slowly became familiar with the system. Not cunning the system was in fact losing the essence of who she really was. She knew how to beat it, and she did that under everyone's eyes. On the other hand, CPS doesn't look for schemes. They don't even try to find out who is lying and who is not saying the truth. They only search for a person to pin down, that person is the man, and that man has to pay child support. For them, a man is guilty already and the woman keeps the children, end of story. Sheebah knew that. She also knew how to go around everything to get to what she wants, even if that man had to go to jail. She knew how to steal food stamps and other advantages from the government. She also knew how to get away with it. For very long time, with Tracy's involvement and support, CPS let her receive food stamps when they knew she did not have custody her children. She received tandiff money while they knew she was homeless. These two were lame lies easy to counter. They chose not to do a thing about it. They knew where the children were living. Tabô and Loylla were with me. Boney was living with her grandma Zora Warner, Kattaya with Sharon Constant and Baby J. was taken care of by Cherin and by Charlene simultaneously. Those ladies were employed by Suzy Dale. CPS knew about them too; they visited the daycare so many times. I complained about all this to Nora, a lady from the CPS Fraud Department in Dallas. When they contacted Tracy Burkhart, the supervisor on the case, she contradicted me. They believed her report instead.

Sheebah accomplished her fraud business, under everyone's nose, by cunning process and carefully planning moves. When she needed protection, she got it from CPS, through Tracy Burkhart. When she needed a physical address or an apartment, Suzy Dale gave it her. When ready to do her income taxes, Suzy Dale was also ready to provide her fake payment stub. She got all these things, not for free. She had a way to pay back. She paid with food stamps. She was not the only woman who sold food stamps to Mrs. Suzy Dale. All female daycare workers did it. This woman carefully selected them for that reason. She considered their social lives and the kind of government benefits they received before hiring them. If they did not have these benefits already, she trained them how to get them. Suzy needed food stamps to feed her daycare children. She didn't even do a good job taking care of children.

Two of her daycares, the Bedford Learning Academy on Brown Trail and the Hurst Child Care Center on Pipe Lane, showed records of abuses and abandonments. These two facilities were putting children's lives in danger. Police were called many times. Parents fought with teachers, mostly with Sharon Owens, because of bruises found on their little ones. Mrs. Sharon Owens used to spank these children with a wooden ruler and claimed that what they had were not bruises but Mongolian spots, and they were born with.

Both facilities were shut down by the order of the court. Mrs. Sharon Owens and Mrs. Cherin, one of the caregivers, were ordered not to be at certain distance of the said children and to never babysit any other children than theirs. But that did not matter anyway because while waiting for Suzy to reopen both facilities under a relative name, and she did it last May 18, Sharon took some of these children at her place.

"It is not like CPS-trained specialists did not see that and other designed and calculated schemes. They simply chose to close their eyes. I am not just saying that. As matter of fact, to answer to your question correctly, to me they are called specialist for the fun of it, they don't investigate anything even if everything is under their noses."

"What do you mean?" Kathryn asked.

"Well, let's go back to what you confirmed with reference to Child Protective Services placing Sheebah in her own apartment in Bedford, Texas, together with her five children. As I was saying about that, when Mrs. Suzy's son went to jail, the rent was paid up to six months. Sheebah moved in. Because of the timing, she…"

"Usually people do not pay six months in advance for an apartment."

"Suzy Dale does just that. It is another of her business. She rents apartments abundantly, signs a six- or twelve-month contract, pays them in full, and leases them out expensively," I said to her.

"Okay, you were saying something about timing," Kathryn asked.

"The 2502 Central Drive # 10 in which she temporarily moved in was not CPS worthy either. Suzy Dale moved her and put her in 2700 Central Drive # 110, an apartment that had already a client. This happened on November 11, 2008. Hoping they will show up the same day and find her in that well-equipped apartment for the visitation, as usual, she called CPS specialist investigators on emergency level. In that same conversation, she added and said that children just came from visiting their father. They are having traces of abuse, their big sister traumatized them by pulling their hair. She said this because she wanted them to see children with her, immediately in that apartment. It was a matter of timing. Unfortunately, CPS was not in hurry to go at 2700 Central Drive, so they fixed an appointment for November 24, 2008. Because she had to vacate as quickly as possible, that delay messed up her timing.

In the meantime, a case worker went to school. She interviewed both girls at Bellaire Elementary. Nine-year-old Tabô said that she does not live with her mother, she lives with the father at Glen Rose Apartment. She confirmed seeing her mother from Monday through Friday at Suzy's daycare. She said that she doesn't like to visit her mom because Daven, her mom's boyfriend, hit her with the stick and calls her names. These things were all facts, under CPS noses, that Tabô did not need to explain. They were confirmed in 2008 Fort Worth Police report and declared in CPS case # 287 495 09. They ignored everything. Their objective was to see me pinned down," I said.

"The report I have does not see Daven beating the kids," Kathryn accused.

"Then, where do these pictures of her taken by CPS, after being in the presence of Daven showing bruises? Tabô was bruised many times around even inside Suzy's daycare too. I gave these pictures to the court to testify of the abuse. Why Tabô declared what she declared to CPS and why do you think she said that she stays with her dad because she's scared of Daven? These so-called specialists closed their eyes on a child's tears. They didn't even start an investigation. She herself confirmed who the two was visiting, the father or the mother, by saying that she has her own room over her dad and Loylla has her own room too? How do you explain the Child Protective case # 287 495 09 in which Boney is saying the same thing and confirming that she lives with Grandma Zora Warner, in Arlington at Park Willow Lane. These things are all over written on her report to cps. Tracy made the same statements in that report. She said in report # 287 495 09 that 'without any doubt, every time children were over the mother, Daven hit Tabô. He left bruises on her body. This had been happening from November 2004 to October 2006.' This case could have been easily investigated because Daven was arrested after hitting her by Fort Worth Police. Please don't tell me that the report you are carrying does not see Daven beating the kids," I responded to Kathryn.

Four days after a case worker went to Bellaire Elementary to interview both girls, Sheebah was arrested. Because she thought she will be out before November 24, the scheduled visitation day, she confirmed that meeting with CPS through Tracy Burkhart. But the amount of her bond, as set by the judge was so monumental, even for Suzy Dale to handle. She was not able to pay. As Hurst Police would report it so clearly later in its case # 08-9786, Sheebah stayed in jail till December. Sarah K Ennis, her CPS case worker with whom she had a prior arrangement to visit, showed up on November 24, 2008, in Bedford, looking for Sheebah at 2700 Central Drive # 110. She had difficulties to find that home address. Her digital GPS she was using to map her way in pointed at the 2700 Central Drive # 10. She knocked at that door to get informed, no one answered. She went back to work. She reported the no-found of address as an incident in the case # 287 49509. It is not like there was no 2700 Central Drive #110 at the Wood of Bedford. The apartment complex had wooded block number visibly put on the doors. Because Sheebah was in jail, someone took the number 1 out of 110. That door then showed # 10 instead of # 110. That was the only reason Sarah K. Ennis did not find the given address. Suzy Dale and Tracy Burkhart did not want her to know that. They also did not feel like letting down everything they have been working on. So they falsified the front door number.

On December 11, 2008, Sheebah got finally released from jail. At that moment, the 2700 Central Drive #110 was already occupied. She obtained another apartment: the 2052 Meadow Park Drive # 110, another suitable and equipped apartment, belonging to Suzy Dale. She then received Sarah K Ennis, after gathering all her kids in it.

"This is quite a story. I know Sarah K. did say something about this change of addresses. How come the CPS was not alarmed?" Kathryn asked.

"You tell me. In normal situations, an alarmed investigator would have looked into it professionally, but it was already decided who to pin down. That person was me. No, ma'am, Child Protective Services did not worry, even a bit, about that constant change of address. By the way, this was most definitely the apartment, the Child Protective Services was placing Sheebah in as her own place, and the apartment you were referring to, in Bedford, Texas. It was in here where Sheebah received Sarah K. Ennis. It was in here where the lady found children. This address and everything were documented down. She was temporarily living at 2502 Central Drive # 10 and still received CPS at 2052 Meadow Park Drive # 110. She did all that to prove that she had children and I did not, but I did not have to prove a thing. Police and Child Protective Services put it in writing for me. In their reports, since when Loylla was eight months old, one can read that kids never lived with her. I personally gave you the whole Confidential Investigation Report, the certified police report and the entire intake report from the CPS. In there, you will find all the proof you need," I answered.

CHAPTER 6

AN ATTENTION DEFICIT HYPERACTIVITY DISORDER CHILD

In their investigations, the main thing the CPS was looking for was to know who lives with children. That was also the main thing that was jumping in the eyes every time they investigated about their welfare. That was also the main thing they failed to see. It was strange to me that they continued to investigate what was written in their own report. Sheebah confirmedly said in the Hurst Police report # 06-875 that Tabô and Loylla live with their father, at Glen Rose. In CPS report # 263 258 15, Sheebah said that she sees both girls every Monday through Friday due to picking them up and driving them to daycare. She added and said that they will remain with their father. He comes to pick them up from this day-care, every day, and brings them back home, at 787 E Pecan Street # 181 because they live together. She wrote this down herself and signed her declaration. On February 5, 2007, Sarah K Ennis wrote that Sheebah stated that Tabô and Loylla live with the father at Glen Rose Apartment. She added and said that Suzy Dale, her boss, sees Kasalobi all the times. He comes and takes her girls home from her daycare. These two conversations are written in CPS case # 287 495 09, of February 20, 2009. They are enough to show that both girls never lived with their mother. Both reports give details of Kasalobi living conditions with them. CPS did not consider them. They were investigating on the preventative measures of things they wanted Sheebah to bring about. They should have asked just one question: how two little girls, who attend Bellaire, in Hurst, go to school from Bedford? On foot or by bus?

"Two little girls you said? It is documented that they are three."

"Tabô and Loylla only," I answered.

"Sir, you are presently involved in a legal action regarding custody of three children. One of them is a bipolar. As it is written here, you don't want her to take medicine. It is important for us to gather information, pertaining especially to the children's needs and relationships with you. It is a fact that you are disputing your ex-wife ordered legal custody and I am personally alarmed about that. You will also have to share with us matters of concern to you. So how about Boney?" asked Kathryn Omarkhail who seemed to lose patience. Her reaction was like the rise of the water in the sea.

"I only have two children with Sheebah. And none of them is bipolar..." I calmly answered.

Even if in the beginning of the interview, I set as a decor, the mood of not being a strong polite type to her that day, I started to answer respectfully. I had to because taking my kids away from me was not an injury that heals by itself. I did not want to live bleeding for the rest of my life. Playing tic to tic with that kind of a woman was just playing stupid. The social order of things obliged me, as we were going forward, to graciously keep my calm to what I sensed to be provocative questions. I said to myself, from now on, she poses questions, no matter how rude they are, I answer them with a clear explanation. I knew I had what one would have called the right stuff. I had the truth in me. I had the truth on my side and much more. Kathryn Omarkhail was not really at my place for my kids; she did not have them in her heart.

Her been there was caused by the court. For her, my kids were just business. They were a list of items that was not even a part of her usual world. She may have considered me as a piece of purpose for her interview, but for the well-being of my daughters, I was the real witness. Been a witness was a thing that was not supposed to happen, but I was there when they were taken. My job then was to justify myself. She was only collecting indispensable pieces of information to be given to the court. It was up to the judge to connect missing dots and to decide. That was the way I saw it. I changed the mood therefore, measured myself to what I stood for and commended her presence. She was there to do her job. That job was to crystallize things for the judge. She was at my place to right all wrongs I was subjected to. That was the reason of her survey and the grounds of that social study. I had to praise the work she was doing because my daughters and I were like a tree and its outer layer skin. Letting Kathryn Omarkhail put her finger in between was a wrong step. That was the sole reason I forced myself to graciously let wisdom lead the way. I decently kept calm to all her provocations. Because I had to assist her search for the truth, I became polite and respectful. We both were two essential persons, ready to implement, for the court principles, all details toward the accomplishment of a fact. And that fact was to establish that in this matter, my kids were kidnapped by two ladies. I had to be very patient with myself in the way I had to answer.

"Are they three or two?" she asked again.

"Two girls only, Boney is not mine," I answered.

"I have to establish who had children prior to what you are calling abduction."

"My yes is a yes and my no a no. I am that kind of person. I have been talking about kidnapping. I never said anything about abduction. In their deep meaning, these two words are different. Sheebah never had any of her children with her, she never had a legal custody of none of them, but she had done a good job of making a liar out of me. What she does better is to keep CPS lying for her. She is pushing that in my face," I answered.

We were in the 325th Judicial District Court. That did not mean there was a court order that gave her the legal custody of any of her children. She had been claiming to CPS specialists that we have decided that both girls, Tabô and Loylla, would stay with her on school days, they will be with me on weekends. There was not such contract or such thing to agree to. She abandoned them. For that reason, she did not possibly have even the natural right that the mother had. She could not claim her children, period. I took care of them, all by myself. I raised them. Therefore, she is not their mother, she doesn't deserve them.

"Who is Boney's father?" she insisted.

"Not me. When she got pregnant with Boney, she was gone already. She became pregnant around the time she was living inside Suzy Dale's daycare. I think I know her father. He is an African dude from Kenya. His name is Boney, just like her daughter. She knows that too. That story never been told. To fatten her purse, in child support money, her lawyer asked the court to record it," I answered.

"Talk to me about Tabô, why don't you want her to take her bipolar medicines?"

I never refused to give her medicines. There was not a reason to do so. She never was a bipolar for the simple reason that she never had an extreme swing in her typical mood, never showed a comportment that could visibly be different and that would affect the way she felt about things. I never noticed her acting differently than normal. She never had been observed feeling unusually great or experiencing a high period of joy. I never saw Tabô affected or imbalanced from things of everyday life. Tabô never was depressive. A bipolar person, as I learnt in psychology classes, is someone with a brain disease, a human being covering a disorder with a strange daily behavior that can completely disrupt his entire life. I lived with Tabô. I was the only parent who was qualified to declare her sick and depressed. She was not experiencing a persistent and difficult mental illness. If she was, I would have given her medicine in a bit, without hesitation. I didn't even see the beginning of consequences that her mother, who was not around, was describing to CPS. I did not see what she was recounting in Tabô. The woman was lying. She was setting things up to get more money. Lots of children are victims of such lies.

In a lot of cases, bipolar phenomenon starts in schools. It is visibly a reporting error that commonly begins in educational institutions. If a child is struggling with his materials, if he is hyperactive, refuses to comply and if he talks back, breaks rules, or merely contravenes, the diagnostic will be brain disorder. He will be declared a bipolar. From that moment, the consequence would be that the child will believe in being sick since he is repeatedly told so and will act as such. He will face a huge number of questions and massive amount of counseling to establish who the school wants him to be, the person he is not. Every institution, like the Child Protective Services, and every department, like the court and its orders, will add to that repeated multitude of remarks, what their world calls investigations and discoveries. At the end of the day, the school will make the child accept as true who he is not and deem what he will become. This will be the time parents will see their child become a fugitive from his own world.

Most of the time, the school does these things when it is a known fact that parents are separated. They create the bipolar business to make a child consume Medicaid. They insist on a child being an attention deficit hyperactivity disorder child to help the government sells their Medicare and to generate income for one of the parents. They get kickback by selling insurance once their investigations and discoveries show that the child is a brain disorder child. This is not normal because in doing so, they hurt everyone involved, including the child himself.

Since CPS accepts the school pressure on declaring the child sick and since they recommend that game to the judge, this bipolar business is not helpful, it gives a child an excuse not to follow rules. The school bipolar business is becoming a new normal; it has been made legal and must be stopped. Tabô was not sick; she did not have to take medicine. This kind of medicine gives an undemanding depression to whoever is taking them, and it also causes a young girl to turn into a fat girl. I was against these pills Tabô was obliged to take, prescribed or not, because usually they come with suicidal thoughts. It was my duty to keep her safe. To be a bipolar is not to be passing over rules and regulations, in a given social environment or to be gifted with over the board natural characters, it is to have a medically declared brain damage. Tabô was not. Her mother spent lot of time teaching her how to behave as such. She wanted to show that I was a bad father. That was the reason she instructed her how to act, talk, and speak the way she was doing. It also was the reason she had told her what to say and how to say it when she was in front of an official. Once proven by the court that I was a bad father, she could get custody. She wanted to be paid. It is a known fact that most of the time nowadays, gold-digger doctors keep creating names of diseases for financial purposes; if you sleep on your break time, it is called break syndrome disease. If you snort, it is a sleeping disorder syndrome. If you have a dispute with your parents, it is a Mendez syndrome and a lips syndrome is when you don't stop talking. All those, including bipolar, are simply created diseases.

"Why I don't want Tabô to take her bipolar medicines, you asked? It is because she is not bipolar. Why would I let her take pills that could increase the risk of her becoming very active?" I asked.

"You are not a specialist in the matter. You cannot confirm she is not."

"I am a parent, therefore I am a specialist. I live with my daughter. For this reason only, I am well placed to know when she is okay and when she is not feeling good. Why would I let Sheebah prove a case and let my daughter take medicines without doctor diagnosis anyway?"

"Your daughter never had a bipolar diagnosis, they never said of her being bipolar," Kathryn asked.

"Not really. She never even received a doctor prescription. The only person who evaluated her once was DuPaul, the Bell elementary psychiatric. That result was full of loopholes, it was opened to doubt. These things that you are talking about is created in Sheebah's mind with the help of CPS. They are designed for the court purpose. They want me to fall. Tabô is fine," I answered.

"Are there other children beside these two, the subject of this custody battle?"

"Yes, I have four here in this United States and one, who is still back home, in Africa."

"Do you currently work and where?" questioned Kathryn Omarkhail.

"I am a driver. I drove a taxi for a while, and now, since 2004, I am driving a Swift truck. I work on a Pepsi account since 2006."

"What do you mean by on a Pepsi account? Didn't you just say you drive for Swift?" she insisted.

Kathryn's line of questions was not designed to bring out of me my known feelings of confidence. To each question she asked, I gave her a direct answer. And each single answer I gave was a door that opened to another question. It sounded like she did not believe what was written in the Bible; she was trying to make me explain in details about how Moses crossed the Red Sea. Her line of questioning was much more designed to drawing me than to finding the truth on a common ground. I answered and said that "I drive for Swift transportation, I said that. Pepsi Co. hired Swift to move his products, I did not say that. Swift then sent his trucks and drivers over Pepsi, I did not say that. I am among those who move Pepsi products, I kind of said that. We move containers full of Pepsi, Frito-Lay, Gatorade, Quaker Oats, and other products from the Dallas plant to Grand Prairie mixing center." I explained to Kathryn Omarkhail.

"Is CPS involved in this dispute?" she asked again.

"I just talk to you about Tracy Burkhart and Sarah K. Ennis who…I mean…Yes ma'am, CPS is actively involved. To the best of my knowledge, one of the last contacts was two months ago on April 9, 2009. I had to meet with Specialist Payne of Hurst office. She called me to talk about this Tabô bipolar business. I explained Sheebah's deal on that situation. I also showed her the rating scale IV on Attention Deficit Hyperactivity Disorder that was done by Hurst Euless Bedford ISD on December 14, 2007. The last time I was in your office, I gave you copies of this rating scale too. I think you had a time to check them up. Did you evaluate their finding? If so, you have already concluded with them that there is nothing wrong with Tabô," I answered.

"Explain me how the rating scale came about," she said as I was handing documents pertaining to the situation.

"I apparently started at Bell Elementary."

"Be precise, do not say apparently," she ordered while reading them.

When the school was told by Sheebah that Tabô was making verbal threats on herself and was acting as a person who was about to take her own life, the campus authorities initiated the wary investigation. I was called in and experienced everything. Together, her teacher and I were asked to sit down. Then DuPaul, the psychiatrist, began to do some psychological tests and more. Many of them were mental evaluations about Tabô. DuPaul questioned me about her behavior. Then, he called her in. He talked to her about people she knew first and exclusively asked her to give answers to questions he posed us. It was here where things became alarming and eccentric. Out of thirty-six questions asked on both tests, Tabô fail short. To the scale of results and through everything, she was bipolar. To the chart of the entire examination, it was determined that she also was an attention deficit hyperactivity disorder student.

"And what happened after that?" Kathryn Omarkhail asked.

"DuPaul called me aside and said to me that something is not right here, I mean she seems okay and yet she is flanking everything as if she is doing it purposely. Apses disorder child doesn't flank all questions even if he/she really is bipolar. Your daughter's answers were not genuine, they sounded pretty much staged. I saw her biting her fingernails, I observed her cutting knobs on both her hands with her teeth, if something was really wrong, at that exact moment, her face would have been twitching and her eyes would have been at least rapidly blinking. This was what DuPaul said to me," I answered.

DuPaul was right. It was his duty as psychiatrist to know these things. Tabô was acting like a child who had headache with a burning fever of more than hundred and yet was still able to play at the park at same time. She was hyperactive and yet paid attention to posed questions. She was impulsive and stayed focused at same time. Tabô thought she was playing DuPaul in his wary investigation. She tried to make him believe in what her mother trained her to show me. DuPaul refused to play in her mother's game.

"What happened after the psychiatric diagnosis?"

"Well, he asked me if I would authorize him to prescribe Adderall to decrease some of her forced activities. I asked him what would be the side effect from that medicine since she was not really sick. He answered and said that this drug was evaluated for her safety and benefit. The first side effect will be to clearing her throat all the time. Addiction to the drug is possible. She will increase in body weight, and down the road, she possibly will decrease her growth during the next eight years, DuPaul said. That did not sound good to me. Since there was nothing wrong with her, I asked him to skip that treatment and find some other suitable thing."

"Why did you refuse her medical treatment? It is my understanding that you always refuse to give medication to your daughter. Why is that?"

"First of all, I never refused any medical treatment to any of my children. Sheebah had been painting me that way to make her case. I am confirming you at this point that up to the psychiatric evaluation, Tabô was simply playing a calculated game signed all over by Sheebah, her mother. All answers DuPaul collected were not coming from her, they were coming from her mother. And this was not the first time, she always wanted her daughters to be declared something so she can keep collecting tandiff, Medicare, free rent, an extra check from the government, beside food stamps she is already receiving," I rapidly said to Kathryn Omarkhail.

Tabô was not an attention deficit hyperactivity disorder student. Even Specialist Payne agreed with me when she invited me in her office. She clearly articulated and said that she made her own evaluation, and that evaluation was positive. She confronted Loylla first. She talked to her on what was written on her school report. Loylla answered and said that their mother coached them to act that way. She had been instructing them to what to declare, to say and how to say it if their teachers ever asked questions about their lives. She had been showing them how to behave in front of a child psychiatrist and when to do it. Specialist Payne confirmed that Loylla refused to play, but Tabô decided to do just that, exactly as they were told. Loylla said to her that she talked back and called you offensive names. She wanted you, the father, to lay your hand on her so her mother can have a substantial reason to go to court.

CHAPTER 7

MIND ABUSE IS A CRIME PUNISHABLE BY THE LAW

Since Tabô's games were noticed in school and because DuPaul's result on her were questionable, Specialist Payne wanted to make sure she won't take a wrong decision, she then took both children in Arlington, at Millwood Hospital for a personal evaluation under the cover of her office. The hospital psychiatrist, a professional for many years on the matter, did not find anything wrong with Tabô either. He didn't even come across something closer to anything or to things that always show on kids with attention deficit hyperactivity disorder that could ring a bell. Tabô did not have headaches, trouble sleeping, or exaggerated excitability. She didn't even have an increased irritability. These things or one of them should have showed up to determine a fact.

"And they did not?" Kathryn Omarkhail asked after taking notes.

"No only these diagnosis did not show up, Specialist Payne said to me that unless what your wife and you want is a check that comes with that kind of business, y'all are not doctors, y'all can't just go around declaring your child a bipolar to obtain money from the government. It looks good on papers, but it is not right. If y'all do not believe our expertise, take Tabô at John Peter Smith Hospital for a third opinion. You cannot be fixed more than that. My job is to protect children against abusive parents, Tabô included, and y'all are abusive parents. Y'all are putting things in your children heads for a purpose. That is mind abuse. That is a crime. It is punishable by the law, Payne said to me."

"What was your answer then?" she asked.

"Specialist Payne was serene and unflustered when she told me all that. And because she was dead serious when she concluded her speech, I saw something different and said to her that I am not married to Sheebah. We don't live together. My kids do not live with her. None of her children live with her. She is homeless. It was not me who declared my daughter to be anything in order to receive something from the government. Sheebah, her mother, had been doing just that with the help of Suzy Dale and Tracy Burkhart. I will never explain this enough, that thing of manipulating the system, is sited deep in her."

"Up to your knowledge, did Tracy investigate on that matter too?" Kathryn asked.

Tracy Burkhart was already at school to evaluate both children. Her conclusion did not differ from Specialist Payne. It was not different from DuPaul's and from the one she received from Millwood Hospital. They all had the same assessment. Their opinion and consideration on the matter concurred: "both children are all right," Tracy said in her report. She concluded that there was not any concern or immediate worry about both children, they were living with their father and they are all right. She visited also with teachers and counselors. No one there confirmed that Tabô was putting her two hands around her neck. No one said anything about her seeking to choke herself to death. Those things were written down because their mother said so.

"Yes, ma'am, she did, and it was strange that she did not lie in her report that time," I replied.

"But why don't you let your daughter take her medicine?" Kathryn asked, sounding like a broken disk.

I agreed with Payne. Tabô was systematically manipulated by her own mother through the entire deal. She was not a bipolar and should not have been considered as such by Bell Elementary School. She was not an attention deficit hyperactivity disorder child or anything near to that, winding up. She was unethically persuaded to conform to her mother wishes, simply. There was a danger of letting her mother keep putting ideas in her head. "Keep on knocking on the devil's door, he will end up opening it," as it was numerously said to me by my pa. That kind of training, from nobody else but her mother, was the most dangerous exploitation done to a teenager; it was a mind abuse, a pure loss and a disadvantage in her future life. And when it comes to your own daughter, Tabô's mother was a criminal, using schemes that was destroying my daughter physically and psychologically. Because of everything that was going on, her down the road became like a river full of meanders. From that moment on, Tabô became scared of the darkness. The night turned out to be a big problem for her. She also was frightened of the emptiness in any room she was in, if nobody was around. She was also jumpy about her own voice. She had to whisper so nobody hears her speak. This was not normal for a child of her age.

When she was alone in the house, and it didn't matter what time of the day or of the night it was, she had every light in every room cut on. She also left the door and all windows wide opened. To me, that was a definite response from a frightened little girl. She felt she was in a potential danger because of what she had been told. That reaction was not coming from a bipolar; it was a panic reaction that was not reflective of normal development. It should not be overridden. When a child is scared that way, although it is most of the time typical on average for each child, something is not normal.

"I am not scared of the darkness. I am scared of the invisible people living inside of the house," Tabô often said to me when I tried to calm her down.

"There are not ghosts or invisible people of any kind living inside this house," I always advised her.

"Yes, there are, and they are not ghosts. I call them 'inside people.' They would never attack me when doors and windows remain spaciously opened. They are scared too, not of the outside light or the darkness of the nights, but of the noise of passing subsistence, like human beings and living animals. That is the reason I open the door, so I can catch some sleep," she always explained.

"Who is the 'they' you are talking about, Tabô?" I often asked, wondering about what was in her mind.

"The 'inside people.' See in the beginning, Mother told me stories of these people to tell to the psychiatrist. She wanted him to believe that I was getting crazy so he can prescribe medicines to take to court and show it to the judge. The judge did not believe me. With the time, you did not believe me either. I started to see these people from my mother's story every time I was by myself, mostly when doors were closed. Now I am seeing them around when windows are closed," she answered.

There were no inside people anywhere near her; there were no invisible persons inside the house. Tabô was petrified for being alone and terrified inside a secured house because her mother was lying to her. Putting this kind of stories in a little girl's mind was a crime. It is a crime punishable by the law. When a child is frightened that much, it is not impossible for him to start seeing things. It doesn't take that much to begin experiencing them, almost immediately. When it is foggy for instance, because he was scared during the day, that child will feel a cold wind crawling in his back in the middle of the night. He will also see ghosts around him. In reality, what he is observing is a configuration of fog moving their shapes around. It was not a ghost. Tabô was experiencing the same happenings. She was seeing a trend of these observable facts, not with her eyes, but with her mind. These things were coming to her in her daydreams. She preferred to leave both doors and all windows wide open not because she was mentally sick, but because it made sense to her. She thought that something bad would happen to her if there was not an outside involvement. Only a normal child in the same age range would have had an instinctual response to his fear that way. Opening doors and leaving lights on was not having her head in the clouds, it was basically a response to what she conceived as a danger. It was in fact a rational instrument of self-defense. She did this every moment and every time she felt threatened. That is self-defense for any sensible child of her age. I tried to talk her out of that out of ordinary behavior so many times. I told her that dead people, ghosts, and invisible people do not hurt people, only living people do hurt living people. She did not accept that as true. Every time I said that to her, she looked at me as if I was the only stranger in Israel. She never listened to my guidance. She was scared. She did not want to upset these uncontrollable inside people of hers. Leaving her personal spaces wide open was a weird way of defense to everyone else, but it was certainly a wonderful survival approach for her.

One thing was clear: she was not nervous of growling thunder, heights, or striking lightning. She was not anxious of a cockroach, a spider, or snake like some other kids of her age would have. For her, these things were natural forces. When time is up, they could end her life in a beat of her heart, on the spot. Inside people at the other hand will torment her body and spirit before finishing her. The danger of being tormented was not coming from outside, she said. She was well alert of the time and the place where she would be attacked; only when she was alone in small familiar spaces and inside enclosed safe areas. The danger of being tormented was already inside the house. That was the reason she insisted of leaving her personal spaces opened all the time she was alone. She paid attention to that observable fact; otherwise paranormal things and some ghostly phenomenon or simply a number of mystical happenings will attack her from inside when doors were closed in. Manifestly, this was the thinking that led to her pointlessly fear. Because there was no immediate danger to her that I knew of, I more than once put her, without hesitation in my Pa family tradition, "Dead people do not hurt living people, only living people hurt living people." That was a secret she should have taken. But the fear of these invisible beings popping up in her life was so intensively fixed; it was deep-seated in her, so much so that it was equally hard to make her change her mind.

That was not how an attention deficit hyperactivity disorder student rolled. That was not the behavior from a bipolar. By definition, that was fear and everything that comes with, a trepidation that was taking over her entire entity. That kind of inside panic was stronger than her will because it was, step by step, becoming her immediate threat. It was a painful cringing situation and a damaging flinching that was worsening. And there was nothing I could immediately do about it. She was ashamed of being found with doors opened while sleeping, she also was offended and showed a define rage about it. I wanted to guide her through that pain, to slowly teach her how to control every bit of her fear. I needed time to have time for that and I needed more of it because she was not letting me in, not because she did not want to but because she couldn't voluntarily ease that situation by believing in herself first.

"You asked me why I don't let my daughter take her medicine. This is my direct answer, it is because DuPaul and Payne investigations concurred, it is because Tracy said in her report that both children are all right, it is because the hospital never said otherwise. Tabô is not a bipolar," I said to her.

"Was she ever depressed?" Kathryn Omarkhail asked, while writing something on her clipboard.

PART III

CHILDREN ARE NOT ADULTS IN MINIATURE

CHAPTER 8

FEAR IS NOT DEPRESSION

I needed time to teach Tabô how to control every bit of her fear. I explained to her that whatever was going on was not a real thing. It was only an imagination from inside her head and an emotion from things she had been picturing with her eyes. I wanted to slowly show her the real cause of her panic disorder. She was not letting me in. Because of that, it was impossible for her to voluntarily ease her situation by believing in herself first. She needed more guidance. I couldn't do it without her help. She told me that she knew exactly what her fear was and what was causing it. The fact that she said that was the difference between her and a bipolar child. Depending of the mood of the moment, a bipolar child would react to different events, but a normal child would always be paralyzed by the fear of something because for some reasons fear is a continuing emotion from some experience in life. Tabô was normal; she was not just taking it; she was putting a fight. Her best defense was to be in opened spaces. She was in fact pulling herself away from that continuing emotion she called inside people. A bipolar child or an attention deficit hyperactivity disorder student experiencing a similar situation wouldn't do that. He couldn't defend herself that way because he is mentally sick. His sickness is an impairment that can be manipulated and managed with medicines. A normal child cannot hide the threat of fear. Tabô couldn't either because fear is an unacceptable pain and a situation that cannot entirely be avoided, even in a time.

"Was she ever depressed because of everything that was going around her or because of that fear?" Kathryn Omarkhail asked again.

"Tabô is vulnerable and petrified, but her fear is not a depression. Her fear is specific, defined, and critical. It is about the inside people. Given that that fear was turning her life into generalized nightmare and influencing her social activities, I observed her becoming irratio- nal. That interfered extensively with her regular routine. Even if her fear did interfere, that did not mean she was depressed. She is not depressed nor had a hyperactivity disorder. Without any doubt, she showed some aggressiveness toward me and toward children of her age, but it was not in intimidating way. She demonstrated manners that could have been qualified as not disciplinary with me. This also was a thing I called house dirty clothes because it was not violence in destructive way. To answer correctly to your question, no, ma'am, she never was depressed. She is not depressed. She doesn't separate herself from other people because she likes to be a leader. A leader can't be a bipolar. Tabô is a people person, her mother is destroying that."

"Well, up to this report, CPS will be involved in this dispute for very long time, why don't you tell them that? Tell them that your daughter had been scared by her mother, she is not a bipolar," she suggested, while reading the rating scale, one more time."

In school of pedagogy, at Bosembo College, the neck of the wood where I am from and where I graduated in genetical psy- chology, I learnt there that children should not be called bipolar. They should not be sent to mental asylum given that things they do are natural things they are supposed to be doing for that age. I was instructed that in that period of time, they are supposed to be swing moody people, and that by itself must irritate parents and caretakers. Their performances, activities, and actions are behaviors that change by every second in a day. Children do shift from fid- gety to restless, from hopelessness to happiness, from melancholy to wriggly squirm. These temperaments should be part of their life.

That is what they do. They are children, that is who they are. They are not adults in miniature, that is who they are.

Grownups, at the other hand, must know that focus impulsivity, poor social skills, defiant behavior, and oppositional attitude do come as a share in growing up business to most children. These characters are idiosyncrasy to them. Instead of identifying these activities as mental illness, adults should know that these are dispositions and reactions that lead these kids to their future. From these natural letters of life, they will exteriorize themselves in appearance, and they will also create a personality in their inner feeling. Children have to release that restless energy, and they have to burn off the steam they carry in them. That is what they do. It is not lack of parenting that leads to this kind of behavior because this behavior is simply their psychology.

More than ever, this was true for Tabô. These commonly particulars had to be found existing in her as part of her normal adolescence. She had to be rebellious because she was going through a normal developmental stage, and this period of time never came to a child without difficulties. It comes with defiance and rebelliousness always. These two are necessary for a child growth; otherwise a child will grow up with lack of feeling and short of sensation. I said this to Kathryn while she was still reading the rating scale as an answer to her question. But she did not get it; she repeated her question and said, "Why did you never tell them that your daughter had been scared by her mother, that she is not a bipolar?"

"That is exactly what I have been telling them and much more since. I repeated it to you so many times already. It seemed to me that you don't want to see it through, just like them. See, how hard it is for you guys to believe the truth? Let me say it to you one more time: my daughter is not a bipolar, she had been scared by her mother, there is no need for her to take medicines."

CPS is like a devil's door. If your child is tired, hungry, and sleepy, and it is dark outside, you go and knock to a door you thought was the right address where you should get the needed help. He will open it quickly than you thought. He will talk you out of not going somewhere else, promising you nothing but good things. Since a fake forged by a good counterfeiter is always better than a real thing, you will believe him because the word on his tongue is always sweet. Then he will deceive you because that is what he does, that is why his door is always built next to the help office. This is what happened to me with CPS. I was told by them to be on April 13, 2009, at their Fort Worth office. I went there hoping to have help for my children. I met Tracy Burkhart again. This time, she tried to play as if she did not know me. She ignored my remarks. Maybe it was because the room was equipped with recording devices. She introduced me to Jenita Talley. She said she was her supervisor. I told her supervisor that for the record, the first time I saw Tracy Burkhart was in Mrs. Suzy Dale's house, she was there because they were trying to see how they would help Sheebah, the mother of my last two girls and their protégée, to get custody of my children even if she knew already that Sheebah was homeless. I told Jenita Talley that I know their relationship and I do not want her in this meeting, Tracy has preconceived notion about me. She will bring nothing but foregone conclusion. Jenita Talley washed up my protest. Tracy ignored that remark too. They asked questions about Tabô's safety. I talked about her well-being. Suddenly, Tracy stopped me and threw her direct upper cut.

She said, "Why are you abusive toward your children, why do you always beat them up?"

I politely answered and said to her, "I do not touch my kids with violence. I love them. I am not abusive toward them. There is a reason you just call them 'my children' because they are not there to be hurt. You see them at my place every single time you arrive there, you ask questions, you observe them, have you ever seen them hurt?" I said by asking her a question back.

"I have been observing them, they are very active. There is no way you do not punish them. How do you punish them?" Tracy asked.

"You had been talking to them in school, what did they tell you? You should listen to their answers instead of being judgmental all the time. As it is written in your own report, CPS case # 287 495 09 and case # 263 258 15, you have asked me and them that question already. They told you themselves that I do send them in their rooms. I take their television away, and if they still not listening I threaten not take them to McDonald or to Chinese. They say to you that I do yell at them sometimes, but I do not hit them, and you concluded and wrote, 'Both children are all right.' Why can't you use that instead of fault-finding things I don't do?"

"You have to declare in writing that you will never lay your hands on them again, particularly on Tabô."

I answered and said, "I will never sign your prewritten document in which you say 'lay my hands on my children again' as if I am confessing something about it. I don't beat my kids. I never beat any of them. That is the end of that story."

"Of course not. I did not say you do beat your children. But you have to declare that down. You have to sign it with your handwriting. You have to say you will not hit them," she insisted and said.

"That won't happen. Everything here looks like you are trying to set me up. I know you and I won't do it. I do not hit any of my children, I never did."

"In order not to traumatize Tabô, it is imperative that you declare something in writing about it, something I will hold you accountable of if it ever happened. This here is a filled page of paper called Plan for Child Evaluation that Sheebah signed already. She promised to never hit her daughters. You have to do the same, it must be done in this present meeting," she said.

I carefully looked at the Plan for Child Evaluation she handed me. It was indeed written by Sheebah herself. I also saw her signature applied down at right end. I felt safe. I told Tracy Burkhart that since the document did not have the mention "will never lay your hands on your children again" for the sake of my children I will hand-write mine. I will sign it only if I don't mention that line. She handed me a Child Safety Evaluation and Plan. It was clear to me that that document was not similar to the first one she handed to me; it is even completely different in its contents. I wondered about that. She said both are the same; they are Plans for Immediate and Short-Term Child Safety. I took it and declared on it that "I don't beat my kids. I never beat any of them. If I have to punish them, I take their television and toys away and send them to time out in their respective rooms." I signed it on April 13, 2009. Jenita Talley inserted her signature as witness. Tracy Burkhart was the last to sign. I asked for a copy.

Tracy Burkhart said, "Only your attorney can have it from this office."

"I do not have an attorney yet." Then again, I just signed it. "Why don't you want me have one?"

"I did not say you can't have one. Go to the office of the Attorney General in Arlington, ask for a copy at public information desk, this office is not authorized to give documents out," she replied.

I left the Fort Worth office without a copy.

"What happened after that?" Kathryn, who was writing everything down, asked.

"Like I said it, CPS is a devil's door. They will talk you out, suck you in, once you believe in them, they deceive you because that is what they do. To my big surprise, that document they refused to give me a copy of was introduced on the trial of June 1, 2009, by Attorney Meda Bourland first and then by CPS Tracy Burkhart just after that. It was a big setup."

I explained to Kathryn that addressing herself to the judge, Tracy accused me of being an abusive father. She said not only I recognized that as a fact, I also confess by writing it, with my own hand, in a Plan for Child Evaluation that I furthermore signed. In that plan, she said, I promised "to refrain myself from using physical discipline on my children and will use other methods for discipline."

I did not let her finish, I stood up and said, "That is a bowl of human crap, I never signed such plan."

To that, she reacted and said, "Judge, you just witnessed yourself what kind of man is this man. He is violent toward his children, and when he burst like that, he uses fists to beat them."

"That is a big flattened pile of horse…horse…" I responded without delay.

I did not get to finish my sentence, the judge asked me to control myself, to not interrupt anymore, to take note, and to use it orderly when my turn to speak arrives. Then Bourland spoke about how caring was Sheebah and how much of a bad father I was. At the end of her speech, she asked to approach the bench. I saw her giving that document to Judge Bronson, the associate judge, and called it some kind of exhibit. She came within the reach of where I was sitting and placed a paper on my table. Judge Bronson asked me if I signed the document on my table. I responded and said, "There is not document here, Judge. What I signed was a Child Safety Evaluation and Plan written by my own hand, just as that woman said it herself. She just dropped two blank sheets from Texas Department of Family and Protective Services on my table. Nothing is handwritten in it. They are not a Plan for Child Evaluation, and they are not even signed. Let me approach the bench and show you what she put down for me, sir," I said.

"Council, what is going on here? The man is defending himself, he has right to the same evidences the court has. I have to question him about this document. You are to abide by the law to provide him with a copy," the judge said

What I received from Meda Bourland was a fake declaration. It bore my signature but was written not by me but by Tracy Burkhart. This was the reason she refused to give me a copy. She said that pertinent to the Freedom of Information and Privacy Act of 1974, they will forward copies of my correspondence to Arlington. I had to go and request it by myself. Fort Worth CPS did not have access to the information concerning me. I explained that to the judge.

"Council, this Child Safety Evaluation and Plan is countersigned by CPS supervisor Jenita Talley which is easy to verify. Following what you just declared, it is my understanding that, using his own handwriting, the father wrote a Plan for Child Evaluation, which is different to this piece of paper I am holding. Now, I just compared both documents, this is not the father's handwriting. Who filled this safety plan council?" the judge asked.

Before Meda Bourland answered, Tracy Burkhart, the CPS specialist, stood up and said, "I did, Your Honor. I filled the empty spaces and the father signed it."

"Is that what happened, Mr. Kasalobi?" the judge asked after calmly looking at me.

"No, Your Honor. Supervisor Talley was the last to apply her signature on the sheet I wrote. She did so as witness. She won't tell you that Tracy wrote, in her presence, what she signed. As matter of fact, the room was equipped with running recording devices. These gadgets will testify in my favor that I personally wrote what they both signed. These gadgets will also tell you, and I am sure of this, that this CPS Tracy Burkhart stayed behind to falsify this very document. If that is so, and if you really want to establish the truth and justice, please investigate her. You will see that she copied the child safety evaluation and plan I wrote, the one that really was signed by Jenita Talley, cut the top out, put on top the piece she wrote against words I said, and copied everything. That is how our signatures appeared to be in the bottom. It is easy to see it by yourself, Your Honor, even with untrained eyes if you compare this to the CPS original. One, on the top of the space she wrote 'Failure to comply will result in further action by CPS,' you will see a black line that is not supposed to be there and that crosses from one end to the other. Two, you will see in the first blank page she gave me that there are three cages cut in the middle by a strong line, this page has one. Three, the second blank page starts with Tasks and Services List. I don't see that head here because this page is also modified. Your Honor, this is the game that this Tracy Burkhart here present, CPS per profession and Suzy Dale, daycare provider, have been playing on me. They want my kids taken away and given to their mother for federal advantages. The mother here present lives in Suzy Dale's van."

The judge listened. Then he said, "I will look into this. If it happened to be so, Tracy Burkhart, you may be charged with perjury."

Kathryn Omarkhail stopped writing. She looked at me and asked if Tracy ever been charged of anything.

I said, "Up to my knowledge, nothing ever happened, but seven days later, she showed up home. It was on her unannounced home visitation. She looked like a lady in charge. As usual, Tabô was on the computer when she entered. I went back in the kitchen where I was cooking. Loylla was outside playing with her little niece. She acknowledged Tabô, but Tabô ignored her, as usual. Tabô never liked her. For her, Tracy Burkhart was up to not good."

"I see the kids are visiting today," she said.

"You called this a home visitation. Why? Because you knew they were here, otherwise you wouldn't have showed yourself up here, in this apartment, in their home, where they belong and where they have been living with me all along. They told you so themselves when you went to visit them in school. You testified it to Specialist Payne and wrote it in your CPS report # 287 495 09. How can you say they are visiting?"

"Sarah K. Enn found them over Sheebah. They live over Sheebah, we can prove that," she said.

"You, Sheebah, and Suzy Dale are buddy-buddy. That is some kind of conflict of interest. It also is an abuse of your moral integrity. In advance of that, you people do tip each other. That is how she borrowed that apartment where Ennis K. Enn found her."

Tracy Burkhart interviewed Loylla and Cui-cui, my grandchild. Tabô refused to talk to her. I did the same. She took notes and left. Kathryn Omarkhail wrote my new encounter with Tracy on her clipboard.

"Any criminal arrest in your name that you remember of? Because for certain reasons, every time I do your criminal background check, a 'not hit return' does come on. Nothing is up."

"Nothing is coming up because there is nothing in my record to come up. I am spotlessly, criminally clean."

"A 'not hit return' doesn't mean no crimes, it simply says that crimes are not available. Is there any charge pending against you?" she insisted.

CHAPTER 9

HOW WE MET

By insisting, she grew my mind in different directions. Kathryn Omarkhail wanted me to have a criminal record. I did not ride a small bus to school when I was growing up. I knew how to analyze a couple of things. It was not hard at that moment to doubt the intellect capacity of this official of the court. I looked at her and fixed my mind on her only. I read her through one more time. The woman was not there to conduct a reasonable investigation. For more than one reason, Kathryn Omarkhail hated me. She hated men indeed. It showed and it is called widow numbness. If she did not hate me, then she just did not like me at all. I let my wisdom lead the way and answered her without a smile on my face and said, "In my book, if it is said 'crimes are not available,' that means no crimes at all. If a crime does not show up in an official record, it means that crime never been committed. Same difference, ma'am."

"Tell me how you guys met?" Kathryn asked.

"How we met?" I asked back

"Yes, how did you meet Sheebah?"

I was separated when I met Sheebah on November 11, 1993. I remembered that as if it was yesterday for the reason that the burning Mount Karmel of David Koreish was still making news on television.

At that time, I was working in morning shift for Intex Security. My section of job to was clean airplanes for Delta Airlines at DFW airport. As I was getting off from the train, on my way home, she was getting in, using the airway stairs main entrance. She looked at me and missed her step. The woman was wearing prescription glasses, the kind that was on Urkel, of the *Family Matter* show. I caught her as she was going down. I felt her. She was about hundred twenty pounds, young, and charming. She positively smiled, then thanked me. I told her that she needed a bodyguard. Without any due, she wrote her number in my left hand and disappeared. When we met again, it was inside her efficiency in Arlington, Texas. I did not feel the sensation that two persons have to have, from one to another when they are together for the first time. Since that bestial commotion of affection did not rouse up in me, I started to ask what put us together. Her place was nasty, trashy, and smelly. And by the mess on the floor, it looked like an eleven-year-old girl was living in that room. On the kitchen counter were pour-out crunches of chips, decant of cereals, and crumpled packages of tobacco. I pointed that mayhem out. She answered and said, "The Marlboro cigarette pack is not mine, it is for a friend of mine. He left it behind."

"Oh! Is that the reason you smell like a pipe?" I said.

"I smell like a pipe? Do I? I tried one though. I did not like the smell." Then she showed me what she called her first cigarette, at least what remained of it. It was a cigarette butt glued inside a glass frame. It was also lying on the same dirty counter. She explained and said, "It is there to remind me to never smoke again."

I saw a picture on kitchen wall.

"That is me, in military uniform," she said.

I was impressed. Under that military frame was an unfinished bottle of Jamaican Bourbon. It was not completely disregarded since a single red rose stick was topped in. It was actually getting drunk given that its stem was plunged all the way down in the liquor. She looked at me and explained, "I do not drink, but the flower is coming from a friend of mine."

"You said you don't have a boyfriend when I met you. That's two friends already."

"I don't have a boyfriend. A white dude who has a weakness for me brought that whisky and that flower over. I don't date white people."

"You don't date white people or you don't like him?" I asked as I was opening her refrigerator.

"I do not like white people, period," she answered.

"You don't like white people and you are white yourself. What kind of fuss is that?"

That refrigerator of hers was empty like a Cowboy stadium on Monday morning.

"How come you receive his stuff inside your apartment: packs of cigarettes, liquor, and red flowers if you do not like him? Up to me, these things are trophies of his attachment to you. I see two plates with foods still fresh in them, which means in return, you do cook and give him all your food," I said to her as if I have known her for long time.

"What do you mean by in return? I don't like white men, I do not date them, and I do not take anything from them. He was the only one drinking out of that bottle. When he left, I wasted that whisky by dumping his flowers in. Of course I made him a decent plate of food from the food he brought in. That doesn't mean he emptied my fridge. I am struggling."

"You are white, and you are segregating yourself from whites. Are you kidding me?" I asked.

"Outside only, I am white outside," she answered.

"You can't possibly show me prejudice and chauvinism against your own people," I said.

"I think I was born into a wrong race. I like blacks, I like your kind. I feel like I am black inside me. Things are just like that with me. It is discrimination and narrow-mindedness in reverse. My refrigerator is empty because I am under big pressure. My one-year lease, which was paid by the state, is about to expire. My Ford Tempo, given to me by CPS is now breaking down. I don't have a good job. I don't have a family to lean on. I don't have anybody to help me."

Kathryn took note and asked me why the State of Texas had been paying her rent and why CPS bought her a car. I explained and said that up to Sheebah herself, she had been a warrant of Texas since when she was eight years old, from the time, Mr. Freeman, her great grandfather discovered that Kathy, her mother, abandoned her at birth, in Ireland. Sheebah was given to the State of Texas before Freeman's death. The state then put her in military school. She lived in different foster homes from Walnut through Lena Pope to Azle. At eighteen, she got her high school diploma. Since she did not want to be in army compound anymore, she was released to go to the Tarrant College. Even if she was not ready to live by herself, she was given an old Ford Tempo and one-year paid rent in Arlington and thrown in the adult society. By the time we met at DFW Airport, she had long passed eighteen and still not prepared to live on her own. It also was the time the state began the process of stopping taking her in charge.

That first day I visited Sheebah, the day I saw a pack of Marlboro, a Jamaican Bourbon, and a stick of rose, she had only two weeks to vacate the premises, by that December. Because she told me she was having difficulties to connect both ends of the month, I invited her to move in with me in The Concord Apartment of Euless temporarily. I shared two bedrooms with Lufungulo Raoûl. He was moving out around that time.

The Concord sits on crossroads of 157 and Highway 10, behind what was K-Mart building. It is Harmony Academy today. It became Camp Mutombo because most of its residents were originating from Kasaï, a region of the Democratic Republic of Congo. Around there, when one was talking a walk, one could hear a resident speak Tshiluba. We called those Tshiluba speakers, the *soso pembe* or white chicken. This was to the reference of white chickens President Mobutu took from China and raised them in N'sele farm. These chickens were sold everywhere in Kinshasa. We said, "The white chicken doesn't lack a country." Because of their culture, les Tshiluba speakers, les Baluba people never lack a place to live either, even in the United States, they made themselves home. So Camp Mutombo was their home. Since Sheebah did not have money at all, I let her move in with us. This was the beginning, Camp Mutombo was about to become her home too.

89

As she was moving her stuff in Lufungulo Raoûl's room, I took a hard look at her military picture, the one that was hanging on kitchen wall. It was here when I remembered her. "Have I seen you somewhere? Your long goldish hair…I have seen this picture some-where. This is the very photo a soldier gave me months ago in…" I hesitated.

"Carson Military Base, you first met me at Carson Airport. I though you forgot, I was not nice to you that day, sorry about it," she completed me.

I was in my first twenty-five hours of solo instrument after being released by Mr. Burt, my flight instructor. I took off from The Acme School of Aeronautics in Meacham field. My assignment that day was to reach Grand Prairie airport, touch and go, and then do the same at Richardson with a left turn to Alliance Airport in Fort Worth. My last landing was in Carson Military Airbase to fuel my Cessna 172. At the second entrance of the pilot lounge, I saw a young woman. She was sitting, lonely, completely lost, on an area bench. She lifted her head up. I glanced back at her. Her eyes were deep in her head, with a look of a sad person. She immediately hid her face. She actually seemed to look in the emptiness of the ceiling. I noticed a big thick pairs of glasses that looked way heavier for her face and understood why her look was so profound.

"Hello!" I said to her. She answered by moving her head back and forth. This notching made her black beret fell on the ground. An overflow of goldish hair ran down on her shoulders. The rain of hair from her head looked like a fountain of water falling from a rock. This soldier was very timid, but she had a massive eyebrow to emphasize the greatness of her looks. That, on its own, revealed the brightness of her facial potential. She was beautiful, and I started devouring her, so much so that I thought if she was an African dish, I would, without any doubt, have put her between two portions of cassava bread and eat it without any soup in it. She stood up to pick her black beret up, her hair flowing all the way down to her hips. That beret was already in my hands at that time. I handed it to her and her eyes crossed mine. I immediately remembered my pa; he told me once that "If she does look at you and doesn't make her look more desirable than needed, at that moment your eyes crossed, she is yours."

"I see from your uniform, you are an American soldier."

"Daah!" she murmured.

A compliment about her uniform would have done it. I did not know how to go about. I was very embarrassed. I did not know what to say at that precise moment.

"I like your uniform. It is making you very appealing," I suggested.

"Uniforms do not make soldiers appealing. Their intent is to scare, to hide and to imprint the authority of the man and woman wearing it," she finally spoke.

"Certainly, particularly this one, it looks like an African leopard," I said.

"It is military sandy cloth," she confirmed.

"I said that because all these soldiers around here are not wearing tach-tach like you. You look good in those. I mean you are an officer, aren't you?" I asked.

"I am a military police officer on the ground. I am off, going home on break, so I need you to leave, you are bothering me now," she ordered.

"Yes, ma'am. I have to fly back to Meacham field anyway, and I think they just finished fueling my plane. May I have your number please? So we can finish the conversation about leopard later on."

Feeling my next step, the soldier went mute again. She retracted herself inside an escargot shell. Her facial look went from nice to somber. She threatened to call the police on me if I did not leave. She looked serious. I decided not to leave. I did not want a ticket or worse for harassing a public servant. At least, this was what I thought.

"No need for that, you are an American soldier. You don't need any police to defend you. Sorry about that," I said even if I knew it was suicidal. I turned around.

I choose not to fight hard. I failed my ancestor dating tradition. Where I am from, when a woman says no, it doesn't necessary mean no. The standing tradition of that "no" means most of the time "date me more, show me what you have for me in your bag of gentlemanhood." A woman's "no" means "insist more, so I know today how you will treat me tomorrow when I will be your wife." I decided to leave empty handed, even when I knew she was just another great person in an American military uniform.

"I said no about my number, but I can give you my picture," a voice said.

I looked back; she was smiling. My pa said once that if you "touch a woman heart, she'll smile at you." That was exactly what I did that day. Women like to be told things they are not and things they won't become just to grow something nice out of them. This young woman who was almost depressed felt pumped when I said, "You are an American soldier. You don't need any police to defend you."

She was all that. She probably forgot who she was just for a moment there and I reminded her. What I said was not a compliment but flowers on her feet. I threw verbal flowers on her feet and she softened my way in. That encouraged me to say to her that if she gives me her number, I will be calling her every morning to tell her that she is shining in my heart to a point that I did not need the sun to lighten my day. I will tell her that even if I do not see her, she is stunning to the infinity minus one. She smiled again.

"Why minus one?" she asked.

"I am not going to tell you everything at once. That is why I am keeping one out of infinity." I saw another smile on her face. This time it was opened.

"Is this what you guys from Africa say to women?"

"Not to women, not to all of them. I am saying this to you particularly, most definitely," I answered.

"I do not have a number yet. I just got sent to Tarrant County Junior College. The army is sending me there. The world is a very small place, you never know, maybe we will meet again. This here is my picture, take it with you," she recommended.

"That works, I will keep it with you in my mind. Thanks," I said in rush. I took my Cessna 172 in the air, made a left turn, and flew back to Meacham Field.

"You don't let a woman who said yes on the first proceed to be the mother of your kids. She doesn't weigh enough," my pa said. Sheebah was not like the rest of American women, she was not easy to get. It is hard to know why American women are so easy to get and if that attitude is good or bad. I felt Sheebah; she was not like an African woman either. African women exaggerate. Not only they play hard to get, dating them is like going through an immigration process. They have to make you feel your own blood runs in your veins first. "It is because they are not club girls," said my pa. Till today, I don't know if he was right or wrong.

CHAPTER 10

SEXUAL DISEASES

Strangely enough, months went by. I forgot all about that encounter and the picture. I did not intentionally forget her long hair and her deep smiles. Nothing sensational happened that could have taken me back to her. She was after all nothing but another numeral to my problems. After that conversation, the first part of it at least, for me as I saw it when I left Carson Air Base, that soldier will be a headache, a bitter person, a discordant companion, and a hard to handle woman just like the rest of them. American women are complicated. They only listen to themselves.

I know this for fact. I dated Banaaba Yakson and married Sylvia Kenny. They were two very crazy bones. Two worse relationships a man can have. Thinking I was having an appointment with love, I ended up having problems on problems just being with them. I realized at the end of the day that they were just numbers, nothing else. These two women were two reasons I did not bother to look at the picture of Sheebah, the young American soldier. I did not want to attach myself to another typical number. Then again, if she did not give me her phone, it was because she did not want me to call her.

"Now explain to me why you kept the one out of your infinity?" Sheebah asked, after telling me that we first met at Carson Airport.

"Why did you give me your picture instead of a phone?" I asked instead of answering.

"Because I wrote my beeper number on the back, I wanted you to call me, so I can give you my number. You never did beep me."

"Oh! I never looked at the picture over that way," I said.

"Why did you keep the one out of your infinity?" she asked again.

"Whatever happened to your hair, they were all the way down to your hips?"

"I said I was struggling, it is expensive to maintain four-foot long hair. Why did you keep your one out of the infinity?" she insisted one more time.

"So I can multiply, in my mind, the idea of me coming to you, watching you dream every night. I wanted to be the one to wake you up every day from my left arm."

"Really? That is so nice."

"Wait a minute, you knew what time I was going home. You placed yourself at a right spot, at the exact moment I was getting off, in front of that airway train entrance. And then you played as if you were missing your step to get me catch your fall. You did that, didn't you?" I questioned her.

"Yeah right, as if I did not have a better thing to do, why would have I done that for? It was just a simple twist of fate. That actually was the first time I was in that airway, I was running late and took a short cut. It was a good pure coincidence that I met you there," she told me.

"This is how I met Sheebah," I said to Kathryn Omarkhail.

"So you guys met. It seems to me that there was only a love of convenience between y'all. You still have children together," she graciously attacked.

"We decided to. It was not a mistake that we had two girls. Before we create a purpose for it, I loved her and named one of my first terminal taxi cabs after her. I took the three first letters of her name and converted them into numbers. This was how my cab was numbered 549. These numbers are her initials."

"You guys never had any dispute since 1993, any violent dispute?" Kathryn Omarkhail asked.

"Come on, ma'am! Like every couple, we had our highs and our lows. After she had moved in with me, it didn't take long for me to find out that she was just too much for me to handle," I said to her.

"Explain what you mean by too much to handle," Kathryn insisted.

In only three months from the time after she had moved in, I realized that Sheebah was bringing home all kind of inexplicable bruises on her body. These bruises were causing open heated discussions. They were visible on her arms and around her neck. I questioned her about the one on the top of her butts and on her private parts. The very suspicious ones were the ones she could explain their origin at all. They were sets of printed four fingers from the left hand and from the right hand and two light skin discoloration marks on the back of each one of her legs. They were drawn on both her legs at equal distance and equivalent height. It was obvious that a man printed them there. Those bruises were still red and looked like they just got convincingly put there, on her skin, by someone who had been compellingly and definitely grabbing her directly from behind. He was holding her and was pulling her simultaneously toward him, and each one of his fingers left a mark on her thighs.

Every time she brought a bruise in, she blamed it on her old prescriptions. She had problem focusing through her old glasses and bumped in one thing or into another at work, she explained. Her justifications were not rational to me. No bruise on her body matched her narrative account. The description of things she called facts was not based on reasons but on fictions. And when she presented details for her defense, her elusive blinking eyes and her twisting hands put in plain words the rest of her story. To help her lie to me more, I even asked her if she was getting into fights somewhere. Since nothing right never came out from her mouth, I then told her what I was thinking about it openly. She became extremely defensive. She said, "Why is it that everything I say is a lie? I see now it is your turn to be hurting me. No one ever trusted me ever since I was young.

Why don't you trust me when I say I have been bumping into things because of my old glasses? Why don't you believe me?"

"I believe you," I said, but she was full of it. To that, she directly stopped being hysterical.

One day, on April, she did not have a swift justification for the puffy bruise that was on the back side of her neck. She couldn't justify the bloated contusion that was on her breast either. Both were skin cupsuckings created by a soft bite from somebody. The ultimate arrogance in all that was the way she tried to convince me what those no-opened wounds were not applied there by a man's lips. She also was short of explaining me why she spent that day trying to hide them. Since she was not able to explain these things, she called them nothing but a red discoloration of her skin. I called them hickies. The one that was situated on the top of her left breast, a soft and very private area of her body, was showing its redness. It was fresh. It was clearly tattooed there by a person who was sucking her skin, period. That person used a row of front teeth against the tongue. That was how it was designed. The whole picture hit me right on the nose; it gave me very bad feelings.

"I may have been hit by an object," she tried to explain again, with tears on her face this time. She was looking in the ceiling when she evasively said that. But it was visible that judging by their sizes, both hickies were not caused by a violent blow. If they were caused by a blow, she should have been badly hurt. The ambulance would have been called in. These hickies were put there as the result of pleasure from a fool-around. The other one that was on her neck was not a game either. It was situated at a place of her body where, if touched that hard, it would have caused her getting knocked out. Sheebah was not bumping into things. She was being gratified by someone who was marking his territory intentionally.

"It is just a discoloration of the skin after been hit, you have to trust me," she said, avoiding my stares.

"Stop digging. Those are hickies. Your justification is like you are still peeing on my feet and trying to convince me that it is the rain, as someone would have explained it to you too. Didn't you say something about trust? I did trust you, this time it is about you lying to me, continuously," I said to her dry up.

"I am not lying…"

"You are. It started with these odd phone calls. Someone is hanging up on my face every time the phone rings. When you pick it up and I approach, you change the conversation. Who is that?"

With a voice that was intentionally leaving things behind, she explained and said that all phone calls were not coming in for her. Only few of her friends have the home number.

"You gave my number to your lovers?" I unkindly asked.

"Not to my lovers. I gave it only to my just friends," she doubtfully explained.

"Where is the difference? Don't tell me those hickies are raining from the sky."

When it comes to married people, the couple should be the only friends that can be. Basically, a man and his woman in a genuine relationship are called to be living as friends. Since these two friends ought to be living as a couple, they should be the only friends in that relationship, period. No one else should enter in their friendship as a friend or a just friend of one of the couple. A thing is, even if it is feasible, that kind of a relationship will be a wholesome comradeship of lie. It will be the kind of slouch story that stretches a proper relationship out, a kind that simply is impossible to achieve and a kind to keep away from. Sheebah did not have friends. She shouldn't have had just friends either. Since they were having sexual activities in a private companionship; those were her sexual buddies. What she had with them was not a healthy friendship. Case and point, one of them went far and applied these black contusions on her body. By definition, that was a forced demonstration of ownership, a show of force of some kind and a message to the person it may concern. Friends do that not apply hickies on friends. They do not do that simply because they are friends. Friends do not do sex with friends. That is a regular order of things.

"What is the difference between friends and just friends?" I insisted.

"Sometimes, in America, people do sex with friends, but never with a just-friend," she said.

I was not that slow to not understand that friends or just friends do not have any level of bond. They are both terms used to blueprint sexual partners, nothing more, nothing less. There is not, on top of these terms, a label showing their real meanings to show who is doing sex with whom and who is not. Nothing is attached to them to show their closeness, nearness, or differences. These two idioms are not there to build a strong root for a fruitful family. The proof, I felt the burning sensation in my manhood three days after seeing hickies on her.

While taking a shower that morning, I became horribly itchy down there. She said that it was due to the fact that we did sex multiple times that same night; it will go away. The burning sensation became worse when I tried to urinate. It was here when I noticed a yellowish and smelly discharge out of my urethra. I showed it to her and told her that I was painfully hurting all over my manhood. She said that that smelly discharged was caused by sexual frictions. I was in endless pain; she realized that and said, "I think it is an STD."

"What the hell is an STD?" I asked her.

"I did not infect you. I am not doing anything with anyone. I do love you and I hope you do understand what I am saying. You have to trust me. If you want to tie me down and to have me followed everywhere, please do so and you will see that you are the only man I sleep with," she said instead of answering my question.

"I don't know what STD stands for. I never heard of a STD burning a wizzle with discharges before. So what is an STD?" I asked her again.

"You know, I don't exactly know what it is…an STD is a…it is an STD. This guy from Nigeria told me that it is a sexual transmissible disease," she explained.

I heard of sexual diseases. I studied them in my biology classes. I was told about some people contracting them and even dying from them, but I never actually gotten one. I did not know the symptoms, which was why I did not see it coming.

"What, you mean something like…do you mean…by whom… when…where…do you sleep with this Nigerian guy?" I disgracefully asked.

"No way, I see, you do not trust me. You are suspecting me already," she shamefully answered.

"Samuel Ndowo, Byron, maybe the white dude? Was it Mondongo, Edward, or Bryan? Is there someone else I did not name? How about Mwangi and Yiosif? Are you sleeping with Ashante or his twin brother Adongho? Maybe it is Akello who just infected me. You sleep with like one of them at time or all of them, together at the same time?" I repetitively asked.

"You just took these African names from the caller ID. I told you, they all are my just friends."

"You just said that this is a sexual transmissible disease. Just like hickies on your neck, it just does not fall from the sky. It is called sexual transmissible disease for reason." I raised my voice.

"Samuel Ndowo told me that his three roommates were complaining of me having transmitted some kind of…I mean…to them. I did not sleep with any of them. They wanted me to. I think they all know you. They are from Kenya. We work together. I am sorry… maybe I got it from shaking their hands. Akello is the doctor among them. He gave me these red pills. I took the medicines, but it did not work."

"It did not work? You mean you knew you were infected and yet you kept sleeping with me? Akelo is the one who contaminated you?

"No, I think it is Samuel Ndowo. He is my first ever. I started to feel sick after sleeping with him."

"Meaning you sleep with Samuel Ndowo. He contaminates you, then per vengeance, you contaminate three of his roommates and all his friends. Now, to satisfy yourself, you deliberately contaminate me too. That is a crime."

We violently argued. Later on during that day, the pain rose to unbearable at work. I noticed that the yellowish liquid changed its body mass and color; it became heavily brown. What also became agonizing was the running out of this gooey liquid and its involuntary expulsion. It was unstoppably making my pants wet and very smelly as if I did not take shower for a while.

At the Parkland Memorial in Dallas, the lead nurse told me that the hospital reserves the right not to treat me. I had to give her twelve names of the last people I was sexually involved with. They did not want to let anything unchecked because they were trying to stop AIDS, she said. I told her that since I was separated from my wife, I only slept with one person, Sheebah. She did not believe me.

"Well, in that case, you need to start your treatment at the county STD hospital in Dallas. It is located at crossroads of Motor Street and I-35 E."

I crossed the highway and went there. There the doctor said that she was obliged to speak with my partner in crime before I receive any treatment.

"A sexually transmissible disease is like a pregnancy, two people contract it together as one individual. It has to be treated at once, together with your partner. This is written by the clinic health division, go back and get me that Sheebah here," she ordered.

We reached the clinic around six in the afternoon, and since it was not an emergency, even if the burning was excruciating and horrendously insupportable, we only get to be received at four in the morning. It was only after the triage that I saw both our names written on the opened blackboard. That board was posted in the entrance of main hall of the consultation room. Every single person waiting to be received was sitting in there. Next to both our names was written the reason we were been received; "STD," it said. It was clear that anyone around there knew why we were there. I was ashamed of myself. I hid behind a rest area magazine. Sheebah was the first to be seen. When the nurse stepped out and called my name, she did it loudly and made sure that I stood and add my face to her voice. It was the biggest shame of my entire life. I was taken in a consultation room; there she took a ten-inch cotton swab, warned me that it will hurt, and then plunged it in the orifice of my manhood. As she was pushing it inside my urethra, she also was twisting it, left and right, to collect as much excretion as possible. It was a real definition of intense pain. I got an instant headache from it. She then pulled the stick off, cut the cotton swab in three parts, and put these pieces in see-through flat containers. With a new cotton stick, she repeated the same exercise inside my mouth, and then sent me in the waiting area. Sheebah was there already. When she called us back in, she said that all tests were conclusive.

I had four active sexual transmissible diseases: gonorrhea, chlamydia, trichomonas. I also had vaginitis in my mouth, which explained the itching, burning, pain, and blood spots in my throat. According to the medical chart, the family of viruses found in Sheebah's body fluid was floating. In the class of floating virus, some were still alive, others were very tired, and none of them was dead. They were still multiplying. That was why the hospital applied the medical procedure called antibiogram culture to find exactly what type of chemical would be stronger enough to kill all of them at one time because they were resisting.

At that, Sheebah looked at me and said, "See, you owe me an apology, I do not have a living STD, and at the other end, you are the one vigorously infected."

"Shut the hell up, we are inside the hospital. Do you want to talk about this now?" I madly answered.

The doctor interrupted her and said, "Do not morally destroy your partner. Medically speaking, he got the trichomonas from you. Only an infected woman gives it to her partner. It lives in him only a little while. It doesn't come from a man. Your man also has vaginitis. It is found only inside the vaginal secretion. He has it in his throat from doing oral sex on you. Lots of these virus are dying or tired because you have been taking antibiotics. Do y'all have kids?"

"Not yet," Sheebah answered.

"It seems possible that the red pills your wife had been taking are either not appropriate for the diseases or not strong enough. It did not work properly. Because of that, you both are contaminated by the virus of next generation. It has become very resistant. You would have been very sick from a variety of complications if y'all did not come over. You have the first warning already: your yellow discharged liquid changed into a mass of heavily brown blood. It doesn't happen that fast. Pills alone won't work anymore. They will miss what we call in the medicine the spike. These viruses had already adapted themselves in you. They could easily mutate to something new. Likely, you do not have young children yet, you wouldn't even know that you have infected them. Trichomonas and vaginitis are adult diseases. They hide in children and develop as conjunctivitis or pneumonia. They must be treated with discrimination. You contracted these diseases together, and you must treat it together," the doctor said.

"We did not contract it together. She infected me. She is the one who is sleeping around. This is my first time to be infected. I always stay away from prostitutes. I did not know I have one in my house," I replied.

I was not embarrassed when I said that. But the lady doctor insisted and said that we got it together. At the end of the day, I received two shots, one in my arm the other one on my buttocks. I directly smelled both antibiotics in my breath. It did not take long. I started sweetening and smelling like penicillin. I also received 60 Doxycycline mixed to Tetracycline pills. I had to take two pills a day, on a full stomach for the next thirty days. The doctor asked me not to engage in any sexual activities during that time.

Even if my doubts were confirmed by the clinic, Sheebah continued giving me unexpected explanations about this bunch of sexual transmitted diseases I had as usual. She continued on her bend-over excuse and said that sometimes, people do get these diseases almost naturally by using the public bathroom equipments for instance. We all went to school, as I said it to her already. There is a reason medical people call it a sexual transmissible disease. People get contaminated only by penetrations with other people.

She broke down and said, "We are roommates after all, we are not married."

"I did not know that we were nothing but roommates. I will remember that," I responded.

At the end of that conversation, I found out that, for a span of about a year, the Kenyan Samuel Ndowo was her fiancé. He was the man she gave her virginity to when she was eighteen. She then found out, after getting engaged, from his three roommates that Samuel

Ndowo was married back home in Africa. To retaliate, she started sleeping with them. Bryan was his high school only white friend. He was the one who left cigarettes and whisky in her apartment. She went to bed with him only after ascertaining Samuel's perfidy. She infected him too. That was why he had been looking for me. He wanted to shoot me, thinking the disease came from me. By the time she was moving in with me, she met Ezekel the Nigerian guy and Byron the Rwandese. She did both of them. At that same time, the Congolese Mondongo was having problems with his wife and the American Edward saw the mother of his kids leaving him. Both slept with Sheebah; both got infected. Since she had moved in with me, she said, she slept with twelve different men. She did them all in my apartment every time I went to work. It was only after she started sleeping with a thirteenth man, another Kenyan called James that she begun having back pain. She also saw a whitish discharge at this exact time. She did not know what it was till Samuel Ndowo's roommates started to complain about being contaminated. To avoid contaminating me, she begun wetting her hygienic pads with the red Nyquil. She wore those things for about two weeks, the time to finish taking these red pills. This was the reason we did not do it for that time period. Then she went to visit Samuel Ndowo in Arlington and brought hickies home. He infected her again.

I felt a drop of blood coming down from my nose. This is a known fact; I do bleed when I am sad. I also bleed when I am mad. I bleed simply because I am having a nightmare. This observable fact is a reality that started when I was child. This time, I bled because of Sheebah. I did not get the reason behind her cheating. Nothing was missing for her to go looking it outside. We made love every early morning at five before getting ready for my first job. We also made it around one, when I came back home between my shifts. This was generally before she left for work. At ten in the afternoon, we met in bed for the third time to indisputably seal the day. Our sexual life was fulfilled; at least that was my every day impression. I was wrong.

CHAPTER 11

PORTOS AND YOLO NEIGHBORHOOD

I did not see how she had time of even thinking about it; we were doing it so many times a day. Apparently, she just was not satisfied. I asked myself what was missing. Maybe it was because she was abandoned at birth and did not know any better. She grew up without a foundation and without a genuine basic knowledge of things. She did not imagine the consequence of what she was doing. Sleeping with different men was something she thought will get her a step closer to finding love she thought she was missing. Sleeping with different men at a time was, up to her, feeling beautifully desired. Feeling she was beautiful was also what she was looking for. She did not know she was doing everything the wrong way.

At this point, I was not angry at her anymore. I decided to be patient. Anger is a fear that only an ignorant carries around with him, as Ma would have said it. I was the one to blame. I should have paid attention to who she would be in my life when she threatened to call the police on me the first time I met her. I made a bad choice and took her in any way. She lay down with other men; she won't stop doing it. I knew we must go apart. She begged to stay. She wanted to have Lufungulo Raoûl's room, fully participate in bills, and stay roommates. I accepted that suggestion since she did not have a place to go. She took a second job at DFW Airport. That was how we both ended up working for Intex and for Hertz Rent-a-Car. She managed to have the same days off I had. We shared the same breaks and same time-offs. She refused to drive her truck and decided to have a ride in my brand-new Mazda 626 to work. Since she wanted to be trusted, we start being together every minute of every day.

Just thirty days after finishing the antibiotics cure, despite the fact that she was in her own room, we started with bed activities. I began discharging again. This time, it looked more like human nose snot. I showed it to Sheebah. She entered the denunciation phase first, then the denial stage. Progressively, she became more and more erratic. Sheebah behaved that day as if I was talking crazy things to her. At the end of the day, she gave me an inconsistent piece of explanation; the virus was resistant to start with, it will take longer to cure, she explained. I did not want to wait an extra minute. I took us back to the clinic.

The doctor said, "One of you guys is still sleeping with old partners."

I said, "That is impossible, Doctor, since that day, we have been together 24/7. We go to bed and wake up at very same time."

"Congratulations for that, still one of you guys is still cheating," he confirmed.

I knew it was not me. I looked at Sheebah and said to her that once home, she will pack and go. She broke down, begged, and confessed once more. She said that it was Byron, the guy from Rwanda.

"When did you have time to do that?" I asked her.

She said that she waited in bed, the time for me to deeply go to sleep. Once I started to snort, she woke up on her toes, took the key to my brand-new 626 Mazda, and drove in Arlington to see him. I answered and told her that she still will pack.

She said, "You lied to me, you said our love should be the kind that would last forever, no matter what."

"No matter what doesn't include cheating, and spraying STD around. Think, what would have happened if it was HIV or AIDS?" I responded.

The doctor approved my speech, gave her a quick counseling, and administrated a stronger antibiotic than before. We left the clinic.

When we reached home that day, she lost it and went berserk when I ordered her to pack. She started to break things in living room. I called Pam, her foster mother. I told her that she spent the afternoon screaming so loudly and throwing kitchen utensils everywhere in the apartment. I wanted her to come and get her before the neighbor called the police. She advised me to calm her down by taking her in the bathtub. She wanted me to pour cold water on her. She was doing it under the same similar circumstances when Sheebah was living with them. I lifted Sheebah from the couch living room and took her in my arms, under the shower. While we were there, someone knock the door. It was Officer Ramirez of Euless Police Department. He asked me if Sheebah asked me verbally to pour water all over her body. I said no, she did not. I explained the conversation I had with Pam D. Terry, her foster mother. I asked him to call Azle, Texas, and verify if what I just said was not true. He said that by me taking her in bathroom against her will, I used force on her. He told me to turn around. When I did, he handcuffed me. I was charged with assault and bodily injury. He wrote in his report that Sheebah stated that "on 04-11-1994, about 11:35 hours, she and Kasalobi got into an argument, over his sexually transmitted disease. Kasalobi got angry and grabbed Sheebah by the hair and dragged her around in the bathroom. The act happened without Sheebah's consent and caused her physical pain and discomfort. I then placed Kasalobi under arrest for assault under the Texas Family Violence Act. He was taken to the Euless Jail where he was booked in via departmental policy."

"You admit that you have a criminal record. If the police showed up and you were taken to jail, it means you do have a criminal record," said Lady Kathryn who spent that time writing down everything I was saying without interrupting me.

"I never laid my hand on her. I never pulled her hair. Things did not happen the way they are written and described in that police report. This is an old injustice. I complained about it inside the criminal court room. Since the Tarrant County Criminal District

Attorney's office has 'a not drop policy' in cases involving domestic violence, the final decision, as to the disposition of the case, rested with the prosecutor. And because Sheebah, the supposed injured party, refused to testify, the decision was not rendered. This is the reason it showed a not-return when you checked my record. Not-return means no crime. I do not have any criminal record. But if you check Sheebah's, besides what I showed you, you will also find that, on March 15, 1994, she was arrested for theft for a $20 check. That was a $200PB, class B misdemeanor, which landed her in jail. On October 18, 1994, she went in jail for assault causing bodily injury. That is a class A misdemeanor. She paid a $200 fine and then was deferred for one year probation. On February 1997, she had an assault with a deadly weapon causing bodily injury, it was a second degree felony. There is an obstruction of a highway passageway on February '98, and another theft by check on April 4, 2000. I gave you the file. You can check the rest by yourself."

"I have the file, I went through it. Even if you never laid your hand on her, the odds were against you. You were arrested, taken into custody, and then entered the guilty plea. That is a criminal record. That is enough for me. What was the name of the apartment complex or a place where you lived on your own? The reason I am asking this is to try to patch things together. I want to learn when your violent behavior started."

"Violent behavior, why in the name of justice…on which base are you calling me violent?"

"Was it in your apartment or in a house?" the lady asked.

It took me a while to give an answer to that question. I had to be cooled off and then be strong like a dry lava, after coming out from an erupted volcano. I closed my eyes before answering. The first image of my first apartment address had Claude Kaloso written all over in my mind. This man swore to be my friend. In reality, he was screwing my woman behind my back. A man doesn't forget when a thing like that happens to him. He has to remember it mostly when it happened in his own castle. Claude Kaloso was bad news for me and for the entire Congolese community. Thinking about him was not an easy task. To give her my first address in United States was to remember, as if it was yesterday, that Kaloso was the reason I raised Tabô and Loylla all by myself.

At the corner of Princint Lane and Bedford Euless Road, located in the city of Hurst, was an apartment complex we jokingly called Yolo. It was called so for a simple reason that a bunch of loving people from Congo Kinshasa lived once there in symbiotic cultural activities. We were an amusing group, the sample of the greatest abroad. From different mentalities and social classes, some of us gathered there just to gossip. We met there to talk about the good time and to eat different African dishes, under the leadership of one person, Roger Masikini, the Mokonzi. He was the boss and he showed it. Yolo was the "Nganda" that collected only the best. It brought us together regardless of the corner of the country we were all and individually coming from. We were one nation. It was here where Claude made Portos Kifunga his first victim.

Back home in the Democratic Republic of Congo, Yolo is a quarter of a pole apart place. In this city, youngsters and completed sportmen expressed themselves in open and legal competitions. Edingwe the "dibanda-man" and Belchika "the boxer" had their days of fame in this component of Kinshasa. Since the street boys and girls of Yolo were mean and mad, they beat the foot out of anyone who did not belong. Police officers avoided patrolling the neighborhood. They entered in only when things settled down. That was how Yolo scared about everyone. When we met at The Hurst View Apartment Complex, beside the police story, similar things happened. We drank as if we were still back home, as if we were still in the city of Yolo. We laughed and had good times. We brawled and gulped uncontrolled mouthful sips of alcohol. And when we did so, we talked about hot political subjects as if there was no tomorrow. Politics divides people, we argued a lot because of that. That led to exchange of strong words, but we rarely came to blows. Those verbal clashes were not that bad, they were almost designed games to throw away boring days. But they were similar to what we survived from when we still were back home in Yolo. And because these things were happening again where we lived, at the crossroads of Princint Lane and Bedford Euless, we called The Hurst View Apartment Complex, the Yolo of the United

States. This place played a big role in the Congolese community. It was the symbol of resistance and the house in which we settled our verbal differences, good and bad. This was the reason we called this place Yolo. We met again and again without bearing a grudge against anyone who derailed. We were a family made in Hurst, Texas, until Claude Kaloso showed up. I also remembered having my first verbal fight with Shadwel Nkuba at Yolo.

Coming from Belgium, Shadwel Nkuba made everyone believe he was a Congolese. He was not; he was Rwandese. He is Rwandese. Byaterana is his real name. He was not the only one passing himself as one of us either. Kalimasi, Kanngubi, Selemani, Jacque Ndenga, Otto Bahizi, and Sinclair were the few in our midst who desperately wanted to fool Congolese. They all said that their mothers were princesses from Bashi in Kivu Province. The difference between them and Shadwel Nkuba was that he bragged about his mother a lot. He said she was a princess from the east side, province of Kivu. She was not from Kivu and she was not a princess. When the lady was young, she had exceptional and nice curves on her body. The kind of curbs Bisengimana urged to take to bed. This was the reason she was brought in from Rwanda in his suitcases as house helper. She was not the only one who was brought in that way, but she was one of the few who helped a lot in the bed. Just like bunch of Rwandese, she changed her identity. She chose to be princess just the way Khamere's mother did. To that end and mean, Sir Bisengimana commended her to be a diplomat at the Embassy of Congo in Belgium. Bisengimana was Rwandese. For strange political reasons, he became one of Mobutu's ministers.

With the time, the diplomat separated from Nkuba, her magistrate husband. She became pregnant during that separation period by a Rwandese boyfriend. That child was Byaterana Shadwel. The magistrate Nkuba is a Muluba. He had strict tradition rules to follow. To avoid a pronounced scandal, the magistrate Nkuba covered that affair. He gave Byaterana his name; Nkuba Shadwel and got together with the diplomat lady. I told everyone that truth. Byaterana Shadwel Nkuba did not like it. He became my enemy from that moment on. The last time we had the same argument, he threatened to kill me once we meet in Kinshasa. I said, "Boy, stop scratching your butt hole, you will wake up with a stinking finger. When we kick the Rwandese Kabangue from the presidency, you need to find the fastest legs to Rwanda because true Congolese will be preventively coming after you. Kinshasa is my country. I grew up there."

At that time, we were fifty Congolese in the community. We were a group of getting along people. Including the amusing assembly dispersed all around Fort Worth, we were a fine crowd scattered in Dallas. We were doing just fine, all together. Even if we all did not live at Yolo, we were one nation. When a new guy arrived, we jointly got together and wished him a warm welcome. Tradition obliged, married women cooked fufu and pondu, and others brought kwanga and makayabu in. Food like mfumbwa and makemba were also present on the table. It was easy to buy these grocery products at Chez Therese, a Mid-City African Market in Hurst Texas. We ate and drunk, kept gossips down and intelligent conversations up to the exceedingly late hours. It was good; this was how we introduced each other. It was in that spirit that Kifunga Portos wanted me at his place, at four that evening. I had to meet a new guy called Kaloso Twaremba Claude, who landed in Dallas a couple of hours ago, he said.

That day, the weatherman spent a lot of time warning people about the outside temperature. He said that it will reach triple digits as it were yesterday. Twenty-seven people died by the heat stroke and more than fifty Mexicans perished in the Texas desert, trying to cross through Arizona into United States, he confirmed. He then begged people not to walk out in the open if it was not necessary. He asked those without good air conditioners to go and breathe safely in the big places like the malls and Walmart stores. It was under that cracked heat that Portos Kifunga wanted me over his place. I accepted his invitation. There was a reason he was called the chief of the clan. For those who arrived from home and first settled in Hurst, Texas, he was a unique pioneer and one in thousands. Congolese from Bandundu, the south region of Congo, he worked for American Airlines in this United States. He received plenty of airline tickets every year. He wonderfully helped people using that advantage. He paid their ways in from Congo. He received them at his place and then he cooked for them. That was very weird for a man of his standard. Where we are coming from, cooking is for women. A grown-up man, like him did not have to go in the kitchen for his guests, yet Portos did just that. He put clothes on the back of anyone in need. He gave rides and shared his couch. There is not a person, from that period of the time, from Bandundu particularly, who can say today that, he did not receive a free airline ticket, a free stay in his apartment, and a free meal from him. That made him a typical well-known person and a guest man. His good deeds echoed far and travelled back to Congo. During one of his business trips home, Portos went to sell some chemicals at Marsavco, a company that made soap in Kinshasa, Congo. Kaloso Twaremba Claude heard of him. He solicited his services. Portos met him. Kaloso Twaremba Claude was miserably working at Marsavco as a cleaner boy. Penny wise, he lacked everything. Out of pure and intense love, Portos accepted to pay for his passport. He then gave him a free airline ticket and enough money, not only to reach Ndjili airport, but to find his way out, once in the US.

As I was turning the apartment inside knob to step out of the door, Jeff Matanga called me back. He advised me to take off the cotton pants I wore and the red jersey sweater that was on my shoulders.

"Your clothes are out of season," he said

"It is burning hot outside, shorts and t-shirts wouldn't certainly do it. They won't protect my black skin," I said to him.

I was right. It is proven that under the heat, heavy wrapped clothing protects the body. North African desert people have been wearing layers of yellow, black, and white clothes made out of silk to generate the sweat. The purpose of that was to produce, from that sweat, the body's salty fluid. That liquid helps these clothes to stay wet and to shield the heat from penetrating the body, protecting it therefore against the sun bouncing rays. In order to balance the temperature in and out, they also drink hot liquid, mostly tea and cocoa juice, when it is hot outside. They therefore metabolize themselves to the surrounding temperatures. That is how they stayed cool for centuries. It was simply by wetting their clothes with their own body fluid and by drinking hot liquid. I told Jeff that it was hot outside; just like desert people, I had to wear long-sleeved clothes and a hat. He called me indigenous. We laughed. I then crossed four blocks and three alleys on foot to reach Portos's building.

CHAPTER 12

THE WHITE ON CHICKEN SHIT

There he was, undernourished and missing hair on both side of his skeletal head, just above his ears. Claude Kaloso Twaremba was standing in the middle of Portos's living room apartment as if he was the man of the house. Congolese tradition obliged, he opened both his hands, offered them to me. I smelled his breath. He was stinking like a scared skunk coming out from the open drain. I refused to give him a hug, but politely met him halfway. I put my right hand on my chest and lightly bent forward to acknowledge his presence. We greeted each other by shaking hands. I did bend forward to show him the score of respect I had in me for every person, particularly him, despite the impression of him I kept in me since we were back home. He then retrieved his right hand from mine, put it on his chest, and recognized my value. The skin tone of the man in front of me was near to the one on people from South Soudan. It was easy to confuse his blackness to the blue marine. He was very dark. Compared to South Soudan people, this man was short and very small for his age. That was the difference. I then remembered how I first met this guy. It was back home in Africa.

Back there, Claude Kaloso Twaremba was a wholesome stretch-out. He had an appalling behavior and had a long arm; Claude stole from his friends. He also had an inadequate sweet verb on his tongue. He was a sitting couch covert with lies; he lied to anyone around, even to his mother, a thing that we Africans do not do. With him around and since people do not really change, I had a bad gut feeling. I knew it won't take long before he revealed himself. I knew that when that happens, the community will suffer from him. Well, as my ma said once, "A dog that chases cars doesn't live long." He will burn himself up.

Kifunga Portos was not there. He went back to work. I smelled trouble. Leaving Twaremba Kaloso Claude home alone with his wife was a mistake I wouldn't have made at that moment if I was him. He just did not know who he was dealing with and what he was facing up to. The man was about to break this house down, I felt it. When we sat, he sucked a junk of snort through his nose, swallowed it, and started his conversation by saying, "I heard about you. You got into it with Aleka Asuka on the first day of your arrival here. Did you know that his big brother is President Mobutu's private pilot?"

"You just landed. Now how did you possibly know that?" I asked with sternness on my stare.

"Your big brother is the mastermind and the founder of the UDPS, the opposition party that is actually fighting against the MPR, the Mobutu party. That is why you both cannot get along."

He had a forged smile on his face when he finished that phrase. That smile made him look as if he was a beggar complimenting a yesterday benefactor who did not satisfy his vagabond expectations that day. He really looked funny; maybe it was because he was also trying to swallow this thick mucus he was generating. Even his voice was coming out very funny. I looked at him and said, "Godly Claude, you are amusing already. How long have you been in the United States again?"

He ignored my question. "Moreover, you told him that the very day you left Kinshasa, Mobutu cried in the meeting, he said, 'Understand my emotions'. I also saw Mobutu cry at that podium. Aleka did not believe you even if it was true. He promised to kill you for that. He even said that he will also kill the Congolese evangelist

Melchior Lecane, the very first day you guys will meet back home in Congo from here," he continued and said.

"I have known you back home as a stretch-out man. It seems to me that you are more than that. You are an emblematical trouble maker. Just few minutes in this great country, including Portos, you have already found four victims. You will never change. A mouth like that in this country, and this is an advice from me to you, will make you sit on a drying branch of the tree. I knew, at the very moment I saw you, that you are still that little snotty made from bad elements. You are a very unpleasant and disgusting person. You should have been dejectedly left behind. It is wise for me to steer clear away from you. How can you be already gossiping on things you are not even well informed, things you don't know their head or their tail?" I wondered.

"Aleka himself told me so. He even said that you never dried up, you spoke loudly and too much."

"Do you know that the white on chicken shit is still chicken shit?" I asked him.

"What is that supposed to mean?" he asked back.

"Welcome to United States of America. Welcome to Hurst, Texas." I ended that conversation, stood up, said bye to Portos's wife, and showed myself to the door.

Three weeks later, Portos convinced me to teach him how to drive. I did it even if my second impression of Claude Kaloso Twaremba was still disastrous. I found it strange that he was a mechanic and did not know how to hold a car wheel. He relaxed on his second day of training. He started talking about his family. He speaks only about his aunt, who lives in Belgium, because he never knew his real father, he said. He never had a father. His mother used to cook kwanga, a Congolese dish.

"My mother used to sell herself for pennies while doing that. I am the fruit of her activities," he explained.

"I heard you. Literally, you are a bastard in the strong meaning of the word," I said to him.

"I did not say that," he replied.

"Sound and clear, you said it yourself that you are a son of the bitch."

Months down the road, while waiting for a way to get his legal papers, Kaloso quickly fit in the American society. By then, he had Portos Kifunga all figured out. We started to see him in his silver Isuzu truck, driving his wife around, picking her up, and dropping her from and to work. That looked safe to anyone but very odd to us. For one, she had her own car. For two, she knew how to drive. For three, she was a cashier at Texaco station that was just at west side on the corner of Princint Lane and Bedford Euless Road. The Texaco station was inside the Hurst View Apartment Complex. She was working inside Yolo, at less than two minutes' walk across the parking lot. She did not need a ride. It was also around that same time period that we started to see Claude wearing Portos's Sunday clothes. Portos did not believe a thing from things we all were seeing. He became suspicious only when he saw Claude, who did not have a job yet, buy new articles from the store. He checked his put-away money that was inside his bedroom. Half of it was gone, taken by Claude. A big argument broke out. Claude was asked to leave before the end of the day. By the time Portos came back home after work, not only Claude was gone, the apartment was also empty. Couches and high chairs, decoration and electronics, kitchen utensils, and bedding were all gone. He also realized his wife was also gone. She was gone with Claude Kaloso Twaremba. They went to live together at Gentry's apartment, across road of Brown Trail and Bedford-Euless Road. That woman he stole from Portos became his wife and the mother of his half-caste child, Claude's firstborn son. It was because of this woman that Claude became a US citizen.

Portos Kifunga was hurt inside and outside by his best friend. That great pain gave him a strong skin; he stood and smiled. Despite his burning pain, he was still among us. He did not let himself down because he knew who he was. He also knew that the night will bring a new day, a tomorrow without another calamity. He still loved Claude, a thing I personally wouldn't have done at that time.

Thousands of days went by; Claude Kaloso Twaremba was now among us. He succeeded to be the story of Dallas. He was much avoided despite the fact that he was actively participating in all community activities. He was known as the malicious snake, given birth from a marriage between a Congolese viper and an India cobra. The man was dangerously venomous of the community. People stayed away from him as much as they could since lots of damages were done by him. No one wanted him in and around his house. He was fond of married women. It was known by then that he had already gone to bed with seven of his best friends' wives. We all knew their husbands. They were common friends of us. We used to joke about it and said that "when Claude visits your house, look your wife straight in her eyes, she knows something." It was near to impossible to know how he seduced them. Each one of these women knew each other; they all knew about Claude. Despite all warnings, they still went to bed with him. Not every woman likes a man because of the width of his muscle, and I am not saying that Claude has a wide muscle, I wouldn't have known. They went to bed with him because they wanted to feel it too. It is a known fact that "a sacred thing attracts" all the time. This is also the reason a married man sleeps with a nun. But Claude was not sacred; he was simply equipped with a soft verb and smarts tactics. Lots of women he slept with were cleanly victims of those tactics. Claude used pills to drug them up. He learned these diabolic methods from Aleka Asuka, the man who promised to kill Melchior Lecane, and me once home. Any woman who willingly stopped at his apartment and accepted to drink at his place was simply put to sleep on "Roche4" and raped.

Claude used to buy these pills from Aleka Asuka, who used to steal them from his little brother. This man worked for Delta Airlines. He travelled home a lot.

One of Aleka Asuka's victim was the wife of a well-known Congolese pilot. That day in Delta break room, she told a group of women she was working with that she took a ride from Aleka. They stopped at Sotogrande Apartment, where he lived. Aleka offered her a can of water soda. She opened it herself and drank out of it. She did not remember what happened after that. She woke up in the couch. Her underwear was wet, and it smelled like sperm. Two of these women concurred; they said it happened to them when they individually drank with Claude Kaloso too. They concluded that they were raped. How Claude inserted the drug in a sealed soda can and how he infused a pill in a potted bottle of a juice remained a matter of investigation. Aleka Asuka's little brother was interviewed by the police about it. He got scared and moved somewhere in Atlanta. To avoid family scandal, these women refused to testify. The pilot moved his wife to Canada where they live to this present day.

Because of the truth that lectures human being that "a friend of your friend has to be your friend," I started to open up to Claude Kaloso, through friends first. We began to frequent each other. We were circled by nice people who loved boxing sports, particularly by Guy Tshiteya, Miteo Ngambwa, Cyril Ndambo, Louis Kipasa, Ngoyi Dezy, and Andi Dimone. We also were surrounded by those who loved to play African football, for the most part by Claude Kabukabu, Shadwel Nkuba, Paul Mokuba, and Réne Ngambwa. Since we were bonded by common nice people, Claude Kaloso found a place in the middle.

Sheebah did not like Claude Kaloso at all. She did not want to see him around; she did not talk to him either. For her, he was a pickpocket. Claude received a payment of $800 to replace the head gasket on her Mazda truck. He opened it and accidently dropped a wrench inside the engine. He was unable to retrieve that piece of metal. He said, "It is okay, it will drop all the way in the low pan." He just did not know what he was doing. I then towed the truck at Vianney, a mechanic shop owned by a Ugandan. It was located on the other side of Adam's gas station, crossroads of Wilshire Drive and West Euless Boulevard. He fixed the truck. Sheebah then asked Claude to pay her money back. He never did pay back. Claude used also to borrow money all over the place. No one had ever seen a dime of that amount back.

That day, I did not go to work; my taxi broke down. I left it in the company shop. We all were sitting in the living room. My front door squealed and opened. That was Claude getting in without knocking. Sheebah got visibly agitated first and mad at him after that. She asked him why he did not knock. He explained that the door was already opened. She madly told him to never show his face again, till the day he will give back her $800. He showed up anyway, couple of weeks later. That also was known from him; he was a pain in the butt. He knew how to bother people. As usual, he was wearing a vest, a white long-sleeve shirt under, and leather shoes. To impress, he put a tie and sunglasses on. Claude was the only man I knew who did not have a penny and yet liked to live big. He liked to show off a lot. I have seen him repairing a car while wearing all Sunday clothes. When he showed, he started by snorting and swallowing his own spittle. He wanted to borrow money from me.

"How did you know I was home for you to just show up to borrow money?" I asked.

Instead of directly answering, he told me a brilliant story about his fiancée. She was stuck in Angola, he said. At first, I did not want to give him a dime. Loaning him anything was always the equivalent of giving it to him, literally. Trying to recover a penny from him was a fight. People do borrow because they do not have any. Claude did not have any to give back. He cleared his spitty throat, swallowed his snort again, and insisted. He said that the woman he was about to bring in the United States was in fact the little sister of Bamassani's wife. That got my attention since Claude himself was telling people that his fiancée was very short. In fact, when she stands up, he said, she looks like an eight-year-old girl kneeling inside a hole. I thought that since Claude had been messing with people's wives, this was the opportunity of making mockery of him. I asked how much he needed.

"$3,800," he said after sucking his snort in, swallowing it, and clearing his throat.

The man had chronic infected nose glands. And what came out of his nose through his throat was not normal. I would have said that he had been eating his own glanders; he was eating himself at all the time.

"I will lend it to you if you pay back with $200 interest," I said.

"I will," he answered without hesitation.

"You better, because it is not given to anyone to be doing what I am about to do for you now."

"Thank you a lot."

He signed a discharge. I gave him the money. He then travelled to Angola and brought his shorty wife in United States. That was the good side of the story, but Claude Kaloso never gave anything back, even a penny. This was another reason Sheebah did not like him. He stole a total of $4,800 from us.

On these days, we used to get together for the fun of it or to eat and drink while watching a sport event, like pay per view boxing matches. We met on May 12, 2001, over Miteo Ngambwa in Irving, Texas, to watch Trinidad against Joppy. Claude Kaloso joined us. Miteo, who had been trying so many times to revive something among us, found a golden opportunity on that occasion. He decided to light the calumet of peace between us. We talked first about my money. He promised to start paying the $4,800 back by settlements. Then Miteo told him, point blank, to stop sleeping with other people's wives. Claude denied everything in block.

"I know about you and Ma Mutombo," Miteo accused him.

"Who, what are you talking about? You mean the American woman who gave you the green card? Ma Mutombo, your wife, and me? No, why would I do a thing like that?" Claude asked repeatedly.

"I am thrilled you dare to deny that fact in my presence. I caught both of you, eyes closed and tongue kissing in the parking lot. You defended yourself and said to me, as if I was your child that she was your friend and it was an innocent kiss. We all know about you and her, Claude. The whole Intex, at DFW, will testify about this. You can deny it the way you want to. The only person who did not know about y'all is Felly Miteo himself. The entire time they were living together, as wife and husband, you were sleeping with her. There was a day, your girlfriend, the Kenyan lady next door to you apartment, caught you with Ma Mutombo in bed. A big argument broke out and the police was involved. You can't possibly rebuff that. I was there, and it was recorded. Can you also deny the fact that in Delta Airline break room that day at work, you started looking for me, calling my house, when I was right there, next to you? We knew you were trying to hit on Sheebah. We confronted you. She testified against you and we all proved you otherwise. Since we are here, explain to us again, what you were doing alone in my apartment that day?" I asked.

"Which day?" he asked back.

"Mr. Felly Miteo, you won't believe this. I went back home ear-lier from work and found this guy sitting on the dinner table, eating my children's food. Say it wasn't so, Claude, deny that also, I want hear it from you. We are not trying to make you confess, we are tell-ing you these wrongs that you have been doing must stop," I plainly explained.

"I did not know about you and Ma Mutombo, I am not mad at you. Don't you see? I have my Congolese wife now. I just can't believe you did that to me. You are my best friend, you were my best friend," Felly Miteo said suddenly.

"This guy is nobody's friend." Ngoyi Banze said, and Guy Tshiteya approved.

We concluded that Claude Kaloso Twaremba was not a sick person. He simply was imposing a control of his negative behavior on every single member of the community. Despite all promises pre-viously made to his friends about not dating other people's wives, he still crossed the line. As much as the white on the top of chicken shit is the unadulterated chicken shit, this man was not the victim. He was the chicken chit despite his denial. He inherited that behavior from his delinquent mother, who was selling herself around. Claude was not a self-destructive man; his brain or lack thereof was riskily setting him to cross to no other man's zone. A question remained nonetheless: was it because of the non-existence of a father that has been causing him to not bring himself to a life of respect for other people's wives?

Somehow, we made him promise to behave. We threatened him and said that if he continues knocking on the devil's door, the devil will end up opening it for him. He will be isolated, and no one will be talking to him, we plainly explained. Felly Miteo decided to forgive him at that point. I then quoted President Dwight D. Eisenhower and said, "I hope to God we are right."

CHAPTER 13

A CUCKOLD IS ALWAYS THE LAST TO KNOW

We didn't even have time to swallow our saliva, we heard from Claude Kaloso Twaremba. This time, it was coming from his own mouth. Paul Mokuba, Vieux Mandefu, Bolens, and I were four assistants to the president of the Congolese Community. We were the community Chiefs des Pools. We met every Saturday to organize the social and all activities with reference to the community. Back then, we were called to write the community by-law. Since one of those days was the last Saturday of the month, we also had to establish a financial balance sheet. And because we were approaching June t30, the Congolese Independence Day, we as well had to do the assets and liabilities for the community. We were very busy. I had to call in from KNON radio, my job.

We needed to collect money for the Independence Party. It was very late when we started calling members. It was around eleven in the afternoon when we reached Bamassani's house. We knew he was in a business trip in Congo. We hoped to talk to his wife. Paul dialed the home number. Strangely enough, Claude Kaloso answered the phone and said, "Do you have a slice idea what time of the day it is? We are sleeping."

"It is forty-five minutes past eleven. What are doing in Bamassani's house, answering his phone, this late?" Paul Mokuba, who knew like the rest of us all, about Claude Kaloso's sinister activities, asked him.

Right there, we all glued our ears to the speaker phone. We first heard the squealing of the bed as if someone was moving on, followed immediately by the voice of Bamassani's wife. She wondered who Claude was on the phone with. He vividly answered and said, "Nobody, it is Paul Mokuba."

"Hang up the phone. Did he hear me talking to you?" Bamassani's wife asked away.

"It is past midnight and you are in the bed with Bamassani's wife. I can hear her whispering. He is your best friend's wife. You bought a house in the same neighborhood, so you can be closer to her? Since he travelled, we have been seeing you with her everywhere. You have been socializing with her in strange places, at the park, in the swimming pool, even late night at parties. Why are you doing this, Claude? You started to sleep with her since the time you moved in her apartment complex in Bedford. We know that for a fact. Why are you always with your best friends' wives?" Paul Mokuba insisted.

"I am not," Claude answered and then the phone went off.

It was said that Bamassani himself knew about their relationship. In the part of Congo he was coming from, in Kisangani region to be accurate, les Baswahili do tolerate this conduct. Their wives do misbehave that way. Husbands believe that a real man hit only on a beautiful woman. So they let things slide when their wives go to bed with their friends. The more Bamassani's wife was seduced by Claude Kaloso, the more attractive and beautiful she was in her husband's eyes.

I was glad that I called in from KNON radio station that Saturday night. I found myself being the most essential witnesses to that conversation. We did not get the money from Bamassani's wife, but I was personally served, on the spoon, for my radio show. I decided to dig harder and I made it a scoop. That scoop made me a black sheep in the community. Some women in the community did not like the way I exposed Claude Kaloso Twaremba simply because

Bamassani's wife was included. The story that was no more about her changed and became about her, a married woman.

"She is a mother with kids. We ought to give her respect and keep her intact regardless of what we are thinking had been happening. She is a married Congolese woman, therefore she should be quoted and pointed out for her qualities, not for her flaws and blemishes," Ma Mukambi, the preacher's wife, advised me.

"I am right all the way. As a married woman, she did not have to let herself open to suggestions that way," I answered.

The next Saturday night, on my show, "The African Ambiance," I exposed the conversation I had with Ma Mukambi. I explained, with vulgarities in my voice, how the cuckold is always the last to know it. Women were cheating with Claude Kaloso Twaremba and their husbands did not know anything about it. Inviting him home was surely killing the entire family. If he did not steal the wife, the daughter will certainly succumb to his charm. I put in plain words the kind of man he was, he will use his polite words to find his way in. Claude was a bad person who wore Satan's ring on the middle finger of his right hand. He was hurting his friends because he knew that in the United States, even if it was suicidal, it was not against the law to sleep with someone else's wife. I also said that he is a tumor in a man's pocket. At the end of each year, using his very polite verb, he steals money from every single person who trusts him. He does that by hunting for parents with more than two children. He promises them $1,000 cash per child on income tax return. At the end of the day, no parent will receive a penny from the transaction when the IRS check arrives. It simply will be a scam and a rip-off. Claude knew he owed the attorney general on child support payment. He knew that by claiming these children, his entire check would be retained by the IRS and decided to steal from one child to give to his own son. The man is a thief; he never honors his debts.

After exposing Claude that he was making his friend a cuckold, I got a feedback from my audience. The best one was from Butera Nkundira. I put her in the air. She said that she was Congolese, from Kivu province. She is not well-known in the community given that her given name is Mitshombero. She is bony and tall, equipped with big forearms in a slender body. With a name like Mitshombero, even if we were in the United States, it was hard to be accepted by Congolese. Because of her Tutsi morphology, one will think that she is a Rwandese, one of 7,200,000 Congolese killers. So she stayed away from the Congolese community, her own community.

"You are right indeed, only a cuckold is the last to know. Your own wife sleeps with the same Claude Kaloso Twaremba you are talking about, did you know that? I do not think so, simply because you are supposed to be a cuckold, the last to know."

It was about two that Sunday early morning when she confirmed that to me. I felt like a jolt of electricity in my entire body. I had been ridiculed publicly while the entire Congolese community was listening. Ibrahim, my Ivory Coast producer, asked me to hang the phone up. I refused.

"That cannot be true. Sheebah doesn't like him since the time he was caught harassing her in DFW airport. They don't even talk the way acquaintances do. He owes her money, one of the subjects of their dispute," I answered.

"They do talk. She owns a Mazda truck, doesn't she? She was here yesterday. She came down to be screwed. For so many years, Claude had been doing that in your own apartment already, under your beard, literally. As much as you know about other cuckolds, your friends know about you. They laugh about you, mostly when you talk about someone else. I know this for a fact. We do talk about you all the time. You believed in your friendship with Claude, you opened your door to him, he entered and took your bed. You are a cuckold, just like everyone else," she said that while my whole French speaker audience was tuned in and listening to my show.

The more she was clearing things up in detail, the more my head was burning hot. If at that moment, anyone had plunged my head in the bucket full of cold water, he would have seen a disappearing hot and dense vapor. By the end of my shift, I was in great pain. TraMadol, a strong painkiller, did not work when I arrived home. That broken news made everything worse. Because I wanted a get-up-and-go stamina to stand up against my pain, I met Butera Nkundira face to face. She gave me a lot of recorded mini cassettes to prove her story. She said she had been recording Claude inside his own apartment.

Not only I heard everything Butera Nkundira talked about, I also heard the voice of Jacques Ndenga's wife. It started with Claude calling her house. She asked him to never call there anymore. She accused him of deliberately touching her breast. Claude's voice responded and said that he acted that way because he loved her. He loved her since the first time he laid his eyes on her, he said. Jacques Ndenga's wife got mad and yelled. She told him that she was not kidding, she will tell her husband. Then Claude said that beside the wife General Likulia confiscated from him, Jacques Ndenga left another woman and kids back home in Congo. The woman responded and said, "If you call again to blackmail me, you will deal with my husband. If you show up again, I will kill you."

I said to Butera Nkundira that this was not just another spot on the leopard skin; it was the mother of all worse situations.

"Why did you record all these?" I asked.

"Claude is my boyfriend. He was. That trollop had lot of enemies desiring to cut his throat. I wanted to be the first to do it. I found your wife with him in his bedroom. I violently kicked her out by tearing her shirt and bras. I took the freedom of setting recording devices on his land line because I needed to know when your Sheebah is there, so I can get in and beat the shit out of her butt."

"I heard him clearly inviting her to come over to Sotogrande apartment and make love to him. As a response, she suggested going swimming at the Hurst public pool, like they did it the last time she was over, after making love."

"Yap, at the end of that conversation, you heard Claude asking her not to forget to erase his number from your caller ID," she said.

"I also heard him asking her to meet him in his brand-new house, the one he just bought," I said

"Mrs. Kasalobi, did you ever receive a letter in which an anonymous person tells you about Claude sleeping with Sheebah?"

"No, ma'am, but people had been accusing me of writing those letters. I did not," I replied.

"Lots of people received these letters. The truth is that Claude sent them. He had been sending these letters himself to his victims. Generally, double-dealing women, even if they are that bad, do not climb on the top of roofs to scream their forfeits. Congolese women, particularly, do not talk, even among themselves, on the subject of being unfaithful to their husbands. Cheating is a prohibited matter. It is a severe taboo and a thing not to speak of. After poisoning lives built hardily, Claude cynically sent these e-mails. Imagine yourself receiving that mail, what would you do? That was precisely the excitement, the stupid pleasure he expected to see from everyone he sent it to. He was there present, as the rust on iron, in each house, spying and waiting to see what would happen. He wanted to find out how the entire family would crumble and gradually melt away. Claude is a human corruption, I wonder why he did not send one to you. He sleeps with your wife," Butera Nkundira explained, and I believed her.

It was Sunday early morning. For a believer like her, this was a day she couldn't create a story. It was a day full of Jesus. Then again, I had all these tapes that were testifying how Sheebah made me go to sleep, on my pillows, when she was doing what she was doing and how Claude put me on his list of his gloomy activities, not behind my back but under my beard. He put me on that list three months after Sheebah had moved in. As we were talking about STD, from the Delta public phone that day, she let me know that an African friend of mine came around looking for me. In the current of that conversation, she said that because of his heavy accent, she did not quite catch his name.

"It sounded something like a car that has either a low or a show in it. I do understand most African English, but that one was definitely out of the box. He is a short, dark-skinned man, well dressed with a neck-buttoned shirt with a tie. He drove an old red car. When I told him that I will tell you that he passed by, the man said it was not very important, he will come back. He just stopped by to say hi."

The only African I knew who had a name that had a car with low and show reverberations in it and who drove a red car was Kaloso. He owned a beaten-up red Volvo. I did not know why he was looking for me. I did not need his visit. At that time, no Congolese who knew about Portos Kifunga's misfortune wanted him around. He was the white on the top of chicken shit. I had feeling that he also was fishing for Sheebah. He had been calling her from the Delta break room public phone, looking for me when I was standing right there by his side.

In DFW airport, our break room had two public phones. We shared that place with Delta Airlines employees. As I was talking to Sheebah that day, Claude Twaremba Kaloso came snorting and occupied the second phone that was at my right side. I heard the picky *click-clack* sound of someone on the other end of Sheebah's line. She asked me to hold on.

"I want to see who this is," she said. When she flipped back over, she said, "It is the guy who came looking for you here the other day, he wants to talk to you, he said his name is Claude Kaloso."

I turned around and looked at Claude Kaloso. He was right next to me, forcing air through his nostrils. The man dared to call my house looking for me when I was at one-inch distance from him. All things considered, he was not looking for me. He was trying to hit on Sheebah, my girlfriend.

"Well, he is still on the phone, I told him to hold on. Do you want to talk to him?" Sheebah wondered.

I told her to keep him on the phone. I went back toward the table where Intex and Delta employees where relaxing, taking their break. Among them were Marcel Tshilombo, Ngoyi Dezy, Miteo Ngambwa, Veron Mualumba, Tshiteya Guy, and the preacher Marcel Tshilumba. They all came where both phones were attached on the entrance wall. They confronted Claude.

Miteo Ngambwa looked directly in his eyes. He asked why he was still holding and who he was talking to. Claude felt busted. He exhaled. A grungy and harsh sound came out through his grungy nose. He said, "Nobody."

Miteo then confiscated the phone from his ear, so violently, I thought he hurt Claude's left jaw.

"Nobody my butt, Sheebah is on the other end of the phone," Guy Tshiteya said.

He took the phone from Miteo and said hello. Sheebah answered, and they started talking. Just the way a person with bronchitis would have done it, Claude snorted again to clear his nose. With the calm voice he was known of, he said, "I do not call people's houses."

"Nobody asked you if you do call people's houses. You are, at this present second, talking to Kasalobi's woman, while he is located at two centimeters from you," Tshilombo said.

Claude Kaloso posed, thinking what to say that would get him out of that mess. He came up with "I don't even know Sheebah's number."

Veron Mualumba looked at him, took the phone from Guy Tshiteya, talked through it, and said, "Do you want another confirmation from Sheebah herself? She is still on the phone?" Miteo said.

"You are thinking we all are idiots, right? Don't be shy now. We all know, no long time ago, you left Kasalobi here at work and went looking for him at his place. Why is that, Claude? Portos's wife you stole from us is not good enough for you anymore? If you want to use a computer, as it was your excuse to show up over Kasalobi's, go to the library or purchase your own, capish? Let's argue just a little bit, Brutus. Why is it that your knife is always deep in your best friends' back? Claude, the truth and a logical conclusion is that you are not a good person doing something wrong sometimes. You are a bad person doing wrong things to your friends over and over. When you plant a bad seed, you will get a bad fruit, simple karma law," Preacher Marcel Tshilumba said.

I saw fear on Claude Kaloso's face that day. We all were mad at him. He knew at that point that he was nothing but a mosquito on the wall that should be squashed on that same wall.

Days went by. We all thought he will never do that again. We were wrong. There was a day that I was not feeling well at work and decided to go home earlier. When I arrived there, the front door was cracked open. I thought that Sheebah had left it that way, an hour ago, after going to work. It was impossible for her to just leave the door ajar. She was anxiously frightened of the kids that were hanging around and smoking marijuana at the park. Then again, it was eleven in the morning. Kids could had left it open before going to school, I thought. When I entered, Claude Kaloso was in my apartment, alone, sitting on the dinner table. I looked at him without a word. He calmly said, "I was in the neighborhood and decided to stop by. I knocked, but the door was already open. And because I was hungry, I entered…"

"And without any restrain whatsoever, you showed yourself to the kitchen, got to my refrigerator, squeezed a plate in, and feasted yourself on my kids' food. What kind of respect is that?" I asked.

"We are friends. There is no need of ceremonies among friends. Your house is my house," he answered.

That was the reason he never sent me the mail he was sending to men he was sleeping with their wives. He did have a million reasons not to send me that letter. Indeed, my house was his house. That kind of letter could have been the equivalent of burning the hand, the very hand that was feeding him. It was by design that he was in my apartment. It was not by accident that he was eating my food. Sheebah was cooking for him. If she was not leaving the door open or leaving him behind, then Claude had the front door key. That explained how he was able to come in the morning and why he was showing only after everybody had vacated to their daily occupations. He was taking over. That explained why he entered without knocking the day I was off. As the rust on iron, he was there present, banging my woman and watching me crumble.

"So you are thinking that my house is your house, right? Are you banging my woman?" I asked him over.

"Your woman…no…we're friends and I…"

He did not finish. I held him by his tie, pulled him from the other side of the dinner table, trailed him outside, and pushed him so hard that he hit my neighbor's door. I yelled and said, "My house is not your house, Claude. If I see you again inside here, I will kill you with the same dull tools Jack Ndenga's wife wanted to use on you." I said to him.

That Saturday night on my radio show, Butera Nkundira showed me something I wouldn't have seen otherwise. Her story touched my mind and opened my eyes. I wouldn't have been otherwise able to understand the meaning of "your house is my house." By ways of spoken testimonies from her, I confirmed that Sheebah had been cheating on me. I also reconfirmed at that same time that Claude Kaloso was a human corruption indeed. I slept on that story for days because it is never good to act when mad. This was the reason I did not raise hell after I saw Claude in my house once again. I needed to compose myself to capture an appropriate moment to confront Sheebah. I wanted a surprise that could make her confess the affair on the first attack. I gave it a moment to rest. I then came to a decision to do my own investigations. If she gave herself the freedom to sleeping with Claude, she could as well be talking to anyone else, I thought. I needed names. I bought myself an Optimus CTR-111 automatic cassette recorder. I connected that machine on the land line and waited. It didn't even take a full day. By mid-June 2001, I recorded a considerable number of men she was actively speaking to. It was clear; she was sleeping with every single one of them.

The first voice belonged to a man called James. This black man did not work, he did not own a car either, but he was married to a nurse aide called Anna. This woman was one of Sheebah's best friends. She worked as nurse aide at Our Sweet Home on Vance Street, just across the Messiah Baptist church, in Richland Hills. She received all her rides from Sheebah. They lived in the apartment F45 in the building behind ours. After dropping Anna at work, Sheebah had a safe and a necessary time to come back and do James. Tyler came after that. He was with his girlfriend in apartment H73, at diagonal direction to the building G in which we lived. They had their mentally and physically challenged little girl with them. John was a robust young man who was still living with his parents in the building B. He was friend to Andrew. Both were friends to my son. These boys were still at Hurst Junior High and spent lot of their time in my apartment. Keith Kenneth was just out of jail. He was a small drug reseller who was living in J81, a building at right entrance of Whispering Run. He was doing Sheebah too. It was hard for me to listen to their conversation. They were talking about drugs, with reference to all positions they made and the one they will make in their next encounter. It was in this section of the tape that I found out that Sheebah was smoking ice and crack with him. She was already a drug addict. Steve Rice was the most dangerous of them all. Up to their phone conversations, they met in Euless through a common friend of theirs who worked at West Park Nursing Home. They started performing their sexual activities inside Steve Rice's big brother's apartment, at Wilshire Manor, on Sagebrush Street. At that time, Sheebah's truck was broken down. She used to drive my Mazda 626. At the same token, she was also using it to drive Steve around. They went together to buy drugs in Arlington. Besides being a small-time drug dealer, Steve was a well-known killer, the tape said. He claimed killing many people in Indiana. He was arrested only once, for shooting a man with a stolen 9mm berretta. Per lack of witness and evidences to bring charges forward, he was released and put on probation. He then beat his wife and went in county jail in Indianapolis. Since he was already in probation, his driver's license was then revoked. He escaped from jail with the help of his niece, a state trooper, working as an officer in the Public Safety Division. In hiding in Texas, he used Steve, his real name, to temporarily live with Glenn Rice, his big brother. He bought a Social Security card and fake driver's license in Bazaar, at the crossroads of Westmoreland and Fort Worth Avenue in Dallas. To make it look legit, he added Rice, the family name, so he can work with his brother. This brother found him a job inside Royal Park Business Center in Euless, at sweeping company called Circle E. Because Steve was dealing cocaine, he had lot girls around him. Sabeth, a sixteen-year-old runaway white virgin girl, was one of them. After being high, Sabeth passed out. When she woke up, she was hurting and bleeding.

CHAPTER 14

WOMEN ALWAYS PICK DRAB MEN

In that cassette, I also recorded the voice of a man called Edo.

He lived at Rogers Apartment in Irving. This man worked for Marriot in DFW Airport. People called him Black Edo because his facial features were exceedingly unpleasant. Edward Phillips was his real name. This fifty-two-year-old homosexual man was not handicapped, he did not have any infirmity either, but he lacked a man's physical appeal. With his horrible gloomy eyes, abnormalities on his lips, the strange position of his existent ears on his head, and a repulsive dull nose, he was the ugliest of them all. Black Edo had a mouth that stunk just like human excrement because of his sexual activities. His body smelled like an empty cotton bag that once contained rotten potatoes. Everything on him, every part of his body was designed in violence with the human nature of things. Even if it was because of the drugs, I did not understand why Sheebah was sleeping with this guy. My question remained: why do women always pick drab men to be with? In that recording was also a voice I recognized. Since I couldn't put a face to it, I stopped listening.

After collecting all elements, I invited Sheebah at Furr's Cafeteria in Irving. In the middle of the dinner, I made her listen to the cassettes. Her tongue was cut deep right in her throat. She apologized, and as usual, she begged to stay.

"On one condition, since this is not your first forfeit, I want you to confess your betrayal by writing, from the first time Claude spoke to you and the last time you slept with him."

She did just that. She wrote a six-page letter in which I found frightening details. That letter was a broken door, not for me, but for her two children. I saw her out of my door, leaving them behind. Loylla was eight months old then. It did not take long; I started raising them all by myself. Claude was the main reason I stayed in that situation. He destroyed what I was building for my children. Per pure resentment, I made copies of these tapes and anonymously mailed them to Tyler's girlfriend, Anna, whom she used to give rides to work, and to John's parents. Tyler's girlfriend reacted violently. She waited for Sheebah outside in the Whispering Run parking lot. As she was stepping out to drop kids in Mrs. Suzy Dale's daycare, she met a scene downstairs. She was physically assaulted. Tyler's girlfriend pulled her hair, tore her clothes, and knocked her down. It was a must-see scene that pleased me. Sheebah denied everything. Hurst Police got involved. For hitting her first, Tyler's girlfriend was taken to jail for assault with bodily injury. I also forwarded the entire story of the allege rape, committed by Steve Rice and his big brother Glenn Rice on Sabeth, a sixteen-year-old virgin runaway to Euless Police Department. The girl testified against Steve Rice. He was arrested.

One more time, Kathryn Omarkhail did not interrupt me. She let me talk and took notes.

"This is going to be the very last time I ask you this question. What was your address just before living with Sheebah? I need to connect the dots and establish your past activities," she asked me again.

"Sorry, ma'am. I was kind of lost there. That question made me start thinking about Claude. I lived at Hurst View Apartment first, I was with three roommates."

"Both girls were born at this place?"

"No, this was way before meeting Sheebah. Tabô was born when we lived upstairs, in E43 and Loylla downstairs in G64. We had both girls in Whispering Run. As Loylla was reaching nine months, barely walking, Sheebah left us. At a certain time, the family size shrunk, I had to change apartments from three bedrooms to two. That is how I ended up in Glenn Rose. Since the day she left her daughters behind, Sheebah did not come back. Up to Hurst Police and to you, she was here yesterday, June 12."

"Since when you two got separated?" she asked again.

"Weeks after knowing Sheebah's distasteful achievements with Claude and ascertaining her cheating with my neighbors, I did not want her around, everything went in the open. From the moment Tyler's girlfriend attacked her, a day after Anna got into it with her husband, my life with her became without a solution. Whispering Run is a small place, every single person knew by then her disgusting sexual appetites with married people around us, with kids, and with friends to my sons. There was not a rationale explanation for her to expose herself that way. It was impossible for a human being, for her particularly, to carry out these devious performances. When did she even get the energy of practically screwing anything that moved around her was a question I stayed up nights trying to answer. Her two daughters were called children of a prostitute. She asked for forgiveness again. I heard that and forgave her, but I was ashamed of myself. I did not have anything to do with her anymore. I listened to me and opened my front door. I let her out. It was after June 2001 when she left. And when that happened, Loylla was about to reach nine months," I explained to Kathryn Omarkhail.

"Did you ever talk to her about all this assumed boyfriends prior to her leaving?"

"If I did? I invited her at Furr's Cafeteria for that purpose. I said she confessed everything in a six-page letter about that. Sheebah openly asked for forgiveness in another letter. It was seven pages long this time. She wrote it a week later, in her very moment of despair. This was the reason I decided to keep both letters safe. When her children reach the age of understanding, they will read and discern things the way I understood them," I answered.

When I read it, instead of finding in my heart a place to forgive her, I got hurt more. She thought that confessing her blunders will soften my heart and I will let her in. I used the second letter against her. I judged her from what she did not write in it. She said that she also was banging Magic, my seventeen-year-old next-door neighbor. Their relationship started around a cocaine puff of smoke, which they shared when my children were in school. Sooner, they got high and did it in my apartment. They continued dirtying my couch ever since then. They also met over Dona, her friend, who lived at Wesley Park Apartment. Magic, John, and Kenneth used to sleep with Dona too. Sheebah knew about it. They all knew about each other, she said. Sheebah admitted in that same letter that while she was in the city of Pecos, to visit her mother in the carnival, she slept with Curby, her own mother's boyfriend. She also was sexually active with Pastor James. Once I read that, I remembered the voice I couldn't quite put a face to but I recognized when I listened to the cassettes given to me by Butera Nkundira.

James is the pastor of Victorious Living Christian Fellowship Church. He had been around my family way before Tabô and Loylla were born. He was a very nice person and a good shepherd who knew how to put seeds deep under the ground to produce good deeds the biblical way. At least that was what I saw in him. Before he located himself eight hundred blocks of Glenda Street in Bedford, this man had his multicultural and nondenominational ministry church directly underneath my apartment. Twice a week, he climbed the stairs just to say hello to us. He loved my kids. It showed by the way he acted. Each time he came upstairs, he had something for them: a toy, a book, or simply a basket full of goods. At one time in December, he brought them a truck full of clothing, games, food, and quantities of gift certificates. They also received Nintendo PlayStations and bikes. Since we did not have enough rooms to keep everything, we had to give some to Bellaire Elementary School. Pastor James farmed the gospel inside Whispering Run apartment with courage; this worked on Sheebah. She started to pray, changed her temper, and begun to get better. I needed that because she stopped fighting, breaking dishes, and hitting her head on the wall when she was mad.

I went back to these cassettes. I could hear Pastor James's television emitting in the background. It was talking about the handicapped black man from Jasper, Texas, three years after his gruesome slaughter. It was describing the horrific way he was beaten, tied with chains to the pickup truck, and dragged all over the highway by white men. That repeat news did not bother Pastor James, the savior of human souls. Instead of praying for his blood that was spread as a carpet over the road, it was that same time he chose to be plotting against me, with vulgarity in his voice. As I was listening to their conversation, Pastor James's credit, as a man of God with a good heart, was getting washed away. My acknowledgment to his accomplishments, as a good preacher who notoriously took my family under his wings, was getting less and less encrypted in my heart. He failed his duty from the moment I put a true face on his story; he simply was a fornicator. I sat down and wrote his name on my list of the most hated enemies. James was an American preacher. Americans are businessmen; they do not give free rides. That common experience identified the real reason he was visiting my family. He did not have a vocation of saving our souls; he simply wanted to be close to Sheebah and easily take her in his bed. He had been doing just that. I wondered at that moment how many married women he used his Bible on for that purpose.

"Let's go far this time. The city of Forest Parks is too close. Let's go to Azle," Pastor James's voice suggested.

"Azle, Texas, is where I grew up, it is not that big. It only has one high school," Sheebah replied.

"Then let's go and make love in Brenbrook. We will finish talking about him paying alimony to you," Pastor James decided.

The rest of their conversation was centered on me. Pastor James wanted me to be paying child support. He wanted her to take both little girls away from me first. With the help of the church lawyer, he already found a loophole into how alimony should be paid, he said. He will use the jurisprudence since we were not legally married to show that she became incapacitated during the time we lived together as man and wife. To the appreciation of the judge, he said, if it is proven that Sheebah won't be able to support herself anymore, my life insurance will pay her for a limited number of years, he said. They agreed on that. That is how they decided to involve the Battered Woman of Texas to train and certain that claim. After listening to that designed scheme, I felt an urge to call Pastor James and curse his church. I put a cork on it; cursing is a language of a person who doesn't have enough words in his vocabulary to express himself. I decided to confront him at the exit of his next Sunday services and create a big scene in front of his followers. I went there, in the very tragic way I did not do it, I hesitated. I did not feel that enormous need of a loud physical confrontation with him anymore, maybe because the delay softened my anger. I approached him as he was saying goodbye to his followers. I held and squeezed his hand so hard and told him in front of his wife, "I know you are fornicating with Sheebah."

His dazed wife and incredulous ushers looked at me first, then shamefully at him. They were very surprised.

I added and said, "I won't be responsible for my actions anymore. The next time I see you upstairs will be your last."

I left. That was a small message from me to him that I planted in his wife. It was small but powerful enough to produce an adequate amount of flames to burn the whole town.

I did not want Sheebah back in my apartment after all these events anymore. She was seen spending her nights on the roof of my friend Eight. I heard that Pastor James bought her a small red Escort. Not long after that, its timing belt broke. Because of the lack of transportation, she got fired from Bedford Nursing Home and from Papa John Pizza. She spent some nights behind the Dollar Store trash bin before going to live in the women's shelter in Arlington. Using back and forth the United Way van as her means of transportation, she nevertheless continued visiting both children at their daycare. This was how she made a social contact with Suzy Dale, the owner. She got hired as daycare caregiver. I did not get to see her till when Loylla reached three years old. That day, Hurst Police knocked at my door. They accused me of family violence. Just like yesterday, June 12, they helped her kidnap both my kids.

"Where is the seven-page letter? I want a copy of both letters," asked Kathryn.

I stood up, reached my scanner machine, and made her the two needed copies.

"Who had both girls when she left?"

"I had them. Do you want proof?"

I plunged my hand in the file case and dug up the leasing records, the Bellaire enrollment forms, all medical documentations, the HEB custodian verifications, the Atna insurance cards, and evidences that was supporting my claim and handed all them to her. I then showed her the last hospital entry when Loylla was bitten by the dog. While she was examining all these copies, I said again, "I have them since their birth. Sheebah herself testified the truth so many times about it. That truth is documented in the government box files, in her police arrest reports, and in CPS records. I gave you these documents the last time I was in your office. They are legal, overweight files and recorded documentations. They will testify that I had them. You should verify the rest of them by yourself." I explained to Kathryn.

The last CPS entry, made on January 13, 2009, and recorded in Suzy's daycare, five months ago, was very vital in its essence. In that last interview, Loylla is recorded confirming that she lives with her father Kasalobi. She is ascertaining in it that she does not live with her mother. The case worker who took the report confirmed that Sheebah read what was written in CPS report case # 287 495 09. She verified all facts, accepted that what was said was true, signed, and dated it.

Because of her long criminal history, Sheebah has a huge documentation and a traceable trail of acts behind her. Everything combined show without any doubt that I do have both girls, despite the fact that yesterday, someone kidnapped them from me. Her involvements with Child Protective Service, every one of her encounters with the police, confirmed as a fact that I have been raising them all by myself, I explained.

CHAPTER 15

FAMILY VIOLENCE

"You repeatedly said you had both girls, all by yourself when she left when Pastor James intervened. You said you had them until yesterday before the police intervened. And yet it is written here that she had physical possession of both girls when Hurst Police helped her run from you for the first time. Because of your history of family violence, Hurst Police was repeatedly called. And the last time they showed up, they witnessed her taking them from you to a safer place."

"Not to a safer place, in the carnival in San Benito. That was where she took them for the first time. Your entire library defines family violence wrongly. I said this many times around and I am saying it again to you: in order for us to be having family violence, Sheebah and I should be living together, at a common address and in the same house. We stopped being family when Loylla was nine months old. From that moment on, we were no more together. She came back, surrounded by Hurst Police, and equipped with that famous story of family violence when Loylla reached three years old. She was prepared by The Battered Woman of Texas. Each incident that followed was dictated by Pastor James., I explained.

In my dictionary, family violence is the transitive use of aggressive and physical means that must start inside of a shared home. It is a vicious and brutal hostility with or without fists as a weapon and on a perso, to impose his or her will when living together in a conjoint residence. Any kind of a way, used to try to overpower each other, while living in a common place, must be defined as a family violence. We never had hostility or exchange of fists. We never had a common place, we never overpowered each other. Nothing of such ever happened between us. She was gone prior to the time she showed up with the police. Actually, Sheebah was the one who was violent and had a tendency of always accusing people of things she was doing herself. She had that kind of aggression behavior that jumped out from her eyes. She never hesitated to use her vehicle as a weapon.

We both were working at DFW airport at that time. After an argument we had in 1994, as I was walking to my car in the parking lot, she brutally moved her Ford Tempo forward and hit me on my butt with it. I was thrown on top of a parked car and landed belly first on the concrete. I was not physically hurt, but I lay down still for a moment. She panicked and called the police on herself. The DFW public safety arrived within a minute. I denied everything and told them that I did not know what she was talking about. They then found out she was on Prozac and thought she was still under it. The public safety wrote a report on it and they asked her to leave the premises. That was a family violence on me since we were living together.

Euless police clearly described in their 94-0076687 report the similar incident that happened on October 18, 1994. She was arrested that day and taken in for using her car as weapon on her live-in boyfriend. While we were living together, she had another live-in boyfriend she hit with her car. She was charged with assault with bodily injury. That was family violence on her live-in boyfriend.

Euless police report # 97-012687 shows, in their files that she repeated the same forfeit on February 13, 1997. Officer Valladares Marco wrote that she used her truck as weapon and hit her common-law husband simply because he owed her some money. She then became hysterical and was booked in on aggravated assault. That was family violence on her common-law husband. Yet again, while we were together, she was living a double life. She had a common-law husband I did not know about.

Sheebah was also arrested on January 6, 2007. She was accused of hitting a man called Christopher with her Mazda P/U over a lady called Stephanie Love. Officer Garner of Hurst Police says in his report 08-142 that Sheebah was taken to jail. That was a family violence behavior on Christopher.

She was also arrested on January 6, 2008, for hitting one of her boyfriends with her pickup truck. As it was reported in Hurst Police 08-142, she used her Mazda truck as a weapon to hit her boyfriend's car when his children were still in. She was arrested and booked. That was family violence.

"Why don't you talk about that kind of family violence instead of creating one on me?"

"We are talking about the violence you committed on her, from you to her," Kathryn explained.

"Please allow me to repeat myself. It takes two to tango. That story of family violence on her, by me, you are talking about doesn't exist. The one you think you know was first shaped, then fashioned and completed by Mahr Kay Byers of the Battered Women Foundation of North Richland Hills, after we were no more a family. The whole thing was the idea of Pastor James. Their plot was to take both kids from my home and give them to Sheebah," I answered.

Sheebah contacted Mahr Kay Byers after her sinister conversation with Pastor James. She was living in the Arlington women shelter. She couldn't keep up with the strict rules of the guest house. She found herself sleeping on the streets because the entrance gate was closed after eight in the afternoon. She was always late. From there, she began collecting foods at church. Mahr Kay was known to hunt for women in similar situations at churches where they were looking for foods. She needed them as much as they needed her. They were her prizes toward getting fat bonuses. They met at the Food Bank of North Richland Hills. She asked her to attend some survival classes and was trained on skills, not to manipulate the system, but all instructions led to it. She learned how to plead her case with tears in her eyes, how to go sentimental in any occasion, and how to soften her attitude when questioned. She taught her how to be in the business of getting advantages put in front of her.

With Mahr Kay Byers, she learned how to act and how to master the game of an abused spouse. In order to maintain child support pouring into her purse, she was told that using nothing but family violence works. By definition, it does; it is among things the court looks deep into first. She graduated in this kind of lies and was ready to win her counterfeit cases against me. In order to take my kids away, Sheebah played the victimized woman first. Then everything was put together on September 26, 2003. It started at 11:00 in the morning by the recommendation of Mahr Kay Byers. The next move was to call Hurst Police to secure the departure of my children. I was surprised to hear the story of family violence when they came knocking on my front door. I told them that Sheebah took everything that belonged to her a couple of years ago and left. Duermeyer, one of the officers, pointed downstairs to a white woman who was crying her eyes out. She was standing near one of the four police cruisers. I recognized Sheebah. It was at this moment that Duermeyer, the arresting officer, showed me a letter, signed by her, withdrawing my two little girls from Bellaire Elementary. He asked me to step aside so she can come up, enter, and get possession of her stuff.

"Sheebah doesn't have stuff up here anymore. She took all her belongings with her in 2001," I insisted.

"Step aside if you don't want to get arrested for obstruction," Duermeyer said.

I did not want to interfere. I took my keys, hopped in my Mazda 626, and left the scene.

When I came back, I realized that not only Sheebah kidnapped my two little girls with the help of the Hurst Police, she also committed a bright-day highway robbery. She took everything that had a selling value: the desktop computer, my personal laptop computer, my television, my VCR and my video recorder machine, my fix Canon Cameras, and my VHS Samsung video camera. She even took a two-gallon plastic container that had quarters and pennies.

"She was dropped at Greyhound bus station, going south in the Valley. She had three bus tickets given to her by Pastor James," Dona said.

"Are you sure?" I asked.

"Well, they thought they were sending them directly to San Benito, Texas. They all mistook Sheebah. She personally told me that she will first go to Lufkin, Texas, to see Katie, her mother."

Before she passed with cancer, Katie was employed by the Heart of America, the carnival that operates in different town of the Valley. Carnival employees, as we know it, move constantly. They sleep outside under harsh weather, windy conditions, and dusty temperature. They work in stormy dust or under the blistering hot sun. They operate when it is raining or when it is simply calm. Children in the carnival do not go to school. They move city to city with them and do not have a stable physical address. They are often exposed to different diseases and infections because of the lack of things like sanitary facilities. They don't even shower as much as needed. Beaten or raped, they are left to themselves. No one reports the abuse because some of the grown-ups in the carnival do deal drugs, others are mentally sick. The rest are illegal. People are basically hidden in there because they have multiple warrants. The carnival adults do not want the law around or near them. Hurst Police did not bother to investigate any of these things before letting two little girls go down south to live that kind of life. They let themselves be influenced by Mary Kay who had a differently perception of the law and Pastor James who did not have any regard for ages and the needs of my children. They dropped my kids in the streets. Instead of directly going to San Benito as scheduled, Sheebah switched her itinerary. She joined her mother in the city of Lufkin, Texas. Only two weeks over the road, she was dry, no financial support at all. My girls started to starve. They went very hungry in New Braunsfels. Tabô became sick. She was four years old. When they reached the city of Nacogdoches, the office of the sheriff department who saw that they did not have appropriate clothing placed them temporarily in the women and children shelter. As it was recorded in his files, the Nagadoches sheriff then called me. Instead of placing them with Child Protective Services, the mother wanted me to go and get them, he said.

I called Mahr Kay Byers. I wildly chewed her about the entire situation. I questioned her on how much she was paid to hurt people and how many kids are on the streets because of her. She answered and said, "If you have something to say, say it to the Battered Woman foundation of Texas, and if you have a complaint, direct it to Hurst Police Department."

"If anything happens to them, I will fight you by different means," I said to her.

"Is that a threat?" she asked.

"You must be the very stupid one to not even know what a threat is," I answered and hung up.

I then wrote four letters. The first went to the Texas Department of Family and Protective Services, the second to the Attorney General Greg Abbot and the third to Kay Bailey Hutchison, Texas senator. The last one was addressed to the US Department of Criminal Justice, Civil Rights Division, and Criminal Section. I proved in it how much Mahr Kay Byers was abusing her official authority for financial gain. I wanted her to be investigated. They all responded. Even if their answers were not quite the clean cut of what I expected for, they were something. It was a start nevertheless. I then drove south, to Nacogdoches, to get my children back. The carnival was not in the city anymore. Sheebah took my girls and escaped with them. I did not hear from them for a while.

At the beginning of December, a telephone message from Tabô was left in my answering machine. She wanted me to go and get them because the carnival was closing for the season. The motel room they were living in San Benito was not paid. Her and her sister didn't have jackets or shoes to face the season. She was happy they saw lots of cities: Brownsville, Matamoros, Welasco, and Laurels, she said. Just after saying that, she changed the tone in her voice and started to cry.

"Curby is mean, he is beating us every day because Big John is my mom's new boyfriend. Grandma Katie said that her boyfriend Curby is crazy because he is sleeping with my mom too. They are always fighting, come and get us." The little voice in the phone answering machine went off.

I found Tabô and Loylla at the Stone Wall Jackson, 226 Stergers Street, in San Benito, in a cheap and dirty motel room that had bedbugs and roaches crawling all around its walls. I met my daughters on January 2, 2004, five months later from the day they left Hurst. I found them in desperate situations. That was the real violence committed from their mother to her own children. By the time I met them, Sheebah was already applying for food stamps. She told the Department of Family that she had been having children by herself. The father abandoned them and went back to his native Congo. They believed that clear lie.

I was a refugee then. Refugees don't go back to their countries of origin. Nevertheless, what she was receiving from the government was not enough. They have to share it with Katie, Katie's boyfriend, and her own boyfriend too. I put my kids in my friend Eight, and as I was leaving, Sheebah opened the back door, where Loylla was sitting, and forced herself in. An argument broke out. Katie, her mother, wanted her gone. She wanted me to bring her back to Hurst because she was sleeping with Curby, her boyfriend. I refused. Sheebah refused to get out of the car. She begged and said she will not be living with us; she will go to Arlington shelter. At the end, Sheebah rode back with us. When we arrived home, she asked to rent my guest room, inside my apartment. I did not want her any place near me or my children anymore. She found her way to Arlington shelter.

"So you are saying you brought both girls back and stayed with them?" continuing with her social study, Kathryn asked.

"Yes, ma'am, I am saying so. I brought them back because I had to. I found them hungry and sleeping on filthy places. The system confirmed that you guys sent them to a better place, you lied. Including the police and CPS, y'all are liars and wrong on Sheebah's behalf since the beginning. Yes, ma'am, I went to get them," I answered.

"Let me get this clear, you are saying the mother never had children after that. That is not true, CPS says that—"

"It is not CPS, it is you. Everything is written in the file I gave you. Didn't you read it?"

The Fort Worth Police report # 04135486 documents Sheebah saying that she used to come earlier morning from Fort Worth to take kids from Kasalobi's place and drop them at Bellaire Elementary. Hurst Police writes in his report # 04-10446 that both girls always live with Kasalobi, who always takes good care of them. Both reports confirmed the CPS report # 287 495 09. CPS says in it that Tabô and Loylla are with Mr. Kasalobi all the time. He comes to pick them up from the daycare and bring them at 787 E Pecan Street # 181 where they live. Sheebah herself went further and took Suzy Dale as her witness. She said Suzy has been seeing Kasalobi taking my girls home, at his place, where they live. On January 29, 2005, Officer Mark Bruner of Hurst Police confirmed in his report 06-875, through Sheebah's own mouth that Tabô and Loylla are okay, they live with their father. March 27, 2006, Hurst Police report # 06-2695 showed Sheebah going to jail for outstanding warrants. Asked about the whereabouts of her children, she told them that the oldest ones, Tabô and Loylla, are with Belinda their sister. They all live in their father's house, in Hurst. The youngest are over friends. This was also confirmed on February 11, 2007, in CPS case # 263 258 15 by Sheebah herself. She was recorded saying that Tabô and Loylla live with the father at Glen Rose and Boney with Grandma Zora in Arlington. This report was made by Specialist Tim P. Bringedahl. Tabô and Loylla testified in CPS report case # 263 258 15, they both confirmed that their little sister Boney lives with Grandma Zora Warner. They said that they live with their father. When he is not home, they stay upstairs with Antonio Rodriguez, their babysitter. Hurst Police established that statement as a fact on June 22, 2007 with its report # 07-5441. I had both girls after her trip back from San Benito.

"Who is Boney? Is he—"

"She, Boney, is Sheebah's third daughter," I answered.

At a certain time, Suzy Dale let Sheebah spend nights inside the Bedford Daycare Academy on Brown Trail. It was at that moment that she started to use her address, the 9160 E. Walter Street, to apply for food stamps and other government benefits. She had strict instructions to never bring a man in there and it was exactly at this location where she got pregnant with Boney. Mrs. Suzy called that a disrespect of a place of work. She got kicked out. She became homeless again. She reached the Kenyan she was sleeping with. The man refused to recognize his pregnancy. At the maternity, she declared that Boney's father was Keith Kenneth. Because Keith was pointed as the father, Sheebah then went to leave with Mrs. Zora Warner, Keith's mother. Time went by, and because she was receiving tandiff, Medicare, food stamps, and transportation from the government, they wanted to know where Boney's father was. She explained that Keith Kenneth was the father, but he was in jail. From his cell, DNA was ordered and performed. He took it. When the results came in, he was ruled out. He was not the father. The bubble was busted: Zora Warner was not Boney's real grandmother. Sheebah did not have a reason to reside in her house anymore. She was politely asked to leave. She had to leave Boney behind. Zora stepped in and became the grandmother to Boney. She spoiled her and treated her as if she was her own daughter. She provided for her recreations and for her schooling. Zora Warner kept her in, and she had been with her ever since. She is the only mother Boney ever knew. This was the reason she is called Grandma."

"Where was Kattaya at that time?" Kathryn asked.

"Daven Williams happened later on. They got a daughter called Kattaya while living together. Kattaya lived at the Sutton Square Apartment."

Sheebah and Daven William did not last long together; they separated from each other shortly after the birth of Kattaya. She then went to live inside the Woman's Haven shelter in Fort Worth for three months. The record shows that she did not have my kids with her in there. She was arrested during that time for fighting in Hurst area. Tim P. Bringedahl of Hurst Police quoted her saying that "Tabô and Loylla are living with their father." That statement is in the report # 07-5441. In it was also written that "Sheebah stops by Kasalobi's apartment to drop things for her kids every time they need them."

CHAPTER 16

IDENTITY THEFT AND LARCENY OF SERVICE

From April 2008, Sheebah was shown living at 1500 Sagebrush Trail, in Euless, with John Andrews and Daniquia Pratt, both employee of Kentucky Fried Chicken. She also lived at 1002 Fuller-Wiser # 4426 as written by Officer Mabry of Euless Police in his report ORI # Tx 2200900. She did not have both my girls with her. She stated, from this address, that I do often let Tabô and Loylla walk to school alone. How would they walk to school alone, from my address, if they were living with her? That accusation left traces that were confirmed in HEBISD truancy report. That report was sent by Brenda Aldridge, the assistant principal, and signed on April 2, 2008 by Livia Mansour, the campus administrator. The truancy letter shows her picking up both girls, every day in the morning, after I left to work, and dropping them late in school. As the sole custodian of my children, I had to deal with the truancy police and the truancy details that started from 2007. This letter showed in detail every single day they were late, absent, excused, and unexcused.

"So Sheebah did not have any of my children after coming back from San Benito. She did not have them at all. She couldn't even if she wanted to. She moves around a lot. She still does. Police had arrested her inside different apartments in which she lived with drug dealers. CPS had recorded her staying with people with histories of molesting children. Friends and family had seen her moving in and out with convicted male friends. It was during this time period that she became pregnant with her last child and started to be evicted from different places she lived in. These evictions show only her names. My girls' names are not written or mentioned anywhere on these lease contracts because they were not with her," I answered.

"Okay, let's talk about something else. Up to you, Sheebah is not a good mother because?" Kathryn asked.

"She never was. It is, as now, recorded that Sheebah was intentionally causing harm to Kattaya, her own daughter, the only child that was in her care at that time. She did not want her from the time she was born. She spent lot of time hurting her physically instead of babysitting her. She was trying to kill her. This is not an accusation, and I do not need to prove it because it is written in CPS files I gave you in your office. After shocking Kattaya that day, she had the presence of mind to take her to the hospital. There she declared that she passed out because she was asthmatic. The doctor proved her wrong and sent his report to Latrell Denise Perkins, a CPS agent. This specialist wrote in her report # 287 495 09 that 'The girl was observed with hand prints on her buttocks, purple bruises on her left side of her neck, black bruises between the rib cage and hip, black bruises on her vital and non-vital body area and on her left upper forehead area. The explanation given by the mother does not match the injuries, and this is placing OV at immediate risk of harm.' That was not short of assassination attempt. A good mother doesn't do that to her child. Carrying that child for nine months doesn't even make her a mother. A mother is a woman who is there for the child, just the way Grandma Zora is to Tony. A mother is a lady who has been there to love, to care, and to protect," I answered Kathryn Omarkhail.

Kattaya was not asthmatic. She spent that day crying because she was hungry. She did not eat because Daven and Sheebah, her parents, had been selling her food stamps to buy drugs. What kind of mother would she be, applying for food stamps and selling them half their given value, instead of feeding her kids? Her screams annoyed Daven who shouted with a voice full of curse words at Sheebah. To shut her off, Sheebah put both her hands around her neck and violently shook her. She did not stop crying. Daven, who at this point was wasted on cocaine, stood up and took Kattaya from Sheebah. He lifted her by the neck and threw her on the concrete floor. That impact was so severe, Kattaya passed out at that instant. And when she woke up, she had breathing problems and she was rushed to HEB. This entire situation was witnessed by Tabô who was visiting her mother that day at Boca Canyon apartment in Fort Worth. She verbally intervened. She was warned by Daven to shut up. She did not; she continued protesting the abuse. Daven got mad. He slapped her. Tabô threatened to call the police if he ever laid his hand on her again. He called her crazy and promised to kill her if she ever said anything like that again. When she picked up the phone to dial 911, he hit her with a closed fist. He then whipped her so hard with the stick, and it left a long and red bruise on her leg. Sheebah witnessed everything and did not protect both daughters. Pictures of these bruises were taken when she came back home. I gave them to you after showing them to Judge Bronson in the family court. Tabô reported Daven to CPS anyway. After that incident, he was forbidden by CPS to be near my girls. He was ordered to steer clear away and at a certain distance from Kattaya, his own daughter.

Sheebah was not a good mother because there was a day when I came back from an exhausting long day of work, just to find out that my electricity was disconnected. Direct Energy representative said that I owed a staggering amount of $1,200. She also said that I lived in apartment # 193 at 5933 Boca Raton in Fort Worth, for a period ending August 2005.

"I never lived at Boca Raton. I never lived in Fort Worth, period," I answered.

"You also lived in apartment # 258 for the period starting on May 2007, and you owe $1,000. This time, the utility was under Kasalobi...wait a minute...who is Loylla? And who is Tabô?" she asked.

"They are both my daughters," I answered.

"It is confusing, Loylla is used here as your first name. The social security number used to connect the electricity doesn't even match yours. The first five numbers are yours. The last four belong to Tabô."

"Exactly, that is a sham called half of social security to confuse the operator. Since you guys do not verify a thing, you sold your services to children, as usual, who did not applied for," I answered

"Who may have done that?" the representative asked.

"Sheebah did that. She is the only person I know who is able to do such thing. She lives in Fort Worth."

I disputed the bill. It took more than a nail-biting two months to set the record straight. I had to live without the electrical power during the entire period. My two little girls paid it dearly. They had to live in the apartment upstairs with Antonio Rodriguez, their babysitter. It was proven after the company investigation that at that time, Sheebah was living at Boca Raton Apartment. When contacted, since she did not want to go to jail for theft of service, she confessed and accepted to pay. Who does that to her kids? I was off the hook and my phone was reconnected back.

Two weeks after the first dispute, I received another bill. I was asked to pay $1,027.70. I felt like I was back in October 2006 all over again. When that consumption of electricity happened, Sheebah was living in Fort Worth at Bleu Valley in apartment # 5901. She was with Daven William. The bill I had in my hands was directly sent to Tabô. She was barely seven years old in 2006. That problem was brought to the attention of Hurst Police Department. They also discovered that Loylla owed $843.17 to AT&T for the land line that was connected in May 2004 at Sonterra Apartment in Hurst, Texas. She was four years old in 2004. They both owed a bundle of $670.12 at 1277 Country Club, $382.23 at Silver Creek, and $517.54 at Valley Park in Fort Worth. The entire crooked deal was discovered by Detective Younger of Hurst Police. Since my daughters' names were used, and given that I was one of the two only persons who knew their social security cards, I was contacted by Detective Younger. He was investigating on a complaint made by Mohan, from Direct Energy customer service, on possibility of usage of fake identity to connected electricity on different proprieties. That, he said, is called identity theft and larceny of service. His investigations were conclusive: Sheebah was found guilty. Younger then handed me the Affidavit INC#07- 3817 certified by Diana E. Sears, Tarrant County notary public and the report # 07-3817 to show me who was the mastermind of the crime. If Sheebah was a good mother, she wouldn't have spent a good deal of time mixing her own children's social security numbers to get utilities connected in her apartment. That was destroying the kids' credits for her own selfish interest.

"So what you are saying is that Sheebah is not a good mother, right?" Kathryn asked again.

"I am saying that she never was a mother. A mother is a person who must excel herself by doing and keep on doing well what she is supposed to be doing. A mother wouldn't have committed crimes of identity theft and fiscal fraud against her own children, as Sheebah was doing. If that is what a mother means, if that is what a mother is called for, then a child will not want any of it. She was doing all this because she was unstable, and quite seriously, she is still unstable. She is on wobbly legs and mentally unbalanced. As of today, right at this moment, she doesn't have a place of her own. If you subpoena the rest of her leasing records, besides the copy I left with you in your office, you will see that she lived in different places and ended up being evicted so many times around. You will also discover that the kids have never been with her in those places. Only the unstable mothers are known not to be living with their own children. Since July 2001, from the day she left, when Loylla was about nine months old, Sheebah had been evicted more than thirty-six times. The last eviction, for no payment, is two weeks old. It was from 600 Boca Raton # 96 in Fort Worth. She was in jail when the eviction went through. As of today, June 13, 2009, she is back on the streets. You said she is the one who kidnapped my two daughters. In all walks of life, where is she going to put them?" I said.

"I did not say she kidnapped your children. If she is on the streets, where are the children?"

"She is hiding them in Bedford, Texas, over at Charlene's, her friend," I answered.

"You know that she lives at 2052 Meadow Park, right? Why would she be hiding them?"

"You are testing me, right? After CPS got involved, the management of The Wood of Bedford apartment got involved too. She was an unlawful occupant anyway. She did not have the time to sign an occupancy contract when she got in. She was hurriedly put in there by Suzy Dale, the undercontractor. She was asked to vacate the premises by the owner. Once more, she was homeless. This time, she was homeless with two of her children: Kattaya and five-month-old Baby J. in her arms. She is not a mother. She is unstable and needs to bring my kids back," I explained.

"She was on the streets, at that period, with a five-month-old child, you said?"

"Almost. At that time, Suzy Dale was selling her school van. Both her daycares were getting shut down by CPS, she did not need it anymore. As she was waiting for a customer, Sheebah was observed driving it, with a For Sale sign on it. Baby J. used the vehicle as her first house, on the first day she was released from the maternity. The very next day, Sheebah turned it into Baby J. and the two-year-old Kattaya's home," I answered.

"How come CPS Tracy Burkhart recorded Sheebah having custody of all children and living, not in the van, but in Sutton Square, from the same day she was out from the hospital with Baby J., her newborn?"

"Ask Tracy that question. She did set that up for her. That statement is in contradiction with Hurst Police report of January 2009. They documented her being in the van with both children and looking for an apartment at Sutton Square. Sheebah was stopped at same Sutton Square and arrested in the beginning of February for outstanding warrants. She went to jail, the van stayed parked in the Sutton Square parking lot, and I was called to go and pick Kattaya and Baby J. up. Both these cases happened way after the birth of Baby J. and before Tracy's report," I responded.

As recorded in her social security documents, she fraudulently claimed all five children in her taxes. It was with that money that she was able to have her first known apartment late on February 2009.

She rented the apartment # 163 at Sutton Square. Instead of making this place, a consign of rest for Baby J. and her big sister Kattaya after nights spent outside in harshly temperature, Sheebah let Daven joined them. Once established, they started setting things in the motion. Sheebah collected Boney from Grandma's house first, Tabô and Loylla from my place secondly. She then called CPS on me. She said that I kicked Tabô and Loylla out after beating them. She contradicted herself and said that Tracy Burkhart, her lawyer, arranged through the court, a five-day guardianship for her and weekends for me. That was a disagreement statement. Tracy, her lawyer, has at that time, already written to the CPS stating that Sheebah has custody of all five children as ordered by the family court. She added and said that they were living with her at Sutton Square Apartment in Hurst. That is certainly the report you read.

Sheebah was living in Sutton Square with her children on paper only. She was not there; she made things look that way. She actually was waiting for an apartment in Sutton Square. That was the reason she was arrested twice by Hurst Police because she was suspiciously driving the school van around and around in the complex, with children inside. Baby J, her newborn baby had been living in that van since her birth, till the end of February. For two years now, Kattaya had been taken care of by other employees of Suzy's daycare. For three years now, Grandma Zora had been taking care of Boney without Sheebah's help whatsoever. For ten years now, my two little girls had been living with me until yesterday. I proved, by the documents I gave you, that I have been raising them by myself. If there was a court order giving her a five-day guardianship, CPS would have known about it. If she had custody of my children, CPS would have known the deal. Tracy Burkhart is a liar, and you keep bringing up lies she ascertained for Sheebah. Did you notice that she never said anything about Sheebah's instability or her lack of a substantial job? That is another set up signed by Tracy," I said to her.

"Let's talk about evictions. I checked there is none on her record. The only address that—"

"Check more. There is a quantity of notices and evictions under her name. The only two places you won't find eviction is at Boca

Raton and at Sutton Square. Boca Raton address was protected by
Meda Bourland, her attorney, and Tracy Burkhart for court purposes.
They needed to show what could be trusted as her physical residence
in court," I answered.

Sheebah was evicted by Flor E. Gutierrez, the manager of
Sutton Square because she did not pay her rent from February 3
to April 30, 2009. February was the first month she occupied the
apartment and April was the last month she was forced to leave. She
begged and told the manager that she was a struggling single mother.
Putting an official court order on her name was just killing her more.
Flor E. Gutierrez knew she won't have money to pay her either way.
She observed Daven and her do drugs all the time, instead of taking
their responsibilities as parents. This was the main reason it took
Sheebah three installments to try to pay her first month. She showed
me Sheebah's payment log. She didn't even finish paying her first
month. So instead of taking Sheebah to court, she locked her out
and kept her stuff in. Even if Flor did make a deal with Sheebah, that
did not make it less of an eviction. It still counts as eviction for the
reason that an eviction doesn't have to necessarily be a legal process.
Once a tenant is expelled, it is a force out. This was not the first time
Sheebah was locked out from Sutton Square, Flor E. Gutierrez said.
Before obtaining that apartment under her own name, she lived there
with friends. Because of nonpayment, they were all dispossessed of.

"She was not evicted at…actually, this address is kept from you
for her safety and the safety of her children," Kathryn said.

"You surely are talking about the 9160 E. Walter Street in
Bedford, Texas. That is another manipulation of the system. When
her daughters want to spend time with her, day or night, she comes
around, parks in front of my apartment, and knocks the front door.
She blows her car horn sometimes, makes conversations with neighbors while waiting for them to get out. I never stepped out with
threats. Her life never has been in danger with me as she had been
claiming it. She is not hiding the 9160 E. Walter Street from me.
She hides it because it is her food stamps hideout. She doesn't live
there. She never lived there. This physical address belongs to Suzy
Dale. Listen to yourself, Kathryn, you talked about Meadow Park

and Sutton Square, I talked about Boca Raton, now we are talking about Walker Street. That is too may addresses for one person. Don't you think? How many addresses can an unemployed woman like Sheebah legally hold?" I asked.

I have already explained to Kathryn who Suzy was to Sheebah in connection with CPS Tracy. Sheebah used the 9160 E. Walter Street in Bedford, Texas, address by connivance with the owner. She did so to obtain government benefits. CPS Tracy Burkhart knew that. By definition, this was a fraud, and by its description, it was a crime. Suzy had been Sheebah's accomplice since the day she hired her to be a caregiver in her daycares. Together, they commit all kind of transgressions, from fraud to schemes. Everything is written in the 2009 contact narrative, a confidential document that the court has copy of. That document was released to me by the Office of the Attorney General. Since Sheebah did move around a lot, that address was the only stable place she kept. She used it to obtain food stamps. For the law, that address was a place for her criminal activities. They committed those frauds and schemes without being arrested. For instance, in order to receive food stamps, Suzy Dale modified Sheebah's Kentucky Fried Chicken pay stubs with her home computer. She reduced her checks to make it smaller, at the amount level consistent with the poverty line. Once the application for food stamps is accepted, they share the revenue. Suzy would also buy a chunk of the rest.

"Where do you think your children are at this present moment?"

"Well, Tabô called. She told me that they are over Charlene's. This lady is one of Suzy's employees. She lives at 1188 Beverly Court in Bedford. Sheebah is hiding them there because, as of right now, she is homeless and jobless. Did you notice how many times I said she is homeless?"

"You said the driver of the Nissan was black woman. Do you think Charlene is the same woman who allegedly hit you with the car?"

"No, Charlene is a chubby, light-skinned woman. She wears Rasta hair that makes her look masculine. The person who hit me yesterday, June 12, was a little older than that. She was darker, shorter and wore natural creepy hair. She was ugly."

"For the security of children, I need you to take me over to Charlene's so I can verify if they are okay. You will drive your own car. I do not want to be liable, insurance wise."

PART IV

POLICE INVESTIGATIONS

CHAPTER 17

THE INSECT THAT EAT A GREEN PEA LIVES INSIDE THE GREEN PEA

We drove over to Charlene's in different cars. Both girls were playing outside with other kids. Kathryn Omarkhail stepped out. They knew her. I took them twice in her office. When they saw her, they ran inside the house. She approached and knocked the front door. Charlene's oldest girl answered. She was twelve. She said she will not open the door; she was not authorized to. With a smile on her face, Tabô waved at me from a left window curtain. Kathryn Omarkhail saw her. I asked her if a child of her age can be lawfully babysitting other children, home alone.

"I do not know exactly what the take of CPS on that is. But the rule says that a child, between twelve and fifty, can be home alone and can also babysit. It is officially permitted until there is a problem," she answered.

"What do you mean by a child…fifty-year-old child?" I asked.

"An adult person, with medical conditions, with Down Syndrome for instance is considered by the law as a child. People with medical conditions still need protection and supervision from responsible adults."

As we were returning to Glen Rose from Beverly Court, Kathryn Omarkhail saw Shanaqua Rangel, my neighbor, coming out from her apartment. She was going to the trash bin. Kathryn stopped her, parked her car, and asked her questions about my two little girls. Two boys happened to pass by on their bikes; she asked them if they know Tabô and Loylla. I heard the entire conversation from these three guarantee witnesses. Not only did they answer, they also pointed to her my apartment.

Kathryn left after four hours of detailed interview.

Six days later, I still did not know who ran me over with the blue Nissan. I didn't have a slice of an idea who was the driver. I decided to go to the police station. I knew they won't give me the license plate number, but since they were the reliable source of information, I hoped for the name of the black lady who was on the driver's seat. The officer lady at the window let me know that those things were of sensitive information nature and the office would not give it to just anyone.

I drove back to Hurst Police on July 19, 2009.

"I am the victim and I intend to press charges against the lady who ran me over," I said.

Instead of receiving what I exactly needed, the officer lady recommended to press charges against Unknown. They will go from there to try to find the perpetrator, she advised me. She then gave me Officer Broome's report police sequence # 090601997 with 17:02:57 entry to start with. That report said, "Sheebah drove to Kasalobi's apartment, her children were getting out of his car. Sheebah told the children to get in her car, the kids got into her car. Neither parent had custody paperwork. Kasalobi was yelling and was uncooperative the entire time. I tried to explain our legal perimeters, but he told me that he did not want to listen and walked off. Sheebah left with the children. Kasalobi was standing in front of Sheebah's car when I drove up and would not let her leave. Sheebah told me that he jumped in front the car so that she would not leave. Kasalobi told me that Sheebah hit him with the car, but that did not appear to be the case. It seemed that Kasalobi got in front of the car in order to keep her from leaving."

Normally, police officers do not side with individuals. They do not have personal opinions to give in regular circumstances either. This was not a normal situation; it was Officer Broome happening. I started to understand what I was facing since nothing was following the normal order of things. His report was jam-packed with lies. After letting my kids leave with women he knew did not have legal custody, he was now weighing in with a different kind of justice machine. His report was a given guarantee. It was full of vital information for the defended to grab. That scared me the most. I posed for a second to think. Then I asked to see what was written before he arrived at Glen Rose Apartment. Officer Kenya Meza handed me the police report seq # 090601943 which was recorded at 13:31:16. It said: "Comment: *Call Compl*RP was arrested several days ago. Her ex took their kids when she went to jail. RP said that yesterday Tarrant Co issued an ex-parte order protecting her and the kids from him. The kids are still with him at his apartment." And the 14:19:32 entry said, "Misc says spoke with RP who did not know if ex had been served with papers, I advised her to contact TCSO further."

There I confirmed my doubts. I was dealing with Sheebah. This time, she had an accomplice in crime. She planned an attempt to my life. She had called the police to justify my death by accident. She knew where we were, stalked us all the way in, and asked her friend to hit me with her car. She knew at this point that whatever she would do after lying to the police will be justified. Police could believe her instead of me. Officer K. Broome did just that. To help her, he wrote abusively that "Kasalobi was yelling and was uncooperative the entire time. I tried to explain our legal perimeters, but he told me that he did not want to listen and walked off." Things did not happen that way.

Police cruisers are equipped with all kind of recording devices. They always testify facts, for or against. Either way, Broome's tape will evidently show that I executed and followed his orders at each second it was given. I never yelled at him at all. I knew what would have happened if I did the yelling. People saw also what happened.

Broome did not talk to any of them. He would have if he wanted to. Any other officer would have done that. He pulled in, adjusted his cruiser, and aligned himself behind the lady's car. He saw me still hanging for my life on the top of the Nissan. He then gave the order to step down. I stood up on my feet. He completely ignored what he saw and decided to write lies with malice in his report. The tape will show that I refused to take his sequenced business card only after he let Sheebah leave with my children. They will also show that it was only after this moment, at the very last second of it, that I left the scene.

Since I was still in the hall, I asked if it was possible to have the video released to me. I also asked to talk to the officer on duty. As I was waiting, Delfeld, Broome's backup officer, happened to pass by. I showed him the report and accused Broome of writing lies. He was visibly confused. The first question Officer Broome asked me when he joined us in the hall was to know where I got the police report. I asked him over if he would give me the name of the person who hit me instead.

"That would be the mother of your kids, of course," he said.

"The mother of my...was she black or white?" I asked.

"She is black and she was the one who was driving the Nissan."

"That is impossible, Sheebah is white. She cannot drive, her driver's license is suspended. Do not be astonished. If you did bother to verify their names, you would have known that. The person who was driving and who hit me was black and she is not the mother, sir. The person you thought was Sheebah was not Sheebah. You saw my kids, they are mixed, mixed black and white, that is," I confirmed.

Broome looked at a complete loss. I asked to talk to the chief of the police. The dispatch lady invited me inside a room that had an egg-shaped table. I sat on one of eight chairs and waited. A man in plain clothes entered from the left side door. He was wearing a golden lone star badge, wallet size, on the top of his blue shirt. Attached to his brown leather belt was a different badge, a bigger badge. This was the symbol of his authority. He introduced himself as the assistant to the chief. He did not need to; it was written on a different ID in a sachet, attached to a cord which was hanging down from the neck to his chest level.

"The chief is not in. I am the officer on duty," he politely said after asking me to sit down. He then looked at me with a blank stare, gripped his laptop as if he was about to write something in it, greeted me again, and added, "You do not look like someone who was ran over by a car. Did you go the hospital?" He asked.

That was a cheap affirmation if measured to the pain written all over my body. I would have laughed to the cynical insult of the assistant chief, but that was not that time. Laughing is a motion that expresses amusement and that has to voluntarily come out from a person, as Muisangic Lumpungu, my ma would have said it. I was on that table to trade my throbbing for justice but not to cry. I was not there to question the seed of meanness on an official's tongue. I did not want to let my discomfort stay in me. I was sitting around that table to seek fairness. So I ignored that remark. I said, "Yes, sir, I went to the hospital. To you, I am not hurting. The truth is that the insect that eats a green pea lives inside the green pea, if you see what I mean."

I handed him the brown envelope in which was the inner CT scan founding that John Peter Smith Hospital gave me after medical examination. He read the first page down, then moved his wrinkled forehead up and looked at me. That move exposed him because I read the man through his facial progress. I saw what he was thinking of at that instant. He looked at me one more time without a word. He then raised his hand to scratch his side hair cut. I saw the *semper fi* tattoo on his forearm. The man is an ex-marine. He saw fights, different kinds of it. That explained why he showed a hard rock emotion. He flipped to the second page and glued his eyes on the third. Meanwhile, I took a glance on the lightened walls and respected what was hanging. I saw pictures of fine officers, present and past. I knew then that I was in good hands. He loudly read the conclusion of the medical founding on the last page and said, "Bruised on lumbar spine and contusion on multiple sites of tibia-fibula lateral lower leg. The right medial elbow completed and no fracture or dislocation on it. Facial trauma has a multiple contiguous on axial section of the left skeleton bone. Paranasal sinuses found and an amount traces of scattered mucosal thickening seen. Displaced facial bone fracture and dentition incidentally noted on tooth." He stopped reading. I handed him pictures of my face showing a chipped tooth, a picture of my bruised elbow, and another of my swelling right leg. He took a look and said, "How can you stand and walk with all these?"

"I am on strong stuff: Vicoprofen 7.5 and Etodolac 500mg. Very strong stuff. Like I said, the insect that eat a green pea lives inside the green pea, as Ma always said it."

CHAPTER 18

THE SMALL HAMMER BREAKS THE BIG ROCK

The assistant to the chief opened his laptop. He scratched something in it and readjusted himself as if he was about to write down all lot. He hesitated and took his fingers from the keyboard. Even if he was sitting down, he distinctly adjusted his belt, on which was a gun, on his left-hand side. That weapon had an encryption of a lone star, visibly incrusted on the bottom of its butt. It was a small machine. Its half cannon was visibly outside as if it was piercing the brown holster it was in. He asked me if I had another documentation to give.

"That's all," I answered.

"What do you want me to do?"

"I want to press charge against K. Broome for his unprofessionalism and for helping these two ladies kidnap my girls."

"Well, there is not enough evidence here to initiate a legal action. Officer Broome acted within his duty lines. I refuse to take your grievances in this office. I won't even make the first move for a criminal survey. If you have a legal action to take against any of my officers, take it to court," he responded.

The thunder hit my ears with the sound of that answer. I looked at him, without a word, begged him to go over everything, one more time, as a normal wise man, he seemed to be, would have done it. He did not bounce. I heard him out, and I ignored what he was saying about the law. I complained one more time. What I was saying to him was not passing through both ears. It was entering in both sides of his head, meeting between his ears, and housing itself somewhere in his mind.

That refusal reminded me of another police officer who did just that when justice called for him. Back then, Bonham, Texas, did not have a noticeable thing built around Highway 5 and its crossroads as it is today. It was late that evening, I was very hungry after my taxi cab fare. I stopped at a corner store and found myself directly behind a nice young lady. She was in line, trying to pay for her goods. Three young men entered and stood directly behind me. They had their heads shaved bald and were acting very funny. A young girl who had tattoos all over the visible parts of her body, even on the top of her shaved head was with them. She cut the line to the counter. I saw a swastika sign on the back of her neck. Instead of paying, she turned around and talked to the nice lady. She asked her if I was with her. The nice lady answered and said that we were not together.

"Good to have said that. Say, man, we do not like your kind over here," she proudly attacked me, using her very threatening voice.

Even if she seemed be talking to herself since she was not making eye contact, I felt it. I ignored her finger gestures because she was high on something and was simultaneously looking on her feet and on the ceiling. I ignored that too. Then, with not distortion in her voice, her attitude changed.

"Nigga, get out of this town." She openly menaced.

"Are you addressing yourself to me?" I asked.

"To yo mama, who d'ya think she talkin' to, stupid?" one of these visibly exited men said.

"We don't say addressing anymore, Jack. Monkeys are forbidden in Bonham, Texas," the other boy said.

"I see four, right here, in this store," I replied.

I saw at that instant the young girl with tattoos do the rooster intimidation; she was getting ready to attack with violence. I backed off just a bit and put myself in a good position to avoid her punch. I needed to hit first, hit hard, make teeth fly all over, and finish the fight before they even started it. I gave me enough space between us to appropriately engage all of them once.

"Oh no, you did not say that, I will fuck you up, nigga," the shortest of them all said. His gang shoved him forward to attack.

"Oh yes, I did. Let it be introduced, this man here is from Africa. I do play different games."

"This Kaffir is out of Africa, freshly off the boat. I will fuck you up, motherfucker," he said.

"I don't even know your mother," I answered, and that visibly excited him.

"I will fuck you up."

"In that case, come and get it."

I pulled myself forward to separate him from other hooligans. At my advantage, he moved back. They all moved a step back. I knew there that if I throw the first punch, cannonball like, and hit one of them first hard and with the mean one, as my pa advised me once, I will control the fight. They will run. I put the apple pie stick, chewing gum, and the Powerade I was about to purchase on the top of the counter. They all saw my position of no return. It was here when, after spitting a river of saliva from the tobacco he was chewing, the man behind the counter intervened. He yelled, reached his bookshelf, and held a big brown bat He stepped over the counter with his intimidating heavy stick. I was sure that these young men will get the beating of their life because he was about to protect his customer that I was, so I thought. Suddenly he cut between us, confronted me, and said, "You, sir, you need to leave my store."

"You, more than anyone here, knows that they started it. They must leave first," I pleaded with him.

"Take it outside. You've seen the mess a dropped watermelon does. Well, your head is not stronger that my club."

"You heard him, get the fuck out of Bonham while you can," the tattooed girl menaced.

171

As I was stepping out, she walked forward and stood guard at the entrance door, as if she did not want me to get out. Just like that, a police patrol car entered the parking lot. She backed off. I approached and explained everything to the officer. He listened and then asked to see my driver's license. I found that very strange. I gave it to him and said, "Officer, I was minding mine when they entered. The clerk is actually my witness. He saw them and heard them. They were about to do physically harm on me. They used the entire dictionary of offensive black names on me."

"Okay, this is what I want you to do…hein…I have all your information here. This is your driver's license. Be in your way. If anything happens, I will give you a call. I have to investigate this problem first."

"I am the victim here. Not talking to them would be defeating the all purpose. It will also be denying me justice. How are you gonna investigate when you don't even know their names? What happened in there is a crime," I said.

"Now you are telling me how to do my job, sir?" he wondered.

"Not at all, sir, I was just saying…sorry about that," I answered.

I felt that the officer was one of them; despite his official position, he had already a sentence. I got out of the town of Bonham and drove as fast as it was legal to do so. I did not want him to follow and stop me for speeding and then give the opportunity to his protégés to treat me like Mr. King even if we were not in LA.

I had the same feeling when I was about to leave the assistant to the chief of the Hurst Police Department. A crime was committed on me; I was run over. I entered that office because my children were taken away from me, not to have him shut off city lights for me, which would have been nice. He refused to help and said, "You put yourself in harm's way and your wife, the black lady who was driving, feeling the life of her children threatened, did not have another choice but to drive forward."

He was supposed to diffuse, not to be escalating the fight. In this case, he shouldn't been trusting what Officer Broome have left him to read.

"Sir, I am not married. The mother of my girls is not a black woman."

"I am reading from this present file," he answered.

"Then, investigate Officer Broome, he wrote the report. His cruiser was facing the Nissan, why don't you check the video?" I said.

"I watched the video. There is not enough evidence in there. The DA won't even take this case."

"When did you watch the video, sir? I just showed up here. Is this the America of justice and equality or am I still in Africa?" I said to him as I was standing up.

"I understand your frustrations, sir. It is better to do things the right way," he answered.

"You know what, sir, my pa said once that natural bald police officers are better public servants. They do greater things for people in need. I think I will reconsider. For now, sir, I am a small hammer, standing on one foot. It is always a small hammer that breaks a big rock," I said to him. I stood up, and started to show myself to the door.

"Is that threat?" he severely asked.

"Not at all, sir. I am not that stupid. I am in your house. This is an African thing, and you wouldn't understand it. See, Mandela was given the biggest rock of them all and a very small hammer. The system thought he will never break that rock with that small instrument. He used it and broke it nevertheless. It took him nothing but twenty-seven years to accomplish the job. He broke it to pieces. For instance, you are wearing a gun on your belt. It looks small. One would think it cannot stand a fight. Not only it would, it will also do as much damage as an AK-47 because it is a 9 mm. You guys are ignoring my pleas and slamming your doors in my face, because I am visibly a small tack hammer. I will stand this fight. I won't back down. I will knock on your doors again and again, and one day, I will carve my way through, no matter how long it will take. I am a small hammer on Mandela's rock. I am a small gun on your belt," I explained.

I stood up, turned around, and as I was leaving, he called me back and said, "I promise you that I will assign a detective on your case. He will take it from here, and we will see what would happen."

CHAPTER 19

CAMERAS HAVE EYES AND EARS

At 8:30 in the morning of June 24, 2009, as I was backing up my eighteen-wheeler off the ramp to the door, I received a phone call from the city of Hurst. It was Detective Duermeyer. He told me that he just got assigned to my case. He asked if it was a bad time to talk to me.

"Not at all, I am about to deliver my first load at Budweiser Distribution Center in Fort Worth, Texas. I can stop and talk to you," I said.

"Did you go to the hospital?" was his first question.

"Yes sir, I did. I went at urgent care of John Peter Smith."

"What happened?" he asked.

"I had a CAT scan done. As written on the report, I left with the assistant chief, the doctor prescribed Vicoprofeh-Ibuprofen 7.5-200mg TAB and the painkiller called Etodolac 500mg. I was discharged on June 14, 2009," I answered and said.

"Why did you jump in front of a moving car on June 12?" Duermeyer asked over the phone.

"I never jumped in front of any moving car. These two women were kidnapping my children. I stood up in front of the car and held my ground. Then the driver, a black lady, moved forward. She

174

purposely hit my right leg, judo like, using her car as weapon. Doing so, I felt and smashed my right elbow on the top of the hood. I also chipped my tooth off, my mouth is still bleeding."

"Why would you stand still in the front of a moving car?" Duermeyer questioned.

"I did not want them to leave with my kids. I did what I had to do to stop them. She saw me and floored onward anyway and hit me," I explained.

"Where are your kids now?" he asked.

"At this exact moment, I do not have any idea. Kathryn and I saw them in Bedford, but they had been moved since. I do not know where they are hidden now."

"So you knew who took them and yet you deliberately put yourself in harm's way, by cornering the car."

"With all due respect, a car cannot be cornered by a man on foot. At that moment, I did not know who those two women were. Kathryn told me who they are."

"She told you that it was your wife who came to pick her children back and—"

"Why is it that the police, including you, a detective, keeps saying that Sheebah is my wife? Can't you investigate to make sure that what you are saying is right or not before saying it? Sheebah never was my wife, and I never have a history of family violence toward her. See, saliva is an important element of the mouth. Without it, teeth will break apart, the tongue will dry up, and everything will be stuck together. Sometimes ago, just the way saliva is to the mouth, Sheebah used to be the companion of my life, the best saliva a man would want in his mouth. She was, at that time, an important breed, and I was the meaning of her life until the day I found out she was sleeping around on me. I kicked her out. Once out of my life, she became spit-out saliva. We all know that spit-out saliva is saliva forced out. It can't be put back in, and it can't be reusable. You know why? Because from the moment it is out, it grows micro animals and it becomes very smelly. Therefore, Sheebah became just like spitting saliva at the time I knew who she was cheating on me with. I kicked her out and she became disposable. I couldn't use her anymore, and she couldn't possibly be my wife. So you guys need to stop telling me who she is in my life. Still, that doesn't give her the right to kidnap my daughters. To answer to your second suggestion, when it comes to his children, and this, I know, in the nick of a time and without thinking, a parent will jump inside the bursting fire to try to save them. I know you would. You will firmly stand your ground, just like I did, and challenge wind and tide for them," I explained with a conviction in my voice.

"We respect life in America. I would never put myself in harm's way."

"I am African. I survived mosquitoes and grew around leopards dens. I admired their nice skins and laughed at their mean faces of the moment. I saw what their teeth can do when they are mad. I am not easily scared, mostly by a car driven by a human being. My kids were in danger, and I refused to move."

"So you jumped in the front of a driven car and put your children in danger?"

"Sir, I did not jump, I never jumped. When she saw me standing still, she yelled a bunch of insanities first. She then calculatedly floored the pedal and ran me over. Gilbert Velasquez and Shanaqua Rangel, my neighbors, were two of so many who saw everything building up. Why don't you talk to them?"

"Your record says a different story. Since you have a long history of family violence and given that you have been in Hurst jail numerous times, I do not think I will investigate this case any longer. After talking to Sheebah, I will close this case," Duermeyer said.

"Record you said? Jail you confirmed? What the heck are you talking about? Hurst Police never had me on any crime related to family violence. I never have been arrested in United States nationwide. When then did you see me put in Hurst jail numerous times?"

"Now you are telling a lie, Mr. Kasalobi. I personally came at your doorstep and put handcuffs on you, not one time but so many times," he cheaply implied.

Through his own words, I discovered that Duermeyer was a lame detective the entire history of all detectives ever had. As detective, his primary job was to question and obtain evidences. He had modern tools and police computers at his disposition for that. His second job was to tell the difference between the truth and the reality. His third was to compare, from the existence of facts in his presence, every find against each other in order to come across the true nature of things. He was unable to do just that.

"Detective Duermeyer, with all due respect to the uniform you are wearing, not only you are being unreasonable, you are a lousy liar. You are also loudly making me think that the house of detective is the school of lies. You are not confusing me with someone else, you are simply not a detective. How can you tell a lie about me and in my face like that? You never ever arrested me and I do not have a history of family violence with anyone in this entire world," I dryly told him.

"The first time I took you to Hurst jail was when you had a warrant for your arrest. I know I put handcuffs on you many times. The last time was when you and your daughter were fighting. I took both of y'all to jail," he said.

"That is so below the belt, sir. I never ever had a warrant under my name, ever. I never fought with my daughter, ever. How did you make a detective, sir, is it by being one hell of a composite liar or what?"

"I do not authorize you to call me a liar. I personally put handcuffs on you."

This man was not playing psychology on me. He was showing me the outstretched extent of his full knowledge. Detectives are not unintelligent at that full length. They don't confirm things they do not know because they are people of vast intellect compass of knowledge. What Duermeyer was doing was spreading out, wide and far and extensively, diluted information to try to gain a cause. Being a detective is not a game of guessing, it is an act of work, it is a technology suited to be used in seeking and recognizing realities. It is a technology that verifies information put in front of eyes and a technology that confirms the truth in it toward 'protect and serve' business.

"You are one hell of a liar, Sir Duermeyer. How many innocents have you sent in jail by confirming things they did not do? You never put handcuffs on me. I don't know what kind of mental illness you are trying to establish on me, it is just not working. I'll say it again, you never took me in Hurst jail or in other jail for that matter. How could you say madness like that? Now I am going to hang up, sir."

And I did.

Having said that, I remembered spending twelve hours inside Hurst Jail. It was not caused by Duermeyer. I walked in myself. I had a traffic ticket and did not have the time to pay it. I gave the money to Sylvia Kelly, my wife then, to go and take care of it. Days went by. I found that evening a police business card pinned on my door. It was a reminder of unpaid ticket. I talked to Sylvia. She confirmed "in the name of God" to have paid it through the city clerk. I believed her because of the tears in her eyes. I called to verify. The police did not find the record of it been paid. It was at that moment that I discovered that my wife was a daring crook. I drove down there to pay it. Since I did not have cash money on me, the clerk refused to take the check. It was late; the ticket had turned into warrant already. I was booked. Ngoyi Dezy, a dear friend of mine, paid $400 bail. This was the only time I saw the inside of Hurst jail, and it was not under Duermeyer's handcuffs.

At 1500 hours the same day, Duermeyer called to let me know that he closed the case. That did not bother me. I knew what he was doing; it was a matter of principle. Bruce Willis would have said, in this case, that the man was performing as if he was a criminal in uniforms. He was not following the proper police procedure because he did not want to expose Officer Broome. For me, he was put there by the assistant to limit the havoc.

I did not want to let myself be intimidated. I decided to report everything to Sergeant Tig of Hurst Police Department. Tig was in his office, at 1501 Precinct Lane, when I arrived. He brought Detective Duermeyer with him in the hall. I looked around and realized that the hall was equipped with live cameras. I knew we will be recorded. I felt good. Both Sergeant Tig and Detective Duermeyer had documents in their hands, in which they were referring to every time they talked to me. When we started talking, Duermeyer insisted in his lies. He exaggerated some of them and added things I never said. Then he said that he has been in the force with the Hurst Police for ten years. He personally put handcuffs on my hands and booked me two or three times.

"That is crazy. You know you just said that with foolishness and persistence in front of Sergeant Tig, your boss? Cameras are running. This entire hall has eyes and ears, they will testify back. Since you have been ten years in the force, when then did you ever arrest me then? This is 2009. The Hurst Police record will show that you were not even in the force when in 1991, I walked myself in Hurst jail for twelve hours. And that was the only time I have seen the color of inside the Hurst jail walls. It is crystal clear that you wrapped your investigations to destroy my defense," I answered.

Sergeant Tig looked at his paperwork. I looked at both cameras. Then he looked at Duermeyer as if he was asking a soundless question.

"If I did not do it personally, then I helped another officer to do it. Either way, that doesn't change the fact that you have been numerously arrested by Hurst Police because of your violent behavior and your long history of family violence," Duermeyer cheaply confirmed.

"How come Hurst Police let you operate in their ranks?" I said to him, looking directly in his eyes.

"With that language, sir, you are now insulting this facility. I won't let you disrespect the Hurst Police Department," Tig reacted with force.

"Sorry, sir, no disrespect toward the Hurst Police Department at all. This man is lying and he knows he is lying. I have problem with that, not with this facility. You have my driver's license, sir, anyone can verify when Detective Duermeyer arrested me," I answered.

Sergeant Tig then looked at Duermeyer without asking a question.

"I think it was on November 2004. Hurst Police was called at Whispering Run Apartment where Mr. Kasalobi, his wife Sheebah, and their daughter Muntumpe were fighting. I made an arrest and took him and his daughter to jail," the detective answered.

"That smells like another pile of cow you-know-what. Is that written in Hurst Police report or is it from your imagination? Sir Tig,

Duermeyer is not setting all facts straight. He is talking about a fight that started in Fort Worth."

"And what fight started in Fort Worth?" Sergeant Tig asked.

It is written in Fort Worth Police case # 041 354 86, that a burglary happened in Muntumpe apartment, on November 10, 2004, at 5716 Fitzhugh Court, the village Creek Towne homes. Sgt. Klein interviewed Sheebah in that early morning about it. She was living at that time over Muntumpe. Since she was the only person inside the apartment, she was a suspect, the report said.

I was getting ready to go to work that morning of November 10, when I heard people fighting in my balcony. I opened the front door and saw Muntumpe and Sheebah pulling each other's hair. Muntumpe wanted her stuff back, mostly her 52" television. She was screaming and saying that Sheebah stole everything from her apartment. I asked them to go fight somewhere else. As they were taking the fight downstairs, Hurst Police arrived. As it is reported in Hurst PD case # 04-10446, Duermeyer Nathan here was actually the first officer to arrive in place. I said hello to him. He did not answer. I tried to shake his hand; he refused. I found that very strange from an officer of the law. Now I understand why. Sheebah told him that she came in Hurst, not to fight with Muntumpe, but to take her two daughters who live with Mr. Kasalobi, the father, to school. As she was knocking on the door, she was attacked. Because Muntumpe was the one who was doing the attacking and who left traces of nails on Sheebah's body, she was taken to jail.

"That was the fight that started in Fort Worth and ended up in Hurst. Sir Tig, you have in your hands the report Hurst PD files # 04-10446, you will found written in it that Duermeyer Nathan did not arrest me. He arrested Muntumpe. That he did. The rest of his story is just a lie, a filthy lie."

"So you never arrested him on family violence?" asked Tig.

"I do not have all records with me right now, but I based my research from what happened in 1994 with the young Sheebah before she becomes a mother. If I did not do it myself, I helped arrest him."

"Oh, now he helped. That is that. This guy has been fantasizing to put me in jail. Mr. Tig, what happened between the young

Sheebah and me happened in the city of Euless, not in Hurst. At that time, Duermeyer Nathan here present was not even in the force yet. How is that possible that he personally helped the police to take me to jail on family violence?" I answered.

Fifteen years ago, I said to Tig, Officer Ramirez of Euless Police was dispatched at Mission Point Apartment for commotion. A week earlier, Sheebah was short of her prescribed Prozac. She developed an unfriendly attitude toward everyone. She was fired from Hertz Rent-a-Car for being verbally sadistic and for using viciously brutal language toward some of her coworkers. On April 11, 1994, early that day, before Ramirez was called in, she also was fired from Intex Aviation, her second job. She was fired for cursing and for being physically aggressive on the job. She then sunk into severe depression and an open psychological struggle. She began screaming and talking to herself. At the end of the day, she started breaking dishes. She was taken to JP Smith Hospital by the Euless Police by the advice of her stepmother. It was after that that I felt a rigorous pain in my low stomach. I saw a relentless discharge when I went to pee. Then, an excretion that was mixed with dark blood wetted my underwear. This was not the first time Sheebah sexually contaminated me. This was happening after swallowing big pills, after receiving painful shots, and after receiving counseling at Dallas County Hospital. When she came back home, I jumped at the opportunity that she was calm and I told her that she infected me again. I asked her to pack and leave. She became very hysterical, began hitting her head on the wall, and started breaking dishes again. She then attached the rope on the air duct.

"Why did she do that? Was she trying to hang herself?" Sergeant Tig asked.

"Yes. You can see her with a looped noose on her neck on these pictures I took the same day. I called her foster mother. She advised me to take her in the bathroom and put water on her head till she cools down. We both got soaked wet. That did not help. She was still going crazy. She even broke her glasses and put a plastic bag on her head trying to suffocate herself. You can see that on these pictures too. With all the screaming and banging on the wall, someone called the police. She was still wet and acting up when Officer Ramirez of Euless Police Department arrived. He asked me if Sheebah authorized me to put water on her. I said no but her foster mother told me so. He said that 'Sheebah is an adult, because you never get her permission, and you put water on her anyway, that means you used force on her. And when that happens, it is called an assault with a bodily injury.' I was taken to jail. Not in Hurst, but in Euless. I was taken to jail way back before Detective Duermeyer here finished his high school. That arrest had been haunting me since. Back then, I tried to help a young girl with comportment disorder and I was charged with a crime I did not commit. Today Duermeyer here present is trying to use it against me as if it was him who arrested me," I said.

"I remember now when I arrested you. You put Sheebah and her daughters in house arrest for two months. We came at your place to secure their departure. We helped them to go to an unknown location to get away from your violent behavior. I think I arrested you that day," Duermeyer said.

"You are thinking that you arrested me that day? I would have loudly laughed, but you are an officer of the law and a detective, why don't you go through your record before saying these ridiculous statements? No police arrested anyone on that September 26, 2003. You were present all right, and this was the first time I saw you. Just when the police arrived, I was ordered to step outside. I left and went to work. Actually, this was the first time that Sheebah kidnapped my girls."

As matter of fact, what happened at eleven in that morning was just a waste of time and money. If they had investigated, they would have discovered that my girls did not need a secured departure. Sheebah held two jobs and was living in Arlington Shelter. I had both girls with me. They were seen walking to Bell Elementary while the oldest was going to Hurst Junior High, which means my door was always opened. Sheebah worked for Papa John Pizza, a job that necessitated driving. Between deliveries, people saw her talking to Kenneth Keith, her boyfriend, at the public phone, inside my apartment. When her truck broke down, she did not have a way to go back to Arlington. She lived on streets and spent her nights on the top of my Ford Escort. So her claim of two months' house arrest was nothing but a fraud cooked inside the Battered Women's Foundation oven to help her. That actually was a crooked landing story that was designed to move anyone's heart and that was given to her by Mahr Kay Byers.

Five days after she left with my kids, Tabô called me. She was hungry. They only ate bananas during that time and were heading south to San Benito, she said. I went down south and got them back.

CHAPTER 20

INTERNAL AFFAIRS

I politely asked Duermeyer how he made a detective. That question pissed off Sergeant Tig. I did so, in the ethic rule of civility, by first giving all due respect to the Hurst Police Department. The question I asked was not necessarily too much of anything because I knew the answer already. I needed to make a point. For me, it was a strategic move. I did not need Tig to prove me how competitive Duermeyer was and what he had already accomplished in his training courses. I just needed to raise a question by speaking loudly about it. If I did not raise that strict issue, Duermeyer would have continued been comfortable making me uncomfortable. That would have been the same as letting him gain a little bit of everything on my expenses, as my pa would have said it.

"I will not warn you again. Your insults to this department are up here now," Tig said.

I did not answer to that remark, but I handed him the report in which Duermeyer wrote nothing but lies against me. It was said in it without explaining why that "In conclusion, following the department rules or procedures, Kasalobi's story about the June 12 event is full of holes. I don't believe when he said to Officer Broome that he did not know the white lady who was sitting on the passenger seat. He said that she was not the mother of his children, but she was.

He also claimed that the vehicle had been following him home since Irving, which meant to say that he knew the occupants. Mr. Kasalobi declared to me that he deliberately jumped in front of the moving car and hopped on top of the vehicle to stop them taking his kids." Duermeyer's report said.

"See what I am saying, Mr. Tig. See it by yourself in that report. If you go through what Broome wrote, you won't see where he reported a 'white woman sitting on the passenger seat.' That is Duermeyer's making. The first time I saw the blue Nissan was when I reached 183 westbound. The second time was when I was exiting the Highway 10. The entire ordeal became suspicious when I was blocked in my parking lot. These two women operated with a maximum speed and took my children. They wouldn't have surprised me that way if I knew them and would never ran with my kids and locked them in their car if what they were doing was logical. I never said that I jumped in front of a moving car. That is simply a bold lie. This actually was the question he asked me while conducting his interview. I clearly explained everything to him. I told him what happened. I also gave him the anecdote about the father, his children, and the fire. Why didn't he put it inside this report if he was sincere?" I asked.

"I watched the tape of the incident from Officer Broome's cruiser, I read his report, I also concluded that there is not enough evidence to keep the case open. This is my opinion," Sergeant Tig said.

"You watched the tape...Broome's tape? And there is not... why am I even bothering? Do you know, sir, that I have been having difficulties to obtain that same tape, is there a reason why? I need a copy of that tape. I want to take it to court on July 2, 2009. I received nothing but excuses," I said.

I was told by the dispatch lady that the police did not have the tape yet. I called again the next day, she said that it was still being processed. Two days later, I showed up there myself. I said to her that this was a public information matter and a matter of public record, I am entitled to a copy. The police must release this tape for court purpose. She said that the tape was the property of the city of Hurst;

she was not authorized to give it to me. A day later, she called me and said that she found the tape, but it was damaged. I insisted to have a copy regardless of its condition. She then said that she will make a copy when the recording machine will be repaired, it was not working properly. To help me with the court proceeding, she said, there was something she could do for me. I must show up at the station, watch the scratched pictures, with the discretion of the chief of police. It was imperative that I take notes because I will watch it only once.

"I sympathize with you, sir but for now…"

"No, Sir Tig, you are not sympathizing with me, sympathy is a very old word from a very old world. It means to suffer with. You are not suffering with me, sir," I explained.

"I understand. I will authorize the duplication of the tape and order it to be released to you," Tig said.

"That would be something," I answered.

"For now, consider this case closed. Is there anything else I can help you with?" asked Tig.

"No, sir, thank you for your time."

I stepped out from the Hurst Police Department. Everything was running around me. Including the baggage of emotion I was carrying in each small part of my muscles, I developed a serious headache in that police hall. In the parking lot, I put my hands in my back pocket to retrieve my keys, a piece of paper fell from my jeans. It was the internal affairs' number Negrita, my neighbor, handed me the day my kids were kidnapped. I called when I arrived home. It was the office of James F. Tomsheck, the commissioner assistant in Washington. I had a quick telephonic interview with one of his staff members. Moments later, he gave me a local branch number. When I called, it was Sergeant Tabor who answered.

I was received by a smiley and tall athletic man, wearing a strong white shirt pressed on starch, his pants were marine blue. With his own Texas country accent, the man said, "Sergeant Tabor, Internal Affairs. Have a seat. How can I be at your service, sir?"

"I have already talked to the police," I said before taking my seat.

"I know, but you did not talk to me. Have a seat. My job is to investigate police abuses," he said while touching his golden police badge.

"But you still are a Hurst police officer. This local Internal Affairs is located in the same Hurst police building, inside which work Broome, Duermeyer, and Tig. You work with them in this very office. You share the same box of donuts and the same coffee table. How are you going to investigate your bodies?"

"You are already here, sit down and tell me your story," he said as I was standing back up.

I sat down, and told him my story from Broome to Tig. When I finished talking, he said that he will look into my complaints. Once a decision is reached, he will call me. He called twenty-four hours later. He sounded very mad. He said that I lied to him. I did not tell him that I talked to the chief of the police already. I answered and said that I never talked to the chief of the police. I talked to the man who said he was his assistant. He answered and said that the assistant was his boss.

"The assistant to Hurst chief of the police is the boss of the Internal Affairs? I thought that the employees of the Internal Affairs and all his members are a body of civilians," I said.

"I won't help you, sir. You lied to me, sir," Tabor answered.

"So in Hurst, the office of Internal Affairs is not a separate organ, situated far from the police department, as I was told by the office of James F. Tomsheck?" I insisted.

As I knew it, the Internal Affairs, in United States, is a division of a law enforcement agency that investigates incidents of law breaking by the police, the officials in forces, and by officers of the law. By that definition and by professional standards, Sergeant Tabor should have followed the government mandated set of rules found in their code, despite the fact that Tig was his boss. And since it was created by voters, he should have been bounded by its stringent rules. Because they all are warrants of investigation, all complaints, minor or not, with lies in it or not, containing sufficient factual information or not, concerning the misbehavior of his superiors or not, should be investigated to their logical conclusion. They should even if there is a misunderstanding.

"I clearly showed that Broome made a professional misconduct. I verified the suspicious acts of Duermeyer and clarified the no concern whatsoever of Sergeant Tig, and I am saying now that an investigation must be opened."

"You lied to me, sir," he insisted.

"Even if there is a lie in my conversation, you are an office of police complaints. You are here to investigate all misconducts filed against members of your department, included this department," I said.

"You are looking to have an upper hand on your wife. There is nothing wrong with the way Officer Broome conducted himself out there when he was dispatched at your place. I will not help you attack this department. The way I see it, you are looking for something to take to court. I will not be your accomplice. Then again, no prosecutor will take your case. I am sorry," he explained.

"Say so, sir, do not accuse me of lying. Say so and I will understand that this department is not fair and just. And that is my observation," I said.

Sergeant Tabor shouldn't be working in complicity with the assistant to the chief. As an Internal Affairs officer, his responsibility is of sensitive nature. He has to report directly to a board of civilians, not to Hurst Police Department. As I learnt it in aviation law and read in criminal books of law, Hurst community should be compelled to do something about this because the goal of Internal Affairs, in the city, is to ensure that the truthfulness of the department is maintained through a structure of internal discipline where equality and justice are assured with purpose by objective, impartial, unprejudiced investigation and review. I went home. A couple of days later, I called Tabor again. I wanted him to send me an investigation refusal letter. He verbally told me he won't do that, but he recognized that I submitted my complaint in person and in writing and within the possible delay limit, as soon after the incident happened. He knew by law that all available complaints should be readily accepted without discrimination and promptly and fully investigated at all time. He knew that no case should be returned with the plaintiff. He knew that the complainant shouldn't be told, for a reason or another, not to file a grievance. He knew that all reports of officer misconduct must be accepted regardless of where the complainant stood. He knew the rule. This was the reason he rejected my case, not through writing, but over the phone. His refusal resolution should have been given to me in a written report form, and he should have explained, in writing also, his department's negative response disciplinary procedures. I would have signed everything as I did on the complainant completed form I filed in his office when I went there. That entire file would have been saved in executive and comprehensive central file. He verbally dropped my case because he avoided leaving traces. This is the reason civilian review and investigation of police misconduct complaints should be reinstituted in Hurst. Civilians who have never been members of any police department should be viewing complaints from the public as a mean of determining where the police department had fallen, actually or potentially, or simply short of its intended goals. Searching for an upper hand on Sheebah or not, whether substantiated or not, my complaint would have provided a helpful feedback to their department. It would have been like an alert to the police executive to identify a need for additional training or disciplinary action and it would have increased awareness of problems between civilians and officers behavior on the field. This, I know. This is what is written in the book of the law.

Sergeant Tabor made me understood why it is not advised to talk to the police without the presence of a lawyer. Every single right guaranteed to a person, by the constitution of this United States, will be violated if that person talks to the police without his legal representative. Kathy Ehmann-Clardy was right when she told me that.

PART V

LAWYERS

CHAPTER 21

HER NAME IS TRACY BURKHART

That day, I was invited at 9160 E. Walter Street in Bedford, in Suzy Dale's house, to discuss the paternity of Boney. It became clear to what they were up to when I entered. This was the second time they were preparing a way to kidnap of my two girls. The first time it happened was when Sheebah took them, on September 26, 2003, down south to San Benito.

As I was knocking on the door, I saw a pile of letters tied together with a rubber band. They were literally sitting on the rocking chair. My name was written on one that was on the top. It attracted my attention because it was sent to Suzy Dale's address. I flipped it just to find out that the three first letters were also sent to me and the fourth was sent to "To the parents of Kasalobi Tabô." A dreadlocked black man opened the door. I asked him why my letters were there.

"Ask Mother, she is the one who authorizes that kind of shit to happen."

"Those are Sheebah's mails. She is supposed to be picking them up each end of the week," Suzy Dale answered.

"Now tell me why they are carrying my name instead of hers?"

"For application purposes, I temporarily let Sheebah use my home address."

"I understand that, but why are these letters carrying my name at your address?"

"To help her with her work force business," she said.

"You need to stop using my name while doing your business because I was not asked to help anyone. Do you know that using someone else's name and addresses is a fraud? It falls under the identity theft section of the law."

"It is not a theft of any kind since I gave her my consent."

"It is theft. What would the law say if a guy on probation gives your place, with your consent of course, as his address to his probation department? It is a bogus address. He does so to avoid the law enforcement to find him. It is intentionally done, so his probation officer couldn't keep track of him. It is as much the same as to register to vote under someone else's address. Even if people let other people use their residences, it still is a crime under the law. I will file a grievance about this. You are protecting Sheebah commit a mail fraud crime and a criminal offense," I said

"What Sheebah is doing with my address is not a crime. It is done with permission. It is a simple good Samaritan act." She smiled and insisted.

Based on her reaction, I concluded that it was a loss of time to try to convince her. She was trying so hard to look smarter than she really was. I collected mails that had my name written on. I was certain that in one of those envelopes lay the upshot of my doubts. Something like a counterfeited credit card or a document from a legal source with my identity for instance was in it. Otherwise why was Suzy's residential address given to her? Why was she using my name? It was to facilitate her to obtain public benefits so they can share. These women were defrauding the government. Sheebah was applying for government benefits. She also was selling food stamps she was receiving under my kids' names. In that context, it was obvious that somehow, these letters had been causing serious damages to me. Since what they were doing was done with malice, sooner or later, the law enforcement will step in. And because it was deliberately done, at the end of the day, there would be a criminal cause of action against them. When that happens and if they ever knocked at my door, I could be able to prove that I was a victim.

"I actually had already asked her not to use my home address anymore. That was the reason her mails were outside. I did not call you to come and discuss the legality of her letters. Sit down please and let's talk," she said.

There, a white woman stood up to shake my hand. Her size was accentuated by a short flowery red dress that was exposing her knees and by the wild and blonde hair she was wearing. She was tall and skinny. I thought I was in the presence of Popeye's wife. Suzy Dale introduced her to me.

"Her name is Tracy Burkhart."

Tracy Burkhart seemed out of place. My presence was bothering her. It showed by the way she was staring at me. She sat back down and adjusted herself in the comfy chair she was sitting in earlier. She was budging in it too much. Maybe it was because she did not have enough meat on her butt. The dreadlocked man sat next to me in the living room. He was Suzy Dale's son. I also met with one of her daughters who was trying to put her two-months little girl to sleep.

"Kasalobi," I said looking at her.

"Mr. Kasalobi is the father of Tabô and Loylla. Boney is also his daughter."

Out of the blue, Suzy Dale explained to Tracy Burkhart.

Even if she was talking to Tracy, Suzy wanted me to say something to betray myself, certainly. I knew it already, the meeting was a setup. I did not say a thing. She then broke the conversation down and said, "Boney is your daughter. Look at her again with the heart of a father, and I know you are a good father, you will see the striking resemblance with Loylla and Tabô. They all look exactly like you. Why don't you recognize her?" She slowly said to me as if I was challenged.

"Boney is not my daughter. I wonder why we are having this conversation again. She doesn't resemble me. She took it after Loylla and Tabô, her sisters. These two are conformed copies of me. Besides, all five girls are baked in Sheebah's oven. They are shaped from the same womb and drank from the same breast. They have to bear resemblances to and from each other. Sheebah and I were separated already when she became pregnant. Did you ever wonder why she is called Boney Malika? Well, Boney is the name of her father. He is a Kenyan. Malika is an intentional misspell of Malaïka, a Swahili word that means Angel. Mrs. Suzy, I am still wondering why we are having this precise discussion again. The last time we had this conversation, I told you that after collecting so much sexual diseases from her, you just don't know how much I hated Sheebah to even try to lie down with her. I said to you that if it ever happened that, from top to bottom, the entire race of human being and all species of human kind vanishes. And God himself comes down to reverse the extinction and finds out that only Sheebah and I are His only remaining hope to multiply and fill up the earth again, I will refuse to comply and positively decline His decision. This Kasalobi here, I told you, will never ever conjugate with Sheebah again. That is how much I hated her. I hated her more than anything in those days. I do not hate her less nowadays for that matter. At this present time, I am kind of vaccinated against her attacks and recurrent abuses. So that daughter of hers is not mine. She is the only woman I know of who is using through her own kids, her ability of doing wrong to achieve her goals to get what she desires."

"What do you mean?" Tracy asked.

"She made her daughters believe that, as long as they are minors, they could do anything they want, even physically attacking the police and getting away with it. She told them that Child Protective Services will always protect them, no matter what. The truth is Child Protective Services will not be there once a crime is committed. They won't be there to protect them once they break a window, physically attack authorities, and skip school or do other nasty behavior."

"Well, we are talking about Boney here. She looks like you. She is yours?" Tracy Burkhart said again.

"People do look alike. it doesn't necessary means that they are related. I heard about a couple that lived together for long, shared almost everything, and physically became a photocopy of each other."

"Well, Sheebah is about to put you on child support. Zora is tired of taking care of your daughter," Suzy attacked.

"And DNA will confirm your paternity," Tracy Burkhart confirmed.

"By the way, who are you talking about my kids as if you were a member of my family?" I directed that question to Tracy Burkhart.

"Mrs. Suzy introduced me already to you, my name is—"

"Tracy Burkhart, I know that already. Since this is my first time to see you, who are you in regard to this matter?" I insisted.

"I am a friend of the family. Sheebah is a friend of mine," Tracy Burkhart answered.

People with the look that Burkhart had are dangerous people. The name Burkhart said it all. She had a heart that was barking at me. Names mean something. Her face was giving me the impression of someone who had the habit of sleeping on the job.

"Sheebah doesn't have a white friend. She doesn't even hang around white people," I said to her.

"You need a lawyer," she replied.

"For what? I have my kids with me. Boney lives with the woman they call Grandma. Sheebah is homeless. Suzy here can testify for me. She knows she is living in her school van. No, ma'am, I do not need anything, more less a lawyer," I answered.

"Sheebah will see you in court on February 23, 2009, at 8:30 a.m." Tracy Burkhart threatened after giving me a copy of the summons to appear in court.

"I will find me a lawyer, and we will be there."

CHAPTER 22

FATHERS FOR EQUAL RIGHTS

I found myself knocking at the front door of the Fathers for Equal Rights, a recognized civil rights organization. I needed a lawyer. After paying my $200 member fees, I entered in the office the receptionist pointed me to. A woman was behind a desk. Every piece of fabric on her, included the handkerchief she had naively around her neck, was out of time, place, and out of fashion. That type of cloths made it impossible to be an attire gear for a woman. I graciously smiled and said, "Hello, are you the lawyer on duty today?"

"Hopkins Laster. Take a seat," the woman said.

With her left index finger, she showed me with notoriety where to sit. She was busy looking at pictures from her laptop. A minute or two passed by, she was still responding to her computer beeps. I invited myself in the chair that was directly facing her office desk and cleared my throat. She still was in her computer. I stood up to leave; she looked at me and said, "What d'you got?"

I opened my file and handed her the summons to appear in court on February 23, 2009.

"How did you get this letter? Where is the rest of it?" Hopkins Laster asked.

"I was not served through a proper channel. Tracy Burkhart, a white lady who was visiting with Suzy Dale, gave a copy to me."

"Tracy Burkhart is a child protective specialist. It is not her place to serve you with a summons to appear. It is not totally illegal for a CPS agent to do so. Summon is from a Latin name that means capture and deliver, it is a current practice since Robin Hood. The law is playing catch up with technology. They want to save about $40 to $200 by sending these legal mails even through Facebook. But you can make it a case. It is not legal in Texas," she explained.

"Tracy Burkhart, the white lady I saw in Suzy's is a CPS agent?" I asked.

"Yes, she is. What is going on here? You only have few days to show in court. You need a lawyer and it won't come cheap," Hopkins Laster explained.

"The reason I am in the headquarters of the Fathers for Equal Rights today is because I don't have the time and mostly the money to hire a lawyer. Are you a lawyer?" I said to her.

She scratched her short military-style cut hair. That "what d'you got" was not a lawyer fine language. I doubted about Hopkins Laster just a little till she started to explain things in a language I was not familiar with. Using words that were hard for me to comprehend, she said that if we are going forward, her first choice will be to request a continuance of the trial setting and serve the mother of my kids with discovery requests. It is never guaranteed that a continuance will be granted and the judge may be disinclined to grant a continuance because this case has been pending for a long time, she added. Requesting a continuance and requiring moving the current trial setting would cause her to incur more attorney fees. She said that she would be more prepared for trial if it could be delayed sixty or more days into the future. Since we were a mere three weeks before the trial and assuming that we were going to have a trial on February 23, 2009, she wanted me to provide her with documents and information she would need to prove and try the case. She was not a magician, she rhetorically said, but she needed to review all necessary documents to my case. To be effective, she required to talk to all witnesses in advance. She said that she would file on my behalf the following legal documents:

A counter petition for $45.

A subpoena for all school records, $70.

An application for CHIPS insurance for $30.

A subpoena for CPS reports for $78.

And court's filing fee, $45.

A total of $3,800 that would include her lawyer fees will cover all costs and expenses.

"With that amount, I would provide you with all necessary documents for the court trial," she explained.

"No problem. We just talked about fees. Are you a lawyer?" I asked her again.

With both her hands, she adjusted the collar of the sky-blue shirt she was wearing under a grey costume-like jacket. Then, she put her handkerchief back where it was. I did not understand the use of that piece of tablecloth-like-material around her neck. The room temperature was just fine.

"Yes, I am. And I am here at Fathers for Equal Rights because I care about children."

Hopkins Laster was a lawyer on duty. She did not care about children. If she did, she wouldn't have asked me for money for $3,800. She was not supposed to charge members. I was a member since I paid my due. Lawyers did not control the Fathers for Equal Rights. This institution was made up of dads who were fighting or once fought to regain the custody of their children. I paid $200 because its revenue depended primarily upon the annual dues and service fees paid by walk-in customers. Even if what I paid was not enough to necessary meet its operational needs, Hopkins Laster did not have to ask me more. As it is written in the FER pamphlet I received, she was in that office to assist me by sharing her educational knowledge with me, to empower and guide me through all meander of the law and around corners of court trials. Instead of asking me for more money, she should have been my strategy and my so many more.

"Do you know where Sheebah lives?" she asked.

"In Suzy Dale's van. She uses the 9160 E. Walter Street in Bedford as her living address. This place is used to get food stamps and government advantages."

"Are you ready to pay so we can start?" she asked.

I came at the Fathers looking for a knowledgeable pro bono lawyer with professional skill in helping dads who had children taken away, but since I did not have enough time ahead of me, I accepted to pay $3,800. I was in real need of a lawyer. I was sure that the power of the money would ready her to teach me some courtroom demeanors. I was right. She directly started to complete a brief and confidential questionnaire about my children and me. After everything was said and done, I stepped out from the fifth floor where the office was located. As I was entering the elevator, I met Doug Clark, the head of the Fathers for Equal Rights. He asked me how it went.

"I think Hopkins Laster is crazy," I responded.

"How come?" he asked.

"She is crazy, she doesn't think right. I regret already hiring her. I think it will be trouble."

"You hired her? Well, that is the reason they are here. They are looking for money," Doug Clark explained.

On Monday, January 19, 2009, three days after the FER office visit, Hopkins Laster called to let me know the status of my file, cause No. 325-428760-07. She said that she had been reviewing the documents I provided. Some pleadings were obviously missing. She wanted, most notably, whatever the Attorney General served me with, to start the lawsuit. Since my trial was scheduled for February 23, 2009, at 8:30 a.m. in the IV-Court # 2, in Tarrant County Family Law Center, Hopkins Laster ordered me to check my house to see if I could find what was missing. She wanted it to be faxed to her as soon as possible. I told her that the letter I received the copy of, which was given to me by Stacy, was the only document I received from the Attorney General. I left it with her.

"Okay, I will check my desk again. Do you have health insurance for the children now?" she asked.

"Yes, ma'am. You should have three Aetna ID size insurance cards with Swift transportation logo on them: one for me and two for kids. They are in the khaki envelope I sent to you on January 17, the very next day after the meeting."

"It is my understanding that you have had custody of the children up to this point, that they have lived with you the majority of the time. It is my understanding that you do not want to delay this matter further and that you will provide me with the names, addresses, and telephone numbers of witnesses who will establish that the children have been residing with you. I need the lease that shows that you had children before October 2008. I also need copies of your paystubs from December 1, 2008, through the date of trial," she asked.

"I gave you everything you just asked already. Check the envelope please. You will find in it all necessary copies, including my lease from 2003 to 2009," I answered.

"Okay. My current course of action will be to file everything once: the order to the associate judge for child support enforcement, adjudication of non-parentage, temporary order establishing the parent-child relation, and SAPCR. I will also send a letter to the attorney general with paternity request for Boney's forensic DNA test, notice of appearance of counsel, attorney vacation letter, respondent's original answer, respondent's rule 194, requests for disclosure to Texas Attorney General, and respondent's Rule 194 requests for disclosure to Sheebah. If a scheduling order has been issued in this case, I would appreciate it if you would fax me a copy. Also, if any discovery requests have been served to you, I am hereby requesting a copy," she imposed.

"The discovery request is one on the top of all documents in the envelope you have."

"Okay, I see from this summons that Ms. Sheebah's address has been withheld from you. I think this is absurd from both a historical and a practical aspect. I'm not sure how you are supposed to conduct this lawsuit without that vital piece of information. I would like also to subpoena someone from the school to testify. I asked you whether you had been served with any questions: discovery requests such as interrogatory, disclosure, admissions, or document production requests. It is very important that I have everything that has been sent to you in the course of the lawsuit," she said as if she was rehearsing.

"Once I hang up, I will resend everything again, including the pauper's oath." I promised her.

Two hours after this phone conversation, about one hour after I re-sent copies of documents and everything she wanted by e-mail, in response Hopkins Laster e-mailed me the following letter.

From: Karambee

To: Kasalobi;

Sent: Monday, January 19, 2009

Hello:

Please confirm that you have received this e-mail. I still need the last three numbers of your social security number and driver's license number. Is Mr. Kasaloba your first or last name?

I need to know whether you filed an answer in this case. If you did, I need a copy. If not, I want to file one on your behalf. If I file an answer, I will assert, based upon your representations to me today that Sheebah accepted government aid, food stamps, or whatever fraudulently during the time you had possession of the children and she did not use that aid for the benefit of the children. Since I did an electronic search of her name, I need $35 from you. This is the information that is listed for her address with her driver's license: 9160 E. Walter Street in Bedford. Do you recognize that address? Of course, do not go there. I have also prepared the attached counter petition. I need a check or money order from you for $45 cost to file it with the court. I think it is important for you to file the counter petition because you may be entitled to back child support from her. The other parties will not be required to respond to the disclosure requests unless the current trial date is moved by at least thirty days. The followings are arguments you will find in the counter petition: the discovery level intended in this case to be conducted under level 2 of rule 190 of the Texas rules of civil procedure and the objection to assignment of this case to associate judge for a trial on the merits or presiding at a jury trial.

As of now, no court has continuing jurisdiction of this suit or of the children and there are no court-ordered conservatorships, court-ordered guardianships, or other court-ordered relationships affecting the children, the subject of this suit. Since you did not live or engage in sexual relations with Sheebah during the probable period of conception and given that you never represented to others that the child was your own, I will make a request for the genetic testing under chapter 160 of the Texas Family Code for Boney. It is called the denial of paternity. You will be, of course, the counter petitioner. It is in the best interest of the children that you should be appointed sole managing conservator of both children.

In accordance with the document given to me, Sheebah, the mother, had failed to support all her five children in accordance with her ability. She will be obligated to support them and should be ordered by the court to make payments for their support, retroactive to the date of filing, and to provide medical and 50 percent of the children's uninsured medical expenses and child support in the manner specified by the court while this case is pending. You have, from the documents presented to me, provided necessaries for the support of the children during their physical possession since their birth. Therefore, I will request reimbursement for the necessaries you had provided for them from Sheebah. I also will introduce a motion to prove that she had been fraudulently obtaining government aid for the children, although they resided with you. She will be ordered to solely be responsible to repay any such government benefits that she wrongfully obtained. For the safety and welfare of the children, I will request that they live only beyond a geographical area identified by the court, acting directly or in concert with you. I will enjoin that Sheebah or any person acting on her behalf from disrupting or removing the children from the school or child care facility in which the children are enrolled or approaching the children at any location other than a site designated for supervised visitation.

I will order the preparation of a social study and request that Sheebah produce copies of income tax returns from 2003 to year 2008, a financial statement, and current pay stubs by a date certain. This counter petition will be respectfully submitted on timely manner in accordance with the Texas Rules of Civil Procedure. All notices for this case should be directed to me as your attorney at the address I gave you. I will make my appearance as your counsel.

What evidence that you have to be able to get into evidence at trial that you think would demonstrate that you should be awarded the children? Do not bombard me with papers that are not responsive to my requests unless you are going to pay me my hourly rate to review them. I will not review piles of miscellaneous papers and prepare a motion for a trial for a flat rate of $3,800. If that is what you want, you will need to pay me $4,000 more, my retainer fee, and my $250 hourly rate. I want this to be absolutely clear because you had been demonstrating that you are not complying with my requests in a timely manner and had been indicating to me that we are having a language problem.

I do want the intact CPS records. I do want the police reports as they came from the police department. I understood from our last telephonic conversation, three hours ago, that you will be bringing those records in with you to Fort Worth FERS tomorrow between 2:30 and 3:00 p.m. Bring also $4,000 in for my retainer. It is my understanding that you have been going to court for your children. I would like to have the transcript of any appearance you made before the judge, prepared by the court reporter, if you can afford it. You have to call her with the case number and the trial date and ask her for an estimate for the cost of the transcript. She will require that you pay the estimated cost in advance. It is possible to get less than the entire transcript, for example, you could just request the testimony of one witness. It is not as good as the entire transcript, but it can be better than nothing.

By the way, we did find your additional leases. We have made copies of your documents and will mail them to you tomorrow. I still need the pauper's oath.

Thanks,

Dorothea Laster

CHAPTER 23

YOU ARE
MISTAKEN, SIR

I knew already that Dorothea Laster was a confused woman. She was taking me for someone else. If not, she was plain crazy.

It seemed to me that that mail was a prewritten document, one of these mails lawyers send to their clients. That was a plausible explanation of why she was still asking me to supply documents and proofs I have already provided, on January 16, the first day I was at Fathers for Equal Right, on January 19, in the khaki envelope, and then by e-mail. She was not checking anything before asking.

It was evident that she did not read my file. She was not reading anything, not entirely at least. The woman didn't even know how to spell my name despite the fact that it was written all over the paperwork I handed her. From that moment on, it was easy to predict why she was at Fathers for Equal Rights instead of making herself known on billboards or in newspapers.

We all know that lawyers are in the business of making money. Dorothea Laster was not a good counsel. She was exaggerating how she was making hers. She was deliberately exploiting the hurting parents instead of focusing on being their lawyer. A good counsel represents and understands the client's emotions as if they were hers. We signed a contract. I paid the total of a flat rate of $3,800 she wanted me to. She clearly stated that that amount was enough. It included her fees and will cover all costs and expenses. Despite all that, she still was talking about me covering different fees by sending her more checks. She went far and suggested that if I did not have handy cash; she would send me a pauper's oath to immediately file. I will sign it in front public notary, send it back to her, so she maybe can get the court to waive some fees and court costs. This was a sorry insult. It was, in comedy, a situation of a bad joke, one doesn't laugh at. With all due respect to her ground academic education, I thought while reading that e-mail that Dorothea Laster did not get it as a lawyer. She was of a diluted spirit and was showing at the same time her knowledge outreached. She was not good. Things she was saying and the amount of extra money she was asking pointed to that qualification. People who helped her graduate should be ashamed of her.

I talked to her in person, with my spoken voice and in writing through a big envelope. I gave her names of my trial witnesses. I told her what they knew and whether they would voluntarily appear at trial. I said to her that their names are written on the copy of the 325-428760-07 Tarrant County Family Services Advisement form I left with her. Anyone in their right mind would have seen written, in black and white, the names of Yvens, Dominic, Romeo, Teo, Mathieux, Masemo, and Cyrus. Obviously, I saw through her that Dorothea Laster was not the one who will destroy, bit by bit, Sheebah's lies. I was not going forward with her; she was swimming in incompetency. I knew from that moment on that she won't rebuild the truth from evidences she had gotten. At this point, I was scared that she will not move people's hearts come the day of the trial because she was not asking for documents, she was after the money. Her games were widely clear, outspread, and well-known. She had been playing them on her clients to increase her fees. A person like that always finds excuses not to do her job. So I decided to drop an e-mail.

From: Kasalobi

To: Karambee

Sent: Monday, January 19, 2009

The pauper's oath was legalized and notarized. It was sent to you in the second big khaki envelope mailed by way of certified mail. I do have a returned receipt from the post office to testify my seriousness. I added in it copies of documents you were still asking even if I either left them with you the first time we met in your office or mailed them the next day. I am sending them again. I know you are a busy woman. If you take a minute to read these documents together and organize all the files you already have, you will find in it a compiled report from CPS. Included in it are also names of prison records. Information about the names and addresses of the shelters where she lived are hard for me to get. I thought that we had that conversation in your office. You said that it would be easier for you, as a lawyer, to get other documents if I pay $3,800. You said that that amount will cover your fees and costs and all expenses. And I paid. Despite that, per your request, I gave you, the same day, an extra check of $210. You needed that money for three subpoenas. Now, what kind of costs and subpoenas are you talking about? I came to Fathers because I did not have enough money. I have already paid you a total of $4,010. To me, that is a ridiculous amount of money, and you are still asking for more. Believe me I do not have $250 hourly rate and $4,000 retainer to give you. I gave you what you asked. I paid because I believed in you. You convinced me you will take care of all paperwork, CPS report, and subpoena services. Something concrete must be done first from your side instead of asking me for more money.

Ma'am, it is abusive manners from your part to keep saying that you believe we are having a language problem, that I have been demonstrating problems complying with your requests in a timely manner. That is crazy and not serious to treat me as an idiot that way. I tell you what; the first time I saw you was on January 16, in your office. I introduced every piece of documentation necessary for the trial I had in my possession. Despite the fact that I paid what you asked, you gave me, the same day, the pauper's oath to file, legalize, notarize, and then send back to you. I did not talk to you until today, January 19. You called numerously, left messages, and asked me for documents I have already given to you. I sent them immediately. Then, you send this mail, in which you are asking for more money and accusing me of not complying. Which one of your requests did I not comply with in timely manner? Ma'am, my English is just fine. If by saying we are having language problems you are insinuating that I do not speak or understand English, then it is you who are having a problem, you are the problem. I will never speak like a lawyer simply because I am not a lawyer. I will never talk like you and this is the reason I hired you. As you know it, I am a DJ on KNON 89.3 FM Radio. Let me be absolutely clear to you: I wouldn't have been hired there if I was not capable of making myself understood. By the way, you are intentionally changing my name. That also is showing how much of bigot you are. Kasaloba is a female name and I am not a woman. About Sheebah, she has moved again. I will get her new address. It was not necessary to spend $35 looking up electronically for the 9160 E. Walter Street in Bedford. I personally gave it to you in the interview I had with you. It is also written on every front page of the CPS reports I gave you. I won't reimburse you because that address is not attached to her driver's license as her residential address as you are insinuating it; the 601 Bellaire is. I won't have $45 more to pay. I gave you already $210 for that. Sheebah sent me a text message telling me that the court date has changed to March 13, is that true?

Kasalobi

From: Karambee
To: Kasalobi
Sent: Monday, February 9, 2009
Subject: Atty Comm

You were mistaken. I have never told you that the $3,800 will cover all costs. And I have never told you that as lawyer, it will be easier for me to get documentations. The only way I can get information is by subpoena. For that, you must either pay for the cost of the subpoena, not by check, or if your pauper's oath is successful, the court may waive the cost. The only other way is to serve Sheebah with discovery requests, but that needs to happen at minimum sixty days before trial. You would need a continuance of the current setting for that. No one has informed me of a change of the trial date. I think it is a setup. She wants you not to show at trial. She had been setting you up since the beginning of this matter. And this was the reason you have never been served by the sheriff from the attorney general's office. She has given them a wrong address and has told them that you have left this United States and went back to Africa. Can you save the text that says that the court date had been postponed? Can you print it?

Thanks.

On February 10, 2009, I received a mail in which Dorothea Laster was complaining about Muntumpe, my daughter. I called her and asked her how she got to her. She said that she initiated the conversation. She found her number through our correspondence. That statement, from her, was kind of lie, but I played the game. She called her, she said. They talked. Muntumpe did not let the interview go on. She attacked her right away about how she was conducting the case, about the pauper's oath, and why she wanted it since she was paid enough to do her job. Since then, Muntumpe had been using my home computer to communicate with her, mostly to harass her. At the end of that mail, Dorothea insisted on receiving the extra pay she wanted because Muntumpe was now harassing her and was telling her how to do her job. If she did not get it, she will take a different route, she threatened.

Dorothea knew how to manipulate her clients. Muntumpe knew how to play games at her ease. It seemed that Dorothea Laster found her equal. In her calculated game of exploiting people, she did not trust Muntumpe to be concerned about this case. The manipulator is always the enemy of other people's perfect manipulations. Muntumpe is a dangerous woman. I would never seek help from her, even if I was at the lowest point of despair. Starting anything with her as Dorothea did was suicidal. She has been terrorizing me and tearing down things she obviously knew I have been building for her.

She also has been destroying every single member of my family and demolishing everything we stood for. Muntumpe has been doing all that since she was fourteen. She began doing them six days after I brought her in the United States. If Dorothea would have called me first before talking with her, I would have told her that at sixteen, Muntumpe was told by a girl called Marie that "as long as you are a juvenile in USA, you can break the law, you can even hit your parents, and police wouldn't do anything about it. If your father touches with violence and hit you, you will see what will happen to him." From that moment, my entire life became nothing but a mess.

Marie was an fifteen-year-old African girl. She was brought in the USA by her parents. Once here, she started misbehaving. Her parents tried to put her back on track, but unbelievably, she played the victim every time they did so. Then she started calling the police and telling them inconceivable stories of abuse. Unimaginably, the police began to believe her. With the time, she was removed from her parents' compassionate house and was placed with the foster parents. She ended up being raised by a white family. Muntumpe heard this numerously and took advantage of it faultlessly. This was the reason she turned out to be an onion. She developed layers of hurt and hate because she wanted to be living just like Marie, with white people. It was without saying that despite her African roots, to arrive to that means, Muntumpe laid her hands on me and hit me, not one time but five times. She physically made me bleed through my mouth and my nose. I have a permanent bump on the left upper corner of my face due to her blows on my head. I have a broken tooth that left a gap inside my mouth on the right side of my lower jaw. She never has been apprehended because, as the police said it many times, she was underage. Her acts and all the beating I received from her undermined my authority as a father. She spent a lot of her time teaching my other children how to disobey me. Makaya, my son, took her instructions seriously. To hurt me, he applied a bunch of that instruction on me. Nothing was pretty. At the end of the day, he also destroyed lot of good things in his own life with the rest of what he learnt from his sister. Like in a dream, I started thinking of how he particularly did it. Rapid review of facts started to present itself in my mind. I remembered the day I came home earlier from work and found him smoking marijuana. His friend Osee was with him. I got mad and asked him to put that cigarette away. He challenged me. I confiscated their smoke. Makaya stood up to challenge me more. I did not back off. I asked him to sit down. He did not, and without a warning, he jumped on my hand, held on to it, trying to retake his smoke. Doing so, he intentionally twisted my right arm. It popped out at the wrist level. I dropped the cigarette. That day, I went to the hospital to have my hand fixed. It was broken. It was twisted, broken by my own son, in my own house, by the instruction from Muntumpe. Things became worse when he pierced his ears. He let his hair grow long to his waist, stopped doing his normal chores, and dropped his pants down. My son's hands began his belt. He held his pants to walk. He quit school altogether after that. The police gave me pictures of him selling drugs on the street. He was underage. They told me that Muntumpe was the one who was providing him with drugs. They also said there was nothing they could do since they did not catch him breaking the law yet.

One day, I yelled at her because she started hiring Dimassa, my other son. She was obliging him to sell marijuana for her too. She denied everything, ripped her pants, tore up her shirt off from her body, shred herself to two pieces of clothing on her back, the bra and the underwear, and started to swing at me. That was the fifth time she hammered my face with her fists. She broke my nose. I was bleeding all over the carpet when the Hurst Police arrived. They put her in their cruiser and took her to the station. They said it was just to separate us until everything cools down. Three hours later, they called me. They wanted me to go and pick her up. I explained how she broke my bones. They did not want to hear a thing about it. They only wanted me to answer their demand. I refused to go to the station.

"That is child abandonment. You will pay $400 fine if you do not come and get her," the police said.

CPS got involved. I still refused to go and get her. They took her to Fort Worth shelter. This was the time I met Glenn, a CPS specialist. She also refused to hear anything about the way Muntumpe dropped my blood. Her main question was to know what I have already done to help her and to create a father-daughter relationship.

"Her problems did not start today. I applied all kinds of tough love on her. I have taken her to counseling, to church, to the elders of my community, nothing ever changed. I even took some family law classes to better myself lately. I wanted to know how to handle her. Nothing I did worked on her. If Muntumpe ever lays a finger on me again, I will go in for a reason," I said.

CHAPTER 24

MY HANDS ARE TIED BEHIND MY BACK

It was after this threat that Glen removed Muntumpe from the shelter. She organized a meeting at her office and took family pictures. CPS took temporary custody of her and sent her to Connecticut. Once there, Muntumpe developed a strange relationship with Stacy Smith, another specialist. Even from over there, she did not stop trying to destroy me. There was a time when, to have kick of a hit, she blocked her phone and spent that time verbally insulting me. She said things a person would never articulate in church. She said those things to me, expecting me to say a thing or two that would allow Stacy Smith to activate her adoption into a white family. It did not work. With the time, she got placed in a group home. It was late that year that she finally got what she has been wanted: a placement in a white foster home.

When she tells the story of her being in a white foster family, she does it with regret and sadness in her voice. In her new home, she said, she used to eat in the same plates with dogs.

"Not as mistreatment, but as a routine. The owner loved his animals so much that he himself shared food with them. They all ate at same time, in the same plates. He sometimes gobbled dog food just like them. It was quite nasty to use these plates for human food. It was equally nasty to oblige us to do the same," Muntumpe explained.

At eighteen, Muntumpe came back to Texas with a high school diploma. I thought she grew it out and changed. It didn't take but three months to reveal who she became to me. She said she was an adult, I gave her that. She said she didn't have to listen to me anymore. I said I understood that, but as long as she was in my house, she had to respect the house rules. She moved out. Days later, she came back and took Makaya with her. I complained because my boy was doing good already since the time she was off to Connecticut. Hurst Police paid her a visit. They explained to her what the law says about her taking a juvenile without parents' consent. Makaya was brought back home. From that moment on, everything I knew as a father went sour. Makaya started to be late home. His grades went back down. We ended up having a student-parent meeting in Mr. Nate Hearne's office. When he entered the office, I saw a different Makaya. His pants, I've never seen before, were four times bigger than his regular size. They were hanging down on his thighs. He had, under there, at least three boxers of different colors. His buttocks were also exposed to anyone's eyes. Makaya had to use both his hands to stop his pants from falling down from his hips. It was certainly sorry to imagine him trying to run from the police. I asked where he got these clothes and why his pants were hanging. He said, "You don't care about me, you don't buy me clothes, and you make me eat out the trash can. Why the hell are you asking me questions like that for? You kicked me out from your apartment full of roaches, you fool. Mr. Hearne, for the past two months, I have been living with my sister, she cares." Makaya said.

"Hold on, Makaya, even if we rarely sat down to eat on the same table together, nobody does eat out of the trash can. What are you talking about? You just spent two nights out of your bedroom and you are talking of two months? And why are you calling me a fool?"

"It is probably the drugs talking," Mrs. Hayes said.

"I do not do drugs. That is a lie my dad keeps telling people. He wants me to find a job after school. I don't want to, and that is why he is not feeding me. He is obliging me to eat out the trash can now."

"Do you see how much confused to the bones your son is? Did you know that not only he smokes marijuana, he is precariously selling it on LD Bell premises as well?" Mrs. Hayes, the counselor, asked.

"The smoking part is not news to me. But the selling part—"

"The money-drug exchange is bluntly made inside CD cases. Your son borrows music from someone, and when he gives it back, the drug or the money is inserted inside the case," Principal Nate Hearne confirmed.

"Your daughter, Muntumpe, is supplying the drug he is selling. She is training him how to skip school and go and sell it. This is confirmed by school police. They warned both of them already. It is just a matter of time. They will get them if they do not stop. When Makaya told us that story of him being fed out of trash can, we interviewed Dimassa, your other son. He told us a different story," Mrs. Hayes said.

"Mr. Kasalobi, your son is about to be expelled for tardiness, absences, unless he gives me a reason not to," Mr. Nate Hearne threatened.

"What say you, Makaya?" Mrs. Hayes asked.

"My own dad makes me eat sticking rubbish, and you don't believe me. He bought a watermelon that day. After cutting it, he put my slice inside the home trash can. He held my head down and forced me to eat it. This is the reason I don't like watermelon anymore. About my low grades and absences, they are caused by the fact that I have been having little sleep because of roaches that infect my dad's apartment. Roaches are eating us alive. Yesterday, when I complained about that, he pulled the jacket off my back and hit me with closed fists."

Since he was sitting on the chair that was behind me, I turned around and looked at him. No parent in right mind, as I was, would have dared to do things that Makaya was talking about to his child. Muntumpe was in his shadow, I thought. She was doing more harm than helping him.

"When did he hit you?" Mrs. Hayes asked.

"Yesterday, he entered in my room and hit me," Makaya answered.

"Didn't you just tell us that you have been living with your sister for the past two months? How did he manage to hit you yesterday, in your room, and in his apartment?" Mr. Hearne asked.

Not only was I flabbergasted and stupefied of allegations that came out from that young man's mind, I also was petrified to hear all lies that timid young man was saying. Every piece of accusation he pronounced that day was an exaggerated recline. It sounded as if he spent lot of time rehearsing. He accused me of everything. The only thing he did not blame me for was the global warming. If it was not because of Mr. Nate Hearne who interrupted him, he would have continued his heinous and reproachful speech without blinking.

"Does your father mistreat your brother and sisters the same way or he only picks on you?" he asked.

"He does that to everyone, even to my cousins. The man is a crazy fool," Makaya said.

"Let's verify that," Nate Hearne said.

He picked the phone up and called Mr. John, the LD Bell school police officer. Minutes later, Officer John showed up with Kanina Musamba and Sanaa Musamba. These two are my nieces. Their father, Brazele Musamba, abandoned them on the city streets when he went back to Africa. I took them in. They lived with us ever since. Mr. Nate asked them questions about when we eat, where we sat down to eat, and what we eat. Then he asked how we live and how they are punished if they do wrong. Kanina told him a totally different story than the one we all heard from Makaya. She told him a story of love and caring. Sanaa concluded by saying that the only three things I ever asked Makaya to do was to cut his hair, raise his pants up, and stay in school. Officer John agreed. He said that he knew Muntumpe like he knows the palm of his left hand. As a Hurst police officer, he spent quite a time with her. She was maliciously manipulating Makaya, her brother. He concluded that Makaya needed to get away from her sister's devil control.

After that meeting, Makaya ran from home completely. I filed the missing person report. Hurst Police refused to take it. They said that it was not necessary because he was still going to school at LD Bell. Since he was missing lots of days, they asked me for his most recent picture to be put in the patrol car computer. If spotted, over Muntumpe's or somewhere else, he will be brought back home. I went to the juvenile office and met with Officer Coffee. His office was located across Bell Helicopter, next to a Texaco gas station on Highway 10. After carefully listening to my irritable complains, he said that juvenile works differently that the regular police department.

"As long as your child leaves your house without your permission, by the law, he/she is considered as a runaway, and whoever opens the door for him/her would be harboring a juvenile," he said and declared Makaya as runaway child.

Days went by. Officer John found him at Muntumpe's. He put him in his cruiser. He then walked back in to warn her.

"The very next time you go and get Makaya from school or from anywhere for that matter, you will be arrested. The law will prosecute you either for kidnapping or for harboring a runaway child. There is an African saying that goes like this: 'Whoever teases the hive bee honey comb must have long legs to run, if you understand what I mean. But in this country, you won't be able to run far," he advised her.

Muntumpe nodded, but Makaya denied having ever run away from home. Officer John brought him back. Makaya did not stay home with us. He did not go over Muntumpe either. He went to live over Osee, his Latino best friend, the same day. This young man had an uncle who was a drug dealer. Muntumpe was one of his distributors. In those days, Muntumpe was doing criminal justice at Tarrant County College. She called me and told me that she will wait for an opening. She will spend that time learning how to turn the law into her advantage. Once she is a lawyer, she will find a clause and end of the law to put me in jail for abuse, even if abuse did not happen, and she will take Makaya away from me forever. That cheap threat stayed in my heart for very long time. I still remember it every time she is around me.

By the police's observation, Makaya and his friend Osee were on the streets. They were openly selling Muntumpe's drugs. I went back to Hurst police station. It was to press charge this time. They refused to listen to me. I wondered why I was archly questioned. For them, it was I who was supposed to be sitting on the bench. I was a suspect. The police told me that I was under investigations from CPS. I spent my parental time hitting Makaya on his sex instead of educating and violently pushing him against the wall and in place of protecting him. They accused me of taking his jacket away while it was cold outside, the jacket I didn't even buy, the jacket that his sister Muntumpe gave to him, and the only jacket he had. And because Makaya was almost an adult since he was seventeen already, he had the right to get away from me, they said.

"I smell Muntumpe in all this again. She did talk to y'all. Didn't she?" I asked.

"We don't discuss anything about who we are talking to," an officer answered.

"This is just bunch of lies coming from his big sister. She is trying to keep him on the streets to deal drugs. I won't let my son live in Osee's parent's house anymore," I said and left.

Days went by. Officer John talked to Osee's parents. He told them to never receive Makaya anymore. Meantime, at LD Bell, Makaya continued sleeping during classes due to the fact that he was spending his nights dealing at the park. His attendance was disappearing and his grades were melting down. Things went from bad to worse. He finally got kicked out from the campus. He was in his last year. I wanted him to have a high school diploma. I enrolled him in secondary alternative education program called Crossroads SOS in Euless. One of that school's strict conditions was that a student cannot miss a day of school unless approved by both parents and by the school. I talked to Mrs. Weryevan, the principal, about Muntumpe. She promised to call the police if she ever showed up there. It did take but a week, Mrs. Weryevan called to verify when I came back from Africa.

"You mean since the last time I was in office? I did not go anywhere. What's happening in Africa?" I asked.

"That is awkward. I just stepped out to talk to you. Muntumpe is in my office right now. She is talking about you. She is telling me how bad of a parent you are. She said that you went back to Africa and abandoned them. Since she is the elder, she said, she is taking responsibility for her sister and brothers. She asked me to forward all official letters and report cards to her address as she just done it with Bellaire. What is strange to me is that she brought with her this notarized letter in which she is officially taking that responsibility. She also has a certified copy of Dimassa's school report from LD Bell. She got it from the guardian of record on Central drive in Bedford."

"How did she get that?" I asked.

"That is a million-dollar question. I did not believe a word she said because yesterday, I saw Belinda. She was playing volleyball. I asked about you. She said that you left earlier. You went to work. You do taxi at Love Field Airport. She wouldn't have told me that if you were out from the United States."

Since it was less than two miles down the street, I drove at Crossroads SOS. Mrs. Weryevan showed me another letter in which Muntumpe was imitating my signature. She was trying to excuse Makaya. He was three times late already.

"Two times, we saw a white Nissan, driven by Muntumpe, drop Makaya on the side of the road. He then disappeared after that. Every time that happened, we gave him a note to give to you. You never answered," she said.

"I never received any letter. Muntumpe is not supposed to be in your facility. I signed documents stating so with you. Why didn't you call the police as decided before?" I asked.

"There is always a police on the campus. They have already gotten my reports. This time, there is no need to. When Muntumpe showed up, we thought she came to get your son out of here. Let's get in and talk to her."

When we got in, a security guard told us that when Muntumpe heard me being introduced, she stood up and ran out from the lateral door.

"It does not matter anymore. Including his three tardies, your son has missed two days already. He can't be here anymore. I need you or anybody to get him off this campus. His release papers are ready to be signed. Even if it is very late for your son to think of getting a high school diploma, there is no dirt that cannot be washed by the water. Take him at the Grapevine, Texas so he can go and start doing his GED there," she explained.

I realized at that moment that Muntumpe just destroyed the last chance her brother had to finish high school. With pain in my heart, I took all release papers, signed them, and directed myself to Grapevine, Texas. As a last action, I enrolled him in a GED program. Four days later, Mrs. Andrew Contreras, the director of program, left a message telling me that Muntumpe showed up there.

"She told me that you stole them and brought them in USA without their mother's permission. You don't love them," she said. "She has already reported you to the authorities, which is the reason you have been mistreating them. She wanted her brother out of the program. She said that GED is for retarded persons. They do not attend a class reunion. Muntumpe needs to learn that her actions will affect her brother in the near future. You need to do something," she told me.

"I had been trying. She is always one step ahead of me. I don't know how to catch up. She is learning the law and CPS is behind her. I just do not know what to do."

The very next morning, Makaya did not show up to school. I knew at this point that he dropped his education. Later on, he was seen on the streets, dealing drugs and spending his nights in Osee's house again. Much later, he was observed fighting to get out from under police boots. Jail was now his second residence. I wanted him out of that kind of life and away from Muntumpe. I went to CPS office in Arlington. I talked to Specialist Linda. The lady listened and then said, "We, the Child Protective Service, do not protect a child from himself. We protect a child against abuses from parents and other adults."

Sheltonia Polk, her supervisor, who was in the same meeting with us, had a different opinion of me. She said that she was assigned to investigate me. Her finding was that there was no abuse toward Makaya or other children as the report said. Nevertheless, she talked to Makaya. She found out that he was a very nice young man, he was willing and polite. It was me, the father who did not understand him. She blamed my son's failures on me.

"Just like every young person of his age, this is his time. It is the time for him to express himself fashion wise. He is showing off himself. "

"See this with the eyes of a parent just for a moment. Let's say for instance that Makaya is your son. He is wearing the Snoop Doggy Dog ironed hair as if he was a girl. Imagine him having on him a size 40 pants while his regular size is 28. These pants are showing three underwears hanging down below his buttocks. See him with two badge earrings on both his ears. Visualize him high on forbidden substances, smelling marijuana all the time and displaying puffy lazy eyes on his face. Now, picture him showing up in your presence at McDonald's where it happens that you are the manager. He is holding his privates with one hand and his pants with the other and he is walking funny as if he had been hurt on his right leg. Will you hire him since, up to you, he is not doing anything wrong, he is showing off, and he has been expressing himself?"

"It is not about me, it is about you, your education, and your son," she said.

"You are a CPS to the core, no mother's heart in you at all. See, Muisangie Lumpungu, my ma, a woman of integrity, said to me once that 'life is not a show, life is what you make out of it. Otherwise it is insanity.' Okay, what do you want me to do?" I asked again.

The lady didn't even move her lips. Her silence was the self-evident answer. CPS officials are good people. I always admire the load of work they do most of the time, but kids do not know better. They always copy from the next person. They copy bad things, bad words, and bad behavior from people they trust. In this case and point, they listen to CPS. Personal advises CPS give to them let to desire. It put them in all kinds of repeated bad situations. As consequence, the child-parent relationship is often completely turned down. She did not answer my question because she wouldn't hire the Makaya with pants hanging down, fashion wise, even if he was her son. That is why the whole CPS institution, as it is today, must be destroyed and then rebuilt from ashes with real parents.

I left CPS and went to precinct 3 of Tarrant County the same day. I pleaded my case there. I needed my son to be sent to the boot camp or to some other institution that will keep him from using drugs. I wanted them to make him stay away from his sister, therefore saving his life. The judge, in office 2, told me that as a parent, he understood my request. And as an officer of the law, his hands, just like mine, were tied together behind his back. If he puts my son in boot camp, he said, he will be charged with kidnapping. I stepped out from there and knocked at the juvenile office 4. The constable told me that both my boys are wild, they are known as such by the law. He then gave me a picture of Makaya holding a pack of marijuana between his teeth and another picture of him and Dimassa, his little brother, both holding respectively an AK-47 and a M16. Both pictures were taken in Fort Worth, inside Muntumpe's house. He said to me that they were aware of everything and they were investigating, waiting for the time to act appropriately.

"Your son is almost eighteen. You cannot save a child who doesn't want to be saved, concentrate your energy on other children," he said.

I went back at the Hurst police. There I was told by a lady officer that "as long as your son did not break the law, we cannot do a thing." I insisted, talked to her about the pictures with guns, his fights with the police, and his street drug dealing. I also asked a restraining order against Muntumpe.

"It is very complicated to have a restraining order against Muntumpe. She is your daughter, their sister, and a member of your family. It would be hard and costly to enforce that court order. Kids will be seeing each other no matter what."

I thanked her and went at Boy Ranch in the city of Bedford. Mrs. Farley told me, "Our boot camp is open to any parent who is able to pay $600 a month. Since it is not government mandated, a child must come in willingly and abide to discipline rules, otherwise at his third strike, he will be kicked out." She said.

At the end of that day, I realized that it was very complicated to save Makaya from his sister. When I thought about it, he was already destroyed. His speech was showing signs of impairment due to his drinking habits and use of drugs. The man was not thinking right. Strangely enough, when I talked to him about it, he blamed everything on me.

I said, "I am not the one selling drugs. I am not the one fighting with the police, and I am not the one going to jail."

Makaya was not the only person who was broken down and damaged by Muntumpe. On December 16, 2003, around 2:00 in the morning, I heard strong banging on my front door as if it was a police emergency. I looked outside, through the lateral window; I saw Nirasanga, my niece, in the parking lot. She was standing and crying. For her parents, Nirasanga was a runaway. As she was crying, she said that Muntumpe helped her run away from her house. She sent a Greyhound bus ticket directly to a girl called Grace Mundum to able her to catch a ride all the way from Maryland to Texas. Everything was okay when she first arrived. Then Muntumpe started to slowly force her to do things she did not want to do, things she had never done before, like selling small bags of marijuana or rocks of cocaine. She also wanted to pimp her to become a sex slave. Since she refused, Muntumpe confiscated her identity card and her social security card. Days later, she applied for food stamps under her name. She also sold her green card to her African friend.

"Today, Muntumpe was forcing me to sleep with her best friend's boyfriend for money. When I refused, this man put his gun on my head. I still refused. Muntumpe then got mad, she collected my things, forced me in her car, and dumped me there in that parking lot," Nirasanga explained.

This was not the first time that Muntumpe stole legal papers. She broke in my closed apartment months before that and took all my children's passports, their I-94 forms, and their social security cards. Equifax confirmed that as a fact. Makaya's social security card was showing regenerating revenues for two years in row, but that money has yet to be reported to the IRS, they said. I made legal noise around it. Mae Jackson, the woman who has been using it, was called by the Office of the Attorney General. She admitted receiving it from Muntumpe. The investigation was opened. In a desperate move, Muntumpe then called me. She said that the police was not a witness to anything, that all these papers belonged to his sister and brothers, not to me. Therefore, she had a birthright to do anything she wished with them. She will keep using them. I reported her to the police. They asked me to replace them while waiting their investigations. It was not easy to do that. To replace their passports, I needed their ID. To have their ID replaced, I needed their social security cards. To have their social security card, I needed their I-94. To have their I-94, I needed the re-entry forms. To have their re-entry forms, I needed their passports. A very complicated process that made me end up in a vicious circle, exactly at the point where I started. Muntumpe had all these papers. She was daring me to do something. I decided to let her in her illusion. In Africa, I learned that it doesn't matter how big the elephant is. It will be eaten one bite at a time.

Nirasanga then told me that the reason Dimassa likes to spend her weekends over Muntumpe was because she gives him beer and smoke. They all deal PCP, marijuana, and ice. That explained why he was bringing in Jordan shoes. It explained also why he was going late to school. When I wondered how he was wearing expensive clothes, he said Pastor James was giving them to him. At this point, Dimassa was sixteen. I believed his words because during that time, Pastor James was nice to my family.

If Dorothea would have called me first before talking to Muntumpe, I would have told her who she became since she was sixteen. Everything she did and each one of her dirty tricks was already written in Hurst Police files. I would have told that to Dorothea E. H. Laster, but she did not talk to me first. I saw this when I went looking for advice from Officer Coffee of Juvenile Division, from Detective John, Ricky Anderson, and John Barrington. As parents, things they put together to help me created nothing but tears and lamentations in me. Muntumpe was not changing. Their best suggestions including their recommendations did not work either.

Dorothea Laster should have been warned about that. Why did she go ahead and talk to her without my consent?

"You are right. I saw in her a potential witness because she saw everything Sheebah did, but I was wrong. She will be a problem in court. I learned a lot about her just by talking to her," she said.

CHAPTER 25

SUDDENLY ALL HELL BROKE LOOSE

Dorothea Laster then invited me to check a mail, full of insults, that Muntumpe sent to her earlier.

"I saw her writing that e-mail, and I told her not to send it. She is always in my file reading and cheaply distributing personal documents. She does this to hurt me. Yesterday, when I came back home earlier, she was on again. She was writing to Karambee, meaning to you. I was mad at her. I told her, at that instant, that she was forbidden to directly speak or to correspond with you. I shut off the computer, but I left without disconnecting it. I didn't think she still will send that mail," I explained.

After that conversation, Dorothea Lanster sent me the following mail.

From: Karambee
To: Kasalobi
Sent: Friday, February 13, 2009
Mr. Kasalobi,
I was hoping that your daughter would be helpful in preparing your case. She has not graduated from law school as you represented to me. She knows nothing of the law. I am no longer taking her

e-mails, which have become abusive. See her attached e-mail, written on February 12, 2009. Who do you intend to testify on your behalf at trial? If your daughter has a drinking or substance problem, please ensure that she is sober when she appears for trial.

I have bent over backward to make representation financially possible for you. If you would like me to withdraw, just say the word and I will file the necessary paperwork with the court. Again, there is no way for you to get admissible documents within the time frame without a subpoena. A subpoena costs approximately $78 each. I will not take a postdated check for that amount. If the court accepts your pauper's oath (which I have not yet received), you may be able to get these fees waived.

Please read the attached e-mail from your daughter.
Sincerely,
Dorothea Laster

Subject: Re Date: 2/12/2009
From: Muntumpe
To: Karambee
Thanks for your comments. Realize that I never told you I was a lawyer. So stop referring yourself to things I absolutely did not say. I was not there present to hear exactly what you are claiming my father told you, it is hearsay. I know my father. He did not tell you that. Besides, what you are saying he said cannot affect your case in any way. My education has nothing to do with your case. I do not understand why you should be bothered about that. This case is not about me. Your opinions about my education level are irrelevant because this is a custody battle case, not a correspondence or a speaking class. If you are concerned about my level of education, and I appreciate all your insults, please direct that question to me. I will explain. I do have a bachelor's degree in criminal justice. In order for me to be accepted, I am taking the LSAT exam, an entry level test law school. Perhaps I offended you, I am sorry about that. I am only concerned about my father and his case. A lot of things that happened should never happen. If you paid attention, gathered substantial evidences, and went through the whole

file he provided you already, you will see that he has a case. That case can easily be solved with your support. My father is not an attorney even if he studied aviation law at Mountain View College. He doesn't have knowledge of court procedures. He doesn't have to; that is the reason he hired you. He is not supposed to be going around trying to retrieve evidence that you need for his case, you should. Because you asked him to, he felt obliged to hire another lawyer to do your job. Veronica showed up in Dallas and got all the information you need free of charge. She then gave them to my father who gave them to you. He gave you everything to satisfy this case as if you were the victim and he was your lawyer. You were paid enough; why do you want him to sign your pauper's oath for? Why are you keep saying that you have bent over backward to make his representation financially possible for him? You have yet to take my father to court, show us what you have already done that worth $3,800. I told you that I will provide you with Sheebah's arrest and criminal records, but there is no need to, my father gave it to you already. You then asked things like CPS case worker names, addresses, and phone numbers to defend your case. I repeatedly told you that pieces of information like that are very confidential information that CPS would never release to me. As a family law attorney, you are award of all that as true. At a certain point in your career, you have come in contact with CPS, you know how they treat allegations made by outsiders. Again, given that he is not a paralegal or your legal assistant, my father gave you case worker names, addresses, and their phone numbers. Don't you think that he has done everything he could to assist you so far? This is all the information you need to start this case. I personally have gone beyond my expectations to provide you with CPS main district office information to make it easy for you to obtain all records free of charge. As an attorney of record, you didn't even bother to go to Dallas. You didn't even request them. What do you still want money for? What do you still want to subpoena? You have been paid fairly. Stop asking for so much extra money. Stop asking for the exact documents you have been given to already. It is now time for you to show something. Do your job.

As a lawyer, you have been unprofessional and a liar. You have been degrading my father. The first day I spoke to you, you made fun of him. You badly spoke about his English accent. You said that you do not understand what he was trying to tell you. Language barrier you said? Is that your best excuse to avoid doing your job? Notice this: my father speaks eight languages. How many do you speak to be my father's speech teacher? You don't even speak English, you speak Texan. My father can teach you how to speak proper and grammatical English. So stop making fun of people. You also talked about his medical issue and disclosed his health conditions to me without his permission. You said that because he just came out from the hospital, he was not thinking right. I found that to be unethically amateurish. It is like you are fighting with the real progress my father and I already made instead of dealing with the real problem. Ma'am, many lawyers queued up for this case because it is so easy to win. What you have been doing is getting money from my dad. That is all. I read the contract of $3,800 you made my dad sign. It is explained that your fees, expenses, and costs will be covered. You then asked an extra check of $210 for three subpoenas. That is a total of $4,010, and no case is filled yet. Are you serious? I have contacted the bar association. I complained about you stealing from him. They have already sent me necessary forms. I will file grievances against you if, based on misrepresentation, you fail my dad's case. My dad is going to use me as his witness, and we will go to court against you.

Please do shift your energy toward something more productive: my father's custody battle. I care about him, and because of that, I care less about your rudeness. Be more careful about what you are writing against me. If you need any assistance, only concerning my father case, you are more than welcome to call me.

Thank you.

Muntumpe

The verbal fight, through their e-mails, between Dorothea Laster, alias Karambee, and Muntumpe did not start on February 12, 2009. It started as a nice exchange during the same time I hired her. I did not know who initiated the conversation first, but when these two users of nice people got together, they did not get along. They started to argue. This is how it developed into a conversation that broke loose from hell.

> From: Karambee
> To: Muntumpe
> Sent: January 30, 2009
> Dear,

Thank you for speaking with me today about your father's case. His trial is scheduled for February 23, 2009, at 8:30, in 325 judicial district court, Tarrant county family law center, 200 E. Weatherford Street. I really need your on trial. Please get together a list of names, addresses, and phone numbers of five to ten of the people who are the most important to the case. I definitely need any information on the CPS case worker, address, phone numbers, and CPS case numbers. I need your adult sister's name, address, and phone number. I need anyone who could help substantiate our claims against Sheebah.

Please also make a list of the most important things that has happened with Sheebah in the last couple of years. A timeline would be very helpful including dates:

1. When she lived with you.
2. When she was in the shelter.
3. When she was selling food stamps.
4. When she was making allegations of domestic violence.
5. When she was allowing your sisters to be outside without shoes and unsupervised.
6. When she has allowed the children to be around her boyfriend.
7. When her boyfriend was on crack or other abusive persons.
8. What information you have regarding the daycare provider, Suzy Dale.
9. What evidence you have that proves that Sheebah has been involved in crime.

Do you think the seven-year-old girl would be comfortable talking to the judge? Would she be able to say what is happening at her mother's?

Thanks,
Dorothea E. H. Laster.

Subj: Re: I need names.
Date: February 6, 2009
From: Muntumpe
To: Karambee

This is Muntumpe. I spoke to the CPS case worker in regards to Sheebah. I was told that I should go to their main office in Dallas to retrieve any information needed for this case. Their main office is located at 8700 N. Stemmons Freeway, Dallas, Texas 75247. Also, I would need necessary forms from you to legally retrieve legal information. I am working on getting some of her police report. I have numbers of two ladies. They are her coworkers at that daycare. They can be potential witnesses. I need time to write a concise statement about things that had happened and the way they happened. You should have that report ready by Friday.

On February 4, 2009, you said that I did not understand what you are asking for. I sent you exactly what you asked in the mail. I sent you the name of the case worker assigned to the case, her address, and her telephone number as you exactly requested. I do not have her specific information. What I sent was general information that everyone retrieves about anyone who is involved with CPS. Because of the privacy law, I cannot get Sheebah's precise information. As a lawyer, you can.

This is the situation regarding Sheebah. She has five children, two with my dad. She doesn't know the father of Boney, her third daughter. Daven is the father of her last two. He is on crack and marijuana. Sheebah and my father have been separated for about six years or more. My dad has been taking care of his two little girls. Sheebah is not stable. She cannot maintain a job. She has not been able to provide for any of her five daughters. She works part time for KFC and cannot even support herself. Since I have known her, she had been homeless most of the time. And when she has an apartment, she never stays in there for two months in a row. She always lives with people, and she had stayed with me twice. The last time she was with me, she stole all my belongings and staged a burglary. She did get away with it.

Sheebah likes to live off the government system. This is mainly the reason she is trying to have the physical possession of my dad's two little girls. It is one of the government requirements to continue receiving benefits. As I am writing this, she doesn't have them, they are with my dad. But she is receiving child support from my dad and other government benefits for them. Sheebah doesn't just get benefits from the government, she gets them illegally. She also gets benefits for Boney, Kattaya, and Baby J. None of these girls live with her.

Boney never lived with her. In fact, people Boney live with are not even related to her. She accused their son for being the responsible of her pregnancy until DNA proved otherwise. Even after the DNA test was done, she still leaves her daughter behind with them. Kattaya and Baby J. are taken care of by other people. Without kids to support and since she never even cares about them, she sells their benefits and gives that money to Daven to buy drugs. People, who care about her children, do drop them at Daycare for Children. Lots of caregivers in that daycare has histories of abuse. In fact, the whole school was shut down because of abuse of children. It is now open under a different name and under a different operator, but it still belongs to the same owner.

Sheebah should not receive custody of any of her children. She is abusive. She used to make Kattaya stop breathing by putting both her hands on that little girl's mouth to hold her breath. The girl passed out one day. She rushed her to the hospital. The doctor suspected that she was doing something to the baby because "this was not the first time that the girl lost her breath," the doctor said. He called CPS on her. Sheebah got away with it by doing some parental classes. That habit of momentarily stopping Kattaya of normally breathing had caused breathing disorder in Kattaya. Today, the girl has asthma. It is maybe caused by her mother's behavior.

Sheebah should not receive custody of any of her children because she let Daven verbally abuse Tabô when she goes over there to visit. She physically beats Loylla with a closed fist and calls her a fat girl. One day, he tied both girls with a nylon rope and left them to suffocate. Their mother was present when he told them that he wished they would die. Sheebah never said a word to protect them.

She doesn't care. Sheebah suffered also from mental distress. She saw her little brother killed by Katie, her mother. He was a baby then, and she was at that time living under the bridge. Katie suffocated him with a blanket. She got away with it because the city of Gainesville, , did not have enough evidence to convict her. They concluded that since it was cold outside and because of the landscape under that bridge, it must have been an accident.

At that time, Sheebah was already living in a foster home. The news of her little brother's death did not arrange her situation. She never thinks right ever since. Most of the time, she doesn't even touch her daughters. She is scared of killing them. She cries and says that she hates them. Sheebah is a con artist and she knows all tricks in the book. She lies of being victim so that she can get victim compensation. To get assistance from the government, she keeps saying that my dad abandoned her and her children and went back to Africa. You saw my dad, is he in Africa?

Sheebah cannot have the custody of both kids because she is constantly in jail for this or for that reason. She got lot of pending tickets and warrants. I am writing these things as I am thinking of them. I do not have material time to revise and summarize them. Hopefully, you will understand the bit of what I am trying to explain. Thanks.

Muntumpe

From: Karambee
To: Muntumpe
Sent: Tuesday, February 8, 2009
Subject: In Re Kasalobi
Ma'am:

I have no idea of what you just wrote to me. None. I think you are having problems with the English language. You are losing something in translation. I wanted to speak with you initially because your father was under the impression that you had graduated from law school. You informed me that was not the case. I thought it would be helpful to your father's case to talk with you, but I see now that it is not. Based upon your recently inflammatory e-mails to me, you may also be too emotional to be a useful witness for him. I will let him make that decision.

I have sought out the identity of witnesses from your father and have already visited with you by phone and repeatedly in writing. I have bent over backward to make arrangements with your father so that he could have representation in this case. I will not take your unwarranted abuse so I will not be accepting anymore of your e-mails. I will not take orders from you regarding this case. Again, if your father wants documents which are admissible in evidence, he will need to subpoena them. The cost for a subpoena is $8 for issuance, $10 for tender (witness fee), and approximately $60–$70 for service of the subpoena. You are mistaken about the cost for CPS documents. No one can obtain them without money. I need more money from your father. You are most certainly mistaken about whether those documents your father obtained as you suggest would be admissible in evidence at a trial. They would not. You are mistaken about whether there is a form I could give you to get documents. The only form an attorney has to obtain documents is a subpoena. I am confident that any member of the bar association or any other reasonably intelligent sober person would be able to understand what I am saying and have repeatedly said in this regard.

Once again, ma'am, I have no idea of what you just wrote to me. None.

Thanks.

Date: 2/9/2009
From: Muntumpe
To: Karambee

What are you talking about? What is your meaning of a subpoena? How many and who exactly are you trying to subpoena because you never told us names of persons that are needed to be subpoenaed? With the information you have, why don't you subpoena them already? You received an extra amount of $210 you said was for three subpoenas. To the best of our knowledge, nothing is done yet, and as now, nobody is subpoenaed yet. Despite that fact, you are still trying to collect more money from my dad. It seems to me that you are trying to milk him more because the man is in need. That is stealing. How about the job you are supposed to be doing, who is going to do it? I need to make an appointment to speak to you personally. And why are you still demanding documents my father has already provided? Why are you still asking for CPS files we have already submitted? I need to see what is going on with this case. Maybe you are not a lawyer. If you don't know that CPS doesn't charge for documents and you are thinking that I am making a mistake about the cost and on the fact that one can obtain them without money for CPS, then, ma'am, maybe you are not a lawyer. Why don't you talk to Veronica? She will tell you she did not pay a dime. I need an appointment to talk to you, face to face.

Thanks.

Muntumpe

Date: 2/10/ 2009
From: Karambee
To: Muntumpe
Ma'am,

You have a real problem. Your contact is unwanted. If you contact me furthermore, I will make a complaint of harassment with the police. If necessary, I will inform the school that you are using their e-mail for the purpose of harassment.

Dorothea Laster

Date: 2/11/2009
From: Muntumpe
To: Karambee
Mrs. Dorothea,

I think you are crazy. My dad thinks so too. Doug, your boss in Dallas, has the same opinion of you too. Dorothea, which part of my e-mail don't you understand? I am getting very frustrated with you. What I am saying is that you do your job. By law, what you are about to accomplish is called a misrepresentation. When that time happens, I will reach the bar association. I will forward the e-mails you have already sent to me and to my dad. We will see then if they

236

would understand what you are doing. So far, you are depending on us to do your job, which is not a problem because we have to assist you. But given that you are now asking my dad to get information you have already received and you know he is unable to obtain, we started to doubt about you. Are you a lawyer? Why can't you obtain the simple police report that is a matter of public information? You are not doing your job, that is why. You are only playing mind games. Guess what, we are far from being stupid. I learned all your manipulations. I know your next move. You are this kind of lawyer, despite all these years you went to school for it, who still read mail between its lines. The proof of that is in the fact that you do not have "no idea, none" of what I wrote. I was not technical when I wrote what I wrote. "No idea, none" is not a language of management. It is a language of exploitation. I hope you did not go to school for that. I gave you the CPS address in Dallas. I told you that Sheebah lives in the woman shelter in Arlington. She falsified everything and claimed she is a family violence victim; they believed her. All you needed to do is to get in their websites or go in person to get her records. You are an attorney; it is your job to prove otherwise, mostly to establish that she is unstable. Why don't you schedule an appointment to meet with me? Better yet, make time available to interview me over the phone. I am your witness, not "a real problem," and yes, I do understand English. If you are busy not to take my dad's case, you're better off to refund all his money to the last penny. He needs a lawyer who cares because this is his life. His children are his life. He has worked hard and he is taking care of all of us. To lose custody and to have to pay child support because of ineffective counseling is unethical. I need you to schedule an appointment to meet before the court date.

Thanks you.

Muntumpe

CHAPTER 26

LAWYER EXCHANGE

It was only after reading Muntumpe's mails from Dorothea Laster that I decided that same Friday, February 13, 2009, that it was time to have a serious talk with her. I had ten days remaining before the court date. Muntumpe was killing me slowly. She did not have the right whatsoever to threaten my lawyer, less again to talk to her. Her involvement looked, on the first sight, as a cry for help. But from the trained eyes that I was, it was easy to see, from a distance, with both eyes that there was a green snake hiding in the grass. Muntumpe always finds some kind of pleasure to see me suffering. She was not trying to help. She was making it hard on me. Talking to my lawyer was one of her games. It was a game to hurt me. I talked to her and told her that she was wrong as usual. I said that Dorothea Laster was also wrong to take her seriously. I then obliged her to apologize. Just when I was talking to her, the "you've got mail" alarm sounded. It was Karambee.

From: Karambee
To: Kasalobi
Sent: Tuesday, February 17, 2009
Mr. Kasalobi:
Do you know of anyone who is not offended by:

- being told that they are liars or thieves?
- being threatened?
- being a professional with eight years of college and eighteen years of legal experience and having a young upstart presume to tell them how to do their job?
- being told that they are not a lawyer?

This is a two-line letter she just wrote as apology; she said that "I am sorry if I offended you by my e-mails. I care about my father and wanted you to see things from my perspective."

This is not an apology. This is not putting this Dorothea Laster at ease. I asked for an apology because I was looking for an indication that she knew she had behaved badly and it would be tolerable to work with her in the future. I don't see that. After receiving these inflammatory messages from your daughter, I don't see any reason to change course. I think it would be best for all concerned for me to withdraw from this case. I think you will have to find you another lawyer.

Please call if you would like to discuss.

Sincerely,

Dorothea Laster

Thanks.

On that Saturday June 27, 2009, I entered the corner room that was located on the second floor of the family court building on time. I waited in there for two hours for what the court called a discovery. I had two scheduled that same day. Marilyn Anderson, the LMSW-AP case worker at family court, opened the door. She called my name. She apologized for the waiting.

"It is due to the fact that Sheebah needed the police to escort her in here. She is scared that you may harm her. When she arrived in the building, she declared that you have been threatening her life. For that reason, she was advised to wait for the first available sheriff to bring her up. She is the reason this meeting, which was supposed to last about thirty minutes, is running almost three hours late. And because of that, Kathy Ehman-Clardy, your lawyer, left. She has another appointment in other court hearing. You are up here alone," she said.

I sat on the right side of the table, facing the entrance. Sheebah took a seat at diagonal side, with her back directly to the window. When Marilyn Anderson opened her folder, she launched her inquiry on me first. She asked questions pertaining to the well-being, the whereabouts, and the residence of my two girls, the subject of the matter. I told her what was going on. I talked to her about June 12 and where my two children were been hidden by Sheebah. I told her that Boney, the other girl added to this legal suit, is not mine, Sheebah knows it. She just wants to be paid. This little girl lives with a lady called Grandma, I said. Baby J. and Kattaya, her last two, are been taken care of by ladies from the daycare.

"Just like a snake, Sheebah doesn't mind seeing her children sprayed around. She doesn't have any concern that other people are feeding and clothing her them. She doesn't care about none of them," I concluded.

To that, Sheebah burst into real tears. Crying was a simple game she rehearsed many times before. It was her main game that led us to this point. Her tears were maybe real, but the act of crying was not. It was a simple manipulation to convince more than one, involved in this case, that she was the victim. My jaw has dropped down more than once when she did that. That day, it also lost its holding power because I just couldn't explain those dripping tears on her face. The woman was created differently; she was the only person I knew of who could lie and cry with tears at same time. How was she capable of letting them drop was a matter of scientific debate. Marilyn Anderson then handed her a napkin. After wiping her face, she gave a strange and different version of facts. She said that we were still married. I left her with the children and went back to Africa. She took care of both girls by herself. She still has them at a not-disclosed location. She wants reimbursement, full custody, back payment, including child support.

"You are already receiving child support," Marilyn said.

"Yes, but I want more. He makes $1,225 a week," she answered with tears still raining from her eyes.

"No, I don't. This woman wants to kill me. Why don't you find a decent job and make your own money?" I said angrily.

I was very loud and mad at this point. The louder I was becoming, the more tears she was shedding. It was here where she played the frightened little girl. She pointed my reaction to Marilyn Anderson. "This is how violent he is. This is the reason why I ran away from him."

"Ma'am, this woman is disaster prone. She did not run away. I kicked her out for cheating. Don't you see she is manipulating your feelings?" I said.

"Disaster prone? See, ma'am, he calls me names, he beats me. Who wouldn't have run from a man like that? This is the reason also I took my children away from him," she said.

"Ma'am, you are not being judged. This is the family court services discovery. My job is to connect missing dots, to establish facts, and to present everything to the judge. For the sake of the children, are you telling me that you are in physical possession of both children?" Marilyn Anderson asked.

"Yes, I am, but I cannot tell you where I live with them," Sheebah answered.

"We know where they are. Up to the county detective, they are not living with you. For the record, what is your real address?" Marilyn Anderson asked at the very moment when Kathy Ehman-Clardy was entering the room to join us.

Kathy was hired when Dorothea Laster quit on me on February 23, 2009, the first day I was supposed to have her represent me on the trial. She did that officially when we stood up in the front of Judge Terri White, inside the third room of the fifth floor. We did not talk about my children that day. That court appearance was changed into Dorothea Laster's exit. My children's trial was reset for July 2, 2009. The whole thing lasted about fifteen minutes. After signing legal papers, just before Kathy Ehman-Clardy's entrance, I approached Dorothea in the courtroom. I asked her to refund the total amount of $4,010. She smiled her teeth off. She said that she worked hard for me. She won't give a dime back because she didn't quit on her own.

"I have bent over backward to make arrangements so you could have representation in this case. You did not see that and let Muntumpe, your daughter, fire me."

She tried to intimidate me. I ignored her approach.

"You will pay back every penny you robbed from me when I was the most vulnerable and then you created a situation in which it was conceivable for you to quit. You quit in your own. Why are you here anyway? You did not file a single piece of paper that pertains to my case in this courtroom. You quit on me when you knew I needed a lawyer the most, just before the trial. Kathy Ehman-Clardy did the work you were hired for. She did that on lesser money and lesser time it took you to crook me. You did not bend over backward to make any arrangement on my behalf, you only bent over backward to steal my money," I said.

Kathy Ehman-Clardy intervened, took me aside, and said that lawyers do spend lot of time working on files. That fact is usually invisible to clients. Since no case was filed, it was understandable that she gave you something back. However, asking her to reimburse will be a lost fight.

"You can sue, but it will be hard to win. Let just call it a loss," she asked me.

"The truth is that Dorothea Laster is not a lawyer. She is a rerun of a lawyer. Let it be known," I said.

I followed Kathy Ehman-Clardy's advice and stayed with bitter feelings on my tongue. For me, the reason Dorothea Laster was talking about bending over backward all the time was because she was a pickpocket bandit. Only a misfired lawyer embezzles money from his customer to satisfy his needs and then justifies it. I had that impression of her the first time I saw her at the Fathers for Equal Opportunity. But I was in need, I let myself be talked out.

At this very moment, when Kathy Ehman-Clardy joined me in that corner room, Marilyn Anderson was telling Sheebah that she knew where Tabô and Loylla were and up to the county detective, they were not living with her as she tried to convince her with tear on her eyes. She continued whimpering because she was unable to say where she lived.

"You mean you don't know your physical address?" Marilyn Anderson asked her again.

"For my security, I won't tell you where I live in the presence of Mr. Kasalobi. He is out to hurt me. Only CPS knows where I live," Sheebah answered.

"You mean 9160 E. Walter Street, Bedford. Well, my deputy investigator talked to Mrs. Suzy Daley, the owner of the place. She said that you never lived there. He then called the Bedford house authority, they confirmed what she said. This here is his report. It says in it that you were last seen living at 601 Bellaire Drive # 163 in Hurst, with a man called Daven. This was your last known address. You do receive food stamps and tandiff for your children and they don't even live with you. Kattaya lives at 1188 Beverly Court in Bedford. Boney lives in Arlington with Zora Warner. Your two oldest daughters are in Glen Rose with their father. Baby J is with you, living as now in…in the van? She is in the van?" Marilyn Anderson questioned.

"I do not live in the van," the very excited Sheebah answered.

"She is a damned liar. I did not want to interrupt because we have to follow protocols, respect formalities, and avoid answering to every provocation. This is too much. You said that y'all still married. He left you behind with children and went back to Africa. There is not a record of any marriage certificate delivered to any of you. You lied about that. There is not an exit or a reentry visa in Mr. Kasalobi's passport since he had been in United States. You lied about that. You also said that because of his violent behavior, you took the kids and ran away from home. How did you do that if he left you behind? Stop telling lies. You live with your newborn in the red van, a school van given to you by Suzy Daley. It is parked outside in the east court parking lot. All your stuff are in there. I just took pictures with my camera for court purpose. That is why it is imperative to give back your two oldest daughters to Mr. Kasalobi. You took them without any legal papers," Kathy Ehman-Clardy intervened and said.

Suddenly, Sheebah went berserk. She started cursing instead of crying. Marilyn asked her to watch her language. She cursed on her again. Marilyn then threatened to have her removed from the proceeding and to have her escorted outside if she did not control herself. She hit the table with her closed fist as if she was the boss. She yelled more insanities at Marilyn Anderson, stood up to leave the room, and clacked the door behind her. Her reaction was self-explanatory; she felt she was busted. In less than few minutes of interview, Marilyn Anderson discovered the truth.

"I did a great job. This is the first case that did not take me long to find the truth. I cracked it open. That was so easy. Sheebah is homeless, fraudulently using a genuine address to obtain legal advantages. It is now proven to me that she never had any of her kids around her," she loudly said to Kathy Ehman-Clardy.

"Lift the tail of the kangaroo from the ground, and it will not hop anymore. You did a good job indeed," Kathy answered.

Just like that, Sheebah reopened the door. Marilyn Anderson told her that if she enters, she will be escorted outside the courtroom building by the police. She started to cry. She apologized and asked the permission to sit down. Marilyn explained that it was too late anyway, she just concluded her investigations. Sheebah begged to be heard.

"If you hide a crime, you became a criminal. I won't reopen this study to help you. It is done. No one pushed you out of the room. My discovery will show that what you have been doing is a crime. I will send a copy to Kathryn Omarkhail and another copy will be available in the building public record," Marilyn Anderson explained while wrapping up her paperwork inside the folder.

CHAPTER 27

EVERY HUMAN BEING IS A PERSON

We stepped out and left Sheebah inside.

"Don't you have a family court services orientation to attend today?" Kathy Ehman-Clardy asked me.

"Not today, it was scheduled on Wednesday, June 24. Something happened and they rescheduled me for July 1," I answered.

"Wait a minute, I have a report that says that Kathryn Omarkhail was already at your place. Was she?" Marilyn Anderson asked with suspicions on her face.

"It should have been done the other way around," Kathy Ehman-Clardy confirmed.

"Yes, the orientation should have been done first and social study after that," Marilyn Anderson said.

"This here is confirming what I have been suspecting all along. Something is not right. Well, I don't think we have a big fight ahead of us. We have a lot of ammunition in the pocket. To be intelligent in the court of the law is to have a right answer all the time. Don't worry, you heard the lady. After her discovery is sent in, Kathryn Omarkhail will make the right recommendation to the judge. I will obtain that record by subpoena, and by next trial, we will have both girls back home. I am going to file a motion to take possession of a child today," Kathy said.

Time went by since I mentioned to Sergeant Tig that I have been having difficulties to receive the video of June 12, 2009, event, from the Hurst Police public record. It was imperative to prove to the court that my two daughters were abducted. They were forcefully removed from the ground up. If proven and because it was done at that time by people I did not know, by the law, it should be considered as a kidnapping. So I needed it for July 2, 2009, court hearing. I called Tig one more time. He explained again. This time, things he said were designed to increase his authority drive. The only thing that matters and I retained from that conversation was "I was watching the tape of the incident moment ago—"

"Okay. That means it is ready. Did you see Broome's mistake in it?" I asked without hesitation.

"I did not find enough evidence to tell me a different story than the one I know already. I cannot keep this case opened. From me to you, I think Officer Broome acted properly and within the law and order."

"Maybe, maybe not, it is up to the court to decide. I won't take your opinion, which is but the police opinion. I still need the video though. It is a matter of public record," I answered.

Not only I understood the man, I also knew what he was up to. He was the boss. In the police business, the boss protects his officers, even if he has to bend the law. His response was a game he gave me more than once, a game I knew so well and I was aware of. It was evident that Officer Broome did not properly do his job. He did let my children go without a court order and without a legal document testifying a cause. He did not properly identify them. Detective Duermeyer was not professional either. He opened the case in the morning and closed it in the very evening. Professionally speaking, that is a significant lack of skill. To me, that is an agonizing liveliness, a horrendous coldness of heart, and a lack of ability to be an investigator. Both officers made unbearable mistakes and their boss was protecting them. Otherwise, why was it taking them that long to have the video released to me?

"I gave the order to have it released. Stop by at r convenience," he said.

I stopped by the police station couple of times after talking toting. The video was still not produced. On the third time, I got frustrated and politely informed the dispatch lady that by law, I am entitled to a copy. It is a matter of public record. I will get hold of it no matter what. That as a declaration of reassurance I articulated to her. She answered and said, "In this case and point, the tape is the property of the city of Hurst. It was damaged, that is the truth. It is now being processed. Since the recording machine is not working properly, it is imperative for you to show up here at the station, watch the scratched pictures and take notes. You have to do so with the discretion of the chief of police."

I did not want to see the chief of the police play politics on me anymore. He probably wouldn't have let me take notes from the original copy, I thought. I experienced him enough. I was one of the people he was called to serve and protect and he was not doing that. The man was capable of letting me watch something that had been reworked on. That was my position and the reason I did not want to meet him again. At the end, I did not show up at the police station and did not get to watch the video. My lawyer and I ended up in the family court on July 2, 2009, without a way to visually explain the kidnapping.

The room V on the fifth floor family court was packed. It was in there that Kathy Ehman-Clardy met Meda Bourland, Sheebah's attorney. Both women started to talk as if they both were some-where else than inside a court of the law. These two women knew each other. It seemed that they went to school together. Kathy became an immigration lawyer. Meda specialized herself in family law. Incidentally, the way they began socializing did not please me, even if it sounded that they were once friends, and it had been a while since their last conversation.

The court was called to order. Judge Terri White had lot on her hands. I saw her going through six cases before calling Kasalobi family to the bench. We stepped forward. She said, "What is going on with the Kasalobi family today?"

Tracy Burkhart explained things that did not make sense to me. She ended her intervention by saying that "Kasalobi is the assumed father. CPS discovery shows that he has a long history of violence. As at this moment, he is not the resident of this United States. His location is unknown. The department had been making diligent efforts to locate him. Our request for search of the paternity registry and a request service of process, since the respondent address is unknown, remain unanswered. Citation by publication and other substituted services, necessary for the reason stated above, in an attached affidavit, remain also answered. We filed an affidavit with the court to prove that both girls have been living with their mother. We visited with them, at their mother's residence and in school and they are well taken care of, as usual—"

I did not let her finish. I jumped forward and said to the judge, "That is bunch of lies, Your Honor. I am right here, present in this court. Why is Tracy saying that I am not a resident of the United States and my address is unknown? What kind of a lie is that? Tracy knows where my kids live. Therefore she knows where I live. She also knows that Sheebah doesn't live with us."

"Counsel, you have to control your client," the judge intervened.

Meda Bourland, Sheebah's lawyer, came forward. With a lawyer explicit language, she stepped in Tracy's foot and explained things her way. After that, she accused me of setting things up in order to have Sheebah arrested. She said that I called the police on her as she was leaving the court on June 1. Once Sheebah was arrested, I went on and grabbed both girls at their school.

"For the security of both children, Your Honor, you have to reinforce the established restraining order against Mr. Kasalobi to stop taking possession of children. He doesn't have rights to them. He illegally removed both girls where they were, from the custody of the only person who cares about them, the mother," she explained.

"There is a parent in this courtroom who does really care about his children. That man is Mr. Kasalobi. Ms. Meda Bourland made a telephone call. She used her position as a lawyer to mislead the Hurst Police. She lied about the unfolding situation and then said things that involuntarily intimidated the officer. Because of that, this man confused the summon order with a restrain order. Mr. Kasalobi did not take possession of children. He had his children with him before the time the police showed up," Kathy Ehmann said.

"In Kasalobi's written complaint, it is said that both girls were kidnapped by two unknown women. Why did he say such things to the police?" Judge White intervened and said.

"Incidentally, Your Honor, that was exactly what Mr. Kasalobi thought when he saw these two ladies lifting his children from the ground. Things happened very fast, he did not recognize the mother of his children. When she left years ago, she was about 130 pounds. With due respect to her weight, she is three times that size today," Kathy answered.

"He is still thinking that it was a kidnapping?" asked the judge.

"Not particularly. He was hurt and he still is. Given all circumstances, I would have done the same thing, Your Honor. There is a video from police cruiser that is showing what happened. Hurst PD is reluctant to…let me put it this way, Hurst Police Department is unenthusiastic to make it available to my client. It will be subpoenaed. Your Honor, it was mentioned in the June 1 hearing that there was a possibility that Daven, Sheebah's boyfriend, had more than once molested Tabô, sexually, every time the girl went to visit them. Prior to this report, Tabô was noticed by her sister scratching. She had pain, which is very strange for her age. This court asked the father to take her to the hospital for a checkup, and that is another thing too. Why did this present court not ask Sheebah to do so, Your Honor? Simply because she did not have the physical possession of children, she never did. Before taking her to the hospital, Mr. Kasalobi reported the incident to the Hurst Police Department. He did so with the respect of the law. Officer J. Ceja wrote the report #090600277 regarding the allegation. It shows that Ceja furthermore advised my client to take her daughter to the hospital. Because both girls were also late for their school annual physicals, Mr. Kasalobi then stopped at Bell Elementary and signed them off. The physical exam was conducted at the CareNow in Keller. The doctor did not find any sign of sexual molestation, but the father was told that Tabô had a yeast infection. She was treated for that. She also showed signs of physical abuse all over her body. She had multiple traces and bruises on her legs and in her back. Pictures were taken and kept in her file. She was released with an extra prescription. You saw the pictures, Your Honor, and you signed the motion to restrain Daven of being near Mr. Kasalobi's daughters. The mother here present is defiant of that order. She comes over to Kasalobi's when she knows he is at work and takes them over to Daven's apartment."

"Where are both children now?" Judge Terri White asked.

"They are over a lady called Cherin in Bedford. Sheebah took hold of them to get benefits from their father and from the government."

"My client doesn't need anything from Mr. Kasalobi. She is running from him because of his history of family violence," said Meda Bourland.

"Your Honor, my client has never been arrested for family violence. There is no record of such arrest anywhere in this United States. So I am urging the counsel to stop mentioning that my client is a violent man."

"I object, Your Honor," Meda said.

"Sustained," the judge answered.

"If he is not violent, why did he call the police on the mother of her children?" Bourland insisted.

"Fort Worth recorded that incident differently. Sheebah was driving erratically when she saw the police cruiser behind her, the record says. Her registration sticker was expired. She was stopped, arrested for outstanding warrants, and booked. The red van she was driving was given back to Suzy Dale, the owner. My client did not call the police on her. Actually, he would have done a good deed to the people of Fort Worth if he did what he is accused of. Let the record show that Sheebah doesn't need to be driving. Not only her driver's license is expired years ago, it is also currently suspended for non-payment of numerous tickets. Likely for her, she just sat in jail for most of them till this June 10, 2009, but she still has to face fees for its reinstatement. Sheebah is an unstable woman. She moves a lot, and she is always in jail. She won't be able to take care of her own children. She never did. Kids need to be returned to the father today, right now, at this present minute, Your Honor. Sheebah never had them. The police video will show how they were removed from my client's custody," Kathy Ehmann explained.

"I would like to watch that video too," Judge Terri White said while writing something down.

Kathy looked at me and winked her left eye as to say that she scored one against nothing. I smiled. After scratching something on her notes, Judge Terri White adjusted her voice and asked, "Is the social study completed?"

"No, ma'am, I still have to interview the mother. For some reasons, her electrical meter was stolen from the main wooden container box. It is interesting to notice that that meter was the only one that was removed from the entire apartment. It happened a day before I went and interviewed her. The mother did not do that to herself. She had been experiencing strange things since this custody battle started. I am waiting for the management to connect new equipment," Kathryn Omarkhail answered.

Kathryn Omarkhail was not a novice. She knew that her word, in that court of the law, was like a Bible for the judge and the social study she was about to conduct will give the children to Sheebah. With that kind of dishonest statement she gave to the judge, even if she did not name me as a person who burglarized the electrical box, she stated there the sample of things to come. That was to say, without openly saying it, that I was indeed the violent father, as described so many times by Tracy Burkhart. Kathryn Omarkhail was telling the court that I wouldn't hesitate to go at Sheebah's new residence to harm my kids, the reason why I stole the electrical box. She was planting doubts in everyone's mind and preparing the court to that aim at same time. That also was Kathy Ehmann's experience. She said that anything Kathryn Omarkhail will say as recommendation will be 99 percent of the time the decision that the judge will take. As she was talking to the judge, Kathy looked at me. She whispered and said, "I think I told you she is a sorcerer, I was wrong. She is an old hag. That is the reason I numerously advised you to weight things before telling them to her and to make sure that while saying them, they don't come out with rage or resignation in your voice. I wish she could also explain to the judge why she hates you that much."

I knew why already. She was trying to hide who she really was by imitating what I do the best, being a man. She hated me because I was a man. That was the reason she had been wearing expensive man shoes and walking like me. She was trying to be as macho as I was, but she won't. She will stay a simple underprovided fraction of my left rib. It is written so. No matter what she was doing to reach that aim, she will never ascend. She will never get higher to reach the level of my foot ankle-bone. It is just impossible for her to reach the exactness put in me by my ma and my pa. That was that because I am perfect, I am a real deal.

"Your Honor, can anybody in this room explain me why anybody would steal a meter that is distributed free of charge, a thing that doesn't have a street value, or a facial commercial significance since it belongs exclusively to an electrical company? Without naming him, Kathryn Omarkhail is assuming my client stole the electrical box. Now how would he know which electrical box is connected to which apartment, less again to her client's apartment? The reason Kathryn Omarkhail did not do her social study on Sheebah is because she knew the woman is living in the van. Let me put this so we all understand the order things happened. Before Sheebah was arrested, Suzy Dale signed the lease contract for the apartment # 96, on Park Terrace, 600 Boca Raton in Fort Worth. She did so in anticipation of Kathryn Omarkail's social study and to prepare Sheebah for her interview. Let it be known that Sheebah herself never signed that contract and never even moved in prior to her been arrested. On June 10, she got off from the jail just to find out she was about to lose that place for lack of payment. On the morning of June 12, Sheebah knew that that apartment will not be ready. The maintenance had yet to cut the electricity on and clean the place. She arranged herself anyway to take physical possession of children since Kathryn had scheduled it to conduct her social studies on June 13. When an occupant evacuates the apartment, it is a known fact that the apartment disconnects the electrical current to save money. Maria Garza, the manager, will testify about that. She will say she did not have enough manpower to quickly work on it. She will also tell this court that there was no light when Sheebah asked to move in. She had to move in because she had CPS on her heels, she said. To do so, she asked to clean that place herself and the manager let her do. I am operating on clear evidence here. I had to pay $20 to Joachim Valderez, the maintenance man. When he entered, he found both girls on their knees, rubbing the apartment floor by hand. They were inside helping their mother. Your Honor, the electrical meter box mentioned here is just another manipulative game from Sheebah's tool box," Kathy said.

"So kids were with their mother, helping to clean the place?" Judge Terri White wondered.

"The father never had them, Your Honor, it was—" Meda Bourland tried to intervene, but Kathy said, "My client was run over by a 2,000-pound car driven by Sheebah's friend. He was incapacitated. Both girls where forcefully removed from the ground, without a proper temporary ex parte protection order. Mr. Kasalobi ended up in the hospital."

"Officer Broome executed the ex parte protection order appropriately," Bourland said.

"Your Honor, Officer Broome says in his report and I read, 'Neither parent had custody paperwork, but Sheebah said she was going to take the children. Since she wanted to have a full custody, I advised her that it was a civil matter. She needed to hire an attorney.' Your Honor, there was not a protection order at that time. Officer Broome would have stated it in this present report, and I would have had a copy. The thing that was maliciously presented to him was a summons. Officer Broome didn't even bother to read it. Do you know why? Because Mr. Kasalobi speaks differently than the rest of us. A great man said once that the justice of all is weakened when the justice of one is impaired. We need to fight this discriminative injustice. Your Honor, this nation was built with and by the people of different backgrounds in the idea that all men are created equal. Another great man said that too. Mr. Kasalobi speaks as himself. Broome judged him already just by talking to him. He found him guilty because of his accent. He believed what a white woman said as the Bible truth. That is not fair."

PART VI

THEY MUST BE RETURNED TO THE FATHER

CHAPTER 28

MOTION FOR A SETTING OF SUMMER

"Council, you are getting me lost here. Are we still talking about Kasalobi's family here?" the judge asked.

"Yes, Your Honor. We are talking about justice and equality here. Sheebah wants to be paid, that is all. She never protected her children even if her counsel is trying to bring this court to believe so. We all know, and this court knows, that is not a safe place for children, can anyone tells me nevertheless what makes a school van a better place for her children compared to Kasalobi's warm and welcoming apartment? My client's two daughters are not a possibility, they are a real promise. They cannot be moved around as a probability to please the mother, her counsel, and the Hurst PD. These girls are not a negligible quantity, they are every human being. And every human being is a person. We all are persons, everyone here present. Nobody is better than anybody else. Therefore, they cannot be taken away from their father because he is black with a simple summons and given to an unstable but white mother," Kathy interceded with fierceness in her voice as if it was done with her last energy.

"Council, no need for that in here. To the best knowledge of this court, there is no court-ordered conservatorship, a guardianship, or other court-ordered relationship affecting Kasalobi's children, the subject of this lawsuit, effective June 12, 2009. May I see both the summons and the restraining order?" Terri White arbitrated.

Meda Bourland stepped forward and handed a seven-page ex parte protective order pamphlet to the judge. After a fast look, she called both lawyers to approach the bench. There was a whispering talk that put doubt in my mind. Then the judge called for thirty-minute break.

As we were stepping out, Kathy Ehmann approached Meda Bourland and they started talking again as if there was not tomorrow. I did not understand how they were able to socialize and laugh at same time after that legal wrestling they pulled up in there. Muntumpe intervened and said, "What we just witnessed, including the argument that broke in there, was just a theater called forward to show us that these two lawyers were doing their jobs. The truth is somewhere else, they know each other. The outcome decision of this matter is being decided behind the curtain. As matter of fact, it is already decided. We need to fire Kathy Ehmann, if we don't, we will lose this case."

I did not answer. Giving her a reply was remembering why Kathy Ehmann, instead of Hopkins Laster, was representing me. I took control of myself; anything I would have said, at that moment, would have been inappropriate. I needed to be calm for the court questioning. I left her in the hall and entered inside the courtroom and waited there. The judge entered. The clerk asked us to sit down. The court came to order. Then the judge stated, "In the interest of Tabô and Loylla, cause number 325-460019-19, in the district court 325th judicial district, Tarrant County, Texas. This is the decision of the court. The temporary ex parte protective order and setting hearing was applied on June 6, 2009, in Arlington, Texas. It has two parts. The first part, the part that is the matter of this issue, is the immediate need for this order to prevent family violence and to protect Sheebah, the applicant, and other members of the family. The orders are in the best interest of Sheebah, Tabô, Loylla, Boney, Baby J., and

Kattaya. It was therefore ordered that the clerk of the court issues a temporary ex parte protective order as follows, and the respondent was immediately prohibited from committing family violence, as defined by section 71.004 of the Texas family code. The order was signed on June 11, 2009, by Judge Judith D. Well and by the Associate Judge Jenny Walker around 04:00 in the afternoon. Even if it was certified the same day by Thomas A. Wilder, district clerk, it left the office on June 15. The copy was given to Meda Bourland, the lawyer of record for the applicant, on the same day. It was served to Kasalobi on June 16, 2009, by the constable of Precinct 2, Officer Robert J. McGinty. The following is this court discovery. To the best of this court knowledge, this court has not participated in any capacity in any other litigation concerning the custody of these children in this or any other state. This court doesn't have information of any proceeding concerning these children pending in a court of this or any other state regarding the person who has their guardianship. This court doesn't know of any person not a party to the proceedings who has physical custody of these children or who claims to have custody or visitation rights with respect to the children. That leads us to believe that, by the time he was served, Mr. Kasalobi's two daughters were already forcefully and physically removed from him on June 12, 2009. Both kids were, therefore, removed illegally and without a proper order. At one hand, it is the understanding of this court that the mother needs help. The court will provide counseling and parental classes. At the other hand, it is yet to be proven that the father is a danger to his own daughters. I here order that they shall be returned to their father. From the moment they are returned, both parents will communicate via e-mails and text messages, not directly or through children. Both parties will refrain from inflammatory language when referring to each other. This matter is reset for hearing on the merits, July 28, 2009, 1:30 p.m. All witnesses are sworn to reappear. This is my decision on this matter."

"Your Honor, this is summer time. Kids are off from school. Tabô and Loylla have expressed a desire to spend this time with the mother, whom they primarily have resided with. I am requesting a setting of summer shared safekeeping and supervision," Meda Bourland appealed.

"Motion for temporary joint mutual to the court received."

"Your Honor, Sheebah is homeless. It is in the interest of this court to know where the children will be. The father also has the right to know," Kathy said.

Meda Bourland objected and said, "For safety reasons, the address of my client and children was sealed by Judge Bronson, Your Honor. Revealing it will be putting their lives in danger."

"Indeed, but since we are in summer break, visitations are here and now order alternating weeks possession. Beginning July 3, exchange of children will be on every Friday at 6 p.m. in the Bedford PD parking lot. This is the decision of this court," Judge Terri White decided.

Tracy Burkhart was then ordered to bring both girls back home. Two days later, a man showed up unannounced at my door. Professionally, he looked as if he was a ready-roady businessman. Dressed in a two-piece black suit and white shirt, he had a black computer travel case with him. He said that his name was Steven Boshuizen of CPS. I let him in. He did not look around as would have done Tracy and Kathryn. He invited himself in the kitchen where I was cooking and told me that he was African.

"You look like a white man to me," I said to him.

"I am not a white man, I am a South African," he spontaneously responded.

"You mean that you are an Afrikaander from the South."

From that moment on, the conversation moved with a pace of an eye-opener. The man did not want to agree with things Africans agree with.

"That sounds as if we still are in apartheid. Do not discriminate me on the unintelligent foundation of who you think I am. To be exact, I am an Afrikaner, not an Afrikaander. We are the descendants of Dutch. Our ancestries were the first to industrially breed cattles, and as shepherds, they commercialized the livestock in the South. They were once called Hollander Taal by black people and South

Westerner by British, but they considered themselves as the Boer," he said and completed himself.

"I see, I consider and respect that side of history."

"The young lady playing a game on the computer is Tabô, I presume. I specially came to see her. Where is Loylla, her little sister?"

"Outside in the balcony, eating or doing something," I answered.

"I would like to interview both together. It is practical that way. It will be easier for me to gather information once. Is there any place we could be alone?" he asked.

He took both girls in Tabô's room and talked to them for about ten minutes. He came out and said, "Well, I think I'm finished here. Everything is in order. We received numerous complaints in which we were told that kids are in great danger. I saw them dandy. I heard from them groovy, it is not even worth to make a report." Steven Boshuizen said.

"Their mother is the one calling CPS. She is forcing her own kids to live in a small bowl placed on the top of the dining room table. She is telling them at same time that they can unbolt their wings and be whatever they want to be. She sounds as if she was a woman waiting to exhale."

"That is so poetic," Steven Boshuizen of CPS said.

"No, that is crazy. The woman is making me sick. Kids are not goldfish," I said to him.

"Waiting to exhale, hein? Well, I'm finished with my interview here. Goodbye, children." He left the apartment on good notes.

On July 9, 2009, Hurst Police Department called me. The dispatch lady said that Kathy Ehman-Clardy subpoenaed a copy of the tape. It will be made available and sent to her per certified mail. She then asked me, to my big surprise, if I still wanted a copy of my own. I said yes. She asked me to come, pay, and get it. I showed up and paid. Back in my apartment, when I sat down to watch, I realized right there that it was not the needed video. That thing I was given to, after spending my two American dollars, had a precise depiction of a different event. To start with, I was immediately annoyed by the pictures. I was not able to see an instructive thing at first. The whole video was grainy and snowy as if the camera was positioned against the light. Its audio was horrible. It was impossible to discern a word. The first few running minutes repeated itself five times in a row. I had to use my hard eyes to see the lights entering the Glen Rose apartment complex. There was then a shadow of a man. I confirmed by his uniform gear that he was the police. He passed in front of the light and disappeared behind a wall. The time was just before midnight, which was off from the moment K. Broome arrived at my place.

I called the police department back. The dispatch lady answered and said that it was Officer Arnold D'Israeli. I remembered at that point that he, in fact, came earlier on June 12, 2009, just after midnight, to investigate Sheebah's over-the-phone harassments. I needed the one that happened at 16:41 precisely, that same day but very late in the afternoon, I said. She promised that she will mail me the good video.

She mailed the video twice, but she still mailed Officer Arnold D' Israel's. I called Kathy Ehman Clardy and told her what I was going through to get it. Instead of directly answering about that, she said that she has filed another motion for continuance. She also filed a protective order against Sheebah. She found out that Sheebah was setting both girls up to testify against me in their next interview with the court. She then said that pictures and video have been subpoenaed. I don't have to bother the police anymore.

Couple of days later, I finally received the self-explanatory and illuminating video I was in need of.

The first day that I was ordered to exchange guardianship of children with Sheebah was Friday, July 10, 2009. I arrived five minutes before the scheduled time. I waited till 6:00 p.m. She was nowhere to be seen. I then decided to go inside the police hall to have them notice us and document our presence. Sheebah was in there. My daughters and I stumbled on her explaining things to officers. When Monique Hall saw us, she moved toward my girls, took them inside the interview room, and shut the door after her. I knew at that instant that she suspected some kind of wrongdoing. When she came out, she did not have both girls with her. That absence scared me. I thought that they were taken away again.

We were asked to sit down. I slid on the bench while Sheebah took a chair. Officer Monique stood near the receptionist table and said, "We do things silly in Bedford. This is how we do them. We sit parents around the table and talk to them. It is not about them but about the children. We know what happens to children living this life. We know this because we have here in the city of Bedford a service that is trying to save such children from their unbalanced homes. When we are contacted, most of the time, it is late. We do start early when we see a situation like yours. So, ma'am, you were telling us earlier on that your ex is a bad father. He had a violent behavior toward all his children. You said that he never cared about any of them. He kicked Muntumpe, his firstborn daughter, out of the house and made his son Makaya eat from the trash can. You said Tabô testified that the father hit her with the belt, causing bruises all over her body, on her hands and arms. Because of that, she was not allowed to eat home anymore. You said that he calls Loylla a bitch and stupid like her mother, that he also took food away from her for a long time. You said that both girls sleep on the floor because the father has one bedroom and the whole house is full of people and guests from Africa all the time. If they were caught sleeping in the father's bed, Mr. Kasalobi would throw them to the ground. You said those things. I then asked you what you do when that happens. You said that you do not do anything because you are scared of him, he is an abusive man. Well, I talked to Mr. Kasalobi. He is confused like a stone. I decided to interview Tabô and Loylla with his permission. They did not make any outcry when I was questioning them about your allegations. They denied being hit by their father. They denied having their hair pulled by their big sister. They denied been left unsupervised. They denied being feed out from trash cans and going hungry. Basically, they denied every accusation you brought forward. They said they love you. If there was any abuse, the judge would have detected it before deciding this custody exchange. My experience with women like you, ma'am, is that they always put things in their children's heads and then accuse other people of things they personally do to others. As a mother myself, I do not like that at all. Children aren't supposed to be in the middle of this mess. Now, this is how silly we do things in Bedford, we confront parents for the good of children. I want you guys to work your problems without involving your children. Think about them first."

Sheebah was not happy with that direct reprimand and exceedingly straight advice. She did not add anything to her first denoted conversation. She took both girls and directed herself toward the main exit.

Three days later, I called Kathryn Omarkhail. I told her that I needed to spend the next week with children in Maryland for their summer break vacations. I called her not because I required her permission but because per my lawyer's advice, I wanted the court case worker to know where both children will be during that time.

"When will be the next exchange?" she asked.

"Let me see, today is Monday, July 13, 2009, it will be the seventeenth. I will have only six days ahead of me. I want to leave the same night so I can be back in town on time," I suggested.

"Well, the only way that idea will work is if you physically bring both children here after the exchange. We then will talk to my supervisor together," she said.

"Okay, I will bring them. The exchange is scheduled at 6:00 p.m. It will be after that then," I said.

"Then bring them Monday morning," she recommended.

On July 17, 2009, I was again inside the Bedford Police Department hall to take possession of my kids for a week. When Sheebah showed up with them, Officer Monique Hall was behind the reception counter. She entered five minutes late. Tabô ran toward me, I opened my arms, thinking she was giving me a hug. Suddenly, she started punching my stomach while screaming. She said she did not want to go with me. Loylla became complicated; she started hiding behind her mother. She did not want to stay with me either. That created a big commotion out of nothing. The police station peace was disturbed to a point that more officers came out to investigate. Officer Hall got involved. She held Tabô's hands and yelled at her. She asked her to stop.

"You cannot lay your hand on your father. Do you want to go in juvee?" Monique Hall asked over.

"I do not want to go with him, I hate him. I don't love him," Tabô answered.

"I understand, but that doesn't give you the right to disrespect him. You don't have to love your father, but you have to respect him, always and no matter what," Officer Monique intervened.

"I don't care," Tabô said with distress in her voice.

"You will care after I put handcuffs on you and take you to juvenile."

Tabô felt that threat; she stopped hitting me. She looked toward her mother as if she wanted to know what to do next. Sheebah became seriously sober. She did not say a word. Tabô felt abandoned. Then Officer Monique Hall took both girls aside. They were now alone, away from their mother and in front of an authority of the law who was not playing their mother's game.

"Who told you to do that that?" Monique asked.

"My mom told us to do that. She said that if Papa hit back, since we will be inside the police station, he will be arrested and we will be living with her," Loylla answered.

"What kind of an underage mother are you? It is you who needs handcuffs on your hands," Officer Monique said after putting her agonizing stare on Sheebah's face.

Incredibly embarrassed for being busted and for being betrayed by her own pupils, Sheebah tried to quickly get in the way of that conversation, but it was late. The message passed sound and clear.

"I did not say that. Did you hear me say that?"

"As I said it to you last week, you have to think of the children first. Whatever you want to achieve, remember that most of the time, children pay for it if you get them involved. You are sending your girls to juvenile, slowly but surely."

"She had been doing just that. She is like facial hair, the more you cut it, the more it grows. She is thinking she is tough, she is not. She is simply a desperate gold digger thinking that I am the honey. There is no way she will leave that alone," I responded

As promised to Kathryn, I took off from work and stopped at the family court service. Kay Rifkin, the LMSW, was in the children's room that Monday morning. She was there to supervise the meeting.

She started chatting with my daughters before I even entered. The place was located on second floor. It was made especially for children. It actually was designed as a kindergarten. The whole room was filled with different toys of different colors. We played with a lot of them. As Kathryn Omarkhail was entering, Loylla showed me a cubical form. She said, "Papa, do you know that when flat opened, this cube figure has six perfect squares that can be connected together to form a perfect cross?"

I agreed with her. Tabô was at that time sitting on my lap. She was chewing the corner of her right wrist. I made her stop. Both her hands were growing two strong nail-like moles. I have been taking care of them with Polymyxin B sulfate, 5,000 units to soften and then cut them with nail clips. I also was putting an ointment of Bacitracin Zinc 400 units, as it was prescribed by her doctor, to prevent infection. I did not want her to be chewing on those chemicals.

Kathryn Omarkhail introduced my vacation request to Maryland. I explained to Kay Rifkin that it was a family tradition for all children. They do get together for one week over my sister's. She asked me if I talked to Sheebah about it; the kids belonged to her as well, she said. She knows, I answered. At the end of that meeting, Kathryn decided that I had to wait till after the next court hearing because she had to bring the matter to the attention of the judge, she said. I understood that decision, but I wondered why I had to drive all the way up there and why it took her that meeting to answer to a simple request.

"You should have told me that over the phone, and I wouldn't have checked them off from school. I wouldn't have taken a day off either," I said to her.

Things went from very unpleasant to awfully biting because of toys, bikes, Nintendo plays, and other things Meda Bourland was promising to give to my girls. They started talking back all the time. It did not take all a lot for Tabô to go off. She began telling Loylla to be rebellious and Loylla started doing just that. She started refusing doing her chores around the house. They both became noncompliant. They both started to openly disobey me. I did not know how to cope with anything anymore. My daughters were not learning from their mother no more, they were growing up to being against me. It did not take long; Tabô embarked herself on self-destructive mode. It started with her drawing unambiguous sexual graffities in her room, all over the walls. When I asked her why she was behaving that way, instead of answering, she went to the kitchen, took a knife, and deliberately slashed all the window curtains. She poured her blue nail polish on the carpet. After destroying her room, she attacked my clothes in my closet. Two of my white vests were painted with the red nail polish. She defaced the frame of my wooden bed with lot of drawings including the phrase "Beauty is not me" with permanent black ink. My room had chewing gum pounded on the carpet and red Gatorade powder crushed all over. With time, she cut all her pants in coochy mama shorts to explicitly show her behind. It was right at this period that she begun calling me "African motherfucka, go back to Africa." It was a serious pandemonium that I knew was not coming out from the head of my little girl. She was barely ten. And it went on and on. I knew she was unleashed. I found myself in a muddled-up mess. I had to relearn how to be patient especially with her after she joined five other girls at Hurst Park.

CHAPTER 29

NOW, THAT IS FUNNY

Together with these Hurst Park kids, Tabô started to stay out late. Skipping school became a game for them. I had also to prepare myself for the worse because her breath started to smell some different kind of funny smoke. A group of Latino kids, from Bell Elementary, called Pewee, were selling what they called weed in school. When Pewee bought two sticks of big Cuban Black and Mild cigar, 75 cents each, they crashed it together with a $10 marijuana stick. Using Swisher and Wild papers, they rolled everything in small-sized cigarettes, about six of them at a time. Each cigarette was then cut in six parts. Each part was sold to students for $10. I did not know where Tabô was getting money from; she was getting high all the time on Bell Elementary campus. And when she did, she came home swinging on her big sisters. Loylla also started to attack them.

"No matter what they say, no matter what they do, no matter how hard they hit you, do not hit back. If you hit back, which is what CPS is waiting for to take them away, you will be playing their mother's games. I will find a way to punish them myself."

I addressed that message to Muntumpe particularly. She was the meaner one. I singled her out because, for a yes or for a no, she never hesitated to strike her relatives. She hit them without further ado. I remembered a day she was arguing with one of them. She asked a question. Brilliantly, the girl answered. Since she was losing the argument, she slapped her.

"Why did you hit me for?" her little sister asked.

"I asked a question, but I didn't say answer it. You only answer when authorized to. Is that clear?" she asked and her little sister ignored her. "Is that clear?" she insisted.

This time, her little sister refused to answer. She did not want to be punched one more time. In a moment there, Muntumpe smacked her on her face again.

"Why did you do that for?"

"I unmistakably asked you a question. You should have answered."

"How should I? You convinced me with a blow to my face to never answer if not authorized to. You are a very mean person. That is why we call you a black cloud. You bring rain everywhere you go. The earth will be sunny if you dissipate," she said.

I approved that little girl's argument. I singled Muntumpe out because since the beginning of this custody battle, I was not sure which side she really was. It seemed to me that she was a bridge. She was helping Sheebah to cross over to my side. Otherwise, why was it that, for the entire fight, she was always with Sheebah and why was Sheebah always one step ahead of me and my lawyer? I suspected that she was helping Sheebah to reach me at her ease. That was the reason I talked to her particularly. At the other hand, Tabô's new attitude was put on display. It was not helping. I knew that at the end of the day, because of that, she will beat her to activate CPS in Sheebah's favor and seal my fate at same time.

We were all dressed up. It was Sunday after church. We were sitting in the living room that afternoon and vacating on different occupational routine conversations. It was dinnertime. Each one of us had a plate on his lap. We were having shrimp rice, mixed with tilapia and mushroom. Some beef meat prepared with tomatoes sauce and red pepper was also on the table. The whole menu was of red color. With glasses of Sangria on our hands, we were having good time. The entire house was nothing but laugh and smile. That joy was also caused by the funniest video from True TV show we were watching. Stupid people were getting caught by police. Then the home phone rang. Tabô picked it up. Her mother was on the other line. She went to talk to her in her bedroom.

When she came out from her room, after a moment of conversation, without a warning, she hit Muntumpe's plate from the bottom up. That plate went flying across the entire sitting area, spitting its red food all the way up to the balcony window side. Flushed grains of rice, including pieces of greens and cut leaves of spinach, found itself perched under the ceiling. It was a shower of red pepper and a rain of the red wine inside the entire living room. We went dead and speechless for split seconds. Slowly, we realized what was happening when the flown food started coming down. By then, Muntumpe's hair was a mess, her white shirt changed to multicolor. She took the chunk of the whole thing all over her body. Tabô looked at her, burst into laughter, and said, "Now that is funny."

I stood up madly to give her whipping proportional to her mischief. Before I reached her, Muntumpe had her already on her lap. She flipped her over, buttocks up, and gave her a monstrous dozen, maybe more, of a dosed beating, using nothing but her open hand. That was a punishment that a parent, in his right mind, should always give to a child, when that child behaves badly, as Tabô did.

I felt, at that point, that I let each one of my children down. Very saddened, I apologized to everyone present in my apartment. I was warned by Officer Monique, a lady with experience in the matter. She advised me to never let Tabô and Loylla use the phone to talk to their mother as long as the final court decision is not rendered yet. Tabô's reaction was obvious. It was not totally unplanned. It happened just after talking to her mother. After Muntumpe's whipping, I held Tabô's ears and pulled them toward me. I started to walk shyly backward. She did not have any choice but to tag along with her ears. She followed them all the way to her room. I forcefully made her sit on her bed. I left her there to meditate why she intentionally reddened people's clothes.

Something needed to be done to protect Tabô against herself. Children do not take actions of that magnitude that easily if everything is on track. I took off from work for the rest of the week. She was going crazy. I needed to be around her. Something somehow had gone loose, and this was regardless of the size of what her mother had been putting in her head. The significance of her behavior, including the way she was going about it, was taking me over. From that day on, I decided to drop her at school and picked her up. I did not want to give her a time to go out and play outside. And on July 24, two days later exactly, they left with their mother on shared custody deal.

On July 28, when we met again in court, Kathy Ehman Clardy was not hiding her worry when she got out from the judge chambers. She had twitching all over her face. She came where we were sitting and said, "It doesn't look good at all."

"It doesn't, how come?" I asked.

"The judge sent CPS Tracy Burkhart to go and get the kids. They are back there in her chambers. She wants to interview them. I know you explained me what happened with Tabô. I gave all details of the confrontation and the circumstance in which things happened to the judge. As a parent, I understand. The fact of the matter is that it was Muntumpe who disciplined Tabô. It should have been you. Tabô is your daughter, not hers. For them, you let Muntumpe beat Tabô in front of her little sister. You did not interfere to defend her when she was crying for you. Therefore, you authorized a stronger sister beat a weaker sister. They don't care about what Tabô did in there. Both girls are prepared to testify against us. Meda Bourland will get us on harassment."

"I brought in witnesses who can easily confuse them," I answered.

"They won't matter today. Meda Bourland came in with a different game plan because harassment is a hate crime. She will fight around that. Do you know that, and this is another problem, Muntumpe had been calling the KFC manager to threaten Sheebah. That is harassment. The Park Terrace apartment manager will testify against us on harassment too, you went there. The testimony of Tracy and the one from Steven Boshuizen, both CPS investigators, will help her big time. She also has a list of people having knowledge of relevant harassment facts and heavy connection with this case.

Meda has an upper hand on us. I say this because I just got chewed up in there. I do not like to say this, but they were threatening me. They want me to quit and get out of this case. Look around you, every single person on this case is white and against you. Your ex is white. Her lawyer is white. The judge is white. The district attorney is white. The assistant criminal attorney is white. The clerk is white. The court police is white. It is going to be tough," Kathy Ehman Clardy cried out.

"You are white," I said to her.

"Having said that, believe me, we do have enough and diverse ammunitions. I know how to present them to the judge. I just noticed a big bruise on Tabô's low leg. She told me that it happened yesterday while she was riding the bike you bought. Loylla seemed not to agree with that version of the story. I will confuse her once on the witness bench. She will remember what happened."

"They don't have bikes at their mother's. They left them home at my place."

"Why am I not surprised? Meda Bourland just told me that Tracy Burkhart told her that those bruises were left there by Boney, Tabô's little sister."

"That is a fomented two versions of lies. Boney doesn't live where they are. She lives with Zora Warner in Arlington," I directly answered.

"No wonder why Tracy Burkhart was stopping her to talk to me. Loylla said to me, 'my case worker told me in the car, when she went to pick us up, not to talk to you. That is why I am not talking to you.' I don't understand Tracy's side taking in this matter. She had been coaching both girls to lie. She also had been telling them to stick with their mother who will receive a house filled with toys for them. By the way, both girls are now hidden over a woman called Dona at Wesley Park in Hurst. She had a one-bedroom apartment, and eight children are living in it. I don't worry about your children's testimony. Steve B…Bo…something shuizen gave me a hundred-page contact log narrative in which Sheebah's life is written in black and white. I will start with that."

The court was called to order by the clerk as Judge Judith Wells was getting in. She was having a bad day. She said she did not sleep well and she was having a headache. Tracy Burkhart was the first to speak.

She introduced and then evaluated herself at same time, as if the court did not know who she was. A show-off designed for a purpose, maybe to openly intimidate me. Since I compared her intelligence and physique to Olive Oyl, Popeye's wife, this woman, Sheebah's partner in crime, had been mad at me. And since then I have been knocking her down by doubting not her level of education but her level of ripeness and maturity. She was not competent to conduct a rational investigation, including a fair survey on any matter concerning my children.

"The principal reason of me being appointed to this case is to do the best job that a case worker can do. It is to examine all pleadings and all allegations from children first and from both sides. It is to stop the family's violence as defined by section 71.004 of the Texas Family Code. I was sent to go and get Mr. Kasalobi's children at their mother's residence. They came and stood in the presence of both counsels and the assistant criminal district attorney, and they talked to the judge. They testified without hesitation that they are both victims of abuse and violence. We heard, through the words of two little girls, the calvary their mother and themselves have been going through. This court will hear their outcries. Unless Kasalobi is here and now ordered to stay away from them and refrained to be near their mother, they will sustain harm. Unless he is prohibited, on the basis of good cause shown by the family law, they will undergo torture. Unless he is forbidden from communicating directly in any manner with them, except through attorneys of record, these two girls will always be victims of violence. They will always go through abuse in his hands. Unless he is prohibited from threatening their mother through other persons or engaging in conduct directly specifically toward Sheebah, that is reasonably likely to harass, annoy, alarm, abuse, torment, or embarrass her, these children will be victims of family violence again. Kasalobi must maintain a distance of five hundred feet away from and near the residences or places of employment or business of Sheebah, child-care facilities, or school of her children. He must be prohibited from removing children from the possession of Sheebah, their mother. It must be ordered that the license to carry a concealed handgun that was issued to him under the Section 411.117 of the Texas Government Code be immediately suspended and he must be prohibited to and from carrying or possessing a firearm or ammunitions even if he is to become a sworn peace officer, a state agency, or a political subdivision fulltime employee, as defined by Section 1.07 of the Texas Penal Code. Judge, I have with me a Child Safety Evaluation Document that this court has possession of. This piece of paper is the evidence of his confession. It proves that Mr. Kasalobi had been abusing his own children. He was confronted in our office on April 4, 2009, on the subject. He tried to deny everything. We insisted and put him in front of accusing facts. We told him that CPS will monitor him until further notice, he broke down. He broke down, Your Honor, and signed his admission of abuse. He then promised that he will refrain from using physical discipline and will use only other methods to discipline his children. With the reference from the Texas Family Code, and since the department just proved to this court that they had been family violence in Kasalobi's family, both children should be now forward remain with their mother who had been protecting and providing for them. This is the CPS recommendation."

"Your Honor, it has been proven in this present court that the Child Safety Evaluation that Tracy Burkhart is still talking about today was a fake. My client explained to this present court how that document was made out from Tracy's own handwriting. Judge Terri White said that Tracy would be charged with perjury. I am asking this court to dismiss this document as evidence," Kathy Ehman Clardy requested.

It was with that Child Safety Evaluation document sentence that Tracy Burkhart, playing the prosecutor and the judge, thought to bury me and close her charges. It was the place certainly but not her moment to do a counsel's speech. Even if she had her back turned on me, inside that courtroom, my eyes were still on her face. I watched her maliciously creating illegal circumstances in order to

exploit them. She was doing nothing but abusing her official authority in front of Melissa R. Paschall, her boss. She had a stupid logic
in her heart that made her think that if she says things under oath
for Sheebah, the assistant criminal district attorney will believe her.
What I saw her doing up there was using her understanding of the
law to intentionally lie to influence the Family Law Center in a very
dangerous way.

CHAPTER 30

MY DECISION IS BASED ON MY SUPERIOR'S DECISIONS

When Sheebah went in jail for outstanding warrants and for driving with a suspended driver's license, Tracy Burkhart was called on June 1, 2009, to investigate. She was told that both girls were been beaten, not permitted to play outside, and they were in danger. When she dashed in my apartment without knocking my door on June 4 unannounced, she found them safe and sound. She saw them vacating on their preoccupations. What she saw was different from what she heard. Once in, she opened every place possible. Not only she saw that I had plenty of food and drinks for them, she also discovered fifty-four cases of Gatorade. She joined Tabô in her bedroom where she was playing on the computer. She asked her if those Gatorades were for sale. Tabô did not answer; she never liked her. Tabô never liked any of these CPS agents, including her mother's lawyer. That room was the biggest in the house; it had a bunk bed, a television stand, and a video game station. Both girls spent their times playing with these things. In Loylla's room, she saw my air mattress standing upward at the left corner side. This was the air mattress

I used to sleep on in the living room. There were two baskets of clean clothes on the carpet. Sunday and church dresses were hung in the open closet. Both rooms were cleaned. On her way out, she met with Muntumpe on the parking lot, and they talked.

Tracy Burkhart did not bother to mention any of these things she saw while testifying in the court of the law because they were positive and in my favor. What she saw in my apartment that day were also what Kathryn Omarkhail saw. They were what Steven Boshuizen saw. But she remained high handed and confrontational. Each word she pronounced was cautiously chosen. Each expression out of her mouth was alertly designed to hurt. I carefully listened to her, and I felt what she was doing to me; she was burying me. She maliciously said that when she visited kids, they did not have food. And when I decided to give them some, they ate out of the microwave, she said. That lie was nothing but a demonstration of excess force. It was overkill intended to turn the truth in good things into a thing that was completely bad. The sole purpose of that untrue comment was to hurt me. The woman was a dishonest and a bent public official, she was not a specialist. By directing the court to have my kids taken away, not only was she putting their life in danger, she also was not fit to conduct duties the state of Texas assigned her to. She was serving Sheebah instead of her office. She exhibited that day a behavior that I characterized in the following: confrontational, harassing, high-handed, vindictive, rude, and malicious. I believed and therefore concluded that she undermined the moral integrity of the court and the authority of the CPS office. Listening to her lies without saying anything was like 'having the person who killed you attend your funeral' as Ma would have said.

"This is the CPS recommendation," Tracy said and brought her charges to close after slicing me like a steak knife on a dice of butter.

"Is there anything else that the department has to add?" the judge asked.

Steven Boshuizen stood up and said, "Your Honor, I was assigned as investigator on this Kasalobi family's case. My main concern was to find who the primary provider of these two girls was. I visited with the children at school and talked to them at their place of residence. I met with both parents, and I interviewed friends of the families. My finding is that the mother is the main provider. And these two little girls had always lived with her. She—"

"I object, Your Honor." Kathy Ehman Clardy got involved.

"She cannot object now, Your Honor. This is not the time for cross examination," Meda intervened.

"It doesn't matter if we are still in deposition, Your Honor. The reason we're all here is to pursuit a crystal-clear justice for the best interest of both girls. It is verified that when you lie in court of the law, you will win, and when you say the truth, you will lose. Not this time, not on my watch. A lie must not weigh through, it should not win. Steven is lying under oath. I read the core curriculum and his CPS Intake Report he voluntarily gave me. What he said in that official hundred-page report, classified as confidential document by the Texas Department of Family and Protective Services is different than what he is saying now. Why would he write his course outline differently than his testimony? This court wants to know. May I proceed, Your Honor?" Kathy asked.

"Proceed," Judge Terri White ordered.

"My course of questioning will be only about the case # 28749509. It is the most recent out of the CPS Intake Report. We will talk about the page 27 of January 13, 2009, pg 29 of February 20, 2009, page 80 of January 1, 2009 and page 25 of December 11, 2008, in which we will find hospital records, leasing records, HEB custodian record, and testimonies from Sheebah, their mother, and from both children. These statements are self-evidences recorded legally by CPS official investigators, Steven Boshuizen included. They will clearly show us that Mr. Kasalobi is the primary provider of these two little girls."

"Proceed," the judge ordered.

"Mr. Steve, who gave me this…eh…this book, because that is what it is. It is a book," asked Kathy.

"I did," Steven answered without hesitation.

"And who underlined sections from the case # 28749509 in yellow?"

"I did," he responded, looking directly at her.

"Let's the record show that Steven Boshuizen, CPS special investigator, underlined the CPS intake report of the confidential investigations he gave me," Kathy said. She continued and said, "Mr. Steven, you voluntarily approached me. You confirmed your discovery and said that Sheebah's children do not live with her. What is now making you change your primary results?"

"I am not changing my results. My decision is based on my supervisor's decisions. It is based on the places I find kids," Steven answered without hesitation in his body language.

"And when and where did you find the girls, Mr. Steven?"

"I found them with the mother at Park Terrace, on 600 Boca Raton, in Fort Worth. I went there one time after the court hearing. It was on June 6, 2009. After that, I talked to the girls a couple of times in their school."

"On June 6, 2009? Well, this confidential intake record you gave me shows that on June 1, 2009, Sheebah was arrested. When she came out on June 10, 2009, she lost the Park Terrace apartment she, by the way, did not occupy yet for no payment. Didn't you write so?"

"I don't recall," he answered.

"Do you still think that you visited with them at that same place on June 6?"

"I have to check my papers to know the exact date, but I visited with them."

"Do you work on weekends, sir?" Kathy asked.

"No, ma'am," Steven answered.

"You said your decision is based on your supervisors' decision. That means you did not go over there. June 6 was a Saturday. Sheebah was still in Bedford Jail and the kids were with the father that Saturday. Which superior asked you to lie? Now, where did you see the kids the last time you visited?"

"I saw them over Mr. Kasalobi's."

"Over Mr. Kasalobi's he says, Your Honor. Now, were they locked in when you saw them? Where they crying, less clothes on their bodies, less food in their fridge, or anything like that?"

"None of that. Loylla was playing outside, Tabô was on the computer. Mr. Kasalobi had enough food for his children. Everything was in place," Steven answered.

"Now, in the last court appearance, the need for kids' glasses was mentioned. Sheebah was brought up, by her counsel, as the only person who ever paid for their prescriptions. What did you find out?"

"Mr. Kasalobi had been taking his daughters to Sue A. Feather Vision Center inside the Walmart store. I went through Walmart's record and found out that the father is the only parent who had been using his credit card to pay."

"How much was the last bill?" Kathy asked.

"$110 for exams and $800 for their prescription glasses. These glasses are expensive. They are transition glasses. They are made to automatically acclimatize themselves to the conditions of the day, to adapt themselves to the light for a better vision, protect, and correct eyes by adapting to the surrounding temperatures and by changing in different colors. They are quality glasses," Steven answered.

"You said you visited kids two times in their school. Which school was that?" Kathy asked.

"Bell Elementary, it is located Southwest of Glen Rose Apartment, just crossroads of Bellaire Street and Pecan Street.," Steven confirmed.

"Now why would the kids, confirmed by you, to always be living with the mother in Fort Worth, be going to school at Bell Elementary in Hurst? Do not bother to answer. Everybody knows it cannot be done because to be enrolled, the kid needs to have a physical address inside the school district he lives in. Let me tell the court for the record that Mr. Kasalobi and family had been living at this Glen Rose Apartment since November 1997. That is being stable. Lease records and medical record do testify so. Now, how many times did you visit Kasalobi's residence and were the children with him?"

"Three times, and at each time, both girls were there with him."

"Did you say, as you were leaving Mr. Kasalobi's residence, that your visit doesn't even worth to make a report, kids are all right?"

"Yes ma'am, those were my words."

"Now, one address in Bedford, the 9160 E. Walter Street keeps popping up as her residence. Who is this address belongs to?"

"Sheebah is a friend to Suzy. She lets her use her address to receive mails."

"Did you ever see Suzy with Tracy together?" Kathy asked.

"Yes, I have been seeing them together. I think they are friends."

"Indeed. So Sheebah is a friend of Suzy Dale. Suzy Dale is a friend to CPS Tracy Burkhart and Tracy Burkhart is the woman assigned to investigate Sheebah. For the record, that sounds pretty much like a crooked deal. No wonder why she sells her stamps to Suzy Dale under the watch and eyes of Tracy. That explains particularly why CPS had let this sham go on this long. Will you tell the court how many times Sheebah went to jail?"

"About forty-six times total," answered Steven.

"Seriously, when will she get a time to share with her children? The truth is that you guys of CPS know that Sheebah is an unstable woman. She doesn't want the kids. She only seeks for advantages that do come with them. Let the 325th Judicial District Tarrant County Family Court know that we are not here, in this room, to leave a mark in history. This gathering is not all about Kasalobi's two little girls, it is about justice. It is not about fairness, it is about all children of this great country, each one of them. This appearance is for unnamed children living in challenged and malfunctional families, in the situation in which these two little girls are now. Sheebah doesn't have a place to care for them. As I am speaking to you, they are hidden over Dona's, her friend who lives in Wesley Park. They are not safe. For more than ever, it is time for this present court to protect children, all children, starting with these two. Otherwise, any unstable woman, like Sheebah, will always show up, tears in her eyes, and this court will hand children to her. For instance, she is dangerously hauling her newborn here and there in the school van. This is the time to stop that. We don't need to wait when that little girl will be hurt, so we can be looking for who hurt her. Let's not listen to Steven who is telling lies because his superiors told him so. Let's not be accomplices of giving children to Sheebah for temporary guardship. It is an unbearable mistake already to have given a week of that temporary guardship to her. This moment of safekeeping exchange is the beginning of their destruction. They are hurting far from their father's home. This exchange should stop today. The defense rests for the moment, Your Honor."

Kathy Ehman Clardy arranged her papers, closed her files, and zipped her big folder. She took four steps backward and stood up in the line with the rest of us.

Meda Bourland took her exact place and said, "Your Honor, according to the Texas Family Code Section 153,075 and this is the legal theory and, in general, the factual base for the claim and for the defense, it is imposed a duty of support of their children from both parents. One important thing the defense left not said was that evidences presented to us are showing that children have always resided with one person: Sheebah, their mother. The defense said that since April 30, 2009, Sheebah has moved four times. It is because the father has not provided assistance to the mother in caring for the children. On finding of good cause, the mother sought services through the attorney general to seek child support from the father, and this case is pending. If the father has had started paying child support, his children would have had already a place they could have called home. Instead of doing that, Mr. Kasalobi is spending his money and time harassing my client. Your Honor, I have the list of witnesses. I will call them one by one to testify. Together, we will ask this court to order Kasalobi to stop harassing my client and to stay clear five hundred feet away from her children. With the help of this court, we will make sure that Kasalobi starts paying child support, his duty to my client and her children. To avoid further harassment, we will ask this court today to authorize Mrs. Sheebah to enroll kids in her school of choice and the judge to order supervised visitations. At the end of my deposition, I will call experts. They are the ones with the correct information on this case. Their personal opinions, their mental impressions, and all documents reflecting such information will be the basis of my accusation. They will produce tangible proofs and data compilations that have been reviewed, by this counsel, in anticipation of their testimony. If they are retained, or if their statements are held on to, otherwise employed, they will be at the control of this court as described in Rule 192.3b. I will call these experts to testify, and they are Kathryn Omarkhail of Family Court Services. She stopped Mr. Kasalobi from running across the state line with Mrs. Sheebah's children. The day was Monday, July 13, 2009. Mr. Kasalobi showed up unannounced at Kathryn Omarkhail's office with one idea in his head: to use this respected court official's name as an excuse. He said he was in hurry and wanted to take, the same night, both kids on vacation to Maryland. Kathryn detected his crooked business on time. She was afraid this man had already carried that action out and sent his children to a sudden vacation to Maryland. Kathryn played psychology on him and told him that the idea was good, but he had to physically bring both children in her office on July 17, so she can talk to her supervisors about it. Your Honor, when Mr. Kasalobi was received in the Family Court service room to talk about his children's trip, he spent that time harassing his daughters. He embarrassed Tabô about two moles that were growing on both her hands and Loylla about her weight. He did not play with them. He did not touch any of them. He didn't even let them play with toys. As a father, he needed to be socializing more with them, and as a man who wants to be their father, he is a disgrace. If Kathryn Omarkhail did not delay the situation, we would have been talking about a different issue today.

"Officer Kevin Broome and Officer James Wilkerson of Hurst Police Department. They both identified Kasalobi on June 12, 2009, as the person who picked up my client's daughters from Bell Elementary and never brought them back. These fine officers bravely stopped him. Thanks to them, both children are with their mother now.

"Officer Mack of Bedford PD did the traffic stop and booked my client. He will identify Kasalobi for harassing him over the phone. He repeatedly, I mean over and over again, called in to have my client stopped, and she was arrested.

"Jac Russ, manager of KFC & Taco Bell, indentifies Muntumpe, Kasalobi's daughter, as a woman with an African accent, who spent all week calling and harassing Mrs. Sheebah at work.

"Maria Garza the manager of Park Terrace, identifies Kasalobi for harassing her many times over by calling and stopping by the apartment. She personally told Mr. Kasalobi to stop stating inappropriate things about Sheebah and to stop asking for details about her lease.

"Suzy Dale will tell us how Mr. Kasalobi went at her place. He asked her to make a written statement in which she would lie and say that both girls live with him. Otherwise, they will go to a foster home because Sheebah is not capable to take care of them.

"Zora Warner, known as Grandma. Even though Kasalobi never talked to her, she knows him and she will tell us what kind of monster he is. Your Honor, this lady is the one taking care of Kasalobi's children. She feeds them, buys them clothes and toys, when the father is out there playing with his money on women. I will call these experts to testify now," Tracy demanded.

Judge Judith Wells asked Meda Bourland to freeze the calling of her witnesses at the stand.

"Before you do, I want to hear from Kathryn Omarkhail. Is Kathryn still in her office? It was my understanding the last time she was, she promised that her social study will be ready today. Clerk, could you get a hold of her, most importantly, will you obtain from her if her study is completed. I want authentications and declarations from her about this case."

"Your Honor, I had Kathryn on line 1. She called to say that she will be ready in one hour," the clerk said, after hanging up the phone with Kathryn.

"Very interesting, in that case, we will take break till two in the afternoon. Kathryn needs to be heard first before taking any decision. I won't be here then. I have to go to the hospital. All scheduled cases will be heard in room 2 by Judge Bronson. It is almost lunch time anyway. Let us take a break."

CHAPTER 31

WE ARE NOT ADVERSARIES

Lots of eyes were glued on the television when we stepped out from room 4. Some of those who watched American football and fans of the Eagles were shedding tears. It did not take long for me to realize that Jimmy Johnson has died. He succumbed to melanoma cancer at the hospital of the University of Pennsylvania. He was sixty-eight, the television said. His death was precipitated by the elimination of the Philadelphia Eagles from the playoffs on January 29, 2009. He resigned his official duty of defensive coordinator on July 24, said those closer to him. I did not know who Jimmy Johnson was, but I was touched to see so many people crying for him. The only time I was excited to watch American football was when the Cowboys were playing their last game. I took out my binder and bought me a bar of jumbo Hershey's chocolate out of the vending machine and sat on the bench to work on its pieces. Kathy Ehman Clardy joined me; I shared some with her. We started talking about Steven.

"What happened there? Why did CPS Steven Boshuizen turn the monk's cowl against us?" I asked.

"What do you mean by monk's cowl…oh! You mean why he changed sides in there?" Kathy asked.

"What a phenomenon he is. See, Africans will always be African. They are fainthearted, weak-willed, and corruptible effortlessly. It doesn't matter the color of his skin and his level of education, Africans are naturally dishonest. They are easily led regardless of which part of this world they live in. They all are easily manipulated. You show them a bone, and they come wagging their tails. You scare them just a little, and they run faster than a cheetah with their tails between their legs naturally. What a turncoat Steven Boshuizen was in there. Just like a chameleon, he changed color on us in a blink of an eye," I stated.

"What are you talking about...who...oh? Steven Boshuizen is African? I thought, because of his accent, that he is originally from Germany. Boshuizen is an African name? Well, what do you know! You are African yourself. Don't be so hard on your people."

"It is just an expression of feelings," I said to her.

"I do not think he changed sides against us. He helped us instead. He openly did not want to go against his superiors, so I led the interview. People like him don't just hang wet laundry out of the wash machine that openly. What you just witnessed is a written old trick. In the book of law, it is a loop called 'let you be nailed without betraying.' It is the game of justice, a game of what always goes down. The man did not turn sleeves up against us. Listen, they are trying to make it a deal in there. They are offering me to give your little girls to their mother because they are girls. Girls are better off with their mother rather than with the father. I said no to the deal because the truth is on our side. We also have lot of ammo against them. I will win and give you back your children, if you let me be on this case."

"If I let you be on, what are you talking about?" I wondered.

She cut a piece of chocolate, melted it in her mouth, and said, "Muntumpe took me off the case. It has been hard to work with her. She has been calling me, almost every day, harassing me over the phone, accusing me of plotting with Meda Bourland against you because we are friends."

"She doesn't have the right or the power to do so. She did not hire you," I said.

Kathy was there to correct things Sheebah was destroying. She was the only person the judge was listening to. Kathy and Meda went to school of the law together. Noticeably, they were friends since that time. In that court of the law, they are lawyers. They are invited to defend their clients. In there, they are not enemies and they are not allies either. Once they finish and step outside, they have to shake hands, congratulate each other, and socialize regardless. Muntumpe knew that too. She was learning the same thing in school of the law at University of Texas in Denton. To be a lawyer is not a business to grab. It is a gift that keeps on giving. If she did not know that by then, if she did not understand their camaraderie, she shouldn't be a lawyer at all. She will be a defeated lawyer. I knew all along that Muntumpe was working against me. Firing my second lawyer was just wrong. Maybe this was the reason she hit Tabô for. She wanted things to change for the worse. The cold truth was that Sheebah and she were birds of the same feather. They both wanted the court to take my daughters away and pay child support. I needed Kathy, so I remained calm.

"She cannot fire you. I am keeping you on this case. I hired you," I insisted.

"Well, she has already filed a motion with my office, it is official. This was supposed to be my last family case anyway. I am going back to my immigration business. If you have to defend yourself, fight Kathryn Omarkhail ferociously. I was preparing to. She is the one whose recommendations will be counted. The judge will be listening closely to her assessments and evaluations. He will take a decision based on what she will say. You will need to attack her recommendations and documents."

Kathy cut another piece of that mouth-melting jumbo Hershey's chocolate I was holding while listening to her and stood up. She touched my hairy white head and asked for the rest of my chocolate if I won't eat it. I gave it to her. Before leaving the hall bench, she added and said, "Do you know when to object? Introduce documents and proof. Give them to the judge as you go. Prove to the court that you are stable, that both girls depend on you emotionally first. Show him that under your care, they will be protected in a social context and you will financially provide their needs. That is what the judge will be looking for. That is what I made Steven spit out in there. If you feel that the court is against you, do not hesitate to remind them that Kathryn Omarkhail is lying on you, and she will be lying on you, we all know that. If the judge starts to get nervous about that, do not say it again. Bronson will not hesitate. He will kick you out of his courtroom."

When she disappeared behind the double brown doors, I started to ask why Muntumpe was still trying to destroy me. By firing back to back two of my lawyers, her aim was defined. She wanted me to lose custody battle. She was acting hypocritically like an African red rat. Once inside the house, this bush animal will eat you alive. It slowly will chew your heels when you are asleep. It will cut pieces of your flesh out from your foot, and it will breathe on it at the same time to num it. Once it smells blood on the wound it just opened, it will breathe rapid and small puffs of air so you don't feel a thing and wake up. This was Muntumpe. This was what she was actually doing. Just like the red rat, she was applying its breathing system on my wounds so quickly that even if she starts panting and pass out, people won't notice what she was doing, what she has been really doing. People who did not know her could think that she was helping. She was not. She was paying me back in monkey money. The whole thing she was doing and every single thing she was saying was finishing me, by simply putting a noose around my neck. She was not helping at all; she basically was handing me a jar of fart. I did not deserve that, I am the father. I sacrificed a lot for her. I did not leave her behind like most Africans did to their children. Not that they left them because they wanted to, but because they just couldn't do it. I fought hard to bring her with me. I thought the right fight for her.

That should have counted for something. She should have been fighting a right fight for me too. That was the way things should be.

For the most part, a good number of children we bring in ends up making us regret doing so and being there for them. It is a cultural shock, they said. I never believed that. This American system was designed to hurt immigrant children, they also said. I still never believed that was the truth. Whatever kids do and hide behind the culture they found in this country and the freedom given to them is just a matter of choice. They choose to do bad things because they choose to. Most immigrant children respect their parents and what they do receive from them. They have a huge regard for their African parents and what they represent for them. Why is it that Muntumpe is not among them? I brought her in this world because she is my seed to sow. Every child is a seed to sow. I wanted to reap high-quality crops from her. When I paid her way into this United States, the greatest country of them all, it was as if I was planting that seed in the very fertile field. I expected the most excellent and abundant harvest from her. I fought hard for that. I fought for her, so that as she was crossing the river, she can also hand the rope to the next person. I fought so hard for her and spent so much money, I made myself poor. As Alvin Hall Junior said it once, I became so poor fighting for her, I couldn't pronounce poor. I have to say po' because I couldn't afford the "or" anymore. About that, people would simply say that is what a parent does. It is my duty to spend that quality time on her. She is your daughter, they would say, and I would not agree less. This was the reason she should also have been there for me too. She should have been as a "right hand washing a left hand" kind of love because a hand cannot wash itself. Why was she attacking me was a question I couldn't answer. Was it because she had her roots already steady in the ground and she did not need me anymore? That was another hard question that remained without an answer. Attacking me the way she was doing was treating me as if I was a negligible quantity; it was also tearing down the path most travelled and the road for the next person. I wiped my eyes using the back of my right hand. This was not the time to start another fight with her. As Ma said it clearly, if you don't want to fight, ignore the person provoking you. If you want to ignore him completely, keep your face toward the sun and you will never see his shadow. I decided to ignore Muntumpe completely. I had to face Judge Bronson first. His courtroom was located downstairs. From the east side entrance, I had to walk past the security post guard. He was inside the first double door on the right inside. I entered and sat down in the room 2. That place was full to its capacity. It was filled by witnesses subpoenaed by Meda Bourland.

Those who were sitting next to me were called in by Kathy Ehmann-Clardy. It did not take long, the clerk police officer yelled, "All rise, the court is now in session, Honorable Judge Bronson presiding."

This man was just and fair, sincere and firm. He kicked butt, they said. I was intimidated. I looked behind me to see if Kathy was in, she was not. She was not coming. I felt abandoned, left to myself at a moment of despair.

"Be seated," the clerk ordered.

My brain shouted inside me too. I got scared. He then introduced the rules of his court while going through paperwork of the case as it was set by Terri White and Judith Wells.

Meda Bourland talked about the law of evidence. The judge excused all witnesses after that. He asked everyone to wait in the hall.

"You will be called, one by one as needed," he said. Kathryn Omarkhail was asked to sit at witness bench. "State your name for the record," Bronson said.

"My name is Kathryn Omarkhail LCSW, case worker at Family Law Center, 200 E. Weatherford, in Fort Worth ,Texas."

"You were called to investigate the case # 325-428760-07, what is your output?"

"During this investigation, although there were concerns regarding both parents, it became apparent that the mother was able to provide a more secure and emotionally stable household for the subject children regarding their day-to-day needs. The primary concerns regarding the mother is her household, it is surrounded by her history of abusive relationship mostly when she was a child. That situation made CPS get involved in her life. The other concern is her living situation: all of her children share one bedroom while the mother sleeps in living room. The mother has lived in multiple apartments over the past five years. However, she appeared to be cooperative, able to protect all her children at this time. She is able to provide the basic and emotional needs for her children.

"The primary concerns regarding the father were his history of domestic violence, his history of hitting the children and allowing the children to be hit by their adult sibling, attempted parental alienation, his extensive CPS history and his living environment. He has at least six children that he cannot provide their names or their dates of birth for. He has not been entered in contact with any of them and has no intention of doing so. His adamant and unfounded allegations regarding the mother who uses drugs and who is applying for food stamps by using an address that did not belong to her and selling it to the owner of that address is just an apparent misrepresentation to this worker. The father sleeps in the living room and the children share a bedroom with other children. Sometimes, an adult brother stays there and an unknown woman from Africa, who reportedly did not speak English, lived also in their home. This woman was never made available by the father for this worker to meet her. The father also reported that different women come and live in the apartment at different times because he is an ambassador for his village in the Congo. Therefore, the father's home environment appeared to be somewhat chaotic and unstructured. The father has lived in multiple different apartments over the past few years, reportedly mostly in the same apartment complex and he could not recall all of the locations he lived in. It did not appear that the father has been able to provide his children with their basic and emotional needs in his home.

"It appeared that both parents could benefit from children in the middle and positive discipline offered through the parenting center. In addition, the father may benefit from conflict resolution through the parenting center and anger management. It appeared that the mother may benefit from individual counseling to work through some of the abuse she has endured through her past adult relationships. It is recommended that the mother avoid romantic relationships until she is able to have an ability to see early warning signs of an abusive person and improved self-confidence so that she is able to set healthy boundaries.

"It appeared that the subject children would benefit from individual and family therapy. They appeared to be distressed regarding the conflict between the parents. Their school records indicate that the subject children had considerable behavior problems at school. This is my assessment and my recommendation," Kathryn Omarkhail concluded.

I have never been hit by a lightning before. If Kathryn Omarkhail's speech was not what it was, then her recommendation was. I felt both of them, and I smiled. Actually, what was visible on my lips at that moment was not a smile, it was a spasm. I was really hurt. It was like the African bee sting, with venom of a different kind slowly crawling deep into my skin. It felt as if one of the venoms was torpedoed from a distance and shuddered strong cramps from my neck to both my shoulders. I was not smiling; hurt people do not smile. They feel the pain. I never imagined a day when I would hear defined lies coming out from the mouth of a licensed official. The family court of the great city of Fort Worth had one licensed official that day who could lie under oath without blinking. Every single word that woman pronounced in Judge Bronson's court was insolence. Just looking at her while she was debiting lies, I felt very sorry for the person who was still kissing her mouth. It was not hard to fairly distinguish which hole it was.

"Mr. Kasalobi will defend himself. For some reasons, Kathy Ehmann Clardy won't be defending this case anymore. Are you ready, Mr. Kasalobi?" asked Judge Bronson.

"No, sir, but I have to," I answered with a distinct respect to the court.

"Let's proceed then. What say you about the discovery of the family court social study?"

"It is said that when you hide a crime, you become a criminal. Kathryn Omarkhail is a criminal. This woman needs to be investigated, she is a polarized liar," I attacked.

"This is not the way to be going with things around here. You will proceed by question-and-answer method. She will answer one question at the time and the court will appreciate. That is the way it works in here. I understand your frustration, sir. I am frustrated as much as you are. You don't have a lawyer, and I just lost Jimmy Johnson, a dear friend of mine," explained the judge.

Question and answer was the only way not to make Kathy lose her control. She was in her environment. By any means of it, I did not want to challenge her because the woman won't be nervous. I saw how things worked for people like me in there. It did not look right with lawyers at my side, things were about to get worse without. As the witness for the court, Kathryn Omarkhail had only two things that counted for her: "If you are a woman, you are in, and if you are a man, stand by." I knew therefore what was coming to me. This was the moment not to fight on my back feet. Kathryn Omarkhail was the patch of the moving sand a step away behind me. I will sink in, if I do the back running. I had to stand my ground. One of the ways we avoided to sink in a patch of the moving sand in Africa was to make use of the understanding of the law of nature and not use the weight of the whole body on two feet at same time. If properly done, I would use the moving sand as my stepping-stone. I decided to fight that fight.

"Thank you, Judge. Kay Rifkin of family court did a parallel investigation. Is it possible to have her in here?"

"I object, Your Honor. Mr. Kasalobi is trying to buy time," Meda Bourland said.

"Why do you want Kay in here?" Bronson asked.

"I want this court to compare Kathryn Omarkhail's report to hers. She will verify my side of story through CPS, police and school documents, and through her own investigations. We will discover here that Omarkhail is an incompetent official who is playing sleight of hand games. She is using her personal opinions rather than her discovery. She made everything worse for me calculatedly and made things look like I never done anything right for my kids. You heard her. What you did not know was that she was bending things from its real meaning menacingly. She lied about the way I live with my daughters. She lied about my residence. She lied about her visitation and ameliorated things to make Sheebah's dream look good and therefore increase her chance of winning. She did so in violation of the law. Kathryn Omarkhail has been making men endure this injustice. These hardworking fathers have been watching their children taken away in this Fort Worth family court because of Kathryn. Not only this is not a thing to do, it is not the way to go with to mound the law for future generations. I need Kay Rifkin to confuse her study," I stated to the judge.

"I understand that. But you need to address your questions to her. The duty of this court now is to hear charges and accusations from different parties. It is you who would provide evidences of your responsibility toward your children. You can subpoena Kay Rifkin if necessary," the judge said.

CHAPTER 32

VERY INTELLIGENT, VERY STUPID

"Yes, sir, it is my responsibility. Kathryn Omarkhail, where were you on June 13, 2009, just after two in the afternoon?" I asked.

"I was at 789 E. Pecan Street # 193 for social study," she answered.

"That was my place. How many closets can you say you saw in entire apartment and what was in it?"

"The first closet was in the hall, it had working gear, heavy-duty shoes, raincoats, and jackets. The second closet was located in a bigger room. It mainly had adult clothes and little girls' Sunday dresses. It also had food and drinks, Gatorade I think. The other bedroom had all kind of dresses and shoes," she answered by consulting her notes.

"If I correctly heard you, which I did, you saw a bigger bedroom and the other bedroom, right?"

"Yes," Kathryn answered without hesitation.

"That makes two bedrooms and yet you said, 'the father sleeps in the living room and the children share a bedroom with other children.' You are otherwise insinuating to this court that my place has only one bedroom in which live my two little girls, their adult brother, and an unknown woman from Africa."

"I object, Your Honor," Meda Bourland said.

"Mr. Kasalobi is not a lawyer. It won't be fair for you to object all the time. He doesn't know how to go about things here," Judge Bronson explained to Meda Bourland.

"That means I should continue asking my questions, sir?" I asked the judge.

"Yes, proceed," he answered.

"Kathryn Omarkhail, are you saying that I sleep in the living room while my two daughters are sharing one bedroom with their adult brother and a woman from Africa, right?"

"I object, Your Honor, this is leading the witness," Meda Bourland intervened angrily again.

"Overruled," replied the judge.

"That means I can continue, Your Honor?" I asked again.

"Yes, continue with your questions," he judge ordered.

"Thank you, Your Honor. I want to expose the complicated side of Kathryn Omarkhail. We all have, in every one of us, a spot that always stinks. But Kathryn Omarkhail is exaggerating. She is misleading the whole system. Kathryn, are you saying that my two daughters are sharing one bedroom with their adult brother and a woman from Africa, right?"

"I wrote what I saw."

"Indeed, you wrote down not the truth, but what you thought you saw. Since the beginning of this custody battle, you have been painting me as a cynical angry man to outweigh what is good in me. I am not a nasty piece of work. On the Advisement Form of the Tarrant County Family Court Services, on the very top of the page 2, you wrote and I read, 'Mr. Kasalobi moved from a three-bedroom to a two-bedrooms in the same apartment complex.' That does sound right. And yet in the assessment this court just heard, you said that 'the father has lived in multiple different apartments over the past few years, he could not recall all of the locations he lived in.' Why is that?" I asked.

"Where did you get that paper? Your Honor, I ask the court to ignore that evidence. It is not a legal report. It is Kathryn's scratch paper, and it must have been obtained from a wrong channel," Meda said.

"I got it from the public record on the second floor of this very building, Your Honor. So, Kathryn, you wrote this down and signed it. Do you still think I live in different apartments? Yes or no?" I added.

"Yes and no are not juridical answers," she replied.

"This court heard you. We clearly heard you and we know you do not want to answer. As a good case worker, you opened all kitchen cabinets and the refrigerator and you wrote everything down. What did you see?" I asked.

But Kathryn did not answer. Her silence was like a hammer blow on my head.

"Your Honor, please ask Kathryn to answer my questions."

There was not a way she could sit up there in that witness chair, in the court of the law full of smart and educated people and boldly be defiant the way she was, unless she had a heavy support beneath her. But we are in United States. In this country, no one is the important brick in the wall. Even that, the brick itself is not the wall, it is not the whole house either, it can be removed and the house could still stand.

"You must answer his questions so we can go forward. Will you please?" Bronson ordered.

"You said and I read it that 'it did not appear that the father has been able to provide his children with their basic and emotional needs in his home.' What did you find in the house cabinets and in the closets that made you say that?"

"I reported everything," Kathryn said.

"Do not be lying under oath now. You did not report everything you saw. Steven and Stacy saw food, lots of it. They saw drinks, including a palette of Gatorade. They saw clothes and shoes. They saw rooms and everything that can be considered as toys. They saw me with them for their basics and emotional needs. And you are right when you wrote, 'His house was crowded with a lot of items.' Kathryn Omarkhail, did you ever taken Sheebah for a drug test?

"There was no need for me to do so. Sheebah doesn't use drugs," she answered.

"Of course, she does. I told you so and I was talking about serious stuff that would hurt her children, my children. It has been proved by CPS that she is using drugs and they are not talking about what you are calling allegations and apparent misrepresentations. It is officially written in their reports and you did not even move a finger to investigate. Even her lawyer has pictures of her using drugs. You just looked at her and decided that she doesn't do drugs, right?" I questioned her.

"It is not up to me to prove that she does or doesn't do drugs. It is up to you. Bring it in the open."

"Was it not your duty, as a social worker, to investigate all accusations brought forth for the well-being of children, to avoid putting them inside a crack house?" I insisted.

"It was and I did what was necessary," she answered.

"Look at her puffy eyes, her dried lips, the way she is trying to swallow saliva from her dry mouth, don't you see anything odd with her? What was necessary then? Okay, I pass. Can you remind me the names of all my children, as I said them to you? You can read their names from the Advisement Form you have."

"Six of them have Kasalobi as their first names. You also have at least six children, excluded one you named Sanaa, you did not provide names or their dates of birth for. You said that you do not have contact with and do not intent to. They are still in Africa, you said," she accused.

"Your Honor, can I approach the bench to show Kathryn's own signed scratch paper in which I answered to that question and said, 'None and no applicable,' but she falsified that answer by writing bunch of lies over the top. Can I?"

"I object, Your Honor, I do not have the knowledge of that evidence," yelled Meda Bourland.

"Since you are defending yourself, Kasalobi, and given that I know where you took all your evidence from, to gain the time, you will give all of them at the end of this trial. But you are free to explain what is written in it to the court," said Judge Bronson after discarding Meda Bourland's objection, asking her to stop challenging every piece of paper I was introducing as evidence.

"On page 9 of the Advisement Form, I wrote that I did not have any other children but those I specifically named. But using the top of my black ink letters, she wrote over bunch of silliness she just said there. It is not against the law to have hundred children and we are not in China where she could restrict me. My living environment is the most steady and established. It is says so on my files since 1989. It is testified by the department of public safety, on my Texas driver's license that I have been living in Hurst, at Glen Rose Apartment, this present address since 1997. That is stability. Now Kathryn talked too much about Sheebah's secured address hidden from me. That address is the 6190 Walter Street in Bedford. We all know that it belongs to Suzy Daley. Did you ever visit the place? Did you ever talk to Suzy to verify if Sheebah does really live there because I know the place and I do talk to Suzy all the time," I explained.

"No, why?"

"I see, you did not because you know the place. This is the address that you and CPS created for her. Have you ever talked to Sheebah to see if she was lying living there? Did you ever call the food stamps office to know why they send food stamps to Sheebah at this address?"

"No and no, I haven't, not yet."

"You said, 'Allegations regarding the mother applying for food stamps by using an unknown address and selling it to the owner of that address is just an apparent misrepresentation to this worker.' Now how did you arrive to that conclusion if you didn't investigate?" I asked.

She did not answer.

"I will take your silence as an admission of your guilty lies. Now what made it to become apparent to you that Sheebah is the primary care taker of my children?" I asked.

"My job was to investigate. Investigate I did and that was my findings," she said, very disconnected.

"Coming back from 18 Beverly in Bedford where you and I went to see Tabô and Loylla hidden by their mother, you talked to a woman called Tiffany, my neighbor. You talked to her at a trash bin about my children. Tell this court where she said my two daughters live and with whom?"

"At that time, she said they were living with you, but they never—"

"This means that she had been seeing my children, in my apartment, for the whole time she lived there. I saw you talking to both her children when they were riding their bikes outside, what did they say about Tabô and Loylla?"

"That the police took them away, but they never—"

"And you did not mention that to this court. Okay, police took them away, as physically removing them from their home ground, the apartment # 181, where they lived, right?" I asked.

She did not answer.

"Okay, about Tiffany how many times she said her kids played with my children?"

"I do not recall."

"Let me refresh your memory. She said, and I am reading it from your scratch papers, 'His kids and mine walk across the street to Bell Elementary. They play together. I saw his kids' mother only one time and I have been living in the apartment # 183, next to his for the past two years. I saw her the day she got off from the maternity. As I was throwing trash, she called me from inside a silver van. She was with her three-day-old new daughter, Baby J William she said her name was.' You wrote that yourself in these scratch papers I am holding in my hands. The question is why didn't you mention that in your deposition?" I asked.

"I dismissed Tiffany's conversation because many of her allegations appeared to be contradictive to yours. She even contradicted your initial and continual allegation against the mother's multiple crimes. None of it was true to my knowledge. She also was observed looking for your approval. That was the reason I dismissed her and did not say a thing about her conversation."

"She couldn't possibly be looking for my approval, simply because I was not there. Anyway, as an investigator and a witness, you should have mentioned that to this court, but you did not. You said, in his present court that 'the father did not provide collateral contacts' while their names are clearly written on page 10 of the court advisement form. They were my witnesses. The question is did you dismiss Tiffany the same way you failed to interview people on my reference list, which I personally gave to you? Why didn't you interview them?"

"You did not make them available to this social worker. You did not bring them to my office," she answered.

"So you had enough time to get out from your office and go to Boca Raton to investigate a stolen electricity meter, and yet as a court social worker, you did not have time to step out from your office to interview my witnesses. From a county official, that is not fair. You easily dismissed Tiffany's declaration, sacked her children's statements, and forgot all about my witnesses. Why?" I said. "To me, your silence adds up to my evidences. Your Honor, Kathryn Omarkhail is not giving an answer to my questions because she lied about everything to protect Sheebah, I mean every single thing that touches me. Since she keeps pleading the Fifth, let me brush for this court some of things she lied about.

"She said that 'the parents met in November 1993 when she was still living with the foster parents. She moved from the foster parent into the father who discouraged her to attend college.' I say that is a lie. When we met again at DFW where we both where working, she was living in efficiency in Arlington already. This was after our first encounter at Carson Air Base. Her used Ford Tempo, given to her by CPS, was giving her a lot of problems. I bought her a brand-new truck Mazda to able her to go to what was called then TCJC. I equipped her with musical instruments because that what she was doing there.

"She said 'the father agreed with the scenario about him jumping onto the hood of the moving vehicle, except that he also reported that the children wanted to evacuated.' I never said such thing. If I jumped onto the hood of a moving car, then I wouldn't have been hurt as I was. I am not crazy. Nevertheless, Judge, Kathryn's job was not to be the sphere of influence in order for her to change the direction of this battle. He job was to be in the middle.

"She said that 'his house was crowded with lot items including a fish tank.' I say, is that all she saw, a fish tank? What a fish tank has to do with a social study, Your Honor?

"She said that 'the father was been married twice before meeting Sheebah.' I say, that should have been recorded in the public record. I was not married twice before meeting Sheebah. That is easy to verify. Kathryn Omarkhail is a big liar."

"I object, Your Honor. Mr. Kasalobi needs to stop calling everybody a liar," Meda yelled again.

"Mr. Kasalobi, you are annoying this court. You will proceed with your questions without calling anyone a liar," the judge ordered.

"Kathryn Omarkhail, you stated that different women live in my apartment because I am an ambassador from my village in Congo. Will you please tell the court what is your exact meaning of the word *ambassador*, then explain it to me how a village can have an ambassador?"

"You said it, explain it yourself," she challenged me back.

When we messed up, which was very often, Ma used to ask us why we were still going to "the complicated white man school" instead of learning how to be deeply rooted from African simple initiations. Up to her, we were mastering in algebra, history about dead people, root squares, European geography, an arsenal of instructions that did not matter to us. This is just being "very intelligent, very stupid" as long as each and every question of life, about things and their answers, was not addressed. She used to say that the white man teaching, among others, was not helping. She was right. Kathryn was the living example. As a university-educated woman, I needed her to explain in front of the smart people of the court if a village can have an ambassador, not because I did not know the answer but because I far reached the same conclusion as my ma. She was very intelligent and very stupid at same time.

Kathryn Omarkhail's statement about me being an ambassador from my village did have one single meaning. She wanted to say I am "an African," supposedly a person a foot below her, as she had been insulting me all along. What she failed to realized was that even the worm helps to catch a fish and the dirty water to stop the flame. I doubted her years of experience in administration field when brainlessly, she thought she easily could drag me in the mud because I am African. For her being me is being lesser of a person and being African is being a second rated human. For a social worker she was, despite her college degrees, that such thinking exposed all her knowledge. If someone could have been looking for her, in that court of the law, he wouldn't have been looking very far. She was easily identifiable by her head, and it was hard for her to change it, as Ma would have said about her. She was an ignorant big dummy made to function among us already when she was supposed to function next year far from us, as Ma would have said about her again. The woman was unable to even explain things she herself wrote down. Luckily, she was fortunate to be imbedded with us, the smart people, who did not limit ourselves with only college degrees.

This is how we did it to avoid using only our college degrees. In the back yard of the village, Kabwe-Kakiele, where I am from, we had a place called baobab palabra that had a cave-like entrance. Past that door was a hole big enough to fit ten people in sitting position. It was naturally carved in by the singing wind coming from lost ages. As its name means to those who are properly initiated, the palabra place was purposely situated in the middle of the village. It was taking place under the baobab. This was the huge and biggest tree not just in Africa, but in the whole world. We sat on the top of its outside mangrove-like roots to enjoy its edible pulps. We also gathered around its thick trunk to listen to elders telling wisdom stories. These elders, the teachers as we called them then, usually stood about ten feet from the front of the tree entrance to educate. They usually begun their lessons by saying, "The elder's mouth maybe stinking…" and we together and at same time answered, "Only the truth comes out of it." They then edified us with what they needed to say. Where they stood was erected a granite pillar measuring about twelve feet. That scissor-cut stone weighed around 794 pounds.

Because it had a cubical head that had five heart designs on it, Catholic preachers called it a Padrão. The whole village celebrated and venerated that stone. People believed that it was a gift from gods because it had broken calligraphic letters written on it. Catholic priests couldn't translate the written language; they did not understand the meaning. They did not know why these calligraphic letters were written under the five heart designs either. It was said that the first white people who slept in that baobab hole detached themselves from Diego Cáo, a 1482 Portuguese navigator, who "discovered" the embouchure of the River Congo. They detached themselves from him and came inland to erect the stone. That story was hard to swallow. Up to Bizen Godelieve, a Catholic nun, the deepest Diego Cáo and his lieutenants entered inland was about 120 miles in the west side of Congo. Because they were hungry, they accosted and entered inland to hunt. The nun said that this was how they met with Yellala, the powerful king of the kingdom of Kongo. She explained that Diego Cáo entered inland but never reached my village, which made it hard to understand how that polished stone ended up there. In world history, the school taught us that he carried only four Padrãos to be used as marker for their "new land." The first Padrão was erected in 1482, in the mouth of Congo, the mighty river. It is still there. I saw it, with my own eyes, the last time I visited the city of Boma. It is majestically standing on the smooth face of a cliff called Shark Point, a rounded headland, up from where the water runs smoothly offshore. This place is one of the beauties of the Democratic Republic of Congo. The second carved stone was raised in Cabo do Lobo, in Angola just south of Lobito. In 1486, his men uprighted the third in Cape Negro, on the Angola Coast, and the fourth on the Namibia Rocky Mountain. These archives of history are counted for and still there to be read. Where the fifth one, planted in Kabwe-Kakiele, my village, with not decipherable and readable characters, came from, is still the question historians have yet to answer.

We paid attention to elders' stories under that baobab tree as we were growing up. They were not just stories, tales, and anecdotes we listened to, they were lessons we learnt from with passion. The sun did not bother us for the reason that that challenge of nature was gigantically tall. Leaves from it branches covered the whole sky. The gourd-like fruits it gave us were heavy; they pulled all branches down to created a giant umbrella. It was there, in that school of the difference, where we were taught peculiarities between being mature and having the maturity for it. It was there where we gained knowledge of the jurisprudence of things. We were judged upon them and their particulars.

To really become skilled, it should have been there, under that same baobab tree, where Kathryn Omarkhail should have went first to learn couple of things regarding what life itself is. What she should have learned were lessons that cannot be taught in a regular schooling by sitting in college sessions or by training in a university meeting. She should have received her education by instruction and with us, sitting on our elders' handmade benches because everyday "white man school" did teach her but lies. On these benches, we took a time to sit and listen. They made the difference in our lives. We grew up on them, and they saw us grow up. We learned on them that lying is just a dishonest activity.

Now, with all its brown benches, the court is also a sacred place that is not far different from what represented branches and leaves of my baobab tree. And just the way the shade of the baobab tree was to us, the inside square in that Fort Worth family court is a sanctuary of integrity for each one of us who enters there. In many ways, both places protect. They listen to ideas, debate opinions, teach new things, and argue on different views. They deserved high regards from people using them. What Kathryn Omarkhail was doing in that family court and the way she was going about it was a total disrespect of the rule of both houses. We were in there to fight for the well-being of children, but her performances were disgraceful and pathetic, mostly because they were coming from a representative of the law. Her presentation completed her open dishonesty, which made it clear to me that the woman had difficulties with her grades once. She spent lot of time collecting zeros in school. That was one of the reasons the woman was trying to give herself a correct appearance. It was intelligent to the core to talk about me being an ambassador of my village. She deceived smart people that we were inside that trial.

When elders had a person like Kathryn Omarkhail under the baobab tree, they separate her from other children first. They made her sit outside the circle that was built for that reason, around the sacred old stone. From there, they showed her how to deal with everyday thing of life. If she still did not learn from her mistakes, she was removed from the entrance of the baobab and then asked not to be around the sacred stone. She was therefore suspended from playing with other children. Without any delay, she was taken out of the village for a while to a place called Ku Sendwe. There, the oldest of elders bid her as a request companion to the wise woman. It was at this time that for the first time, harsh scary techniques and yellings were used by this wise woman. She inculcated good manners in her using butt weeping over and over again. It was only after that insensitive and unsympathetic reeducation that she was able to be readmitted back under my village's big tree.

Because she was part of the record, this is the thing that the Fort Worth 325th Judicial District should have been doing for all Kathryn Omarkhails it is full of. These Kathryn Omarkhails needed to be taken out of that courtroom and be reeducated and sanitized from their lies. This should stop the excess of their unfairness recurring. It could be good news for the rest of us. And all decisions taken inside the judge's chambers would be fair. Then again, if they have to be sanitized them, this Family Law Center court would surely lack its human substance because it is filled with nothing but these Kathryn Omarkhails. So I persisted on ambassador utterance and asked her again, "Kathryn Omarkhail, what is the exact meaning of ambassador?"

"Explain it yourself," she talked through.

"I will be obliged. Regardless of the spelling, ambassador or embassador is the highest diplomat. He is a special representative in diplomatic mission that a sovereign state sends officially to another country. Therefore, an ambassador is an official emissary, he is a special envoy to a particular country to represent the authority of his country. Now nobody here thinks that a village is a country. No one in here imagines me being a civil servant accredited as a diplomat from my village to whenever place because my village is not a country. The question in everyone's mind now is to know why you, Kathryn Omarkhail, an official of this court is changing a good function of a useable word to absolutely a bad thing? Your Honor, I never said that I was an ambassador. I am not that unintelligent. I told

Kathryn Omarkhail that we, people from Congo, have a community named CCDFW. In that community, I am the Chef de Pool, meaning one of four assistants to the president of the community. As such, I do help settle newcomers from my native Congo. I do give out my share of help. This was the case of the lady who provisionally lived in my apartment. She was already gone when Kathryn Omarkhail came over. I had to tell her that story to connect dots, and she decided to put lies around my well shared story. From what I just said, Your Honor, could you conclude with this woman that my home environment appeared to be somewhat chaotic and unstructured as she said it? I do not think you would.

"Your Honor, I just demonstrate in here how this woman, Kathryn Omarkhail, is undermining the moral integrity of this present family court. She lied in her investigation, and on the top of her own words and by her silence, she also lied to this present court. The woman is not working for this 325th Judicial District Court. Her assessment to this court should be thrown out. The woman took sides. I have been raising my children without Sheebah's help. I do provide a home, basics, and emotional needs to them. An investigation must be opened against Kathryn Omarkhail. She is trying to change the time. She cannot change the time. She is simply trying to put the life of my children in danger. Change must be considered. She must be removed from the Family Law Center and must be replaced by a competent specialist and a hardworking person.

"Since I am through with her, may I now approach the bench to submit all evidence in support of my assertion? You asked me to give it to the court at the end of this intervention," I said.

"I object, Your Honor. By the Texas rule of evidence, Mr. Kasalobi cannot introduce any of his evidences anymore, even if they are circumstantial. He let his date limit expired," Meda Bourland attacked again.

CHAPTER 33

WHY DIDN'T YOU ARREST ME?

"Your Honor, all documents I am about to introduce offer to this courtroom the direct proof of the truth. They are a compilation of dates and times of events as collected by the police and by CPS," I responded.

"Again, Your Honor, just because he said he got them from the system doesn't mean we know how he got them. We are not familiar with any of them," Bourland said.

"If all of your evidences are from CPS and the police, hang on it just a bit till I verify if your time limit has indeed expired. I did not request them at the end of your intervention, I said at the end of this trial."

"Actually, Your Honor, you said at the end of the day," I said.

"Yes, I recall saying that. It means at the end of the trial. We are not yet finished. Steven Boshuizen gave me the assemblage of all CPS investigations. I think you have a copy of it. Before this trial, I went through it, and to prove that I did, I read in it that Devon William, Sheebah's boyfriend, beat your daughters consistently, often with a stick, and leaves bruises on her every time he does so. This situation cannot be tolerated. I will verify with the clerk to see if your time limit has expired. We are not through yet. Let's take fifteen minutes, when we come back, Mrs. Meda will call her next witness."

Officer Delfeld Jason was the first to be called on the witness stand after the break. Meda Bourland tried by different ways to get him to say things he visibly did not know a thing about it. He explained to her that he was not the arresting officer. Bourland insisted and pushed. She wanted him to say that I was harassing Sheebah, and that was the reason he was dispatched to my apartment.

"Okay then, you were there as a backup officer. But as an officer of the law, you heard him harassing my client, tell us about it," she insisted.

"The only time I personally heard about Mr. Kasalobi was when the agency received a priority 4 call, on early June 12, 2009. It was about six in the early morning. The ex was calling and harassing the RP about their children and the RP wanted an officer to go and tell her to stop calling, the priority 4 call said. Officer Arnold D'Israeli went to talk to RP. I talked to the ex who was very upset that the ex-husband took the kids while she was in jail and won't give them back. She said she has filled for an ex-parte protective order because her two girls always live with her and Mr. Kasalobi is intervening. I checked, there was no such thing on file, and there was no protective order either. The only thing present was the mutual exchange of children order and an order for communication between the two to be done by e-mail or via text messages. So I advised her that until the protective order is served, it is a custody problem and she needed to contact her attorney. That is how I first heard about Mr. Kasalobi. I then saw him for the first time in that afternoon, he was sitting on the curbside."

When Bourland realized that her method of questioning Officer Delfeld was misfiring, she started to lure him in by explaining how well I was known by the law, that I am abusive toward my children, that I had been distressing Sheebah for a while. That line of questioning confused Delfeld Jason more.

"Explain to the court how violent and uncooperative this man was when you guys arrived at the scene?"

"I would not say Mr. Kasalobi was uncooperative. When I reached the apartment, he was sitting on the curbside as I told you. He politely spoke to Officer Kevin every time he was asked to."

"But he stood up and refused to follow Officer Broome Kevin's orders. Didn't he?" Bourland asked.

"The only time Mr. Kasalobi stood up from the curbside was when he was about to show me the summon paper he said his ex introduced to Officer Broome Kevin as a protective order. And he stood up only after being permitted to."

For simplicity of purpose, I did not want to let pass that opportunity. I decided to cross-examine Officer Delfeld Jason.

"Officer, at that time, where do you think the children lived?"

"With the father," he answered.

"What made you arrive to that conclusion?" I wondered.

"Since Sheebah was not answering her phone, I went at the address she gave the police dispatch. Nobody knew her there. The neighbor said she did not live there, but her children live with their father. Then, by her own admission, she was in jail for two weeks. The truth is that she has been going to jail quite often, she doesn't have time and stable environment for the children."

"Would you say then that Sheebah is causing huge scenes and creating altercations around the children for the sole purpose of getting food stamps, child support, and other government benefits?"

"I guess so," Delfeld answered.

"I rest my case, Your Honor," I concluded.

Officer Broome Kevin from the Hurst PD was called up to sit down on the witness stand. Meda Bourland approached and focused her examination on me harassing Sheebah and on children. She questioned him about how they voluntarily got off from my car and why he thought they were running from me and getting away from an abusive father. She also asked him to explain how much I was yelling and how much I was uncooperative.

"It seemed that Mr. Kasalobi was not hit. He got in front of Sheebah's car in order to keep her from leaving. I tried to explain our legal parameters, but he told me he did not want to listen, he walked off," Broome explained, completing his June 12 report.

"Officer Broome, your speech is different from Officer Jason's deposition. Why?"

"He is speaking from his point of view, I am speaking from mine."

"Police speak the same language unless one of them is lying. Officer Broome, are you lying?"

"I am not!"

"You just said 'our' legal perimeters. From you to me sir, what does 'our' stand for?" I asked.

"What I mean by 'our' is what we do here in United States," he answered.

"Oh, I thought it was the police perimeters you were talking about. Who is the 'we' in that?"

I directed the "we" question to K. Broome personally. My aim was the court attention and my intention was to make everyone in that court to see the light about the person K. Broome they considered their public servant. I asked that question because he was out of control that day. He acted just like Officer David Eric Casebolt of McKinney Police Department, the day he was filmed wrestling a black teenager girl to the ground at a Texas pool party. I did not have another way to put it but to draw a parallel. Even if I was not wrestled on the ground, these two officers used the same methods toward two black people, her and me. Therefore the "we" of K. Broome was the pushing down of David Eric Casebolt.

"Who is the 'we' in your speech?"

"I said 'we' as we, Americans," he answered.

"Are you racially prejudiced, Officer?"

"Racist? No, I am not."

"Yes, you are. You just dismissed me when you said 'we'. This great country, the United States, is my country. I am American. You started your xenophobic bigotry on me on June 12 on the basis of the color of my skin and the accent in my speech. And you sacked me today in front of this large audience. That is being racist. Right?

"Don't answer that, Officer. I object, Your Honor," Bourland said.

"Sustained, I need to hear his too," Judge replied.

"I am not racist, Your Honor," Broome answered.

"Officer Broome, why didn't you arrest me that day?"

"Arrest you for what?" he asked back.

"If I was yelling at you, as you said it in your report, it means I was making noise. If I was uncooperative, that means I did not follow your orders. How come you did not arrest me or simply give me a ticket?"

"There was no need to."

"There was no need to arrest me because I was following your instructions. You lied on me in your report because I am African."

"Your Honor," Bourland intervened.

"Was that necessary, Mr. Kasalobi? This is your last warning," said Judge Bronson.

"I am through with this witness, Your Honor. May I call Sheebah at the stand, please," I requested.

"I object, Your Honor, Sheebah is the applicant of this legal action. She can't be called at witness stand."

"Overruled. Sheebah is the primary witness. She needs to be heard," Judge Bronson responded.

When Sheebah sat up there, I said to her, "Both your kids wear glasses. Will you tell the court the prescription size of each glasses for each child?"

"Objection, Your Honor," Bourland yelled.

"On the starting point of what? Your objection is baseless for this court. It is ludicrous to me. She is the mother. You said she has been buying their medical prescriptions while the father is playing with his money. You declared in your accusation file that the father went back to Africa. She has been raising her children by herself. Do not object. She is their mother. She must be able to know," the judge said, overruling Bourland's objection.

"Thank you, Judge, for that clarification and for calling their claim what it is: baseless and ludicrous. So what are their sizes?"

"I don't recall," Sheebah answered.

"Good, what is the name of the doctor who writes their prescriptions?"

"I can't remember right now," she answered again.

"In which hospital do they go to for their eye prescriptions?" I asked.

"I am sorry, I cannot recall," she answered again.

"Of course, there is no way in this world you would have known all that. Not only do you not provide for your daughters, they also do not live with you. Your claim is wholly inaccurate. It is offensive to me, divisive to your daughters, and inappropriate for this court of the law. Loylla's vision is 50/20. Tabô's prescription has expired since June 2009. What do you do with the child support you receive every month?

"Your Honor, please find on page 3 of the file you said you received from CPS Steven Boshuizen, copies of prescriptions from Doctor Sue&Feather inside Bedford Walmart. All paid receipts have my name, credit card number, and signature on it. Your Honor, this court doesn't have to force squares into triangle holes to understand these 'I don't recalls' from Sheebah. 'I don't recall' means I don't provide for my children, I am here to try to get paid. Tracy Burkhart, Kathryn Omarkhail, and Meda Bourland have unjust theories and silly correctness about my children. This court should cautiously and suspiciously listen not to what they are saying but to what they are not saying. They all are wrong and unjust. The answer that this court should be looking for is in their charges against me and in lapses in Sheebah's answers. Therefore, this case shall be dismissed and both girls should be given back to me."

"I object, Your Honor. Mr. Kasalobi is leading the court. My client is the only person who had been providing for her children. She—"

"Providing? How long are we still on this? Your Honor, to start with, can her client tell us how she reached this court building?" I asked.

"My friend dropped me. It is not a secret, my driver's license is suspended for now," Sheebah said.

"Very good. This court thinks that Tabô and Loylla both live with you. Am I wrong?"

"You are not, they live with me since 2006."

"I am excited. Where do they go to school?" I asked.

"For the moment, they are enrolled in Bell Elementary," she answered.

"Which school have they attended since 2006?"

"I object, Your Honor, I don't see where this line of questioning is going," Bourland said

"Overruled," the judge answered.

"So which school have they attended since 2006?"

"Bell Elementary," Sheebah answered.

"So they walked every day, back and forth, from Fort Worth to Hurst, Texas?" I asked.

"I drove them. I drive them every day to Bell," she answered, after rocking herself in the court chair.

"Every day? Now I am very keyed up. How do you do that? You just said that your driver's license is suspended. And it is suspended indefinitely since September 1, 2006, as certified by Joyce E. Stevens, manager of Texas Department of Public Safety and custodian of records of the Driver Records Bureau. It is a serious problem because your driver's license is suspended pursuant to the authority contained in the Texas rules of evidence 902, Section 4, and Transportation Code, section 521. Why don't you say the truth? Say it the way you said it to Officer Mark Bruner and the way he wrote it in his Hurst Police report 06-875, on January 29, 2006, through your own mouth that Tabô and Loylla live with the father and you were living with Daven William since. Say it the way you said it to CPS, in their report case # 263 258 15, on February 11, 2007, and on May 7, 2007. You were living in Arlington Shelter and told them that Tabô and Loylla are living with their father in Hurst, Texas. Say it the way you said it on February 5, 2007, as it was reported on page 11 and page 58 of the same case that Tabô and Loylla live with the father, at Glen Rose Apartment. On page 62, you added that sometimes you do pick both girls up from their daycare and do take them to their father at 787 E. Pecan Street # 181. You said that if the father is not there, you leave them upstairs with Antonio Rodriguez, their babysitter. Say it the way you declared it on June 22, 2007, to Hurst Police when one of your boyfriends attacked me with a gun. You confirmed in their report 07-5441 that you came by the Glen Rose Apartment to drop something for Tabô and Loylla, your kids, who live with their father. Now, January 13, 2009, is a very important date because it is CPS' last interview with the children. It happened five months before June 12, the day you kidnapped my daughters. Say it as it is declared on the page 27 of their case # 287 495 09, when Loylla was interviewed in her daycare. She confirmed that both her sister and she live with their father Kasalobi. If you dare to deny that too, then explain to the court why you signed the report as confirmed by the case worker on the case. She stated that Sheebah signed and dated the report on January 13, 2009. Did you sign the report?"

"I do not recall," Sheebah answered.

"Of course, I did not expect a different answer. Your Honor, I just demonstrated to this court, with the help of Sheebah herself, following what is written in CPS and police report, handed to you by CPS Steven Boshuizen that this woman never had my children. Both girls lived and live with me. They walk from Glen Rose Apartment to Bell Elementary, back and forth. She never provided for any of them despite her claims. As matter of fact, she spent a lot of her time sending Tabô to steal food and drink for her in my refrigerator. And that is how Tabô ended up thinking that stealing is okay. She was caught stealing from Kroger and from the dollar store. This woman is not a good mother. I need my kids back home where they belong. I rest my case, Your Honor."

After a long silence, Judge Bronson said, "Is there anything else to add from the movant in person or from her attorney before I render my decision?"

"No, Your Honor," Meda Bourland answered.

"Respondent, do you have something else to say?"

"No, Your Honor."

"Attorney General?"

"No, Your Honor," said O. Settle.

"CPS?"

"No, Your Honor," Tracy answered.

"I listened to each body in this room. Up to evidences collected by Child Protective Services and given to me by CPS Steven Boshuizen, up to support of confirmations and proof of evidences given to the court by Kathy Ehman-Clardy, the father's attorney in record, I do not have other choice but to declare inconsistency in CPS Tracy Burkhart's defense of children, subject of this matter. It is clear that children always reside with the father. That is a proven fact. There is also visible lightness and nimbleness in Kathryn Ormakhail's investigations. She failed to tell to the court that the father was the sole parent providing for the children while the mother was without job, either in jail or in shelter. Because of these irregularities, I have authority to give Mr. Kasalobi's two girls back to him, but I won't do that. Mr. Kasalobi did not prove to this court that his children will be safe in his home. As long he keeps letting his older daughter beat his young daughters, they will always be in danger. Therefore, while waiting for the social study to be redone and completed, I decide to temporarily apply the Article 153.317, the Alternative Possession Election as follows:

"The father, to be the Possessory Conservator. The mother, to be the Sole Managing Conservator.

"The father will have one hour supervised visitation with his daughters. These visits will be supervised by CPS at Tarrant County Visitation Center on the first, third, and fifth Saturdays from five to six in the afternoon. He will arrive promptly at four forty-five in the afternoon, register, enter, and wait in the waiting area. The mother will deliver the children to the visitation center promptly at five and leave the premises. Children shouldn't be in the visitation room before the father's arrival. The mother will promptly return to sign them out at six.

"Both parties are to provide age-appropriate table toys or activities for the child's visit.

"Kay Rifkin, LMSW, will be the coordinator at Family Court Visitation Services Center for any question brought up.

"The father will continue paying $649.25 for child support per week. The payment will be done from now on, in person through the court State Distribution Unit.

"Any retro child support is reserved till the final.

"The medical, health, dental, and eye insurance for children should be paid by the father, at the appreciation of the lawyer of the mother.

"Children will not have contact with their older sister, Muntumpe.

"Children will not have any contact with the father except as set forth for the father's day and visitations in this order.

"Children will be interviewed by Judge Judith D. Wells to collect more information about their welfare.

"All sworn in witness will be heard by Judge Terry White at reset.

"This case is reset by me, Judge Bronson, on September 8, 2009, at 1:30."

CHAPTER 34

FOCUSING ON A WRONG THING

It was very hot outside, about 107 in the shade. I felt like I was about to pass out when I sat inside my Mitsubishi Mirage. It was not the heat; it was what just happened in that family court that day. As I was thinking about the next step, O. Settle, the prosecutor for the attorney general's office approached and knocked at my window.

"My man, I am not supposed to give you legal advice, but I am telling you straight that you did well in there. You defended your children logically, but you are not a lawyer. You have a good case, with lot of ammunitions, you still do not know how to present them. You have evidence needed to win, but you don't know when to introduce them to the court. And I do not like that. My job is not to counsel you, it is to prosecute you, which I was doing in there, but it would be unjust to see your children ending up with an unstable mother, which is the reason you were fighting against. Besides you and me, every single person in there was white. They will not cut you slack. They will crucify you and then take your children away if you don't aim your gun from a different shoulder. Too many black children are taken away, every day, by CPS, and I don't like that. Your case is reset for September 8, 2009, it will be heard inside Judge White's courtroom. The way I know her, she will reset it again to allow you to obtain a new counsel. From that time on, all prior orders will remain in effect. Do not expect her to give the kids to you without you showing her one or two things. No judge in their right mind would. Your ex and you need to sit down and talk, maybe in mediation meeting, to try to stop this foolishness. In there, you will learn couple of reasonable tools. If you cannot meet in the middle, then, my man, you have to fight to stay the primary provider you had been. You convinced me, but you did not convince the court, and this is the reason I am talking to you. Find you a lawyer and stop focusing on the wrong things to try to reach a right horizon. Find a white lawyer, a female white lawyer who has children. And you will see, she will focus your fight on showing how you have been providing and protecting your children. That is what the judge will be looking for. Well, my man, I did not tell you a thing about anything. This was not a legal advice, and I did not talk to you. Have a nice day, my man."

"Thank you, sir. I will find me a lawyer," I answered.

I knocked at main door of the Bedford office of Bailey&Galyen on August 1, 2009. It was early in the morning. No one answered. As I was leaving, I saw the lady touching the knob from inside. She was the secretary. I hired Chuck Rowland. I talked to him. Before he shook my hand, he pulled his pants up, which was a pure waste of energy. His belt was not there to underline his waist as it should be. It was there to hold his pants from falling down. He was small, very small, around the size of the musician Snoop Dogg. The man smelled like a drinking salon, and it was only nine in the morning. He was drunk already and his speech testified that. I explained the reason I was hiring him. He stood up to fetch a dictionary in the main cabinet. The blue shirt he was wearing came loose. It looked on him as if it was put to dry on the wire hanger. He put that dictionary on top of the cabinet and read it as if it was a document. After taking a look at each paper in the evidence file I presented, he decided to request a new social study. It was here that the name Kathryn Omarkhail came through. He said of her that she was a witch. He beat her more than one time in the court because she was a liar.

"She lies a lot in her reports and then confuses herself in the hearing. She is an old hag who hates people around her," he explained.

This was how I knew couple of things about Kathryn Omarkhail. It was through Chuck Rowland. During that first meeting, he also came to a decision to file for a novo hearing, in timely manner, to appeal all portions of the Judge Bronson. He asked me to be inside the courtroom, on the trial day, fifteen minutes before the scheduled time so we can have a briefing. He also explained that he will need to file a motion for substitution of counsel, not because he wanted to delay the matter but to have him granted the permission of him becoming my attorney of records, in accordance with the Texas rules of civil procedure. By doing so, Chuck Rowland hopped that the court would set the matter on the docket for hearing on September 4. And they did; he became my attorney of record.

When September 4 arrived, Chuck Rowland avoided my presence twice. At ten minutes before the hearing, I saw him entering the chamber located at the right side of the room 5. He was there talking to Meda Bourland when I approached. I knocked the frame of the entrance door to let him notice my presence. He stood up and slammed the door on my face. I did not suspect a thing. I thought he did that because he was busy preparing for the trial. Lawyers consult each other before trials. I left and went to wait in the hearing room. At minus five minutes, as he was passing by the bench I was sitting on, I stopped him. I asked if we were still going to have the time for client and lawyer consultation, before standing in the front of the judge, as he promised.

"There is no need for that. I am quitting. That is why you did not hear from my secretary. I have already filed a motion to withdraw."

"Why is that? Why would you do such thing without warning me? You took my money," I said.

"You will be advised very soon. If you don't want me to quit, object when the judge announces the motion. She will ask me to stay," he advised.

The man's breath was already smelling as if he had the whole bourbon brewery in his mouth.

"But why would you quit at a critical moment like this one?"

The court was called to order. The only person absent was Kathryn Omarkhail. Chuck Rowland requested the court to grant him permission to withdraw as my attorney. The judge asked me if I agree with that motion.

"Your Honor, Chuck here just advised me five minutes ago, in this present court, to object to his withdrawal. May I ask why Chuck is quitting? Chuck was paid, he is quitting. Kathy Ehmann Clardy was paid, she quit. Dorothea E. H. Laster quit after being paid. What is going on here?"

"Your Honor, the cause for withdrawal as Mr. Kasalobi's counsel is that I am unable to effectively communicate with him in the manner consistent with good attorney-client relations," he said.

"That is a bowl of shit, Your Honor. I was in his office on August 1. I first talked to him on August 3, and this was the only time I had ever seen him and ever talked to him. He told me he will call after filing all necessary paperwork. On August 28, his office called me to confirm today's hearing. What kind of communication was I supposed to be having with him?" I asked.

"Mr. Kasalobi, you need to watch your language when addressing this court, and please do not interrupt. Wait for your turn. Counsel, is there another reason for your withdrawal?" Judge asked

"Additional cause exists, Your Honor. The client has defaulted in the financial obligation in accordance with the contract between client, Mr. Kasalobi, Bailey&Galyen, and the lawyer, me, Your Honor."

"That is a bigger bowl of…Your Honor. I have here two contracts: an Employment and Fee Agreement and a Contractual Agreement for Legal Services, both from Bailey&Galyen. May I approach the bench to give copies of these documents to the court?"

"Your lawyer has already provided the court with some copies. Please continue."

"The initial non-refundable retainer fee was $2,500, excluding $250 for attorneys and $100 for legal assistants. I gave him a money order of $350 separately for that. A deposit of $1,500 was paid. I was given the receipt # 242888. The first payment agreement of $333.33, as stated in the contract of employment and fee agreement on page 3, was due on 09/01/2009, the second on 10/01 and the last on 11/01/2009. I mailed the amount due for 09/01 payment on Tuesday. Today is Friday, 09/04/2009. By now, it must be in their office. What Chuck needs to do is to call his office to verify, Your Honor."

"It is not my place and time to call to verify. Mr. Kasalobi was supposed to hand his check or to drop it in the night box in a timely manner," Chuck Rowland said.

"Your Honor, I do get paid every Tuesday at 11:59 p.m. I work in the early mornings. On my break time, I bought a money order, and I directly dropped it in the mail. So it is late...We are Americans...We owe a lot and sometimes live on credits. Most of the time, we pay our debts late. If we are late, we pay with late fees. Chuck Rowland himself doesn't pay on time all the time. I know lawyers are crooks. Chuck here is trying to rip me off. How come he never sent me a letter notifying me of any of these?"

"Counsel, your office doesn't accept late charges?" Judge asked.

"The contract gave him specific instructions, Your Honor."

"Did you inform Mr. Kasalobi, on time, about your withdrawal?" Judge asked.

"Yes, Your Honor, a copy of this motion was delivered to him. He was notified by writing of his right to object to this motion," Chuck answered.

"That is another bowl of...a moment ago...he just...Your Honor, this man is on drugs or something. He must be. What he is says is nothing but the truth. As matter of fact, he is too insubstantial, frail, and too yellowish not to be on drugs. Just look at him, he has been drinking already, can anyone smell his breath? Coming inside the courtroom drunk is a mockery of your profession. Your Honor, this man just told me moment ago that he is withdrawing. He also tried to set me up by saying that if I want him to stay on this case, I have to objet. He can quit, Your Honor, anytime he wants to, but before he does, I need my money back, to the penny," I said.

"I myself do not have a copy in which you are notifying Mr. Kasalobi of his rights. When was he notified?" Judge asked.

"Your Honor, I worked nine hours on this case and on the office basic rate. The total fees and expenses spent on this case is $1,325.

As of now, Mr. Kasalobi owes me. On this pace of hiring and firing lawyers, he will not have a representative in this town. If he tries to hire another lawyer, he will see what will happen to him. My advice to him is to make a deal. He needs to negotiate with his ex. She has the kids with her, she has an advantage on him," he said.

"Your advices are nothing but commentaries from the sheep and the reaction of the shepherd. You are a not a lawyer. Because of lawyers like you, the book needs to find another definition of a lawyer. Please do not threaten me. Do not ask me to negotiate. I am a reflective person. I am a circumspect human being. I am an intelligent and ingenious man. I will fight to my last penny, and I will win because I am in the true side of the story. No matter how long this night will last, the sun will rise. It always rises even for people like you," I said.

As I was thrashing out the liquor reeked and puny lawyer turned drunkard, a police officer entered with a dossier. He handed it to the clerk. When the judge read it, she said, "Counsel, Kasalobi never been officially notified of your withdrawal. You just filed these documents today, at 11:35 a.m. with Tarrant County. This case doesn't even show an oral deposition. It is clear that Mr. Kasalobi did not know anything about your withdrawal. Therefore, he can agree or disagree to this motion. Another hearing should be set. You should provide him with the originals of all discovery responses and documents. Mr. Kasalobi, you are hereby notified that if you wish to contest the withdrawal of Chuck Rowland, as your attorney, you should appear at the next hearing. If you do not oppose Chuck's withdrawal, you may notify him in writing of your consent to this motion. This case is still set for hearing on September 8, 2009, at 1:30."

On September 7, 2009, a day before that court hearing, Amie Gardner, the legal assistant to Chuck Rowland, called me. She wanted to know if I will be on September 8 to object the withdrawal of Chuck Rowland.

I said, "What you need to do is to give me back the money that Chuck Rowland stole from me."

"Which money are you talking about? Sir, are you going to be in court?" she asked.

"I won't. Give back my money, the money Chuck took to represent me."

"Then, please sign the bottom of the motion for withdrawal of counsel, on the dotted line that says cause for refusal, and send it back to this office. It was our wish to resolve this matter and continue to represent you. We would very much see your case through to its completion," she said.

"I don't have such document, ma'am, and I really do not care," I answered.

"Yes, you do. We sent it via certified mail RRR # 7004 2890 0001 8808 2922, and you signed for it."

"I did not sign for any certified mail ,ma'am," I answered.

"Sir, we sent it on the address Muntumpe, your daughter, gave us. She had a no-charge telephone conference on August 3, 2009. It was for status check, with this office. She also had about a couple of telephone talks with Mr. Chuck. She was charged fifteen minutes for each conversation. In one of these conversations, she asked me to forward all correspondences to the new address she gave us."

"Did you say Muntumpe?" I asked.

"Yes, but that was not her who signed on the US Postal Service certified receipt for the correspondence we mailed. You signed your name 'Kasalobi,'" the lady said.

"Muntumpe called your office and talked to you? Look, I do not sign my name. My signature is complicated than that. You have it on your document, why didn't you compare it? That being said, I still want my money back."

"What money?"

"My $1,850, I personally gave it to you for Chuck's representation. The man quit in the heat of the court session with the judge. He never defended me. He accepted my money only to legally steal it from me. He said that I did not pay the next installment of $333.33, I told him that it was in the mail. Did you receive it? "

"Yes, we did."

"That makes a total of $2,183.33 that I need your office to give back to me before I reach the Office of the Chief Disciplinary Counsel of State Bar of Texas. Your lawyer is a robber. Can you believe that I even begged to write him another check on the spot, right there in the court, and he refused? He stole my money and I want it back."

"Well, take that to the bar then."

CHAPTER 35

SHE CONFISCATED ALL PAPERS BECAUSE SHE PAID FOR

I did not talk to Muntumpe about her interfering in my court fights again. Asking her about why she signed my name would have caused lies from her. I knew it would have ended up with her using her negative experience to win. I had a custody battle fight ahead of me. I did not have the time to fight her fight. I was, by then, used to her trying to constantly destroy my life. Signing my name to steal important documents was not her first either. This time, she did it in front of a witness, the office of Chuck Rowland. It would have been begging for a lie if I spent my time talking to her about it, as it was the day when she stole my passport and my immigration documents, including her brothers' and sister's.

I had it that much that time. I wanted our legal papers back. She challenged me. To show she was challenging me, she openly started to use them to connect her utilities. She also leased them to obtain income tax returns. I sued her. Once in the city of Hurst court, she cried to move the feeling of the jury. They watched her drop tears, crocodile tears. When she realized that she had the jury's attention, she began to play with them. She lied and lied. They listened and listened. She said I stole her sister and brothers from their mother and brought them in the US without her consent. Once in United States, I started to mistreat them. They went hungry without clothes on their backs. I assaulted them and fed them out of trash cans. She made me look like a monster when she said that, one day, I entered her room and touched her breasts. When she complained, I kicked her out of the house. That was the reason CPS sent her to live in the foster home in Connecticut.

CPS was involved indeed. With the testimony Dimassa gave them, they found out that Muntumpe had been lying. What she was saying was nothing but fabricated lies.

At that time, Muntumpe was a runaway child. She was giving me all kind of troubles. I decided to send her back home to Africa. I bought a ticket for that aim. When she found out that she was about to be sent home, she claimed being touched on Saturday night. She wanted me arrested so she can stay. When confronted by the police with Dimassa's testimonies, she broke down. She said that she spent that very Saturday night upstairs in a lady's apartment. The lady gave her that idea so she can stay in the USA and go and live with her. She was given a police ticket and was brought back home. CPS did not send her to Connecticut because of that claim. They sent her there because she badly beat me. She broke my tooth and caused two bumps on my head: one on my face and the other on the back. I was tired of her and sick of everything she was causing to my entire family, so instead of being sent back home as I proposed, CPS gave her a second chance and put her in a foster home.

In Hurst court, she told the jury that she was eighteen when she came back from Connecticut after her graduation. She still witnessed me mistreating her brothers and sister because I did not love them. I did not worry about her accusations because she got these stupidities from Chantal Yaone, a cousin of mine and another burned-head woman who never respected her father. Muntumpe marked off when she said she was the only person, in the house, who had been taking care of Makaya, Dimassa, and Belinda. She took these papers because it was easy, that way, for her to enroll them in schools, to take them to the hospital in the case of emergency, and to find a safe residence for them. The other reason she confiscated all papers, she added, was because she paid for them. That was a big lie.

At that time when Sanaa and Kanina were living with us, she made my kids believe that I cared more about these two grandchildren than I cared about them, my own children. It was not so. My two grandchildren, including Belinda, refused to play her games. They followed my advice, stayed in school, found jobs, bought cars, and started to help themselves. She hated them for that. Makaya and Dimassa spent that time selling her drugs. They quit school for that purpose. They then were found most of the time under police boots and spending their days in police stations. Muntumpe helped them to turn their blaming fingers on me. They accused me of abandoning them in profit of other children.

When I applied for work permits, I applied for everyone in the house. INS needed $25 each for fingerprints. Sanaa and Kanina paid their fees. They were working using their I-94. Makaya and Dimassa were not working. They both were selling her drugs. They also were smoking cocaine and methamphetamine. Because she was their boss, I asked Muntumpe to pay. Not only did she refuse to pay for them, she also refused to pay for herself. I paid. She started her campaign of denigration when she realized that I paid for every single one of us, including her. She told Makaya and Dimassa that I was setting them all up to have them arrested and sent them back to Africa. It did work, almost.

At the end of the day, we got work permits. Muntumpe and Makaya did not get theirs. They did not show at the fingerprint office.

After the work permits, we all needed to change status from refugees to residents with Green Cards. Sanaa and Kanina paid out of their pockets. They paid $240 each. Because I needed everything to be done within the given delay, I paid for Muntumpe and for Makaya. I paid $240 for each of them. Because Dimassa and Belinda were still underage, I paid $170 each. Makaya was not living with us at that time. He was with Muntumpe. He was wasted on drugs. Again, Muntumpe convinced him that this deal of change of status was a setup. I simply was trying to trick him. Once in the immigration building, I will have him arrested and send him back to Africa because he is on drugs. I tried to do the same thing to her when she was still living with us. I had wind of that lie and they told me that Makaya was very scared. I sent Dimassa, his little brother, to go and get him. When Dimassa came back, he said that not only Muntumpe asked Makaya not to come, she also pleaded with him not to go with me at immigration office. Makaya did not go to biography data and to eye prints with us. We all got changed from refugee status to residents and obtained our Green Cards, Makaya and Muntumpe did not.

So I was not really mad at her for saying in court that day that she confiscated our legal documents because she paid for them. She never paid for any of them. She lied. She stole them, used them, won in the court, and then kept them. I did not wait till they expired, I applied for new ones. They did not come cheap. That was then. I had a custody battle fight to attend to. I did not have the time to fight her fight this time because there was not any blessing in doing bad things. I left that fight and its consequence to the law of karma. Mr. Kasongo Senga Kaswatuka, my pa, said once to me, "Son, the benediction doesn't come from God. The malediction doesn't come from Satan either. We make our benediction, and we make our malediction in this world. When people appreciate things you do and say it loudly about you, that is a benediction. You are blessed because you are doing good things. When you are constantly doing bad things and people are noticing them, and they are all the time declaring them openly, that is malediction. You are cursed because you are doing bad things."

Muntumpe was cursing herself. She was doing bad things. There was nothing to gain by giving her address to the secretary of Chuck Rowland.

She did the same thing once because she wanted Dimassa to continue selling her drugs. She changed my address to hers and said in the court that I was not able to protect none of my kids, particularly Dimassa. She loved him, and she wanted to save him from me. Despite the mistreatments she endured from my hands, she always brought food and money for me to pay my bills, she added. That was why, as required by the law, she has the right to claim all my children on her income taxes, not me.

When I realized that, at just sixteen, Dimassa started also to believe in Muntumpe's ephemeral reality of life, I began to slowly let him see what Muntumpe was really doing. I told him over and over that she will never give him the basics of the real life as promised. Instead of complaining about things we all cannot change, I asked him to stay in school and to stop following her snake advice. I advised him to go back to work because it was there where the rest of us found money. At that age, I kept saying to him, Kanina Musamba followed my advice, found a job at Kroger, and bought a car. Sanaa Musamba did the same, but Makaya, with Muntumpe's guidance, preferred the easy life of a thug. He did not accomplish a thing. He is where he is today, without a high school diploma, because he did not want to empty his ears. I said to Dimassa that Muntumpe will never teach him to be tough, to canalize his goals, and to correct mistakes that kids do make. Her advices and decisions will deepen him, as it did to Makaya. I said to him that with Muntumpe, he will never get the power to stand on his own, because she produces nothing but the white stuff on chicken shit.

"That is what you will receive if you continue hanging around with her. The white on the chicken shit, not worth a thing, it is still the chicken shit. Giving you drugs to sell and making you run from school is not love, it is pain. That kind of money doesn't last. Your sister will destroy you because she is the chicken shit," I said to him more than often.

I brought my children to the United States to give them a good life. I brought them in here for them to have a piece of this American dream, not to be changed into sponges of beer and drugs. Because I was trying to save Dimassa from her, she sent Makaya to beat me. It was the day I found him and Osee, his Latino friend, smoking marijuana in my house. I told them to put it out. Makaya challenged my authority. I snapped the marijuana stick from his fingers. He stood up and hit me twice in my ribs. As I bent down, he went for his stick. He then twisted my left hand to get his small cigarette. I dropped it. With my foot, I squashed it on the floor. He twisted my left hand harder and broke it. If it was not for Osee, he would have done more damage. Muntumpe explained that attack by saying that what Makaya did was biblically authorized. It is written in it that parents do not provoke and incite your children. Because I was aggravating all my children, she sent Makaya to beat me, I got what I deserved, she said. Muntumpe always wished me pain and suffering. She always wanted me to confront her so I can spend some of my times in jail.

CHAPTER 36

YOU DO NOT GO TO COURT WITH- OUT A LAWYER

I refused to listen to Amie Gardner, Chuck Rowland's legal assistant. I said to her that he quit, I need my money back, and I won't show up in court on September 8. I did not have to object her boss's withdrawal. So these documents Muntumpe received was not worth a penny to me anymore. She could sign my name, steal my files, and transfer them to whichever address she wanted to it would make any difference. I will not give her an opportunity to argue with me anymore. I am her father. As such, I knew deep in me that she owed me in thousands. Even if she kept all my papers then and I lost my children's documents, I stood my head up and said the truth in that court. I did not have anything to lose that second time around. Therefore, I did not want her behaviorism to obliterate the rest of my day and her demeanors annihilate my inner peace anymore. I told Amie Gardner that my daughter's act confirmed what she was still capable of. She won't do anything with what she received just the way she did not know how to go about with all INS legal papers, our passports, and social security cards she stole from me when they expired. My triumph was when they expired. My other victory was when she herself reached me after they did. INS did not let her renew any of them. She did not have the authority to do so. A bird needs two wings to fly, as my pa always said. When you are telling lies on someone, you are stealing his dignity. And when you rob someone of his dignity, you rob a piece of your own at the same time and you won't have any remaining in you. Muntumpe did not have enough feathers in her second wing to fly because of her calumnies on me and because of her trying constantly to steal my dignity. She humbled herself, turned around, and reached me as she found herself at the end of her road. She wanted me to renew all papers. I accepted. I even applied for her I-94 and her social security card because a Congolese preacher stole these documents from her when she was living in foster home in Connecticut. It was from these new documents that she obtained her green card and her driver's license.

I hang up with Amie Gardner, Chuck Rowland's legal assistant, and called Qi. I called her for advice. I had a big legal fight ahead of me that I was risking facing without a lawyer. Qi was a lawyer. She was my redskin American Indian friend. I met her, for the first time, when I went down to Nacogdoches. I was after my two little girls. This was the first time that Sheebah kidnapped them on September 26, 2003. Detective Duermeyer chose to lie on me because of that same occasion.

I called Qi for advice because she was my friend. Our encounter happened when I was driving to Nacogdoches. It was also after talking to CPS Stacy Smith. I told her that my children were stolen from me by Sheebah, their mother. It was not parenting, as she insinuated it. Therefore "I am going South East to get them back. Up to Tabô, Sheebah is hiding them in the carnival called Heart of America." Stacy did not give me the time to finish, she threatened me. Then she said, "You put them in house arrest for two months, and now you want them back."

"That is the most ridiculous statement I have been hearing since. I said it once, I am saying it again, her claim of family violence and her two months' house arrest were nothing but fraud cooked by Mahr Kay Byers of the Battered Women Foundation. It was a crooked story inside the oven of Pastor James. What they gave her was a landing hand designed to move anyone's heart, and Hurst Police failed for it. Think about it for a second: my door was always opened, why didn't they arrest me on that September 26, 2003?" I asked.

"This time, police will arrest you for stalking. There is a reason they came at your place to secure their departure. It was because of your violent behavior," CPS Stacy Smith said.

"Tabô just called me. They are hungry and cold. I am going to get them. Call the police if you want to."

Hours after that conversation, I jumped in my car, my friend Eight, as I always call my '98 Ford Escort. After a long day of work, I descended toward Dallas on 183 E. I took US 175 from Dallas after merging on I-30 E, I directed myself south toward the city of Nacogdoches. I was very tired and was forcing myself to drive hundreds of miles by night. But those miles were special; they were far removed from the rest of all miles I have ever driven. My two little girls were at my final destination even if they were constantly moving as the carnival was. I began talking to myself as I was entering the city of Reese. I was at that moment completely lost in my dropping tears because I was scared to have already lost them. I saw an unbelievable event, something that people do not see very often. I first thought that it was a strange flying bird, directly coming down from the sky, toward my windshield. I had to reconsider right there. Since it did not have wings attached to it, what I was seeing was a flying cord, long and with lot differences, that was flopping without flapping. Its body was wiggling like a long pigtail. And that pigtail sounded like a living string when it hit my windshield. I was completely woken up by the impact. I stirred to my right, adjusted my wheel, and stopped my car over the curve to scrutinize. For me, what I saw was a snake that was flying, a phenomenon nobody ever saw before. I set my windshield wiper on to throw it off from the car, too late, it spread its blood all over the windshield instead.

Just as I was stepping out to get it off from my windshield rubbers, where it was already tangled up, a lady pulled in the front of my friend Eight. She jumped out, leaving her driver door open, and started screaming as if she was a little girl. I looked at her. I saw a silly, well-dressed, and beautiful woman. She was silly because both her hands were doing a special dance on her head. Not only she was undoing her hair as if she was been attacked by African bees, she also was scratching her ears off. Her face had this expression I was not capable to explain. What she was doing and all her gestures were worth to be kept in memory, stopped for times to come, but I did not have my camera with me. Women are strange people, for a snake, even if it was coming from the sky, the lady was showing she was a very panic-stricken woman.

"I saw an impressive thing that one doesn't see every day. I saw a snake that was flying," she said, biting her lips.

If doctors are right when they say that it takes seventy-two muscles to say a single word, then this lady spent her reserve of brutal force to speak that sentence. The woman was out of control, strangely active, and equipped with a smile that was glued to her lips. This brought forward all her facial features.

I answered and said, "That is also what I said to myself too, but it is only a snake, the way it has always been since ages."

"Oh yeah! I know that. This one was crossing the road, which by itself is strange enough, because the concrete is very hot. Snakes have sensors under their tummies for that. Anyway, the truck that was on my right hand side, your side of the road, just in front of your car, runs it over and ejected it, flip-flapping behind. It ended up flying on your windshield. As a matter of fact, this is a diamondback rattlesnake. You recognized it by its rattles. This one is old, less venomous. It has, let me see…about twenty-seven rattles, that means, relatively least potent venom," she calmly illustrated in plain words.

"That explains it all. That truck did not have its mud flaps attached to it for sure. But it was not flying."

"Oh yeah, it was. You have an accent, you are not African."

"You are kidding me. I thought it was the other way around. When you have an accent, you are African. Anyway, it doesn't matter. Bob Marley said, 'It doesn't matter where you are coming from, as long as you are black, you are African.' I am African, my lady."

"African-American, I meant to say. You are not an ebony black man." She insists, her reddening face looking directly at me. She had very long hair I called blanket of magnificence. That blanket not only was dropping behind her head, it also was covering her shoulders.

"Look at me. See this encircling facial front around these big eyes? That, my friend, is one of the features of a black man. This large, flattened, puffed, and broken nose in the middle of my dark-skinned face is also one of a black man's characteristics. I have frizzy, nappy, and woolly hair, I also have huge and great lips. These two describe the beauty of a black man. Yes, I am black. I am an unadulterated African black man proud of his exaggerated frontal forehead. Ebony is a language I do not speak, black is what typifies me, and African is who I am," I said to her, admiring her slender body. The woman was sculpted in a hot spirit materials; every part of her was a rare draw from a darned good artist.

"Anyway, my name is Chetanh. Qhwanakc Qi Chetanh. I am a lawyer. I am from the frontier country, way up there in the west, in a little place beautifully perched in the cliffs called Mesapagodas, in Utah."

"The name is Kasalobi. I fluently speak French. Qi you said?"

"Yes, a pure red blood from the deepest of Ute Mountain. I am a Cherokee Indian. We live around the Mancos, a spiritual river full of sacred fishes," she answered.

"You do not look Indian to me," I said

"They don't make us the way they used to anymore, but we are still the same. I am a Chicana, a mulatto between a pure male Navajos of Opy-zuni tribe and a beautiful female Kakoo from the Comanche family."

"How did you become a Cherokee if you are a mixed blood from Navajos and Comanche?"

"It is an Indian thing, you wouldn't understand. Where are you coming from, Mr. Kasalobi? I like the way you are verbalizing words, using your French intonation. Even if, to a certain extent, I do not easily catch your enunciation, I still like the way you are rolling your tongue and the way you are saying it. I like your accent, Mr. Kasalobi." She asserted that idea to me so loudly.

Qhwanakc Qi Chetanh spoke fast, she still does. If it is true that it takes two liters of air to a singer for his catchphrase while on stage, it took her more than that to combine phrases together. The woman is a machine of raw speeches. She did not like my accent as she tried to make me believe it. She only put that sweetness forward, right on my nose. She was being polite. People do make fun of other people's accent all the time. And from different ways we speak to each other, they also formulate diverse kinds of entertainment because we are human beings. From time to time, we have the ability to laugh about things. We significantly like it. We considerably hate it some other time. At that point, Qhwanakc Qi Chetanh was jokingly making fun of my African accent in Texan English. It did not bother me at all. Actually, I did not consider myself as a person who spoke with an accent. People don't speak with accents. It all depends on the language we use and the corner of the town each one of us is coming from. I spoke like me and they spoke like them.

"Well, my accent is from Kabwe-Kakiele, a well-known place in Congo Kinshasa. But for now, I am after my children. Their mother took them from me and went to hide them in Southeast of Texas," I explained to her.

We talked around the flying snake and she advised me how to get my children back. Just the way she appeared, Chetah Qi Qhwanakc faded away in the middle of the morning traffic, behind the mass of speeding vehicles. This was how I met Qi.

We stayed in touch. We met many times in Texas. She even showed up in one of my trials. I visited her in Arizona. She showed me her beautiful Mesapagodas village and we spent times fishing in the Mancos River in Utah. I took her to Zambia twice. The very last time we went to Africa came very afterward. It was in 2013. On our way to Jomo Kenyata Airport, on September 21, we stopped at Westgate mall for the last shopping spree. As we were leaving the parking lot, around noon, we heard gunshots. At the airport, we saw horrible and very atrocious pictures on television. The mall was attacked by the Islamist group Al-Shabaab. One minute later and if we did not leave sooner, we could have been among those who innocently lost their lives.

So Chetah Qi Qhwanakc has been my best friend since the moment we all saw a flying snake. That day, because I had legal fights that I was about to face without a lawyer, I used my phone and called her for a legal advice. I explained what I was going through inside that court of the law.

"You do not go to court without a lawyer. Representing yourself in the court of the law, even if you are a lawyer, is suicidal," she said.

"It is indeed. I agreed with you. I wrote letters of complaint and sent them to different institutions that deal with justice and the protection of children and to the attorney general, even to Kay Bailley Hutchison, the senator. It did not make a difference. What else should I do, now that my children are taken away?" I asked her over the phone.

"You don't have to do anything else. Anyway, as my people would have said it: the real problem here is the life itself. If you get married to a bad woman, you will become a philosopher. They are right. Listen to you, you have become one already. Why didn't you marry an African woman? I heard they are good people, they are also friends to their husbands," she explained.

In my culture, she continued, people do not get married because they are in love. They marry first and then become friends. Love would eventually knock on their door. Friends are like a family. They don't divorce because they are family. You marry a white girl, let that life happen to you, and you are complaining now, why? Remember, you are African. African men walk only on one leg. They have two to stand on, but they don't walk on both at same time. They use one leg after the other to walk. The left touches the ground while the right is still in the air. Before the left completely touches the ground from top to bottom, the right is already lifted away, absolutely. Do not let yourself be grounded. It is not too late. Help your kids. They are the essence of your life. They should be sacred.

"Get you a lawyer because a flow of water that doesn't reach the ocean is not a river," she advised again.

"What do you mean?" I asked.

"You are not a man if you don't get your kids back. American women are strange people. In the beginning they show themselves as one thing and later on, you sturdily find out that they are not what they said they were. By that time, kids already started to pay for being alone even if people see them with their mother. Kids cannot educate themselves, go get them back. Bear in mind that rivers have meanders because of running by themselves."

"Man, Qi, you are good in giving advice. That flying snake we met was the providence. Do you believe in external circumstances or maybe in outside influence, like everything is already planned?"

"I am a tribal Indian woman. I believe in signs. I believe in the rain, the wind, and in destiny. Where a white man sees God, I read that message as coming from the living spirit. When an Arab sees Allah, I contemplate the weight of a spirit in a river and in the cloud. I am philosophically fatalistic. I am not pessimistically defeatist. I see fate everywhere even if I was educated in a white man school. Like I said it, find you a lawyer and go get your children. Remember that the belt is not designed to hold the pants but to underline how well the hip is cut. Don't go looking for her behind them. When it is over, it is over. You told me once that you are from Kabwe-Kakiele, right?" she asked after advising me about what to do about getting my girls back.

"Yes, it is the most beautiful among all villages. It once had Sankia, the biggest snake ever that scared almost anyone but me. That snake was the dragon. It spit fire through his nose and needed a sacrifice, a living animal every month. If not it would get out, swallow children, and curse the dry land, they said. That story was not secrecy at all. Everyone in my village knew about it. Children explained it with ease. But we have never seen anyone feed it. People believed in these stories until Kasco, my cousin, and I put end to the mystery. But as incredible as it sounded, that story was not a fiction, not in its entire narrative.

"My village had seven hundred men. Some of them were married to at least two wives. Each family counted an average of five children. We were many. I remembered what it was in my village when we were growing up. Boys swam naked in a spot called Kialume River. Girls sang marvelous songs with terrific sounds under the moon. We all played the Tembi together in the village sands. We went to the same school wearing yellow and blue with black shoes as uniform."

"Courageous few children went inside the forbidden bat cave in which Sankia lived. We went in there to collect gwanas in order to get pocket money. I was one of them. We collected these bat droppings for Mr. Thassé, the only village white farmer who lived among us. He sprayed them as fertilizer on his crops. For one Congolese Zaïre, we gave him four buckets of it, each. That was nothing but slave wage compared to the job we were called to doing for him, but we did not have choice. The collection of these droppings was a dangerous and unhygienic business to deal with. The cave had big black roaches that crawled on top and all over them. They carried different virus that gave us skin infection. We itched a lot, had tear, and coughed a lot because of the gas coming from the gwanas. Village elders forbade us to hazard ourselves in the cave to avoid being swallowed by that spitting fire, Sankia.

"One day, Kasco, my cousin, and I descended in that open cave to fetch gwanas. We decided to investigate the forbidden side, where the dragon was supposed to be living. We followed the whistling that was coming from the breathing we thought was coming from the animal. We saw a human shadow. That was Alphonse Deckonick, the Catholic father, who was actually snoring while walking. The man was overweight. He was in there, dressed in black robe with a goat strapped on the leash.

"Another story around Sankia was that catholic missionaries imported that big snake to my village because of the green color of its skin, so it can easily hide in the grassy green water. They also talked about the size of the imposing body to scare people. My village people suspected, for very long time, that Father Deckonick was the guardian of the cave. Kasco and I saw the father. We confirmed and concluded that allegation when we distinctively saw the goat disappear in the mouth of the snake. We crossed fingers to pray. We made the cross sign to scare the devil in it. It was at this moment that Father Deckonick tried to stop us. He said, 'Sankia is a representative of Lucifer. You children don't have a powerful prayer to command it or a spiritual mean to stop it appropriately. If you fail in your quest, which you will, he will take you with him to hell.'

"'Good, so I can go in there and beat the hell out of Satan. I have been dreaming of beating the son of the bitch. Look, we are under the ground, in the dark cave, with a spitting fire dragon facing us. I will be damned if we are not already in hell. If we don't kill it, it will kill us. This is a tradition rule against sorcerers and old hags. We need to apply it right here, right now,' Kasco explained, just when Father Deckonick was picking up a sizeable stone from the ground.

"One of things I grew up admiring in Kasco was his reckless courage. He was a foolhardy person. He never showed how scared he was. And when he was, if he was ever, he attacked first. As a daredevil he was, the man taught me two more things about ghosts.

"He confirmed what my pa always said: that ghosts do not exist. If they do, then they are dead. They do not harm living people. Since it was known that ghosts and ghoul spirits operate at night, to prove his theory, we visited different cemeteries. We went in at twelfth gong of midnight. We screamed at soundless burial grounds to challenge them. We yelled at those inactive graveyards for them to come out and fight with us 'if they were men.' Nothing has ever happened. They never came out and attack us. That convinced me of their no existence. So I did not have any problem participating when he was about to rashly destroy the snake. We burned amulets and African gris-gris that were placed on public places to scare people. We dismissed village wizards, ridiculed the power of witches, and nothing never happened. We did not die from any of these beliefs, we actually became Kas' and Kasco, the Kabwe-Kakiele terrible kids. So one more time, I stood by Kasco, ready to go to hell with the Sankia to kick the hell out of Satan."

PART VII

WE ARE AFRICANS, WE ARE GOOD PEOPLE

CHAPTER 37

"ARE YOU STUPID OR WHAT, THAT IS WATER"

Kasco did not believe in Satan; he even had a problem believing in God as brought forward by a white man. When he saw Father Deckonick picking up a rock and approaching me, he knew at that point that we were about to be fed alive to the animal by this Catholic missionary. He did not want that to happen and I did not want to be killed under there. He persuaded me to attack first while he was distracting the snake. I hesitated. With one adjusted punch on his jaw, Kasco knocked the father down. He tried to stand up, and I knocked him out with a superman kick to his head. We then turned our attention toward the animal. This abnormal thing was about thirty feet long with a circumference looming the size of a middle-sized car tire. Our hunting skill taught us that after swallowing a dinner the size of that goat, that constrictor snake would be unable to defend itself. Kasco attached his khaki bag he brought in to collect gwanas on a rope. He threw it to that giant crawling animal. Sure enough, it attacked the bag. It definitely thought that the bag was a prey. Its instinct kicked in, and it began to constrict around. Kasco pulled the bag back. The giant fought more and its teeth get stuck on threads. I jumped ahead and put my khaki bag all around its head to cover its tongue and confuse its eyes. We completely tied both bags on its neck and head. To make sure that we had an upper hand, we used another rope and tied loops all around its long body. The idea was to make that monster not to expand its ribs out enough to breathe. The fight was over at that point. At that certain moment, the father disappeared as we were trying to get the animal out of there. We did not see when he left the cave.

Including the goat inside, the animal was very heavy to carry out. By only looking, it weighted about 460 pounds, maybe more. With palm branches, we built a heavy-duty mat. We laid different straws on it. That helped us to pull it all the way to the open village. We did so to impress girls. For them, we were heroes for bringing it, alive to their eyes, for everyone to touch. We did it with ease and without any preparation. The whole village was intimidated. Adults talked about killing it for food, but they were all scared to touch it. They thought it was a spirit sent down to torment them. Since we both were grandchildren to the chief of the village, they thought we had special magic. Mfumu Senga, our grandfather, confirmed these rumors. He lied about the power transmitted in us by him. Per respect, we agreed with him. We did not have any power. We did it because of his recklessly foolish manners, Kasco was an audacious and bold young man. The village elders examined the animal. They said that it was not a fire-spitting dragon. It was not a Sankia either, but a huge, very cold, and green reticulated python.

Even if we solved yet another mystery, the oddness of that experience was that reticulated pythons were not African animals. They roam in South Asia. Why missionaries brought the snake in my village and why Deckonick was entertaining that enormous reticulated under there was a question we all knew the answer since the beginning. It was to keep people away. When white Catholic missionaries came from the water side, they asked our fathers to close their eyes and pray to Jesus. When everyone bowed to worship their God, they took the land of my fathers. When they complained, they cut their children's hands. They kill them and raped their wives. They threatened everyone with things no one could ever explain, things like fire-spitting Sankia that cursed the land. This snake was one of the multiple ways they kept people at bay. Now Africans are already landless in their own country. This Father Deckonick, just like his predecessors, used the same scary techniques because he stood robbing diamonds, the wealth of the village from and around the cave. That was the reason he planned to build a big church on the land he was cultivating already.

"What happened to him anyway?"

"Likely for him, he was seen jumping in his Land Rover and leaving the village in a hurry. He would have been mobbed," I said

"And that abnormal python?" Qi asked.

"We cut its throat."

"Snakes do not have throats. They don't even have necks."

"Yes, they do. The belief was that when a python's esophagus was cut, it will poop white stuff. Sometime, a big diamond is hidden among that white stuff. Since women do not eat any kind of snake in my village, the diamond was to be given to them. We did not find any. We shared the meat nevertheless. I cooked my split in the pepper soup. I had a very delicious meal. With the python out of the way, the cave myth dissipated. That dissipation opened the way to the Ebambula brothers. They felt free to descend in the big hole. Instead of guanos, they hunted bats. These animals were meaty, alarmingly big, and had a body the size of a rooster. My village was fond of that flesh," I explained.

"You don't say," Qi asked.

"By the way, Qi, you are beautiful."

"What? What are we talking about here? How can you curve the corner driving hundred miles per hour like that?"

"Because I did come across today, before this conversation and tell you how a beauty you are. A lady like you deserves an undressing of eyes. Not once but a bunch of times, with an adequate amount of interest," I said to her.

"We are talking over the phone from a distance. There is no a possible way to undress me with your eyes. Anyway, I am wearing an appealing Navajos Opy-zuni Indian tribe garb. I know you would have liked it if you were here. It matches the bright blue eyes of mine, purposely, just the way I wore it last time you visited. I see you. You are getting all excited now," she said.

"Excited? How did you know that? You can't see me."

"Lawyers always put the X and the Y together. They do perfectly Q all the time. It is a straight line that makes sense because nothing comes out after Z. Hey, since you are a real son of Kabwe-Kakiele, explain to me why your village was once called Zamunda?" Qhwanakc nicely asked.

"Who is now curving the corner driving hundred miles per hour? It was not my village, it was my entire country. Zamunda is a deformation and a mispronunciation of the word Nsadi, which means water."

The first white man known to reach the African bank of the Pacific Ocean was a Portuguese navigator called Diego Cáo. He was with his two lieutenants: Christopher Pero Dias and Bartolomeus Dias. Christopher Pero Dias became well-known under the name of Christopher Columbus, the guy they said discovered America. In 1482, they accosted Africa, exactly where a mighty body of water was throwing itself in the ocean. That mighty water was charming, and it still is today. Because of that charming effect, it was called N'Tsayidi by autochthones, which means "engaging water." It still is engaging as I am speaking to you. The whole land was called N'Kongo. That engaging mighty body of water, the N'Tsayidi, is known as Congo River today. With its excess of 821 feet, it is the world's deepest river, and by its discharge of water of 1,447.915 ft 3/s, as we learned it in school, it is the second largest in the world. Congo River has a length of 2,920 miles. Even if it is the ninth longest, it has the first greatest bed of transportation the whole world has ever seen. Diego Cáo, his two lieutenants, and his men stopped there not because they were short in provisions, but because of its beauty. They then entered 120 miles inland to hunt. They went up all the way to a city called Boma. It was there when, in their first voyage, they met with frizzled-hair people. Those were black people. They were Kongolese. These Kongolese did not pay attention to them. They were interested in these dug-out canoes. They wondered what kind of baobab tree they used to make them. They also were amazed with these "bamboo sticks" spitting lightning and fire that they were carrying around.

By waving his extended right hand, trying to somehow make himself understood, Diego Cão asked them the name of the dry land they were standing on. In almost a language near to the one spoken by children among them, a peasant farmer, who was observing him and who obviously did not understand the question, though that the albino, as they considered them, was asking them what was the name of that body of water. He answered and said, "E nge n'zoba, wena mama maza mena, N'Tsayidi," which means "Are you stupid or what, that is water. It is called N'Tsayidi." The farmer, as were other black men around there, thought that Diego Cão and people accompanying him were albinos. They did not respect them as guests. As matter of fact, this was the first to them, to see albinos who were not scared to openly talk to them.

Back then, in many African places, ignorant people didn't consider albinos as human beings. It was a spoken shame to even give birth to one. They were thrown in prairies after birth for wild animals to feed on or simply killed on the spot because they were considered as bad spirits. The lucky loved ones were hidden, most of the time by their mothers. In this particular case, they grew invisible, far from public eye. And when they grew, they made themselves too small to be seen; some kids did not want to openly socialize with them. Even their dead bodies were segregated. To avoid a bad omen, the family did not mourn and the village did not express grief for the body. Female or male, their afterlife was not respected. They didn't even bury them. They were exposed to the elements on a pit, to have their flesh rotten and their bones dried. The superstition made village people believe that because they were part of the revenant ghost, if exposed to the sun, the wind would blow their bad spirit away. They wouldn't be able to come back in any body possible. That belief is still current and it is at hand in today society. Albinos are still mistreated and killed at this present moment in Rwanda and in Burundi. They are, at this present moment, killed in Uganda, in Tanzania, and in Malawi. Because of their grim distinction, they are hunted and dismembered in these named African countries.

Contrary to what the United Nations testified about it years ago, they are not killed because they are discriminated. They are killed because ignorant people are badly misinformed, inspired by witch doctors who makes them believe that they are born with supernatural powers. To get rich, witch doctors say to these ignorant people that they have to kill albinos for their limbs. He spreads rumors that albino hair, used into fishing nets, brings good luck. The potion made out of an albino's genital makes a person's sexual activities aroused. Any body part, cooked in an argyle pot, brings luck to the buyer, and when cooked with blood in it and skin still attached, it makes people wealthy. So rich misled people buy albinos' bodies. They are sold to witch doctors. When captured alive, an albino costs up to $75,000. Any of his body part is worth $350 if it is from an adult and $500 if it is from a child. Foolishly enough, this practice is current and albinos are not respected in named African countries. They were not respected in 1482 when Diego Cão accosted and was mistaken as one of them in Boma either.

Even if he did not get it, Diego Cão took note when the first black farmer with frizzled hair said, "Are you stupid or what, that is water. It is called N'Tsayidi."

He looked around and saw a man he thought represented the place. That man wore a leopard skin and a pair of raffia sandals on his feet correctly. His left arm had an armlet made out of a boa skin. His right had a copper bracelet. He also had a necklace amulet made out of ivory, ornamented on wild animal teeth. By that image, Diego Cão thought that he was the chief of the village. He was not. The man was simply dressed up. Diego Cão pointed the east side of the ocean and repeated the same question.

"What is the name of this dry land you all are standing on?"

The man followed his finger, looked where it was positioned, answered, and said, "Nsaka zoba kibeni. Inki n'sadi," meaning, "The albino is really stupid. That is the water."

Bartolemus Dias, who also was the group cartographer, got confused. He did not know what to make of "N'Tsayidi" and "n'sadi" even if they both signified nothing but water, pronounced on different accents. Because of the language barrier, he wrote down that Diego Cão "discovered" the land called Nzadi habited by indigenous. In a letter he wrote to the King Dom Joao II of Portugal found on top of the Shark Point Rock, near the city of Boma Padrão, Diego Cão mentioned that he discovered the mouth of the mighty river that was falling into the Pacific Ocean and called it Rio Ponderosa. That place is the embouchure of the River Congo. He also said in it that he went inland and saw a place he called Nzadi Mundo. By that he meant he discovered the world called Nzadi. With the time, that Nzadi Mundo was transformed to Zamunda by the habitants of Goma.

"Zamunda sounds nice. Why did you change it to Zaïre?"

"Well, when Mobutu became president, the country's name was Congo already, but he decided to go back to the roots to when it was N'Tsayidi or Zayidi as it should have been pronounced then. He changed Congo back to its authentic name. Zayidi became Zaïre. I don't see why Diego Cão claimed to have discovered the embouchure of the River Congo. Both the river and its mouth were there before he arrived," I said to Qi

"Right. So Zamunda is the original of Zaïre," she confirmed.

"You got it. To discover a thing is to create that thing, by accident or by purpose. It is to make something from nothing. It is to build a little sample that did not exist before. So for me, Diego Cão did not discover a thing," I explained

"Anyway, I have to go. About your children, what the government did then, the first time we met, when the snake came out flying, is the same thing they are doing today. I am on my way to Laredo, Texas, to settle a divorce. Call Nwokoye Violet. She is a friend of mine. She went to the University of Denton, Texas, to try to change this kind of misbehaviors. Besides being a good lawyer, she certified in counseling. She has a practice in Arlington. The lady never lost a trial. She will get your kids back. Good luck."

Just like that, she hung up.

I did not call Nwokoye Violet. Prior to talking to Qi, I had already some engagement with Vincent Ndukwe. He was from Nigeria and I was precisely warned to stay away from Nigerians.

"They are so crooked, they can kill you for a dollar," I was told.

This was how people talked about these Africans before I even arrived in this country. Despite that, I hired Vincent Ndukwe on September 9, 2009. I was also told that the first taxi cab driver you will see as you will be exiting the airport will be a black man, a Nigerian precisely. Sure enough, the first taxi cab driver I met in United States was a Nigerian. I was his last fare from DFW airport. The man was not mean; he was not menacing at all. I told him that I was freshly arriving in town, out of Congo Kinshasa, and I was going to Bedford, Texas, to meet with Masikini Mombole, the president of the Congolese community. He greeted me with respect. The man sounded well educated. He took me to Bedford, Texas. It was around eleven in the afternoon when we arrived there. Masikini Mombole was not yet home. He was still at work, as we were told by the next-door neighbor. We stopped by the motel 6, at the corner of Main Street and 183. The price was $60 for the rest of the night.

"I can afford that price," I said to Ondungide.

"Man, $60 is four times the regular motel 6 price. It is raised because they are having the Arbor Daze carnival in the city on Ector Drive. Besides, you will need that money. It is going to take you about a full year before you establish yourself in this country. Let's go spend the night in my apartment. We are Nigerians, we are good people. We must help each other."

"I am not from Nigeria, I am Congolese."

"What is the difference? We all are Africans, We are good people. Let's go to Irving," he answered.

I did not want to go with him, but for some reasons, this African man was different from all known Nigerians. He was so welcoming despite everything I heard about his kind. Once home, he said, "I have an 8:00 test to take at North Lake College. If you are hungry, in these kitchen cabinets, there is everything you need to cook fufu and soup with. Man, we cook in this country. We do not need women for that. If you are thirsty, the fridge is open. I have Sangria red wine and some Johnnie Walker."

I did not have a choice. I spent the rest of that night on his couch, watching television while he was sitting on his dinner table, studying. Before I slept, I made sure that my 500 dollars were hidden inside a secret pocket of my jeans and under my belt. In the early morning, before leaving Irving to Bedford, Texas, Ondunginde gave me back $21 I paid for taxi fare. The man was not a crook.

"You're gonna need it," he said.

That proved it. Not every Nigerian is crooked person. I realized at that point that wicked people say mean things about other people just because they can say it. They criminally plaster mud on everyone's face for what one person did. The real crooks are Hopkins Laster Karambee and Chuck Rowland. Are they both Nigerians? Maybe they should be considered as such. Half of lawyers flocking the Fort Worth family court are crooked. Are they Nigerians?

CHAPTER 38

"THEY STEAL FOOD TO FEED THEMSELVES"

Thanks to Ondunginde's attitude of sincerity, I trusted the Nigerian Vincent Ndukwe. I did not want to give my fight up, stand still, and be a road kill. I come to a decision that he was the lawyer to show up in the court with. To let myself be condemned by Hopkins Laster, Chuck Rowland, Tracy Burkhart, and Kathryn Omarkhail for a crime that did not happen yet, like in Tom Cruise's *Minority Report* and lose my kids, was out of the question. I paid $950 and I hired him. I then handed my file to Roxanne, his secretary.

"This is the first custody battle I am receiving today. Since 8:00 this morning, we have, let me see, thirteen cases of divorce, four assaults, and six traffic violations," she explained.

"No wonder, your waiting room looks like JPS hospital triage room. It is full over its capacity. Maybe it is because you guys are less expensive around here."

"That might be it, but mostly because we are good in what we are doing," she replied as she was opening the folder I just handed her. Then she asked, "Are they with you?"

"My daughters?" I asked back.

"Yes, are they both living with you in your house?"

"Officially," I said to Roxanne, "Tabô and her sister Loylla where supposed to be staying with their mother, far from me and in an undisclosed location. They also were supposed to be living inside Fort Worth county city limits. This was ordered by the family court, on the request of Meda Bourland, the mother's attorney till I was called at Kroger."

"Your two little girls do come here every day to steal food, mostly small cakes and donuts, to feed themselves. I don't blame them, they are abandoned," the lady from the bakery said.

I wouldn't have known this if she did not asked me to go to Kroger and meet with her. Without a job, the only thing Sheebah managed to do was to hide them from me. She did not have enough food to feed them, so she gave them strict instructions not to come back home. She also obliged them not to answer their phones when called by me. Those were phones the court forced me to buy and to be monthly paying for both of them. My daughters were not really free of their movements even if they were seen at Kroger. Because she was high all day long, they were left unattended all the time.

"That is kind of impossible. My kids are with their mother in Fort Worth," I said to the Kroger lady.

"She made the court believe she lives in Fort Worth. We are in the same apartment complex in Sutton Square. Your kids are hungry, when you are not home, since your front door is always open, they enter and take food for them and for their mother. Your neighbors know that," the lady answered.

"That makes sense. I complained to the office about my food and accused the maintenance guys of stealing from me. I have to go and apologize."

"I know your two little girls. I see them all the time running wild inside Sutton Square apartment and inside this store. I know what you are going through, and I don't want to call the police on them. They don't live in Fort Worth, otherwise they won't be going to Bell Elementary," the Kroger lady asked.

She moved in Sutton Square as a stay-in girlfriend to Washington. This man was renting the place. The chunk of food stamps she was receiving from the government was sold. The money was used to purchase drugs. Both Washington and Sheebah were on drugs. She chose an apartment at crossways from Glen Rose where I was living, so the kids can be near my place and not go totally hungry.

"You are right, they wouldn't be going to any Hurst school as long as they are living in Fort Worth. I just can't be five hundred feet around them. Temporary ex parte protective order obliged, you know. The last time I hazarded myself around their school, the secretary threatened to call the police on me," I said.

"So you don't even know that one of them, the chubby one, just got bitten by the dog. I saw everything as I was getting ready to come to work. She was walking outside her mother's boyfriend apartment, unattended as usual. The dog attacked her as she was approaching apartment # 134 of building J. She got bitten on her thumb. The owner of the dog asked her mother to take her to the hospital. She will pay, she said. The mother said that it is not a big deal because the dog is vaccinated. She is unable to take her there, not because of the dog had been vaccinated but because she has bunch of warrants for her arrest. If the Child Protective Services or the police got involved, she will be taken to jail. Fuck the temporary ex parte protective order, those are your kids. You need to go and get your child and take her to the hospital. Her thumb is bleeding," the Kroger lady said.

I went to Sutton Square apartment. Sure enough, I saw both girls at the park playground. Loylla came running toward me. Tabô took a different direction. She went to call her mother. Loylla's thumbnail was crushed and broken. It was still bleeding. I took her to the owner of the dog. I wanted to know if the animal's shots were current.

This lady said, "Your daughter trespassed. She jumped inside my balcony to pet my little Chihuahua. She is always outside looking for trouble. This is not the first time police arrived here because of her. She broke the laundry room door before being bitten by my dog. I reported her to the police for that too. They know her delinquencies already."

It was hard for me to argue with her. As I was talking to the lady, Sheebah showed up. She asked me not to call CPS on her. I promised not to. She added and said that she authorizes me to take Loylla to the hospital. When we reached the Methodist Hospital, Lisa the nurse was bothered by the way Loylla looked. As a mother, she found my daughter very dirty. Which was true, Loylla did not take shower for a while. She was stinking. I told her that Loylla, as well as Tabô, was living with their mother, following a pending court order. To the sound of that, Nurse Lisa called Tabô in. She started checking her hair. She had lice. Because she was also itching, she told me, "Both girls have scabies, they can go back to school till they finish their treatments."

Tabô threatened to kill herself. Kids, in her school, will be laughing at her when she will go back, she said. Nurse Lisa talked to her. She said that no one will know. She took both girls at the hospital store and bought chemical products against lice and scabies with her own money. Using medical products she bought for that occasion, she obliged them to take shower. They changed into hospital scrubs. She put their clothes in plastic bag and dumped everything in the trash can. She then cleaned their hair to get rid of lice. It was only after that that she took care of Loylla's thumb and gave me prescriptions. I did not take them back to their mother's.

"If both girls live with me in my house, you asked? Yes, Roxanne, they are living with me since the day I took them at the hospital, even if their mother has temporarily custody. The mother cannot provide their primary needs. She cannot afford to feed them either. The woman doesn't take care of them despite the fact that I pay an astonishing amount of $ 649.25 a week in child support. That money is used on beer by Daven William or on drugs by Washington, both their mother's boyfriends. Because of her lawyer's advice, the court obliged me to be on Etna insurance, meaning the most expensive dental, eye, and health insurance ever. I am financially cut into pieces," I explained.

"Did you tell them that you don't make enough to pay that amount?"

"Of course I did. I complained about everything to the judge, to the district court first, and to the attorney general. I even included my taxes return."

Cherryl Lopez responded for the judge. She called me in her office and said to me, "The court received your correspondence. However, I will not forward it to the judge, as it is a violation of the code of judicial conduct for the judge to participate in ex parte communications with the attorneys or litigants in a lawsuit. Basically, the judge is prohibited from discussing this case or gathering information on this case without both sides being present or presented. Ex parte communications cannot be placed in the court's file. Therefore, I return this complaint letter to you and urge you to follow correct legal procedure in communicating with the court."

Bill Stephens responded for the attorney general. He wrote and said that the office of the attorney general is prohibited by the law from providing legal advice, legal counsel, or interpretation of the law to private individuals. Federal law prohibits us from intervening in matters that involved child custody or visitation. In Texas, family law determinations regarding custody and visitation are made by the court system. You may wish to contact Texas Access, Allied Legal Services or a project of Legal Aid of North Texas with questions about child custody and visitation and family issues if you are not able to afford an attorney.

"Otherwise, what they are saying is 'We don't care.' It is like they want you to fail. Tabô and Loylla are not the only children I have, Roxanne. This child support is making my whole family suffer. It is destroying my other kids' dreams and future. My rent is $640 a month. Now, I bring home $230 a week, which means I have to face my other bills with that amount. I just can't feed myself. This is an impossible life to live. Clearly, I am dying, Roxanne," I carefully explained.

"How do you get around with all your expenses?"

"For now, I am tapping in my savings. I still have about $62,000 remaining."

"You guys are supposed to share your children's medical bills, as ordered by the court, why don't you ask her to pay her share?"

"Legally, she should. But she had people like CPS Jenita Talley who keeps protecting her. For instance, I sent a text message to Gcs@ dfps.state.tx.us, with an annexed mail for LCantu@sao.state.tx. I wanted them to have the mother pay her half of their prescription so they can have glasses. Jenita Talley of CPS, supervisor to Tracy Burkhart, called back to intimidate me by using scaring tactics on me. 'If you ever send another mail like that to my bosses, I will personally see into it and press harassment charges on you. If your daughters need glasses and if you think they have to have them, why don't you pay for their prescription yourself instead of waiting for their mother?' she said."

"You should write another letter of complaint to her supervisors," Roxanne said.

"I did. I sent it to Steven Boshuizen. I wrote in there that Tabô had a big bruise on her upper left arm, larger than a quarter. I showed it to the case worker when I went for supervised visitation, inside the family court. The case worker reported it directly to her supervisor. She was pinched by Washington, her mother's boyfriend. Even with that info included, Steven Boshuizen did not answer. I sent another complain to the Txabusehotline. The office of the Consumer Affairs for the Department of Family and Protective Services called and told me that Mr. Hugh Simonich was reviewing my concerns about CPS Tracy Burkhart and Jenita Talley. Ms. Tiffany Lee will be investigating Tracy for misinformation to the court and for allegedly telling my daughters to lie, and Ms. Marilyn Glenn will be looking in allegations that Jenita Talley withheld information about their abuse. At the end of these investigations, I received a letter that said that both CPS agents took appropriate actions during their investigations according to CPS policy and procedural guidelines. Like I said it already, they do not care."

"Hold on just a minute. How do you go to supervised visitations if you have both kids with you?"

"It is a complicated situation, Roxanne. Every Saturday before 4:00 in the afternoon, I let them walk across the street. They go to their mother's at Sutton Square. She catches a ride with them to Fort Worth court family court. The rest is the game she plays so well," I explained.

"Whoa," Roxane exclaimed.

"Yup, whoa indeed. I let her use me that way because I want to see my kids. The visitation center knows I have both kids with me. To avoid continuous tax fraud from her part, the Department of Treasury/Tax Fraud also knows I have them," I explained.

"For them, you will need to document everything. They need proof of what you are saying to them. For this office, I want details of any representation you used, elements of any contract signed or promises to appear that were made, what you paid for, and what happened," Roxanne said.

"Everything is in this file here," I answered.

"I see. We have a private investigator here. If there is a need of, you can talk to him to testify for you."

"I hired Jim. License # C-6679, state license A1352 and EIN #27-2682216, at ABPS abpsmail@gmail.com and at jkkacorp@sbc-global.net. I did not think he was legit investigator, yet he said he was working with Kithas&Associate of American Bureau of Protective Services. I hired him anyway."

Jim's service was on the front page of Yahoo in the Fort Worth Private Investigator section. Jim and I did not meet in his office, even once. All business gatherings were held in his house, in North Richland Hills. I smelled the presence of a skunk as I was entering the house. The man had cats of all colors living in his house. Domesticated or bred in feral conditions, many of them were mixed, and I did not know if they were spayed or neutered. They were so many I thought I was inside a city cat barn house. I was asked to sit in the couch full of hairs, which made me sneeze a lot. Jim's cats were not fed cheaply. I observed glass bowls in which was poured ice water. They did not eat vermin such as rats, mice, or lizards; they were healthy. I saw special sittings and expensive litter pots. By the smell of it, they had exclusive dishes for their foods. It also was evident that they received veterinary care because they were tamed to be friendly to visitors, so friendly that they were trying to sit on my lap. That bothered me a lot. I saw about five fat raccoons in the backyard. I saw a skunk, maybe the one I smelled the presence of when I was entering.

"They belong to my husband," the woman who was present in the house said.

"The raccoons, the skunks, or the cats?" I asked.

"Well, raccoons and skunks are friends to cats most of the time when there is food around. My husband is mental. He thinks he is a special agent or something like that, he feeds every animal around here," his wife said.

For his surveillance inquiry, Jim was paid $500 retainer. His rate was $60 per hour, plus 40 cents per case miles. He established surveillance in the vicinity of Bellaire Drive. What I wanted from him was to put everything he will see in writing for the judge. I needed him to establish things we all knew already, things that CPS did not want the court to know. I wanted him to testify in the court how long my kids were left unattended by their mother. I needed to have in him a witness who would picture their mother using drugs. He did just that.

"Okay, I think I got everything I need. What happened with your trial subpoenas? How did you serve them? Any witness we can talk to help us?" Roxane said.

"As I was getting ready for my October 8, 2009, appeal, which I lost for trying to defend myself, I did indeed subpoena Monique Hall, officer of the Bedford Police Department, and Suzy Dale, the lady who has Sheebah under her wings. Officer Monique was served by the deputy of the Hurst County Precinct. Suzy's subpoena was prepared inside the 325th court, in Fort Worth. She also was lawfully served. Those two people did not talk to the court. If they did at that needed time, they could potentially have held my motion for appeal together, but they did not meet the judge. They were served and they did not show up. Maybe it was something that had to do with Bourland. She spent a chunk of her time using the rule of witness and the rule of evidence I did not know anything about it against me. Because she blocked my first witnesses, I guessed that she also blocked Monique and Suzy too. They never had been punished for not showing up. Ma'am, I went through hell."

"I see. By the way, I like your outfit. Do you always dress like this? " Roxane asked.

"Of course I do. I am an expensive man, highly proud of myself," I said.

"I like African dresses. I like their colors and the way they are put together. Vincent Ndukwe doesn't really wear them. See, you are handsome in them."

"I am a handsome even without them. Thanks for noticing that anyway. I wear African clothes at work and at parties. I wear them, most of the time, when I feel good. People look at me, not because I am fine-looking guy but because I am always dressed up when I am in these clothes. Dressing up is the key to being good-looking and handsome. This one here is the Congolese three-piece expensive stuff. In my language, it is called a thousand five hundred boubou. This is the kind I put on most of the time, because of the way it comes across people's eyes. However, Pinsela, my female Swift supervisor, hates me in them. She hates my handsomeness and she hates me in my boubous. She hates my African roots, my culture, and the way I look in it. 'Swift Safety Department never had a problem with the way I fit in them. They never talked to me about the kind I am always wearing, why would it be matter to you?' I often asked her. 'One of these days, one of these days,' she always threatened me."

"That is discrimination. It is against the law. You should have filed grievances against her," Roxane said.

"I thought she was kidding, but she was dead serious. The woman was jealous. Her last attack was in June. That was when I filed the statement of harassment against her," I answered.

"You did, hein, tell me how it went. Even if this story is not related to your lawsuit, tell me how it went. Was she fired?"

Every time Pinsela was present and in charge on Pepsi Grand Prairie site, she brought in a bunch of unwritten rules. Often, she did so to make some Swift drivers, working under her, including me, very uncomfortable.

"Having been trained by Richie Pope, I am from the old school. And old-school drivers go by the book," she constantly said.

Pinsela did not go by any book. She gathered self-taken decisions and maliciously created illegal circumstances in order to exploit them. Instead of ascertaining her right as a supervisor, she lost respect of the drivers. And by abusively using her official authority on me and by harassing me, she therefore lost mine.

That day, when I arrived at Quaker guard shack in Grand Prairie, I stopped to have my trailer seal and paperwork inspected. Pinsela who was inside the guard shack, standing directly behind Will and Chrystal attacked the way I was dressed.

"Who are Will and Chrystal? Are they your coworkers? Are they drivers too?" Roxanne asked.

"No, they were security guards on duty. Pinsela was inside their guard shack. She was not supposed to be there. She was waiting to see what kind of clothes I was wearing that day. She said, 'I numerously have told you not to wear this kind of African clothes and this leather shoes here at work, why are you still wearing them?'"

This was not the first day my African clothes bothered her. It was not the first time she showed aggression toward the shoes I had on either. When she attacks, like that day, I always reply politely, "These are my working dress. You should have seen my Sunday clothes."

She never stopped. She continued demonstrating discrimination against anything on me. That same day, she said, "Sir, you were asked to wear nothing but Swift suggested shoes, like sports or tennis. Why are you still wearing this kind?"

I lifted one of my feet when she said that and showed her the way my shoes were built.

"The bottom outer sole is a rubber, the rest is leather. My shoes are legal by Swift standard, they are oil resistant, and they are covered all around. Nothing is wrong with them," I told her.

The very next day, she was standing inside the guard shack again, away from her desk, out of her office, and far from the Pepsi building. I knew she was waiting for me once I saw her. As I started stepping out from my truck, she approached and yelled at me once more. She said, "From now on, if you dare wear those shoes again, I will write you up and you will be terminated. You will be the next Jerrod to be moved off from this account."

Jerrod was the driver she removed from Grand Prairie Pepsi account.

Instead of being on her desk and doing her job, she intentionally made mine much unsecured. She threatened me every time she saw me dressed up and looking good. It was easy to conclude that Pinsela was prejudiced, in an unadulterated definition of the word.

"As I have asked you many times around, what is your real problem, Pinsela? Why are you always intimidating and threatening to fire me?" I replied.

"Wear those shoes again and you will know why. I will officially write you up and then I will send you to talk to Orlando at Lancaster," she said.

"There is no need for me to go and see Orlando. I have been entering Swift terminal yard at Lancaster almost every day. If my clothes are not within rules and regulations, Orlando would have had me stopped long time ago. We both know that there are two fashion inspectors at the fuel island who mainly checks shoes. Why do you think they never said anything about mine? Do not write me up, Pinsela, that won't quench your thirst. Please fire me because I will never stop looking good. I will never stop wearing my shoes to satisfy you. I won't go talk to Orlando. I will talk to Ted instead," I said.

What she said after that was unjust roaring to ruin my day. Instead of proceeding the way any supervisor would have done it, she preferred yelling at me some more. This time, she shouted at me in front of four over-the-road truck drivers. They were waiting there to be checked in.

"You don't have any right whatsoever to scream at me in front of everyone like that. You shouldn't scream at me, period," I said to her.

CHAPTER 39

HE WAS NOT "TRUE SELF A LAWYER" YET

This is a thing: Pinsela never acted like a leader. She constantly operated like a prison guard. She was always inside the guard shack, behind the tinted window, spying on drivers. She even did it on her days off. She comes on the first shift, the shift she does not run, in the darkness of the early morning, and sits in her car. She hides to see who is coming when and to hear who is saying what. Then she takes everything in the afternoon in her own shift and discusses it with other drivers. Pinsela went far that time when she told them that I was the laziest of both shifts combined. And the reason I was bringing in two or three loads every day was because I was wearing these African long ceremonial robes. They needed to stay away from me because I was making all of them look bad. Leaders don't do that. They do not criticize an employee to other employees when that employee is absent. A leader is a person in charge, a person who makes sure that his or her followers do not tumble. She said these things out of the hatred she carries in her heart against me. My productivity file was contradicting her. It was telling another story; I was one of the best ranked. She only was denigrating me because she knew they will tell and I will confront her. From that moment on, a lot of drivers did not want to be under her supervision anymore. I was among them. She wanted a fight with me and I was not up to that fight, but I decided to report her to Ted, the Pepsi manager. He was still off. I did not want to bother him about Pinsela that time because he was home sick. I waited a whole week before saying anything.

As we were looking for empty trailers that other day, I started talking to Blessing, the lead driver, about Pinsela. She heard her name and joined us. Directly, she said, "Sir, you are not listening to me. You are wearing another clown costume on Pepsi property. You will be sorry for not listening."

She then told Blessing that we can bobtail to the plant, the mixing center did not have empties. Before we exited, Willy, the yard dog joined us. He asked us to wait. He drove back and got an empty for Blessing. He sent me to pull mine out on the spot 982. That spot was located at the right side of the security shack, on the right side of the entrance. That side was always blocked in by entering trucks. I stood there, waiting for the security guards to stop the traffic, so I could get in and pull it. When they finally stopped the traffic, I hooked my truck to the trailer and proceeded to the exit gate. Just like that, Pinsela came running toward the guard shack. She was almost out of the breath. She said, "Sir, you have been in the yard for a long time. You were with Blessing here. He has already left. You need to leave now."

"I was stuck. I had to wait for the security guards to check drivers in first and then to stop the traffic. For now, as you can see, there is a truck in front of me. I will be gone just after it goes," I answered.

"You need to leave now. If you bring in less than four loads, I will send you back regardless of the time of the day you will be in," she intimidated me.

"I move five loads every day, ma'am, you know it," I answered.

"Y'all are getting away with lot of things. If I was in charge of this account, y'all will be bringing in twelve loads per day, one load per hour because y'all are dedicated and the plant is fifteen minutes down the street. It takes only fifteen minutes a lap of time for each run to be completed," she said.

"That would be against the department of motor vehicle law, against the department of transportation rules and regulations, and against Swift safety policy. It will be against the law, period," I explained with a smile on my lips that told her right there that she was stupid.

Ashley, the security guard, intervened. She explained what happened and why I was still in the yard. Pinsela looked at her and said, "When I tell him to leave, he leaves. I am going to write him up."

That hesitation in Pinsela's voice was a visible sign of disrespect. It scared Ashley. She backed off and put both her hands in the air, symbolizing deception. She went back in her office without further ado. Pinsela was becoming ridiculous at this point. She was still ordering me to move even if there was a truck directly straight up and in front of mine. I stood up there, my hand pointed toward Willy who was bringing another trailer. I asked him to explain why I was still inside the mixing center yard. He did, but Pinsela refused to believe what she was told about me being in the yard that long and been impeached moving forward by bunch of trucks. She continued harassing me. I ignored her, drove forward, and left.

At the end of my shift, she offered me a chair in the main office and said, "Sir, I told you about your African garbs…"

"Hey, ma'am, these are expensive clothes made out of high quality materials. They are not objects of ridicule. This long-sleeve shirt only, and only this long-sleeve shirt, cost more than everything you are wearing right now. So stop hating before I file discrimination grievances against you."

"I am not hating. I told you to stop wearing these clothes because they are diminishing your movements. You are not listening. I asked you not to wear this kind of shoes here because you can lose your ground, slide, and hurt yourself. You still do it. Today, I told you to leave the yard, you did not do it in a timely manner. When I say leave the yard, you leave the yard. This is your last warning. You will be removed from this account the next time around."

"You have been saying 'last warning' so many times now. Do something about it. You are mad about my shoes. That is a fact. I will keep wearing them to show you how much rebellious I am about it. Regarding my clothes, you are off beam. You are wide off from a normal mark, and I don't want to talk about it anymore. About me leaving the yard, you are awfully wrong. I am not equipped to fly above a truck that was in front of mine. Having said that, you are the boss, and bosses do what please them. You have been harassing me for a long time, and I have plenty of witnesses to prove my case. Enough is enough. I will talk to Ted once he arrives," I answered, stood up, and left the office.

For a black person, Pinsela was not a woman of strength; otherwise, she wouldn't have been spending her time hating my African roots. A balanced black woman is not jealous of any man's ethic culture, she embraces it. She also cannot be either mind porous about where she is originally coming from or having opened pores in the intelligent part of her body about a man's race, his civilization, and his traditions. Being a black woman is being the matter, not the question. It is to set things right and let them keep going right. To be a black woman is to have the mental state of being a black woman. By her ability of thinking, a black woman should show the difference. She must act as if every ethnicity, every existence, and life itself is at stake because a woman is the cradle of humanity, as Sedar Sengor of Senegal said it. That is who Pinsela should have been, the source and the cradle of humanity, instead of hating other people's culture and hating their ways. As an African-American woman herself, she should have been the mother of humanity to keep producing nothing but positive attitudes. She should have been the power that represents the African culture and the source from which she hails, because everything considered, she is aboriginally and primitively African woman. She is a person of color, and as such, she should have known that any mental porosity from a black woman or a property of having one reduces to fragments all way of life.

Pinsela thought she despised my clothes, my shoes, the way I wore them, and the African way of life. She did not despise me. To be despised is to be despicable, it is to be contemptible. I was neither one. I was proud of being me. I represented my culture and dressed consequently. I spent my time teaching who wanted to learn how we live back there because the African culture is not only a matter of dancing and different dances or wearing fancy colored clothes, it is a school of life. She did not get it or dare to learn. She was ignorant, and that was the reason she became a lost person. Instead of learning, she kept losing herself by entering claims against established African structure.

"She was thirsty of learning. Ignorant persons are like empty cans. They make lot of noise. With her harassment, she was only making lots of noises, in reality, she needed to be taught. The lesson you taught her was in fact what we call damage control. Was she fired?"

"Actually no, but she was passed by for a promotion. She was not the only person who was thirsty of learning my culture. Black Americans need to learn about my culture. It is very current to see them make a mockery of us, their congeneric Africans, simply because we do not speak like them and do not act like them. It is the responsibility of Africans themselves to give them a lesson to control the damage. I did it once with my Swift instructor."

"What are we talking about again?" Roxanne asked.

"We are talking about the harassment of Pinsela on me because of my African outputs."

"And what your Swift instructor comes in about? You are not going to tell me that story too? I have people waiting," Roxanne said.

"I just want to make a point here. My Swift instructor used to curse all the time, mostly at me. Instead of concentrating his efforts on teaching, he spent a lot of time insulting my African roots. With him, I learnt that there is no bad student, only a bad teacher. He called me nigger this every time I scratched the twelve gears on the company Volvo 440 and motherfucker that because I did not ascend them properly. I told him one day that I am not a motherfucker."

"Yes, you are. You are a motherfucker."

"That cannot be. I don't even know your mom," I said to him.

He got mad and called me Bonobo. He said that I did not have any business learning how to drive eighteen-wheelers. Driving is dangerous business. It is not like running bare feet from a hungry lion. I could hit a tree because there are no roads in Africa. What I needed to do is to go back there, marry me a female Bonobo, and engender some ugly little Bonobos, he said sarcastically.

"Bonobo is an African monkey. Call an African what you want, just do not call him monkey. This is a highly offensive term. It brings back the worse colonization memories. Coming from the mouth of a black man that you are, that provocative name is awfully odious," I said to him.

And then I intentionally scratched the gears again, he called me stupid.

"Okay, because I am stupid and you are smart, tell me the name of the current president of the United States," I asked.

"What is the meaning of current?" he asked

"That means right at this moment, today, on this third day of April 2004 in progress."

"Hell if I know his name. But I know the President of Africa, his name is Nelson Mandela. The capital of Africa is Nigeria. You thought I did not know that, didn't you? I know all about Africa. What kind of question was that anyway?" he answered.

"You are right, my brodaa. You know all about Africa," I answered mocking him.

"Yeah, why are learning how to drive trucks anyway? Y'all don't have a modern way of transportation."

"Yes, we do. The president of my country bought two brand-new buses for us, after building only one mud road, which goes from north to south," I said to him.

He hesitated about ten seconds, then said, "He only built one road for two buses? Now how you guys do to go from east to west, from one corner of the country to another?"

"Well, we fly helicopters," I said to him. And without showing it, I smiled inside.

"You don't have helicopters in Africa. You sleep in trees."

"Not everybody lives in trees, rich and old people do," I answered.

"Now, how do they do to climb all the way up?"

"They don't climb, they have elevators built in," I answered with no smile on my face.

"Cool. That is a blessing and a very nice thing to see. I want to visit." He smiled.

Just like Pinsela, the man was brainless. He was jealous because of what I carried outside. He also was bothered by the baggage of knowledge I demonstrated around. He called me stupid for all the good reasons I represented. For that, I decided to quench his thirst for knowledge. I taught him the different between watching television and reading a book written by an African, about Africa. I told him that Africa is not a country.

"And that is the difference between the truth and the reality," I said to him.

"I have people waiting, answer this for me very fast, was Pinsela fired after being passed by for a promotion?" Roxanne asked again.

"Nope, she never was. With her, it was a different story. From the moment she said that 'your garbs can not be put on anymore. I will talk to Pepsi. They will ban you on this property. They will ban you, not today, not tomorrow, but they will ban you. Mark my word. I will be on your ass to make sure you do not wear your African comedian clothes at work anymore. I will "black and white" on your ass. Believe me, you will be out of here, maybe not today, maybe not tomorrow, but you will be out here.' I did not want to lose my time. I said to her that since she was the boss, she could do what that pleased her instead of harassing me. I called Ted and explained in detail what was going on. I filed the statement of harassment against her, and Ted stood up by me. He called Jo Right, his boss, at Lancaster terminal. They all ended up calling a meeting with Melisa and to Joe Mack McFaul, the safety guy. Pinsela was written up."

"Despite all that, she was never fired?"

"Actually, it was I who, at the end of the day, got politely fired. In complicity with Jasmine, a check-in girl, and her boyfriend Eldred, they created a story I did know the head and the tail. Pepsi believed them, and I was asked to go over the road. I refused and this is what happened…"

"Okay, I got it. People are waiting. Tell me that story later on. I think I got everything I need to go to court with. I will call you if I need something else."

After calling him numerously, I finally met Vincent Ndukwe in his office on November 3, 2009. Well dressed, the man was in a three-piece suit and tie. He had his feet inside some black Stacy Adam's shoes. What he had around his neck was not your typical scarf. It should have been called a banderole streamer or something of that kind. Even if days started to be cooler than before, that thing he had on was not in its place because we were inside a temperature-controlled building; it was also ridiculously hanging all the way down to his waist. That scarf was not supposed to be around his neck.

It was hard to communicate with Vincent Ndukwe. He spoke softly and his office had the radio blasting rap music. He also was drinking Evan Williams Bourbon, right there in front of everyone. I judged him right on the spot for that. I judged him because he was not yet the student of the game. Lawyers don't openly play that game in front of their associates. He thought he had already arrived, but he still had a whole yard to run. He did not show me the maturity of being a "true self a lawyer." He opened my file and went through it.

"Ambassador of your village? Obviously this Kathryn Omarkhail doesn't like you. She doesn't like you or she is plainly a stupid investigator. How can she put that in writing? Well, I have seen worse. You are not a Dallas county resident. Roxanne should have told you to pay $1,500."

"I will find the money," I said to him.

"I reconsider in that case. But your files are not written in the language a lawyer can easily read. Roxanne will finish putting the whole thing in a legal way. I will then study everything when it's ready."

"My final is scheduled for July 12, 2010. I will lose it if I try to defend myself. Please consider my $950 as a deposit toward $1,500," I said to him.

"Well, call Cheryl Lopez, the 325th District Court Coordinator. Call her and request to have it rescheduled. When you are at it, ask her to have your trial by jury," Vincent suggested.

"I don't think she will do that. She refused to move my October 8, 2009, appeal, the first time I asked her the same thing. She said that once the case is on deck, only a lawyer can change the date, with the judge's approval of course. I lost that appeal, trying to defend myself. She also said that come July 12, 2010, if I still do not have a lawyer, the trial will be sent downstairs."

"To Judge Bronson the associate judge? I will take the case. $950 will be the deposit indeed. But by July 10, I need you to pay $1,500 more," he asked.

"Yes, as matter of fact, I am going to write you a pre-posted check right at this moment," I responded.

"Okay, now what is that business of you having a restraining order protecting both girls against you, being on supervised visitations, and still having them in your house?" Vincent Ndukwe asked.

"The system, specifically Kathryn the court case worker and Tracy the CPS case worker, wants the mother to have my kids. They are saying that kids, particularly girls, are better off with their mother. But the woman is homeless and jobless. When my kids are wherever she is temporarily living, mostly over a friend, they go hungry. They are often beaten and also late for school. The reason she kidnapped them last June was to show to the court that she had them. She did show them in the court, won the case, and got them for the time being. She won because I did not have a lawyer. She, since then, brought them back to me," I explained.

"And the orders remain in place. I understand. Does the court know what is going on?"

"Yes, it has been reported to Hallmark, the room supervisor by Kay Rifkin, the visitation coordinator. Kay approved with me that there is no need to continue going every Saturday to the supervised visitation anymore. The clerk said that the verdict was already rendered. I have to report what is going on to the judge the next time he will be in court. It is complicated situation."

"Having your kids back in your house, after the judge has ordered you not to, is not a complicated situation. It is a choice. You may go to jail for contempt. You are also allowing your ex to set you up. It is not good idea to disrespect the judge's decision. Bring me pictures and video showing when their mother brought them back to you. I also want to talk to your witnesses."

I agreed to bring the video and pictures. I paid. Roxanne fixed the second appointment for January 15, 2010. I left building 1 of Stemmons Park, exited from Inwood, and gave my back to Dallas on 35E.

On December 27, 2009, I received a mail from the court. That letter said that Meda Bourland was going on vacation during the period covering the first scheduled date. Therefore my final court date has changed. It will be on January 25, 2010, instead. I let the office of Vincent Ndukwe know about the situation.

"Of course, it is a well-known line of attack. She is using it very well. It is a strategy to throw you off your balance," Roxane explained, using her singing voice.

PART VIII

FIGHT FOUGHT BY A TITAN

CHAPTER 40

ENTER NWOKOYE VIOLET

Meda knew about Vincent Ndukwe being hired to represent me. She expected me to show up without a lawyer. Since Ndukwe would be at my side, she put another clip in her gun. Now she was playing it against me. I met Vincent Ndukwe for the second meeting. He was wearing a pair of ripped jeans this time. He had a Dashiki on top. He told me in that meeting he was sorry.

"Beside the weekend, I will only have five days to study your case. That is not enough time to review your files."

"What am I going to do now?" I asked.

"The best option for you now is to go without a lawyer again. Once there, insist on the fact that you don't have a representative. Say it clearly that you did request a judgment by jury and the room is empty. That is not a genuine excuse since you did not pay the fees, but it is a game to gain time. To each asked question, make sure to answer that since you don't have a lawyer with you, you cannot defend yourself. The judge will rule against you. I will appeal her decision."

"That is a stupid advice I have heard since I am a lawyer. Vincent Ndukwe, a lawyer, told you that really? You don't say," Violet Nwokoye said.

She wore an appealing African kinky hair. I did not wonder why, I just liked it. I also liked the way it was done.

"He sure did. I followed his advice and I lost again," I answered, looking directly at her.

"I can't believe he advised you to do so. At this stage, lawyers do not appeal the final. We file the motion for new trial. Professionally wise, this is just being a loser. Vincent Ndukwe is a shame for a lawyer. He gives lawyers a bad name. Teddy Roosevelt was right when he said that if we could kick the person in the pants who is responsible for most of our troubles, we couldn't be able to sit for a month. I know the guy. A leopard doesn't change his spots, as we say it in Nigeria. With that kind of money you paid him, Vincent should have done better than that," Nwokoye said to me.

"Actually he gave everything back. He is not a crook like Dorothea E. Hopkin Laster, alias Karambee, or Chuck Rowland. He wrote me a check of $ 2,450," I explained.

"Not all Nigerians are bad people. Thinking of me as one of them is an intolerable rudeness. They hate us because of the behavior of few. People should be talking about our level of education instead of what single individuals are doing. Nigeria is not Africa and Africans are from Nigeria. I read the final hearing. In your own words, explain to me what happened on January 25, 2010," Violet Nwokoye asked.

"Well, after the regular mumbo-jumbo court ceremonies, it was ordered that Sheebah should be the sole managing conservator and I was appointed possessory," I explained.

"How about visitations, supervised visitations, are you still going?"

"I stopped going to supervised visitations simply because I am tired of playing Sheebah's games. I have both girls with me and a restraining order against me. I have both girls in my house, providing for their clothing, food, and recreation needs, and it is me who pays child support. So I told Kay Rifkin, the visitation coordinator, that I have both girls and I won't be going to supervised visitations anymore. I was tired of playing that game."

"Okay, explain to me everything that happened on that final day," Violet Nwokoye asked.

On January 25, 2010, I was ordered to pay a one-time fee of $50 in full to have supervised visitations with my own children. Prior to these visitations and to have that right, I was also obliged to pay, through CPS or district clerk, an amount of $35 per hour in cash to the lady supervisor who would bring the children, every time she would bring them, which would be once a week, for a period not to exceed three hours per visitation. I understood right there why some parents refuse to follow these kind of orders. I also understood why they run with their children and go in hiding. They disappear because they don't want people, judges particularly, to tell them how to raise their children. The judge ordered that I continue paying $649.25 a week, until Loylla, the youngest daughter, reaches the age of eighteen and graduates from high school. Sheebah twitched the corner of her eyes when the judge said that I was $387 behind in temporary child support. She smiled when the judge said that I owed $20,776.00 in retroactive child support for the period of time going from January 1, 2007, through August 31, 2009. This was the highway robbery fomented inside the mind of a pickpocket that Sheebah was. I explained it by showing facts and proved it many times around that she never had children with her, but no one in that court of the law listened to my plea. That was the reason people grow doubts and stop trusting the system.

It was ordered that, besides the $649.25 I was paying a week, I should add $51.00 per month. That mount was to be given to Sheebah on the post judgment interest at the rate of 6 percent per annum. The first installment of that amount was due and payable on February 1, 2010, time to which my employer will be ordered to withhold it from my earning. That disposable earnings, the court said, was for the support of both my children.

It was ordered that I have to maintain, in full force and effect, my children's medical and health insurance and I should pay an additional $60 per month to Sheebah beginning February 1, 2010, for the children to continue receiving Medicaid, regardless of whether I have them covered on my health insurance.

It was ordered that each parent should pay 50 percent of the non-covered medical, dental, orthodontic ophthalmic, psychiatric, psychological, and prescription drug expenses incurred on behalf of the children within ten days of notice of the bill.

It was ordered again, to always go to Walmart, in Bedford, and cause both children to have a new ophthalmology eye exam, every time it was needed, at my sole cost and expenses and pay 100 percent of the costs of the lens and glasses frames needed by both girls as result of the eyes' exam.

It was ordered to me to pay $ 2,700 to Meda Bourland for attorney's fees, expenses, and costs incurred in relation with children to both children and during the trial with interest at 6 percent per year compounded annually.

At the end of all these court-ordering ceremonies, Sheebah was confirmed the managing conservator of my children.

"On the phone call I received from…by the way how do you know Qi? Is she your…do you…" asked Nwokoye, showing her hesitation by touching her kinky hair.

"No, Qhwanakc Qi Chetanh is what I call a friend. We never did it, if that is what you want to know."

"And yet she said that you guys did the world together and went overseas for pleasure."

Nwokoye Violet was a very beautiful black woman, visibly strong, about six feet tall, and living her life. She was the kind that intimidates a man because of her physique. As a woman, she was the very breed that you do not want to start with when you are not ready because it seemed to me that she always went by her day. If she says yes, when you mess with her, you are in trouble, and if she says no, you still in trouble. Pa said once that a woman like that is like a spoon of salt. If you do not use it wittingly in a good way, you will spoil your earnest soup. Either way, she was a fine-looking woman, the class apart you do not find everywhere. So I kept my crush inside, far behind my tongue, and admired her African skin. It was striking soft, at least from where I was sitting.

"Actually the only overseas I have been together with Qi is Africa. We never went to bed together…let me rephrase that: we spent nights in the same bed, but we never did it. Letting me do anything intimate with her, she said, was like taking a cup of coffee together. It would mean a thing to her. She is a traditional woman with long established principles. Qi is in that class that waits until married. And she was not getting younger, I said to her many times."

"Well, I did not want to be in breach of your secret, but I wanted to establish a fact. She told me that this was not the first time Sheebah, to use your words, kidnapped your children. What happened the first time when you went to get them? Were they happy and willing to come back with you?" Nwokoye asked.

"Of course, this was actually the time I first met Qi. It was on my way down to Nacogdoches. They were more than happy when they saw me in San Benito where they were been hidden by their mother. They were willing to come back with me and leave their mother behind. She was starving and letting Curby beat them. When she saw her children leaving her, she upped in my friend Eight. I did not have another choice but to bring her with us."

It took me two cans of Monster energy to try to wake me up. I couldn't keep my eyes opened while on the road looking for them. I was very tired and my car started to drive by itself; at least this was the impression I had until a flying snake hit my windshield. I met Qi at this place. She explained me where that snake came from. Hours later, I reached the town at eleven in the late morning. From US 259, it didn't take me but minutes to find the Greyhound. This bus station was the point of reference. It was next to Pine Hotel. Once I reached my destination, Kirby, Sheebah's stepfather, did not want me to knock on hotel room 211.

"They are sleeping. Do not go in there, Sheebah is not alone."

"I just want to see my kids this morning. I care less who she is with," I answered and knocked on the door.

"You are going to make trouble, aren't you? It doesn't worth it." Kirby advised me.

I knocked again. Sheebah cracked open the door. Without her glasses on, both her eyes were conked out, more or less loopy. To me, it looked as if she spent that night partying. She was unmistakably wasted. Just after opening, she turned around, giving her back to the door, and without considering who was standing at the entrance hall, she said, "Why are you knocking? You knew the door was opened."

Then I heard a pitchy little voice blaring behind the door. "Papa!"

I froze up. That was accurately one of the faithful voices I was after.

"Papa!" My legs refused momentarily to support my weight. I pushed wide open the door.

"Papa!" Loylla screamed one more time. That last screech woke almost everyone in the room, besides the man who was in the bed.

"Loylla, Loylla," I answered.

Sheebah turned around and saw me standing there. Her face looked like the mug of someone who just witnessed a rush hour train hit the crossing eighteen-wheeler truck. She always had that face. She opened her half-baked eyes when she heard my voice. This time, her jaw dropped to a broken point. With her crossed eyes, their countenance, and the aspect of their appearance, Sheebah looked very complicated. She did not say a word, which was good; it improved her verbal communication. She mistook me earlier with Kirby when she first opened the door, the reason she asked why I was knocking, knowing that the door was opened. I looked where Loylla's voice was coming from. She was dangerously kneeling on the top of a four-feet-high unprotected shelf divider. That was where she spent that night. She spent that night inside an opened unfilled place in the wall. A television set was between her and Tabô. She also was on that ledge. Both children had to fold themselves in half to fit in that wall cupboard, used as a closet and as an entertainment center at same time. Sheebah was insane to let her own little children spend nights in that perilous place, in the hotel room wall. That right there proved to me again that she really did not care about her own kids. She was dragging them place to place for her own interests, not because she loved them. Loylla jumped off from there into my arms.

The whole hotel room was chaotic. It looked more of a small children home playground than a space to rest. It had piles of unclean lingerie all over, even on top of the dining table. That space was not an agreeable "send off a real mother's rest" as Ma would have described a nicer place than that. Built for two people, it was occupied by nine. They were sleeping almost everywhere. Draining the last liveliness she had in her legs, Sheebah turned her all body to her right side suddenly. She raised her shoulder near her right ear. That move attracted my attention. In the crinkle bottom of the neck was an inch-long bruise she was trying to hide. It was a very red starchy hicky. Drawn on the white person's colorless skin of the neck, there was not need to hide it; it was visibly red as if she just got bitten by an African bee. At that split second, I felt resentment in my heart. I didn't know why I felt that way. It was over between her and me.

"That is what I was trying to tell you when I asked you not to make trouble. Something never goes away, and because another man is sleeping in her bed, you may react with violence and make trouble," Kirby said.

"I am here for my children. Let me tell you something about trouble. Tabô told me that you have been striking them. Talk to me again, and I will give you one left that will stamp a big souvenir on your face. I will make sure you remember it for the rest of your miserable life."

"Papa, let's go to Chinese, we did not eat since yesterday," Tabô asked.

"How did you know where we are?" Sheebah asked.

"White pages, internet white pages. I have to take my daughters back home with me. I can't let them watch hickies on your neck," I answered.

"Your Momma, she did that," she replied.

I felt like popping my right on her kisser for disrespecting my ma. I had to think twice because that was exactly what she would have wanted me to do to her at that moment. Smashing her face would have been an unnecessary pressure on me; it would have impeded me from quietly go back. I did not want to go back without my daughters and have to have a strain syndrome of nerve breaking, hallucinations, and nightmares, every time I was about to put my head to rest because I acted stupidly. So I let it slide.

"You need to leave my daughter alone. I told my daughter that she needed to stick with her own kind. She did not listen. She went ahead and got her a nigger. Look where we are now. We don't need your kind here. As matter of fact, I don't even want you to hold my grandbabies," Katty Kaykey, Sheebah's mother, said.

I did not answer. I let her vomit her extreme dislike of black people on me. She was the most ignorant person I have ever seen. That was also the reason I needed my kids away from that place. Despite her hate for me, including all niggers' names she has ever used to qualify me, I still kept a big deal of respect for her. She was the grandma to my daughters. I respected her for that reason. I held my two girls close to me. The beats of their hearts made them sealed to my chest. Since all animals run in packs, I was at that moment the final point of the pack. I was the leader and the animal in charge of my pack.

As I was getting ready to leave, Sheebah came out. She asked me to buy her some foods. I refused.

"This is the kind of must that a woman must have a man for," I said to her.

"You are starving me. It is against the law to starve someone," Sheebah insisted and said.

"You are not a minor child of mine or my elder parent. Go and ask the hicky man to buy food for you."

"Are you jealous? See, you still care, well, I am already taken," she said.

"Exactly my point, so beat it," I said and jumped in my Friend Eight, made sure all doors were shut off, and starting leaving with my daughters.

"That is right. Qi said that she jumped in your car and forced herself in. You brought her to Texas. I overheard you say that you left her behind. Was that not so?" Nwokoye asked.

"Of course, we were in the Valley and the day was January 2, 2004. If she did not jump in my friend Eight in Brownsville, my daughters and I would have left her behind. I asked her to step down as I was getting ready to leave with them. That was when a strange thing happened. Katie Kaykey, who minutes earlier was calling me nigger, came out from the hotel room, from 226 Stergers Street, and asked me to take her with me. 'She is sleeping with Curby. She needs to go,' she said. I insisted, I called for Sheebah to get out of my car, but she persisted. I did not want to create a scene. I drove forward. I would certainly say that even if she was in the same car with us, she followed us to Texas. I did not let her live with us when we reached Hurst, Texas. She went to Arlington Shelter for Women. That story is in the files."

"Can you prove that your children were mistreated in Brownsville?"

"Unquestionably, I recorded the conversation I had with Tabô. It was around seven in the afternoon when I picked up the phone. She was crying at the other end. She said that Grandpa Kirby beat her. He wants to kill Loylla too. She desperately wanted me to go and get them. I took her grievances seriously and considered her tears as an eminent treat of bodily harm, even if her mother was there with them. About that she said, 'Mom is not strong to defend us, come and get us.' Do you know in which city y'all are now?" I asked.

"No, I don't know, but Grandpa Kirby keeps beating Loylla and me for no reason. Hey, Papa. I need one dollar to buy food, we did not eat yesterday. Today, we used Coca-Cola to eat cereal with. I don't like Coke in cereal," she replied.

CHAPTER 41

AMERICAN OR CITIZEN?

The caller ID showed at moment the area code 956. I looked in my Texas time pad and realized that the first three digits, the 399, were assigned to towns down south, in or around San Benito. If her call was coming from a mobile phone, then it was set in the way that it has to jump from signal tower to signal tower. That way, it was hard to pinpoint the exact location that call was coming from. If it was coming from a fixed, then it was easy to find the carnival Heart of America, in which they were been hidden. They were in the south.

"You are in the Valley. Are you using a cell phone?" I asked.

"What is a cell phone?" she asked.

"Do not worry about that. Why are you using Coke in cereal? Don't you have milk?" I asked.

"No, Mom did not buy milk. She said she doesn't have money. The refrigerator in the hotel room doesn't work. I need one dollar, can you come here please? She needs to sell her food stamps to have money," Tabô said in the tape.

"Of course, where is your mother?"

Suddenly, the phone went off. I dialed back, a long beep came on. It sounded like a public phone that did not take incoming calls. Calling the police was out of the option. First I did not have my kids' physical address. Police would have wanted it before doing anything. Then I did not know exactly what Sheebah has told them. Because they are also her kids, police would have said that my girls were not in danger, they were with her. As they have been telling me, they would also have said that it is not a kidnapping. They would have said she did not run away with your kids. She has taken her own kids on the trip without your permission, and it is not a crime. It is called parenting, as they insisted many times around. If it was a man who had taken his own kids without informing their mother, the outcome would have been different. He wouldn't have been the father anymore, but the "last person to be with them," or "the person of interest" or simply "a wanted man." His picture would have been on television. I knew what to do; I did not need the police. I did not want to wait and find myself in a situation in which I would have to try to pick the yellow of a broken egg up from the ground. I drove to the Valley. After the usual fight with Kaykey, I got my children. It was here when she hopped in my friend Eight, compelling me, for no reason at all, to take her back with us. Driving with her inside was the most depressing moment of my life. She did not stop talking, attacking, and cursing. I got distracted because of all kind of rudeness she was pouring on me and took the US 59 North instead of South to Lufkin. I found myself at the edge of Logansport town at the immigration temporary checkpoint. The border patrol officer asked me if I was coming from Louisiana. I hesitated. Before I even answered, she asked me if I was an "American or citizen?" I hesitated again. This was not a difficult question to answer, but it was selective. It was easy and selective, the discerning kind that calls for a rain of other questions and the very kind that immigration officers always ask to confuse those who enter illegally in the United States. This lady knew the difference, but she wanted me to make a mistake. I answered and said, "Hein? That is a very strange question. There is not a difference between an American and a citizen, as long as we are in the United States. American is a citizen and a citizen is an American." I said.

An American, she said by reading it in a pamphlet, is "an indigenous and untaught inhabitant of this great nation who can willingly make a choice of taking part in any determination that will decide of the becoming of his country. He is naturally an intuitive home-grown aboriginal. A citizen, on the other hand, is a city dweller. Even though he owns the equal loyalties by naturalization to the protection of this state, and may enjoy other privileges, he is only a chosen local occupier of a place alternatively given to him by this nation. Even though both of them have the right to vote, a citizen is the one who may feel that because he became national, he is obliged to mark a ballot. So there is a big difference between an American and a Citizen, which one are you?"

The ICE patrol lady educated me with that explanation, contrary to this man who attacked me at Love Field Airport. He was coming out, looking to catch a taxi. I was in the queue waiting for a fare. In order to ride with me, he asked me if I was an American.

"Yes, sir, I am," I answered.

"You have an African accent. I won't take a ride from you. Do you even know what American means? You are nothing but a citizen. Believe me, I know what I am talking about. I am a real American."

"What is the difference, sir? You called yourself an American ,and you just called him a citizen. What is the difference?" Andrew James, the front desk attendant, asked.

"He is not an American like me. I don't like his kind. He doesn't speak like us," he answered.

"I can hear him just fine. He has an accent, so do you. The difference between my accent and both of yours makes this country a great nation. It makes us the United States of America. Actually, it is you who has a native Texan accent. You are not speaking like him, and that is not a reason to be disagreeable. With all due respect, sir, I will not deal anymore with your racial discrimination. You are an idiot if, for you, the difference between an American and a citizen lies in the accent with which people use to talk to each other. You are probably going to catch a ride somewhere else," Andrew said.

Just like that, things went out of the hand. The man lost his composure. His verbal communication became nothing but curses. Police got involved.

"The person's accent, his size, the tone of his skin, his language don't decide anyone's citizenship in America. We live in tolerance of different countries. Unless you want a ticket, you need to leave the Love Field Airport premises now since you don't like his kind," the officer explained.

"So which one are you, American or citizen?" the ICE officer asked me again.

Like I thought earlier, the lady knew the difference. She wanted me to make a mistake. For instance, around Laredo, Texas, or in any port of entry, that officer would have formulated that question this way: "In which great nation is Texas located?" If the given answer is "United States," that person passes the test. He really lives inside the US territory. If he says, "United States of America," then he will be suspected of illegal entry and maybe subjected to deportation. Americans don't say. "I live in the United States of America," they say, "I live in the US or in America."

I still had my kind of pronunciation that the Love Field airline passenger did not like.

If this officer is thinking like him, I will be here for very long time, I thought. I looked at him vaguely and I said, "Up to your explanation, there is no difference between an American and a citizen."

"Do you have your green card, sir?" she asked me.

"I don't have my green card anymore. This is the first time that I am asked to show my green card as moving identity. I have a certificate of citizenship, but I do not carry it around. Let me give you my Texas driver's. You can verify my identity with it. I have it right here with me in my pocket," I said.

"We are border patrols, we do not do driver's licenses. Every time you arrive near a border town, you have to have your certification on you. It is the law. Where are you coming from, sir?" she asked.

"Brownville, ma'am," I answered.

The officer got very nervous when I said Brownville. With her right hand on his gun, she yelled and said, "Put your hands where I can noticeably see them. Put them on the dashboard. Now, slowly step out of the vehicle."

I was very tired, sleepy, and lost after being harassed by Sheebah, I did not have any intention to get shot by an immigration border patrol. I stepped out.

"Who is the lady in the car?"

"Nobody really, she is the mother of my two daughters."

"Can she drive to Hurst, get your certification of citizenship, and come back with it?" she asked.

"No way, she will steal my Friend Eight and run away with my children again," I said.

"Ma'am, will you please park the car in the waiting area? Bring the kids in break room. It is going to be a long day," she explained.

The officer made me enter a lockup place full of screaming Spanish people. Without committing a crime, I mistakably swung by the immigration checkpoint, and I was very tired and in detention; what's the worst that could happen to me in there? They were in confinement already for some other reasons, and she caged me with them behind prison bars. Their noises did not bother me a bit; it was a lullaby to my ears. So I laid down on one of two long benches, built in inside the wall. I submitted myself to my incidental fate and closed my eyes. I did not understand why Sheebah was not there with me. She did not have any documents on her. Maybe it was due to her skin color. Hours later, the officer woke me up. She asked the same questions she already asked, and I gave her the very same answers.

"Once I am out, I will file a complaint for false imprisonment of my underaged children."

"Your children are okay, they are not in any prison," she explained.

"They have been detained for twelve hours. That is false imprisonment. I will complain," I said.

"This is immigration. We are the guardians of the land. You can complain as much as you want."

She did not say anything after that. She closed the door behind her. Moments later, another Latina officer entered. She apologized and said, "I am the overnight on-duty supervisor."

"My children are illegally detained..."

"They shouldn't have been held in this place at first place. I am releasing you so you can take care of them. You are free to go."

"I will file a complaint, still."

I was not sorry for being briefly in jail. This was what a father takes for his children. It took forty-five minutes for the Latina officer to make me sign all release papers. I was then let go. We left the checkpoint and I took my kids home. Sheebah went to live in the Arlington shelter.

"Okay, she went to live in the shelter. Unless she had children with her, it doesn't make any sense for her to claim she had been there for them. They were unattended, exposed, and hungry. She ignored their tears and spent that time on drugs. That there shows that the woman is really irresponsible and unstable. Well, she has legal custody of children. Let's not blame the judge here. It is the recommendation of the case worker and Child Protective Services. The judge is there to study evidence and to deliver justice from all given testimonies. I will represent you," Nwokoye said. She touched her head and fixed her hair while directly looking at me.

"How much is it going to cost me if you represent me?" I asked her.

"I am not that expensive. The rate is $200 for the attorney and $80 per hour legal fee. If you pay an estimated amount of $1,200 today February 16, 2010, and agree to pay the total value of the extra time that will be spent on any new petition, I will take your case on," Violet said.

"That is not cheap, but agreed. I have my booklet with me. I pay by check. Do you mind?" I said.

"I did not say it is going to be cheap, I said I was not expensive. In the contractual agreement you will soon sign, you have also to agree to reimburse reasonable incurred expenses, including but not limited to copies, travelling, and filing of documents." She fixed her hair again, which attracted my attention

"Agreed, I will pay to the last penny," I said while looking directly at her this time.

"Is there something in my hair? You keep looking at it."

"I love African natural hair, and I like the way you beautifully dressed it."

"Thank you. You should have seen it yesterday. I was late today and did not have enough time to make it appealing," she answered.

She then stood up and passed by me to reach the cabinet in which were documents. I looked at her from a different position. She was natural. She did not have makeup and fake nails. That started to excite me. Her body was sculpted by an art master who carefully used diamond scissors. I did not need to imagine her in shorts or even in skinny jeans. She had a superior physic that a lot of women lack when wearing body-dresses. That excited me more. Next to Serena Jameka Williams, she was far better. My crush for her grew just by looking at her, but she was about to become my lawyer, I had to put a cork on it. She took a big folder from her secretary's cabinet and started to bring it back. I quickly took my eyes off her. She entered back, coming from the main office, and said, "Can you prove to me that you had both children from 2007 to 2009?"

"No question about that. I have everything, pictures, records, addresses, and witnesses. Sheebah never brought any of these in that court. They don't have anything. These are reports from CPS and from the police. You will find dates of interviews that were made by my daughters, prior to her kidnapping them. They never lived with her ever. I need a trial, not a negotiation," I said to Nwokoye.

"Do you know where she claimed to have been with the children from 2007 and 2009?"

"She fraudulently uses the 9160 E. Walter Street, in Bedford as if it was hers. She uses that address while she claimed living at just one place with my children: the Sutton Square Apartment. She only lived there from February 3, 2009, to April 30, 2009. The manager, Flor E. Gutierrez, gave me her eviction records and this payment log that shows why she was evicted. She just couldn't pay," I said to her.

"This is my plan: they set you up and get both children from you. I will get your kids from them and give them back to you by setting them up. Before I do anything, I need to make sure that Meda Bourland, her lawyer, convinces her client to forgive everything or about a total of $12,000 on back child support. The calculations are all so confusing for me. I cannot tell exactly how much or the exact amount they will be reducing. I have to leave for my vacation. I have to go to Nigeria, but I will have my office print the letter for you to pick up. There are some classes you have to attend for the judge to approve the deal."

"I did the two classes I was obliged to. I have certificates to show for. One more thing, she took both kids with her. I do not know where they are. She said she can do that because she is the main custodian."

"I will find them," Nwokoye convinced me.

I signed a "legal services contract" with the office of Violette Nwokoye in connection with my custody battle. Violet was therefore appointed to be my agent and lawful attorney in fact.

It did not take her long, on February 25, 2010, just a month after the January 25 ruling, Nwokoye called me for a meeting in her office. She told me that she brought in a motion for new trial. She wrote and told the court that the new trial should be granted to me because the other party did not introduce concrete evidences. Whatever they introduced, she explained, was legally and factually insufficient to support the January 25, 2010, judgment. She wrote and told the court that the father shouldn't be indebted with the amount of $ 20,776 in retroactive child support to the mother for the period of time from January 1, 2007, through August 31, 2009. New discovered evidences show that the respondent intentionally lied to the court in her testimony. She led the court to believe that the children lived with her during that period of time. It was not so. Not yet seen evidences from different police departments and intakes from the Child Protective Services are showing a different story. The respondent's lack of evidence obliged her counsel to hide her physical address and the place where she supposedly was living with both children. New evidences will show that the respondent was either in jail or in shelter during that period of time, and none of these places show the kids living with her, Nwokoye explained.

On the visitation court's ruling and on access to the children by the father, especially on the order beseeching him to have supervised visitations and based on this ruling, the respondent's evidences are clearly lacking. It is legally and factually insufficient to support her case. Newly discovered evidence, pictures, and testimonies show that the petitioner has not, in any way or the other, intentionally put the children, the subject of this suit, in harm's way. The mother has done it numerously. She also has let her last two boyfriends hit his children with sticks and closed fists, leaving bruises on their fragile bodies. We are intending to bring forward evidence to prove this case, Nwokoye wrote to the court. The petitioner did not harm the children, the subject of this suit, in any way possible, emotionally or physically, and evidence will show that subsequent to filing the lawsuit, the children lived with the petitioner and he had been the sole caretaker for them.

The above errors amounted to such a denial of movant's rights as was reasonably calculated to cause and probably did cause rendition of an improper judgment in the case. Tex R. App. P 44.1 (a)(1). Kasalobi has a meritorious defense to the cause of action alleged in this case, Nwokoye wrote to the court.

The granting of a new trial, Nwokoye concluded, would not injure Sheebah and justice will not properly be served unless a new trial is granted. The court has to set aside the judgment signed on January 25, 2010, and grant a new trial because all evidence brought forward, in this court, by the respondent is legally and factually insufficient to support that judgment.

Violet Nwokoye gave me a copy of that letter inside her office in Arlington. I stepped out from there. I took left, passed Rooms-to-Go furniture store, and directed myself to the University of Texas in Arlington. Belinda had a volleyball game. Her team was scheduled to play with Louisiana Lafayette.

Early that day, about three hours before, I called Belinda to confirm if the game will still be inside the Texas Hall. I wanted to watch her play. She said yes. Minutes later, she called me back and said that she locked herself out of the Taurus. The car was left in front of Albertson store on Washington Street. The ignition key was still inside. She wanted me to go, use my spare key, park my Mitsubishi Mirage there, and bring the Taurus at her campus, as I was going to watch the game. I knew what she was doing. As usual, she did not want her friends to see me with her. She also did not want them to see me coming to her university inside my 2000 Mitsubishi Mirage. Besides its black color that was getting washed out by the Texas heat, nothing was wrong with my Mirage. The fact is my daughter was not proud of me. She never was proud of who I am. My presence always shamed her, mostly when she was with her friends. She denied me many times around. She refuted who I stood for and who I stood for her. Some of her teammates had rich parents, and they drove expensive cars. She wanted to be like them, which was not wrong. It was okay to aim high, but it was not okay to dismiss me. I was the source of her life. I am the source of her life. She once told them that she was not African from Congo, she was French from Paris. I never played her game. I did not feel like playing that day either.

"I will be there in my Mitsubishi Mirage. Remember, you drove this car when it was new. When it broke down, I bought you the Taurus. Now that the Mitsubishi black color is washing off, you don't want your friends to see me in it. This is me, Belinda, I cannot change who I am. We will go fetch your Taurus after the game," I said to her.

When I showed up at her game, there was already a man sitting on his bench, the bench I was supposed to be sitting. He was sitting on my seat. He has been introduced many times around, by my own daughter, as her father. Lots of her friends knows this man as such. The man was built with the same physique and stature just like I was. He was black, had white hair, and stood the same height as me. The only difference was that he had more pennies than me. Well-known in UTA, he drove nice cars and showed it. Every time the University of Texas in Arlington girls won, they individually received trophies and flowers to give to their parents. This man received these things from Belinda. He received my stuff. He received them pretending that he was me and took them at his home, at his place instead of mine. I did not blame him; my own daughter authorized him to take my place. He was the reason Belinda hid calendars of her game schedules from me.

CHAPTER 42

BILL OF REVIEW

The man sat two rows down, on the right side of the bench. It was his habitual place. I sat where parents were supposed to sit. The game did not go the way UTA planned, but it was a good game and the whole Texas Hall stayed vibrating. At the last whistle to mark the end of the game, UTA players came up to meet families and followers, but Belinda disappeared. I saw the man getting out from the hall. I think he did not have lot of patience. The coach was the last person out of the locker room. I asked her where Belinda was.

"In the sports room, I am going to fetch her for you."

I sat there and waited.

When she came back, she told me, "Maybe she is meditating. She is on the bench with her head down. I did not want to bother her. I left a note telling her that you are waiting for her. I was supposed to lock all doors. Since she is in there, I made it the way that once she closes them, they lock from the inside." The coach said.

I sat again and continued waiting for Belinda till the whole hall became completely empty. At the end, I stepped out from the west door. I got out at the right time; the security guard was closing the front gate already. One more minute of hesitation and my Mitsubishi would have been locked in. I saw the player number 9 talking to her parents. She was about to drive off. I sent her for Belinda. She came out and told me, "Your daughter is the only person in the room. Everyone is gone. She is sitting on the bench, doing absolutely nothing. But I told her that you are outside."

The player number 9 confirmed what I knew already. Belinda was hiding. She was hiding from me. She did not want to be seen with her. She probably did not think that the other man and I will show up at same time.

When she finally came out, her first words were "Which car did you drive in?"

"Is that the reason you went hiding in there? You did not want your friends to see my car? Well, I did not drive your Ford Taurus if this was what you hoped," I said.

"No, that is not that, I had to wrap things up, I am always the last to leave the locker room."

"Now you are thinking that I was born yesterday. You should have started this conversation with words of excuse instead of talking about the car. The coach is supposed to be the last to leave, not you. She has the keys. She just told me so. Talking about that, Belinda, why didn't you come up where I was sitting on the stairs and recognize me. Every girl from both teams did so at the end of the game but you. Why?"

"Papa, we lost. I got disappointed and left."

"Each one of your teammates lost just like you. And just like you, they were disappointed and yet they climbed the stairs. They come up toward where their parents were sitting and gave them sticks of red flowers. They recognized their parents by doing so. Your coach and her crew lost the game. They did not pretend to hide themselves behind the curtain like you. The whole campus lost, they did not go in your locker room to sit on the bench. I know you were hiding, and this is not the first time you are doing so. Belinda, you never wanted your teammates and friends to see me. You did not want me to be seen with you today. This is me, Belinda, the whole package, I cannot change who I am. I am where you are coming from, I am what you will become, so be proud of me," I asked her as we were going to get the Taurus.

As I recalled it, this was not, in fact, the first time. Belinda had to have her knee operated on at Texas Health Harris Methodist Hospital in Fort Worth. When they finished, her coach asked for my presence. I had to go sign insurance papers and check her out. Belinda called also. She said she was at 1301 Pennsylvania Avenue in Fort Worth. When I reached the hospital, she was not in the actual room, as she said. I called her back she confirmed being in room 420. I told her that I just left that actual room. One more time she said she was in the room, waiting for me. I went downstairs. I talked to the receptionist. She said, "Unless she is talking about the West Campus on 10864 Texas Health Trail, Fort Worth Texas 76344, she is not my patient here."

I dialed Belinda's number again; she confirmed been in room 420 of the Texas Health Harris Methodist Hospital, on 1301 the Pennsylvania Avenue, in Fort Worth Texas 76104. It was at this point that I decided to go at the West Campus, about two miles down the street, to verify that as a fact. There, she was. Not in the room 420 as she kept repeating it, but downstairs. Her bed was in post-operation lobby. She had packed and was ready to leave. Two of her friends, including Bianca, were helping her. They also were getting her ready to walk on crutches. My presence was not needed. She did not expect me that fast. It was not needed in the first place, and that was the reason she gave me a fake address. Because she was with her friends, she wanted to leave before I arrived. I took some pictures. She left with Bianca in Bianca's car.

As we were reaching the Taurus, I advised Belinda to stop hiding from me.

"Just a reminder, this situation keeps happening. It happened already when you had surgery at Texas Harris Methodist Hospital. Just like today, you hid behind excuses. This is me, Belinda, the whole package. I am where you are coming from and who you will become, so be proud of me because I am everything that is me. I will never change who I am called to be."

"Papa, I did not mean to offend you," she said.

"Yet you keep offending me. The proof, only the car ignition key is inside the Taurus. Where are the rest of keys? They all are supposed to be attached to a set, to one set. You can't lose one without the others."

"What set?"

"Belinda, it is a common thing that all keys are kept on one ring together and on the same key chain. The only reason you would separate the Taurus ignition key to others is to…"

"I don't keep the car key and the door key together."

"Yeah right, since when? The reason you were hiding in the locker room today was the same reason you hid the real address of the Methodist Hospital. It is the same reason you separated keys. See, I named you. I gave you the name Belinda for a reason. One names a child only to show to the world who that child belongs to," I said, hopped in my Mitsubishi, and left Arlington.

Days went by. April 6, 2010, trial happened. That judgment was made possible by Violet Nwokoye under Level 2 of Texas Rule 190 of Civil Procedure. She brought a suit forward regarding the final order of January 25, 2010, affecting parent-child relationship. The court heard a motion for a new trial. Because of new discoveries, Violet Nwokoye asked the court to set aside and to cancel the order rendered on January 25, 2010, as it spoke about the retroactive child support, visitations, and access to children. Both lawyers put Sheebah and me on the stand. The court heard our testimonies. The judge made a ruling in the open. That court ruling reduced the retroactive payment from an amount of $20,776 in back child support to $6,000 to be paid to Sheebah, the mother. I was ordered to attend two parenting classes after which I would be able to be granted unsupervised access to my daughters.

I told Nwokoye that I have already done four as it was ordered previously.

"Those four were ordered by CPS, these two must be done to satisfy the court," Nwokoye answered.

That motion was granted by oral pronouncement. It was entered in docked sheet by the court. I attended the ordered classes. When Nwokoye presented my two certificates to the court, I was still unable to claim the court's rulings of April 6, 2010. Nwokoye found out that that was due to the fact that the order was not signed before the court-allowed time. That situation complicated the judgment and every other decision that came with. That was also the reason Sheebah was still hiding the children, and my retroactive child support obligations were still not reduced. I did not have an adequate legal remedy available to avoid the effects of the old order. So I asked Violet Nwokoye, my lawyer, to go back to court on both issues as it was decided on April 6, 2010. I wanted her to be there for the portion of the judgment in the cause number 325-428760-07 that incorporates the retroactive judgment, visitations, and access to be set aside and vacated. I also wanted her to go back there for the April 6, 2010, ruling itself, on decided issues to be upheld as required by the law and to enter into judgment. And for a general relieve to be sustained as it deemed to be just and right to the court at the time of its decision.

It was done. Nwokoye succeeded one more time. I did not know anything about it till the day I got frustrated with what Sheebah was doing. It was about eleven in the afternoon when the manager of Alameda Village Apartment called me. Both girls were found by themselves, after hours, playing inside the closed swimming pool. They jumped the fence to get in and were swimming without supervision. They were trespassing.

"They did the same thing yesterday. I kicked them out and called their mother. This is the last warning. I will call the police if they show up here one more time," the Alameda manager told me.

"Where are they?" I asked.

"They ran when I was using the phone to call you. Quincy, the black maintenance man at Glen Rose who recognized them, was asking them to leave. They did not listen. You guys cannot leave children alone. This is child abandonment," she answered.

"My kids walked miles from Arlington to come and swim here at Alameda? You said you talked to their mother. When did you talk to the mother?"

"They did not walk miles, they live at Sutton Square. I talked to their mother yesterday, just after kicking them out from this property. They were with Kim, the chubby white girl," she said.

"They live at Sutton Square again? I thought their mother was kicked out from there."

"She was. Up to Quincy, she is now living back there, not as the owner of that apartment, but under someone else's name. Your kids are on the street all the time. The mother works late nights. She had to close the Kentucky Fried Chicken restaurant."

"She works? I did not know that she was working," I said.

"Why are your kids outside anyway?"

"I want to know that myself. The kick in all that is that CPS knows about this situation. I hired Kithas & Associates Private Investigator for the job. He found a bunch of stuff after his investigations and reported them to Specialist Amber Young. CPS knows that their mother leaves them by themselves," I said.

"These two children will end up in juvenile. Why did you let her have your daughters? She lives with a male friend who spends his time mistreating them," the lady asked.

"No, she doesn't live with a male friend. She lives with Oscar Washington in apartment 176. We were supposed to spend a night there, but they are not getting along." Tabô appeared from behind the bushy flower where they were hiding and answered.

"Actually, I verified that already. She doesn't live there. That was the reason I asked you guys to go home at your father's instead of staying outside in the middle of the night," Quincy said.

"I said that because Mom sleeps in her car with my sisters. Sometimes, we sleep in the car with them. Sometimes, we go over Kimberly's. Kimberly's door is closed already," Loylla said.

"Don't say that. Mom told us not tell, not matter what," Tabô replied

I took both girls home. I personally went to Sutton Square Apartment in the very morning. I knocked at the door 176. I was told that Sheebah was kicked out for not participating in the bills. I went to talk to Sheebah. Her car was parked behind Wesley Park Apartment washetaria. She did not want to talk to me. Her other children were still sleeping in the car. I called Nwokoye and told her what was going on.

"Did you read the court report I do sent to you?" he asked

"Yes, I did," I answered.

"It is written in there, by the court, that you have to have the kids. Keep the kids, it is a court order. Do not give them back," she said.

"But I do not have any written decision from the case worker yet. If I do that, I will be playing her game, I will be arrested."

"It was ordered in the last hearing that you have standard and not supervised visitations. That means you do have access to your children any time you want to. You do not need any caseworker to approve it. You also do not need any CPS to be around from this time forward. The new orders say also that it is your right to have them for the whole month of July since they are on summer break. You need to come to the office, sign some papers, and get court documents that will protect you."

"Thanks, I did not know the court already ordered standard visitations," I said.

On July 5, 2010, I arrived at Nwokoye's law office in Arlington and sat on the waiting area couch. She was very beautiful in red. The short red Sunday dress she had on fit the black sandals on her feet. One of things I always admire in a woman is the shape of her legs. When standing up, Nwokoye's legs had more than a simple shape. Not only were they well cut, they designed her height at her waist level. They were given to her at right moment to make her a well set-up woman. God designed her beautifully. *Michaelangelo did not have anything to do with that,* I thought, looking at her again. We sat inside the hall office, on the left side of her working room. I signed the court orders she handed me.

"Did you talk to your ex today?" Nwokoye asked while giving me copies of the court-signed orders.

"Hell no, there is no way I would continue spending my time talking to a person whose main job is to see me hurting. I stopped answering her calls since yesterday night," I said.

"What happened?"

"Well, it was late night two days ago, at exactly three minutes before midnight. She said that by the time this conversation ends, it will be July 3. It will be my birthday and she had a gift for me. Her wish will be to change the ways we were going with things, mostly with the child custody battle. She will go to the office of the attorney general to stop child support. She will also ask them to stop collecting the rest of back child support. This will be a gift for my birthday. She will do that in one condition. She suggested that we get back, get married, and raise our children together. I answered and said to her that if we ever stay, you and I, the only remaining people in this world, and God comes down to keep us alive as His last humankind on tracks to recreate His humanity, I will stab Him before he says another word. And if He becomes adamant and obliges me to be touching you so that we can continue His work of multiplying and filling the earth, I will make sure that He is dead before suggesting again some other unintelligent idea. I dryly answered her."

"What did she say?" Violet Nwokoye asked.

"She threatened me and said that she will then be moving out from Texas. She will take both girls with her if I do not change my mind. If asked, she will tell the judge that she is running from me because I put salt in her car fuel tank. I hung up and went back to sleep."

Nwokoye listened carefully and wrote something down.

"You know she cannot take the children out of Texas, right?" she asked.

"That is why I did not respond. She wanted me to fight around the children."

"Talking about the children and this was the reason I asked you if you do talk to her, do you know that she took Tabô to a psychiatric hospital. She declared her crazy. She knew exactly what to say, and the doctor believed her. Your daughter is on medications now. The mother put her there so she can collect an extra check from the government. Most stupid mothers do so to collect advantages. You will have a zombie for a daughter because of that kind of medicine prescribed to her. If she continues taking them, she will be a super-active and problematic child while the mother is receiving government money."

"That is also the reason she still wants both kids kept in daycare after school. Now when did she take her there because both girls are back with me? I picked them up from the street, literally, with the help of Officer Jimenez, when they were trespassing at Alameda Apartment? How does she do that and when? That woman is something. She is too much for me."

"I understand your frustrations because they passed the age of being still in daycare. She wants them there to justify a point and to continue receiving advantages. I prepared another order to stop all these, but Bourland and I are still having a little problem agreeing with the attorney general on the understanding of some terms. When we agree, she will forward the issue to the judge to give directives on what Sheebah wants. I will thank Ms. Bourland when she reaches that deal even if she said that 'thanks aren't due yet' the last time I talked to her. Sheebah had to sign her part of the deal. She has the affidavit already, but her lawyer cannot force her to sign it. Pressure is inappropriate. While I am dealing with that, I believe you received the invoice I sent you on the balance on your case. That will have to be taken care of to completely finalize it. I am expecting you to do your part in this matter," Nwokoye answered.

"Oh yeah, I brought you a check of $500. Thank you for reminding me. You said that if I have a question about any bill to feel free to openly ask. I just paid $600 on April 28, 2010. You said it was for the preparation of documents. Before that, I paid $400 you said was for final order. Why do I still have to pay $300 every month? That is not in the contract," I said.

"This check of $500 is really needed. To answer to your question, I filed papers with the court, the CPS, and the attorney general. Remember what was written in the contract: the rate is $200 for the attorney and $80 per hour legal fee. When you signed, you also agreed to pay the total value of extra time and new petitions. $300 is my retainer fee. You need to be sending that amount by mail starting August. Talking about starting, Ms. Bourland asked me to tell you to back off just a bit and not be so harassing and improper with the mother of your kids. I think she is right because it would help. As it was ordered, the communication between you and Sheebah must be made by texting. She said that your messages to her are always demeaning or threatening. She said that you have to knock that off, to be neutral, and not try to re-hash everything with her. She asked me to pass this along, and I am passing this along," Violet said.

"Now, Violet, that is crazy. I don't call or text that woman. That is how much I hate her. Actually, she is the one who calls and texts. Now I will hate her even more for putting Tabô on medications. I will have a word with her this time."

CHAPTER 43

YOU ARE NOT
A MOTHER

"I'm working on the access here. If you want to go fast, go alone, but if you want to go far, find you some playmates, as we say it in Nigeria. I am your playmate. Now we are together, do not mess thing up for both of us. I did thank Bourland after she had told me that. I thanked her for all her efforts in this matter first and then I said to her that I will relay the information to my client, to you. I also reminded her that I will be looking forward to receiving the amended order from her. She showed me her concern about my dad who is sick in Nigeria. Did you know that I am going back home to Nigeria?"

"No, ma'am, I did not know that you are going home. Sorry about your dad," I said.

"I appreciate that very much. Do you really have your kids with you? When I spoke to her, she gave me the impression that the kids live with their mother. They have a place of their own and her client does not sleep in the car, neither do the other kids."

"Like I said, that is crazy. I have them with me. Officer Jimenez of Hurst Police Department will confirm what I am telling you. I also have bunch of pictures, right here, taken with them in my apartment dated yesterday, July 4, on the Independence Day. I took them to watch fireworks in Arlington. Why don't you stop by my house unannounced to see them?" I said to her.

She looked at me and smiled. That grin made her more significant. If I did not see, in her eyes, how important she was for my fight, I would have asked her, on the spot, if I could take her out, go, and drink a glass of margaritas together.

"That is the job of La Casa. They will be there. Your case that you hired me for is almost completed. Besides Ms. Bourland and Sheebah, the holdup is to have other attorneys sign the order so that I can take it to the judge for her signature. I however did not check up on the status because for a while, you ignored the bill I sent you. I ceased the work, but now that I have a portion of the money, I will start back. I will need the rest to be paid before the conclusion. I will get back with you by Friday to let you know what the status would be since I will start working on it today. I will need some time to get to everybody. On the issues you and Bourland just raised about text messages, I will not be able to do anything with that right now until this first step is concluded. Remember, I told you that we will win this case. We will win it, not by using evidence, but by setting the other party up, as they have been doing it to you. All evidence we have, evidence that Kathy Ehmann Clardy introduced, are not good anymore. Bourland had been using the law of evidence on them and against us. They have shut us up, and new evidence are not really that good. They are coming from the old ones and I don't want to solely depend on them. We will win by setting them up, as they have been doing it to you. I am good in the game of jujitsu. We will use their own forces to pin them down, and they won't even see it coming. If you retain me for the second part of this fight, I will go back to court for modification of the suit. It is only after that that I will be able to file and yet another petition. This one will be concluded, not by jury as you requested it but by the judge. Once concluded by the judge, it cannot be reopened because there has been a trial. And a new trial is all that you will get. If you want an appeal to the appeal court, I don't do that kind of work. You will have to contact another attorney for that. By the way, I need the class certificates you said you have. I did not get any response from my previous mail. I need to receive those in my office by tomorrow to enable me take care of things I need to take care of," Nwokoye responded.

"That will be done," I answered. I thanked Nwokoye one more time and stood up.

Before stepping out, I told Nwokoye that for constantly lying on her income taxes 1040 EZ form, Sheebah was audited. For eight years in a row, she had been fraudulently claiming both girls and receiving about $5,000 every year in income tax returns. The IRS wants her to show school, hospital, and lease documents, including addresses where the kids lived with her. She can't lie to them of being the sole provider anymore. I know this story from Suzy Dale, her accomplice. She is kind of scared now since Sheebah had been using her street address. She feels exposed. I think we can use her as a witness.

"Send that as proof to IRS. Tell them that you never went back to Africa as she had been claiming. Include all documents pertaining to that matter, proving that you always have kids. Talking about the kids, did you stop going to visitations because I received a mail that said that your use of the visitation center was terminated effective immediately. The letter was written by Kay Rifkin of the Tarrant County Domestic Relations Office?" Nwokoye asked.

"They did not cancel, it was I who…"

"They did cancel. It is the policy of family court services to cancel visitation privileges when there have been excessive cancellations. If you wish to have your visitations through the visitation center reinstated, you will require a court order to do so."

"I don't want any court order. There never was any excessive cancellation. I had my kids, except moments when she goes and rent an apartment where you pay $1 for the first month and accept to pay the full amount at the end of the next month. Just the way she just did at Manchester Apartment, at 825 Norwood Drive, in Hurst when they had that promotion. The apartment her lawyer is calling a place of their own and had an impression that kids live with her. Well, up to Alma Campos, the manager, she did not pay and she just got evicted again. Those are the moments she let people visit and told them she got my kids. I have been having them. I talked to Hallmark, Kay Rifkin's supervisor, about it. I said to her that the purpose of me going to the family court supervised visitations was to see them. Since they live with me, in my house, I don't want to be taking them at Tarrant Visitation Center just to see Sheebah have all the glory. I just don't see the need of playing Sheebah's game," I said.

"Actually, you just got played. She just set you up again," Nwokoye said.

"How? Kay Rifkin agreed with me. I was losing the court time. I was also taking someone else's place."

"Oh yeah, like I said, you just got played. They made you be in contempt of the court direct order."

"I just can't let her get credit for the children she doesn't have," I answered.

"Oh, I was about to forget, the opposing counsel wants you to go and get your children's glasses replaced at Walmart since the old ones are already broken. Walmart is willing to replace them for free," Violet Nwokoye said.

"I have already done that. In order for them to watch fireworks yesterday July 4, I have to have both prescriptions replaced. Tabô's glasses were already expired before being broken. Loylla's vision was at worse point. I took both girls at Walmart and made it done. And no, it was not for free. I had to pay. Loylla cost me $45 for eye exams, $16 for dilation, $75 for frame, and $370 for eye lens. Tabô cost me $45 for eye exams, $16 for dilation, $120 for frame, and $430 eye lens. Here are all receipts. This is how much both prescription glasses cost me every year when I take them there. Nothing is free, even the replacements. By the way, my daughters wear transition glasses. Etna Insurance only covers a small portion of that medical prescription. The January 25, 2010, court report says that each parent shall pay 50 percent of the non-covered medical and prescription, within ten days of the notice of the bill. Why did the court never force Sheebah to pay her half?"

"She never paid, ever?" Nwokoye asked

"Never ever, and this was not the first time either. Kattaya Williams broke both her big sisters' glasses on March 10, 2010. I bought them new ones. Sheebah never paid her share of the bill. Tabô lost her pair on the night of April 24 when they went playing outside in the parking lot. We went looking for them, but we couldn't find them. At the end, I replaced them. Sheebah did not pay her half. On June 25 in the mall, Kattaya twisted and forcefully scratched Loylla's new glasses. Since she was not able to see, the medical technician decided to replace them. Sheebah did not participate. Now, this is the kicker. Every time I pay, she is the first to go at Walmart to pick them up without my knowledge so she can tell lies around them to make herself proud. She even changed my phone number in the file to hers the last time she was there. She wanted to be directly called when ready."

This was not the first time I replaced my daughters' glasses. The mother never participated. This time, it should have been her turn to do so. That was what she promised to the judge the last time we were in. She first said she did not have the necessary money. The judge then ordered me to give her my children Etna Insurance cards and support the co-pay. I gave to her on spot. She ordered her to cause kids glasses replaced and to show receipts the next time she will show up in court. That next time was actually on October 8, 2009, the day I showed up without a lawyer and lost that appeal. When the January 25, 2010, final court date arrived, the glasses were still not done. The reason the glasses were not bought, she said, was because both insurance cards were under my name. Walmart did not let her use them. That was just another excuse since both cards were given to her to be used for the medical needs of both kids. She claimed they were not good so she can continue receiving Medicare advantages and have child support increased to $60 more.

"I know you begged the judge to ask Sheebah to give those cards back to you, so you can take your daughters at Walmart yourself and she said no," Nwokoye reminded me.

"Yes, and I begged her more. I asked her to give me two officers to help me take both kids at Walmart to have their glasses done, she still did not move. You read the report, it doesn't say that I begged for the sake of my daughters on January 25, 2010. It says, 'Father and mother are ordered to meet at Walmart. Father shall cause an ophthalmologic eye exams at father's sole cost and expense, and it is ordered that father shall pay 100 percent of the costs of the lens.' That is exactly what I always do. That what said to the judge when I was begging her. I said I pay 100 percent of all costs. So I was not ordered, I begged for it."

I thanked Nwokoye one last time as I was stepping out. Once outside, I dialed Sheebah's number. I talked to her about her putting Tabô on strong medicines. Her answer was "Doctor signed the prescription. Do what you do best, call the police. You cannot prove anything anyway. You are just trying to hurt everybody, your daughter included. That is why you are always sick. You need Jesus, you need to come to God, when you do, you will see changes. You lost in the court. You can't say a thing anymore. Go away."

"George Forman said once that everyone has a plan until they start punching him in the mouth. What you are holding on are temporary orders. That is what the court put in place. It is not over yet. I won't rest till I prove to them that you are a liar. You will be exposed. You don't love your daughters. What you are showing to them is hate. What you are doing to them is actually destroying them. In case you don't know, Tabô is mad at you. As you know it, she was selected to be a figurant in Hanna Montana's play. You pick both girls from school and took them to Arlington on Friday afternoon because you did not want her to go. You knew at this point that the promoter was expecting her to be in Dallas at Marriot Hotel. They had a one-day series of rehearsals in the morning of Sunday, June 6, 2010. You picked her up anyway. You told her that you loved her very much, if she is hired, you said, she will be away from you and you don't want her away from you. Is that love? You made her miss her appointment to shine. You also made her lose her opportunity to grow wings. Who knows what could have happened down the road. Because of you, I am now asking that question to myself. Because of you, Tabô is getting the worst of your stupidities, and I am wondering if anyone will be able to control her behavior in years to come," I explained.

Tabô was indeed getting out of order. She was out of control. Just the other day, she was at about twenty inches from the television. Being that close, she was blocking her little sister to watch the same program. I said to her that this wouldn't have been happening if she had her glasses on. She talked back. At the end of that conversation, she called me stupid. I sent her to her room, but instead of obeying, she hit the front door and ran outside. Then she called me from her mother, she was crying. She said, "Papa, I am okay, but Washington hit me for nothing. Mom doesn't want me to tell you that."

She didn't even finish talking to me, Sheebah knocked at my front door.

"Why was she beaten?" I asked.

"I am tired of Tabô. She keeps creating problems for me. I don't want her there, at my boyfriend's place anymore. Please do not call the police. I have a warrant. You are a good man. I am not trying to hurt you. I am scared, that is all. Look at my situation, if you win, you will put me on child support. If you win, I will end up in jail," she said, talking almost to herself.

"So it is appropriate for you to steal money from me because I am a good man?" I asked.

"That is why I am begging you not to call the police on Washington. I am ready to negotiate. I do not want to go to court anymore," she said.

"Yeah, right. I let you slide this time. Do not think you are controlling everybody. You are only hurting your own children. You even stopped them to attend the summer break activities. To avoid both girls spending this time outside, Officer D' Israeli planned to have them in the basketball camp, and I paid for it. I also bought gears for that occasion. What did you do, one day before the camp starts, as usual, you showed up and took both girls. You then left a message in my phone for me to go and get reimbursed. Officer D' Israeli was confused for your lack of maturity. What type of mother are you?" I asked.

She turned around and left without proposing another of her idiocies. As she was leaving, I called her home number. Washington picked it up. I threatened to badly hurt him if he ever touches any of my children's hair again. I hung up before he answered. Tabô came back and entered the house. She refused to apologize. And she showed it.

"My mom's lawyer told us that only Mom can tell us what to do, not you," she said.

"That is your mother talking, not you. You are not that crazy to challenge me. Now go to bed."

"She also said that I have rights in this house. I will go to bed when I will go to bed. If you force me, I will call the police."

That was the most defiant Tabô I have ever seen and the most insubordinate child I have ever heard. I immediately stood up, ready to shut off the mouth that was spitting her mother's idiocies with a blow, but I had to think twice. It was not her. My daughter was not dangerously rebellious as she was appearing to my eyes, her mother was to blame. She was teaching her how to disrespectfully behave.

"Actually calling the police is a good idea. Go ahead, they will tell you that you only have three rights in this house. The right to be fed, the right to have a roof on your head, and the right to have clothes on your skin, that is all. After telling you so, as they leave, you will be going with them. I will not let you in after calling them on me. Just ask Muntumpe, she will tell you why she was sent to Connecticut," I said.

After that heated conversation, I cut off the light and sent her to bed. It was at this moment that Sheebah sent a text message. She wanted me to meet her in her friend's place to talk about Tabô.

I did not answer. She sent another one and said, "Why can we get back together?"

"I don't feel like talking to you, you are constantly hurting me," I answered.

"You just don't see it. Maybe I am doing so because I still want you. I am here for you," she said.

"There is no way in the world you can be there for me now. Where was I when you were fucking my friends? Where did you put me then?"

"That was then, it is in the past. I am here for you now. Why can't we still make it? Actually, I am outside. Can I come in and use the bathroom?" she texted.

"You have issues. Go to Kroger, they have bigger restrooms," I texted back.

"In that case, give my kids back. I don't want them around Muntumpe, your daughter, anymore. She is telling you not to be with me. You will see I will punish you. I will increase your child support payment," she texted.

"It is increased already, go away," I said to her.

Sheebah called the office of the attorney general. She complained about the amount of money she was receiving. I did not know how she got my pay stub, but she found a way to send it to them. She chose the one that showed more earnings. That is to say that I do make more money than the amount I claimed to be making. Sheebah did not forget that I was a truck driver. She knew that I did not work the same amount of time every week. What I gave the court was the average of what I did that time, an average of five days a week and the average they did asked. What she gave them was a check stub that showed seven days of work. From that, the attorney general increased my child support to $60 more. That was $60 on the top of the $60 that I was ordered to pay by the judge for insurance despite the fact that she had my daughters' Etna insurance cards. This was her plan all along. She wanted to bring me to her knees so I can beg. I did not want to be her slave. So I sent her to hell.

"I said to you that the fight is not over yet. I said to you that George Forman, heavyweight boxing champion, said that they all have a plan until I start punching them in the mouth. Keep on increasing whatever you want. The sun will rise tomorrow, and when it does, the tables will be turned over."

"I did not increase a thing. I did not talk to the office of the attorney general," she replied with a voice that was telling me all.

"The same office of attorney general you did not talk to gave me an appointment for this next Friday. They want me to bring the new orders for April 6, 2010, and all my last month's pay stubs so I can be able to discuss that increased amount of money you just forced upon me. See, it not over yet. It is not over yet, Sheebah. Very soon, I will make you drink from the same cup, and your big mouth will taste your own bitter wine. For now, I will continue paying. I will pay," I texted back and shut off my phone.

I think Muntumpe did print that pay stub with more earnings from my computer and gave it to her. She had been working against me for a while now. I never understood what I have done to her and why she hated me that much. She should have been spending that energy to see in me a man that made a nest to protect her against all open weather. She should have been recognizing that what I have done for her was certainly a challenge. Undoubtedly, it was my duty, but I had to challenge all inclemecies of four-season weather to unstoppably protect her against freezing and unstoppably confine her against the summer heat. I grew her wings and kept her alive. I nurtured her with great love. And what was coming out of that supreme sacrifice was treachery on treachery.

The truth was that at that point, I was not able to pay anything to anyone anymore. I was not even capable of feeding myself. I had kids; she was receiving child support from me. She was using that money for drugs and beer while I was providing for them. I told my story to Joachim Lopez, a Mexican friend at work. He said he knew a place where I can work without using my social security card; it was his friend's restaurant. He doesn't ask for work permit or for any green card. This place, he said, is where his people from Mexico work without papers and make just enough money to send back to their families. Therefore, I can work there, and the government won't know that I am working. I applied. I was the only black in that taco restaurant bar. The work was not easy. I had to close the club, which means I had to clean everything, from dishes to the floor. My under table money was the salary of undocumented immigrants. It was $120 cash per week. That was $3 per hour, the amount paid to people living illegally in the United States. With that slave wage, I still had a hard time to pay the cost of living while on child support. I did not have a choice. I stayed, but the restaurant job did not give me a break I expected; it was dirty and all the time tiring. The work started at eleven in the afternoon and ended up at four thirty in the morning. I only had thirty minutes of sleepy driving before reaching my Swift Truck at Pepsi. The money was not even enough to buy groceries for my kids.

"Do not worry about groceries, come early tomorrow, we will go to Walmart," said Rafina Maria, one of the undocumented women.

"You will buy me groceries at Walmart?" I asked.

"Hell no, we will go and pick groceries at Walmart from inside the Dumpster."

"In the trash? You eat from the trash?" I asked.

"We do not eat from the trash. We take home the food wasted by the white man. With the money saved, we buy beer. Come with us, it is fresh and not expired food."

"And why do they put it in Dumpster then if it is not expired?" I asked.

"The federal law says that cooked food and groceries must be disposed of past seven in afternoon. If they sell it, the government will collect on them," Rafina Maria explained.

PART IX

THE BALL CHANGES HANDS

CHAPTER 44

THERE ARE REASONS TO BELIEVE

At the moment Rafina Maria explained that the government will collect money on these stores if they ever sold definite foods after a certain time, the word "collect" clicked in my head with IRS. I remembered what Nwokoye said. She advised me to send proof to the Internal Revenue Services to show that from 2003 forward, I was living in United States as Assylee. I never went back home and left her raising children by herself, as she claimed. Nwokoye counseled me also to send all documents pertaining to that matter and evidence confirming that I always had both kids with me from the second she left.

I sat down and wrote the following letter to the IRS.

From: Kasalobi
To: Internal Revenue Service Po Box 2986
Austin Tx 78768-2986
To whom it may concern
On your decision letter 525, please find included:

I. An October 31, 2008, letter written and signed by Julie Moreno, the community manager of Glen Rose Apartments. She states in it that Kasalobi is the head of household. He leaves in the apartment 181 at 787 E. Pecan Street in Hurst, Texas, and lives with all his children including Tabô and Loylla. Mr. Kasalobi had been our resident since 2003 to today's date. Included are copies of lease agreements with Glenn Rose that cover the period from January 2003 to December 2009. Mr. Sheebah never left with them or in this complex.

II. A two-page Chase Bank statement. These statements contain a list of cashed checks used for the lease payment from November 2004 to today's date. They clearly show who had been paying the rent at Glen Rose during the questioned period. They bear only my signature and the amount paid. Please find all my children's names written all over them. These documents prove also that Tabô and Loylla, my youngest children, never lived with Sheebah, their mother.

III. A letter from Bill Clayton, Reliant Energy vice president and customer care. This letter proves that the electricity account # 7118522-7 is connected under Kasalobi's name at 787 E. Pecan Street # 181 since December 23, 2008, through today. I have been paying by check.

IV. A report of payment history from Charter communication. You can confirm it on the account # 8246 10 029 0152649. You will find that I was the only person paying this bill. I have been paying it with my JPMorgan Chase Bank credit card.

Therefore, I disagree with the statements sent to you by Sheebah concerning the custody my children. She did so to keep claiming them in federal tax return, as she had been fraudulently doing since 2003. Sheebah never had custody of any of my children.

Sincerely,

Kasalobi.

On my way to Walmart, I dropped that letter in the mailbox. Around seven in the afternoon, we met at the crossroads of Ester and 183 in Irving with Rafina Maria and her group. We were not the only people up there. Some of us were up the hill in the StarPlex Box Office theater parking lot. When the store service exit door opened, everyone got out from their cars. The lady forklift driver showed some human kindness. It was nice of her not to dump the palette inside the opened blue container. She put it down and went back inside. We all approached without hesitation. I picked all kinds of unwrapped fresh food. I scraped cooked and raw meat together and collected vegetables and fruits. The forklift lady came back out with another palette. She deposited it near the next container. The first one had still uncollected provisions. She picked it up from the floor and dumped it in the Dumpster. That new palette had all kinds of breads and cakes. I did not eat carbohydrates, but I collected some anyway. She repeated the same maneuvers four times because the store had four blue bins out there for waste food. After everyone had picked good food, she locked the bins and went inside. The reason Walmart management was depositing food on the ground was not to help the neediest, it was to follow the Federal Department of Agriculture guidelines since it was against the law to directly hand the unsold food to anyone. They did not want to be sued for food poisoning or for something near to that. So they put it on the ground. If Walmart store bins did not have presentable food, I went pleading my case at the food bank. I visited Kroger and Target. I also went to the church located at Central, behind Pipeline. This was how I got food for that day. This was how I continued collecting rejected and unsold food to feed myself. I did not go hungry for a while.

I had my food, my kids had theirs. Their food was coming directly from inside the store. Loylla was in charge of my credit card. She bought their grocery and the ready to be consumed food with it. Both girls preferred what I called junk food; they did not like the way I put my kitchen together. As a matter of principle, I made sure that they did not eat what I was bringing from the street. My street food was all the time hidden in the back of the closet or under my bed. I cooked what I ate most of the time. They liked the oven and the microwave.

I continued working for a slave wage at the taco place and for $3 per hour pay under the table. Then I heard a strange story on the radio. I don't remember which one. They were talking about this assistant manager of a restaurant in Dallas. When she came at work that early morning, she found all lights off. She entered and cut everything on from the switch boards. She heard at that moment a short, suffocating, and smothered scream followed with a big *woof*, as if a bag of some weight just got dropped down. It was in fact the electrician tumbling from the ladder. The man was working on some kind of electrical wire problems. He was electrocuted and killed on the spot. Even if it was an accident, the assistant manager was arrested for negligence. She did not read the memo sent to her earlier on, telling her that the electrical current will be cut off all night for maintenance. She lost her brand-new car and she almost lost her house while she was in jail. When she came out, no one wanted to hire her because of what has happened. So she hit the street, not to prostitute herself but to become a beggar. She spent her days at different corners of the city streets. Since she was a good-looking and well-dressed woman, she made about $100 a day. She did not squander it on drugs, throw away on cigarettes, or misuse it buying beer. She did not waste a penny on stupidities. She paid off her house, bought her a new car, and put herself back in school. She stopped begging only when she found a job as a lawyer after graduating. She became a lawyer because she confined herself within the walls she was building for herself and succeeded.

That story inspired me. The restaurant job with its chicken change was not mine to do. I decided to fight the assistant manager's fight. I hit the street to beg. I chose the city of Plano, not because I was trying to hide from the Congolese, my people, but because Plano was entirely a commercial city. Lots of late model and expensive cars were being cruised around. To make myself understood and well explain my story, I dressed well, just like the assistant manager. I made sure that I had nice shoes. I wore Stacy Adam, Giorgio Brutini, Aston Grey, or Borelli under my feet. Every time I was out there, I had to have a three-piece clothing on me, including expensive pants, a chosen vest, and a well-dressing shirt to match each one of my shoes. My sign said, "Child Support Is Killing Me," so that no police could accuse me of panhandling. I was a signer and was not asking for money per se. I stooped on my feet for five hours or as long as the sun was still in the sky. It did not matter to me if I happened to be recognized. Lots of corners took me seriously, others received me with smile. People had jokes; they gave me bags of condoms. My favorite place to beg for money was West Campbell Road and Central Expressway. My best spot was Arapaho Road across Dallas Parkway. I made about $100 a day in average, more or less. It was this way that I kept myself alive, took care of child support, and easily paid Nwokoye's $300 retainer a month. I asked for money on the street.

Nwokoye continued working on my case with my help most of the time. She advised me that day that with CPS, even if it is the same system everywhere, if you want things to bring about quick results, do not be contacting the same people every time around. CPS agents have different channels to reach their goals. So I took my story to the city of Watauga. I talked to Amber Young. She was a CPS draftee, still in training. Rookies always go by the book, they said. This was the reason I trusted her. I needed another investigation that would help me break through.

Amber Young thanked me for previously submitting the Internet report in reference to what was happening and to the injustice I endured in the hands of those who were supposed to protect my children. To ensure confidentiality, she asked me not to name my children in any report anymore. She recommended me to always use their initials in future correspondences. Those initials will be their identification numbers that will be associated with the Internet report. The information I gave, she said, was entered into the database and forwarded to the main office.

"When did Tabô get beaten?" Amber asked.

"It happened the day before yesterday. It was Monday, August 16, 2010, in the afternoon. She crossed Pecan Street to go and visit with her mother. Oscar hit her with a closed fist because she did not knock the front door before coming in. Tabô took the phone outside to let me know what was going on. Oscar Washington chased her. When he reached her, he held her on the ground with both his hands around her neck. He then lifted her and pushed her against a parked car. Tabô dropped the phone. He took it. He still hit her head on the ground. He pushed her so hard on the ground, she bled through her nose, scratched her knees, and got badly bruised all over her fragile body."

"If she was that badly bruised, the school may have noticed something."

"Ms. Swayze, the Bellaire Elementary social worker lady did. She made a report in which she talked about 'numerous and visible bruises left on Tabô's turned-blue body.' She also talked about the big black bruise that was left on her upper left arm. She reported everything to her authorities who sent their reports to CPS. CPS never reacted. They have agents like Jenita Talley who always intimidated me and always threatened to sue me for harassment every time I complained about my two girls. Sheebah is protected by CPS through people like Tracy Burkhart," I answered.

"Did you talk to your lawyer already?" she asked.

"Yes, ma'am. I called her at her personal phone. She asked me to call her office and make an appointment to meet and conference about it on Friday. I never placed that call. I did not see the need since I explained everything already. Her office called me later the next day to remind me. They also had some papers for me to sign. I think it was a Motion for Judicial Review. They wanted me there at the end of that same day. I got upset and complained over the phone."

"Why is that you got upset for?"

"Nwokoye's office does that all the time. They do not ask you the best time to come in, they just tell you to show up without warning. That pissed me off. I went there, did not have time to read everything, took the motion with me, and left the office. I then forgot to return it back. She e-mailed me and said that I have made it impossible, at that point, for her to do her job. I was putting her in a difficult position with other parties. She had already told them that she filed the motion and will send it to them. Because I did not return the paper, she thought that I wanted her out of the case," I answered.

I explained what was happening to Amber Young. I said that my daughters Tabô and Loylla are consistently been beaten by Oscar Washington every time they go visit their mother. This man had been mistreating them, seriously slapping them on their heads, and causing them to have headaches. Oscar had been doing so while Sheebah is standing by, witnessing these abuses, and doing nothing. She never tried to stop any of his assaults. As matter of fact, she was approving of it. She said once that Tabô deserved it because she said a curse word. That curse word was "damned it." "Damned" is not a curse word. Damned is in the Bible. Therefore, it was not fair to receive such a beating from saying it. The woman is an active participant in her own children's pain. My daughters are beaten using closed fists. They are beaten with the belt. They are beaten for telling me what they are going through. They are threatened to be beaten again if they ever say anything against their mother's boyfriend. My daughters are coached not to say a thing, they are even scared to have the police involved. Sheebah's three other daughters are also beaten daily. CPS knows the excruciating agony they are going through. They are going to be killed under the Child Protective Services watch. When that happens, CPS, as they are known to doing, will engage their best specialists to investigate. They will also send their expensive lawyers to defend a dead child. That is what they do the best. A little girl called Zahra Baker was killed. Instead of them doing something about her throbbing while she was still alive and they knew everything about it, they waited till she was dead to investigate her death. They always wait till a child disappears or something big happens to show up. After many physical warnings, Zahra Baker disappeared first. They then spent lot of money and time trying to find her, and they did. When they did, she was already dead, cut in different pieces. Her body parts were all over, purposely placed in different places for people to see. CPS knew what Zahra Baker was going through. They spent the precious time doing politics and waited instead of protecting her.

"This is exactly what is about to happened to my daughters. CPS knows what they are going through, yet they are closing their eyes. I am accusing them for not doing anything and for still not doing a thing. They know what could arrive," I said to Amber Young.

"Well, the first thing I will do with your case is to go and interview both kids in school, first thing in the morning. Sheebah won't continue having everybody's hands tied behind their backs. She cannot be getting away with lot of things all the time. The second thing I would do is to intelligently talk to her inside her apartment and to interview the kids again in her presence. I will then take pictures of bruises and document the assault," Amber Young said.

She called me after her investigation, thanked me on behalf of CPS for sharing my concerns about my children. She said she volunteered to investigate and completed her investigations. All alleged abuses and neglects, involving not only my children but other kids living with Sheebah, did occur. She made her report to the Department of Family and Protective Services in which she stated that with a preponderance of the evidence supports she collected, there are reasons to believe about their medical neglect by their mother. There are reasons to believe about their physical abuse by Oscar Washington, the mother's boyfriend. There are reasons to believe about injury to a child by Oscar Washington. She asked the Department of Family and Protective Services for assessment and services to my family. The next step, she wrote in her report, was to remove the rest of children from Sheebah's home.

I took the report and ran with it to Arlington. I gave it to Nwokoye. She smiled. I loved that smile on her lips. Nwokoye told me that that report was one of the things she was waiting for to break through my case.

"To enable me to take care of this case, I need the class certificates you said you have. I sent you two mails about it. I did not get any response from you. Please bring them tomorrow," she asked.

"I am sorry, ma'am, my blood sugar was so high. I was under medication. I couldn't answer your first mail on time, but I did send four certificates already. I was sure you have already received them," I answered while my eyes were scanning her beautiful body.

"Not yet. After all is said, you were supposed to legally have your kids on July for summer break, as it was decided and written in new orders. It did not happen that way. It still needs to be done the legal way in case something happens. I will also need to get the judge sign this child support issues. Any other issue can be brought after. This order is not ready yet, but it will be finalized by Friday.

It has taken me three hundred hours to complete it. I am still working on it because most family lawyers are in conference this week. I will be out of town myself for another conference this same week, however when Sheebah's attorney responds to the petition, I will be setting it for a hearing. I will let you know the exact date of hearing when I get back in town. As for this petition, it is concluded, believe me. You will hear from me next week. Thanks for this CPS report," Nwokoye said.

Days later, I received a mail from Diana H. Tijerina, the paralegal for Nwokoye. She was advising me that a hearing was set for November 17, 2010, at 1:30 p.m. on the original petition for bill of review. I did not have a question to ask about it. The presence of the woman was making me lose control. At this point, the crush I had for her was making me confused. I was this close to telling her that every time I was in her law firm, I paid more attention to her beauty well connected to her body and more consideration to her than to what she was telling me about my case. My crush for her was my weakness; it did have a comparison, but I had to keep it professional, which was becoming harder. I have been avoiding telling her that. I met her anyway for the bill of review conference.

"Yes, I got a letter from Ms. Meda on the tenth. Her client will be forgiving about a total of $12,000 more. The calculations are all so confusing for me to tell exactly what the exact amount will be. I will have Ms. Diana H. Tijerina print the letter for you," Nwokoye explained.

Ms. Meda Bourland was playing a different game, she said. She had drafted a letter with instructions from Sheebah on the said amount. This was not what we decided on the retro forgiveness. The new order had to relate back to the January 29, 2010, written order from January 25 judge's decision since that was the last order of record. The child support was directly withheld then. The interest for 2010 should have been reduced as well in its overall. Bourland said she needed to take a final drafted letter from Sheebah, and together, they will get the reduction order from Diane Conine. I know this is a game from Bourland herself. Sheebah did not have anything to say about it. She did not decide this. Bourland also said she will get back to me with that executed letter and that order of reduction.

"That is so confusing, but I do have an upper hand. I will play her game to the last minute and my uppercut will knock them down, both of them, together. For now, I need to make an important call to the counselor. I have to recommend Tabô. She needs help. I just got back into the country. I told you I was going to be gone for a while to take care of my dad. I will not resume work fully until next week as I am not physically strong to do so at the moment," Nwokoye said.

"Thanks. As I said it before, I need a trial, not a negotiation," I said.

"I heard you the first time. The tree that cannot bend will fracture with the force of the wind, as it is said in Africa. We will win. You can decide after that moment on how you wish for us to proceed for the second part of this fight, if you want me to stay on this case or if you want to hire another attorney. The second part will be rounding up on giving back your child support money," she said.

CHAPTER 45

WARRANT FOR PHYSICAL CUSTODY

Days went by. I found a phone message that said that Nwokoye's paralegal office has been looking for me. She wanted to discuss the developing situation in my case and the letter Bourland has sent to my lawyer. The number they had in the file had been saying that I was not available. I had Metro PCS and my job was driving. I moved a lot inside my truck. This company was known of losing signal every time their customer was out of town or just far from their rooming area. That was a fact. So Nwokoye's office left a message for me to call back. I did not call, but I sent an e-mail in which I said that I will be in Arlington the same day, after work, around two in the afternoon. I stopped by the office without an appointment. Nwokoye was in the main office. She was delightfully ravishing as usual. The day was March 21, 2011.

"Do you still have the kids at your place?" she asked.

"Yes, ma'am. They are in school by now."

"Sheebah is currently in jail. She was incarcerated in Arlington since March 17, 2011. I just filed a motion in which I am requesting a warrant to physically take custody of both children and a motion to modify the order in suit affecting the parent-child relationship. I filed both of them today with the family court in Fort Worth," she explained.

I felt very good. The woman was protecting my rights. She was looking after me even when I did not ask her to. She said in the motion that currently, the children are in the possession of the mother. Sheebah should be served at that address. The children's present physical address is unknown. This court issued the child custody determination. It still retains continuing jurisdiction. The following proceeding, she said, has been commenced. It could affect the current proceeding, the motion to modify parent-child relationship. The court should issue a warrant to take physical custody of Tabô and Loylla because the mother, who has primary custody, is currently incarcerated in the Arlington. Her release date is unknown to the father. The father, the petitioner of this motion, is unaware of the children's present location or residence. Based on that, the father believes that his children are imminently likely to suffer serious physical harm. In that motion, she is asking the court to direct the law enforcement officers to take physical custody of the children immediately. She further asks the court to authorize law enforcement officials to enter private property and take physical custody of the children because a less intuitive and intrusive remedy would not be effective. The petitioner further asks the court to authorize law enforcement officials to make a forcible entry at any hour. He asks the court to provide the placement of the children with him pending final relief. He also asks the court to impose any necessary condition on the placement of the children to ensure the appearance of the children. She asked the court to oblige Sheebah to pay reasonable attorney's fees and expenses, then to grant the request for warrant to take physical custody of children.

After that conversation, Nwokoye then showed me the other letter Bourland sent regarding the retro forgiveness.

"She is mad. What I was saying, a simple letter to IRS, as I advised you, opens their eyes. After verification, they now know the truth. This is actually the second battle we are winning. The first was when Amber Young testified against your ex. The family court will know soon that she had been lying all along. The letter to the IRS made them nervous for now. At the end of the day, they will sign the motion. This is how you fight a custody battle. You use the

African lion technique to kill a water buffalo. The lion lies down with four feet in the air as a sign of submission, and the buffalo attacks head first, letting himself be open under the neck. The lion moves just a little and grabs the neck, and the game is over. It is called jujitsu, the game in which you use your adversary's own fight against him," she said.

The e-mail Nwokoye showed me reminded me of Judge Bronson of IV D Family Court when I was sent downstairs to be heard by him.

"What is the truth when it comes to your own children?" he asked me after I have said that what Sheebah was telling him was nothing but lies and what I was saying was the truth.

I inspired myself to the lack of answer thereof as written in a living tale of a greatest man in the history. He was asked about the truth by a sitting judge, a representative of the government just like Judge Bronson. The greatest man of them all did not want to answer. He knew what the truth was and what it stood for. He did not answer because he was aware of the fact that even after giving him explanations and telling him the whole definition of what it was, the government representative wouldn't have understood him. They were not emitting the same frequencies at that point, so why waste his energy. If I tried to explain myself to the judge Bronson that the truth about my children was the truth about them and the only way to know that truth was to know my children, the judge wouldn't have understood me. He wouldn't have because the truth goes up very slowly walking the stairs and a lie reaches its destination faster because it takes the elevator, as it was said by Koffi Olomide, the Congolese artist. There was a reason Judge Bronson asked me what was the truth when it came to my children. The established institutions, like CPS, were listening to a bunch of lies that came running toward them and reporting to the judge so he could decide against me. There was also a reason I did not answer; the truth was slow. I knew it will eventually swarm out. Meda Bourland was getting agitated. She knew her client was about to get the beating I was receiving, but with intense pain this time and on the top of unbearable headaches. So she wrote the following letter:

February 13, 2011 13:33:30
From: Ms Bourland mbourlandlaw@yahoo.com
Date: Sun, -0800 (PST)
To: Violet Nwokoye Violetnokoye@yahoo.com
Subject: Re: Kasalobi - Retro forgiveness letter

Hello, Violet, and happy late New Year to you. I apologize as it appears this e-mail did not go through earlier. Mr. Kasalobi decided to tell the IRS that my client is not the mother of her children, and again, he keeps asserting that the children live with him in spite of the social study and CPS findings. His claims are completely false. The IRS confirmed he made the report. And until she can spend the money to get all kinds of certified records for the IRS, she owes many thousands of dollars to them. Dealing with this has been a huge pain to both me and my client. His actions have not put her in a forgiving mood. I am certain this was motivated by some desire to get back at my client. Continuing to berate and harass her is not helping this situation, the children, or my client's disposition toward him. Needless to say, she will not sign any affidavit now.

Meda Bourland, Attorney at Law

The reason Judge Bronson asked me what was the truth when it came to my own children was because the government decision was already made. For him, as for the court officials, "children are better off with their mother." He refused to find the truth in open records and documents given to him as he wanted their mother to have them. On one hand, Bourland's e-mail showed that I knew what I was doing; I had the truth in me. On the other one, as once advised by Ricky Anderson, now that the IRS believed me, the time was up to my lawyer to provide the rest of evidences of my responsibility toward my children. Sheebah was in impossibility to prove whatever she had been saying about them simply because she never had them. Nwokoye then asked me if I brought with me my children's new school records, their registrations, their report cards, and new CPS records that I obtained from Dallas headquarters. She needed to take these documents to the judge to complete the new orders, as we discussed it in our last meeting. As long as Sheebah was in incarceration, she did not want her lawyer to find a reason to reset the hearing. She also asked me to scratch something down with the same guidelines, using my own handwriting. She wanted me to confirm what she said in her letter, as if it was me who was requesting a warrant to physically take custody of both children. I did just that.

Date: March 21, 2011
From: Kasalobi
To: Nwokoye Law Office.
Re: In the interest of Tabô and Loylla.
Ma'am,

I have reasons to believe that Tabô and Loylla are imminently likely to suffer serious physical harm because;

I. Since January 25, 2010, the day the judge's orders were rendered, Sheebah, their mother, leaves them alone and unsupervised after school. She doesn't hold a serious job, and when she does, she works late in the afternoon. She also goes to the club every weekend. At those times, all her kids, including Tabô and Loylla, stay dangerously unguarded and treacherously unattended. This was confirmed by Kithas & Associates, my private investigator. Included in this exhibit A is a copy of this investigation.

II. When the mother is home with them, Oscar, her boyfriend, uses closed fists to beat them up. Exhibit B shows both girls with bruises all over their bodies. One can see them on their legs, faces, and knees also. For having have said, "Damned it," Tabô was beaten with the belt. Pictures were also taken. These pictures show big red bruises on her low stomach, black circles on her upper leg, and light scratches on her neck. These girls don't come back home after being beaten; they are always kept inside and out of school. One of these days, the school notified Amber Young. Because they were badly bruised, Sheebah did not open her apartment door. Amber reported the incident. Included are two copies of the last CPS investigations she completed. Included also is the investigation made by D. Pace, of Hurst Police. Officer D. Pace couldn't do his investigation earlier because "he was not authorized, by the mother who he said 'has legal custody' to lift 'an eleven-year-old girl's clothes up.'" After being authorized by his supervisor, and with the help of a female officer, he finally discovered hidden bruises. He was still able to find bruises on Tabô's stomach and legs and light bruises on her neck two days after the abuse. Oscar Washington was taken to jail. When Tabô went back to school, Swayze, the Bell Elementary psychologist, took pictures of Tabô. One can still see bruises on her neck. These pictures are included in exhibit B.

I believe therefore that Tabô and Loylla are in immediate danger of serious physical harm because their mother is now in jail in Arlington. They are left home with Oscar. They are alone and in danger. Would you please request a Warrant to Take Physically Custody of a Child for me?

Sincerely,

Kasalobi

On March 22, Tuesday morning, the warrant to physically take custody of both children was on the judge's desk. Before signing, she called Arlington Jail. She was told that Bourland, Sheebah's lawyer, just bailed her out that same morning. Judge Wells did not sign the motion to attach to the warrant. It did not matter to Nwokoye at that moment; she set the temporary motion to modify the parent-child relationship for April 4 at 8:30 a.m. We actually met again in the court for the third hearing of the year on June 1, 2011. This time, it was for temporary order concerning Tabô and Loylla.

On that day, everyone appeared clean and well dressed, ready for battle. Paschal, from the office of the attorney general had a bigger group of people. CPS was there to hang me. That did not intimidate me; I had Violet Nwokoye at my left side. When she touched my right shoulder and I felt reassured, the judge was already presenting the court. I asked her what I should say if the judge ever asked me where both children are. She answered and said, "Bourland doesn't know who has both girls either, she things your ex has them and your ex won't say a thing to betray herself. Let's play their game."

"You know I am paying child support and still taking care of both children too, right?" I asked.

"I will address that question after my upper cut. Remember what I said to you, they won by setting you up, we will win by setting them up. It is not time yet. Bear with me here, my brother. Next time, do not interrupt the procedure. If you have a question, please write it down on the piece of the paper and complain later," she explained.

At Judge Wells's first question to know if everyone in the court was ready, we all answered individually that we were ready. Then the court examined the record and all written agreements. After hearing the first argument from Bourland and after seeing the first evidence from Nwokoye, my counsel, the judge declared that all necessary prerequisites of the law have been legally satisfied, that the court has jurisdiction of the case and of all parties. She ordered that for the safety and for the welfare of Tabô and Loylla and for their best interest, all orders previously entered and dated on January 29, 2010, orders that would not be changed by the present order, should remain in full force and effect.

At the end of that introduction, she said that Oscar Dave Washington, Sheebah's boyfriend, is ordered to not have any contact with Tabô or with Loylla. She specifically told Sheebah to make sure, from June 1, that she doesn't authorize him, not only to be five hundred feet closer to my daughters, but also to be in the same apartment complex with both of them at same time. She ordered that I should have possession of both children for summer time: from 2:00 p.m. to 5:00 p.m. starting June 4. I should have them overnight in July starting Saturday, July 2, from 2:00 p.m. through Sunday, July 3, at 6:00 p.m. Hurst Police should be notified and around for all weekend possessions of children: at drop and picking-up times. I should have access to them again pursuant to the standard possession order as detailed beginning July 4. The exchange point for children will be inside the Arlington Police Department Building located at 620 W. Division, at corner of Cooper and Division. The officer on duty should read the order and must be a witness to the exchange.

The judge ordered that each parent shall administer prescribed medications for each child while that child is in their possession. She ordered that each conservator shall comply with all terms and conditions of this standard possession order, which applies to all periods of possession occurring on and after the date the court signs the standard order. She ordered that the conservator shall have possession of the children at the time mutually agreed to in advance by the both parties. In absence of mutual agreement, it is ordered that the conservator shall have possession of the child under the specified terms set out in this standard possession orders. The judge went on and gave orders for holidays, vacations, thanksgivings, father's and mother's days. She even gave orders of even-numbered and odd-numbered years. She said that the duration of this order and the periods of possession ordered above apply to each child while the child is under the age of eighteen and not otherwise emancipated or until further order of the court. She ordered another social study to be filled with the court when completed. She said that the new social study should be prepared into the circumstance and condition in which children will be, and it should be done in the home of the conservator. The primary focus of the new social study, she said, was the custody access, the principal criterion for children and for governing conservatorship. The pre report conference date for that social study was set on Thursday August 25, 2011, for intake. She then ordered me to pay $300 by June 30. Sheebah fee, as usual, was waved.

Terresha D. Stevens was appointed as the amicus attorney to provide legal advices necessary to assist the court in protecting the best interests of both children. The judge ordered that I pay $150 per month to her, with first payment been due on June 15, 2011. She said that I had to pay on the fifteenth of every month until further order of the court. What killed me was when she said that "the mother's fee shall be determined at a later date and balanced against any average I may owe."

I directly interrupted the court right there. I refused to pay any money to anyone. I said, "The court hired her, the court pays her. Just how much money does this court think I make every month?"

"Counsel, advise your client to conduct himself in orderly manner," the judge advised.

"I told you not to interrupt. I will argue this case later on." Nwokoye said.

The judge continued and said that the payment to and the order appointing Stevens shall be effective immediately and remain in effect during the pendency of this suit or until further order of the court. All parties were enjoined from disturbing the peace of children, withdrawing them from school, hiding them, secreting them from the other party, making disparaging remarks regarding the other party in their presence, cancelling, altering, failing to renew their insurance coverage.

"This court is adjourned," she concluded and said.

I did not wait for the usual signing of paperwork, I left. Nwokoye came after me.

"You need to cool down. Things like this happen all the time in the court of the law. Nothing to worry about."

CHAPTER 46

UPPERCUT

"Ma'am, I did not see your uppercut in there. What I saw was Terresha D. Stevens being appointed as an amicus attorney. With all respect to what you have been doing, even if I have to use all my strength and determination, it is financially impossible for me to be paying, beside $300, an additional amount of $150 per month for a total of unspecified amount of money. Why didn't you say anything?" I asked.

Nwokoye should have said something. She had my four last pay stubs for June in her hands, an exact total of $ 926.94 take-home. That was barely enough to pay my rent. I was this close to tell her that I was able to pay her $300 a month, her retainer fee, because I was a street beggar. It was not a struggle to stand under the sun and beg for money; it was dying, a slowly but surely dying experience. A diabetic, under more than 100 degrees and eating out of waste bin food, doesn't last long.

"I will die if I spend one cent on Terresha instead of buying my diabetes medicine regularly."

"I understand that. Let the court do his job first, and I will continue fighting for you," she answered.

"When? Why didn't you do that today? Why didn't you tell the judge that Sheebah should pay also her social study instead of waiving her fees? She is not an indigent as she is trying to make you guys believe. I pay her a total of $701.76 on child support now. She receives $585 child support from Daven William, her other babies' father. She works at KFC for about $1,280 a month. She receives $750 on food stamps. The woman makes around $3,316.76 a month. She should be ordered to pay $150 a month for the amicus lawyer, not me. When are you going to fight for me? When?" I said.

"The real fight just started. I just told Ms Bourland that her client is lying to her. She doesn't have both children, they reside with you."

"Now, why would you possibly do a thing like that for? You told me not to," I said.

"This here, my brother, is the beginning of my uppercut," she answered.

She continued and said that this was the reason I did not see her fight that hard in there. See, Bourland will tell her client to go and take physical possession of both children because I threatened to expose her in the next meeting with the judge. I said to her it is not fair for my client, Mr. Kasalobi, to be paying child support and taking care of the children while her client, Ms Sheebah, is using that money on her boyfriend. By the way, in the case you did not know, lawyers do communicate about the case before appearing in the court. They do so all the time, she said. Bourland promised her that Sheebah will come at my place and get them. When she does, it will be the beginning of the end, she said. The order is that Oscar Dave Washington cannot be near your children. He will be because he leases the apartment they live in. Sheebah doesn't have a place to stay, she needs him. Once both kids are officially there, because Oscar doesn't like them, something will happen and that will be an endangerment to a child. It will be a reason enough to have both girls removed from her. That is the first setup.

She also explains what we will do on visitation orders. She said that on the first day, June 4, 2015, I have to show up on time, meet with my children, and make sure that the officer on duty signs my presence. For the rest of June and July, I will have to call Sheebah and tell her that I cannot make it because I am far from Arlington, in

Waco or Houston for instance, but I still have to show up there for the officer on duty to notice me.

"Remember, this was how they did set you up on visitation days inside the family court. Sheebah said to you that you did not need to show up there because you had kids with you. The reason of visitations was for you to be see them. You did not go. They found you in contempt and kids were given to her. Well, karma is a bitch. It is payback time now. Do not text her, all communications must be over the phone only, hoping she is not recording. Did you understand? Can you repeat that?" she asked.

"Yes, ma'am, I should be at the appointment thirty minutes before the time. I will make sure my presence is signed in. I will wait. I will leave from there only after consuming the entire time, the whole three hours. At the end of every visit, I will ask for a report to keep jealously," I explained.

"Good boy."

"How about the overnight weekend visits?" I asked.

"Look, you will see your kids anyway. They will come to you. It doesn't count if they cross the street and come to you, which they will be doing because they are used to you. As long as Hurst Police is not aware of their presence in your house, it won't add up to your credit. If the police did not notice their presence, it will not count either. So let's do that."

And it happened just the way Nwokoye predicted it. On June 4, 2011, Sheebah brought the kids at Arlington Police Department. She brought them one hour late. She said she did not have a ride, her car was broken down, and she was waiting to catch a ride from her friend. I told her not to worry.

"If you can make it, just call me and let me know. I see Tabô and Loylla every day anyway," I said to her.

With the same excuse, she picked them two hours late. This time, she added a sorry to it. She was late because she was waiting for her friend to get out from work, she said. Officer P. Ramirez took note of that irresponsibility. She was on duty that afternoon. She told me, "I just checked Sheebah out. She has multiples warrants for her arrest. Maybe that was why she was hesitant to show up on time. We don't arrest people recommended by the judge or those that show up by the court order. Your lawyer can subpoena me if she wants to. I will testify and tell the court that she was late." She said.

That was also the last time she brought kids in Arlington for court order exchange. I sometimes called her to tell her that I was not able to attend because I was still working. Some other times, I said that my blood sugar was so high; I couldn't drive. She bought everything I put in front of her because she did not have a ride all the time and I showed up there every time. Things worked in my favor. She was absent for the rest of June: on the eleventh, eighteenth, and on the twenty-fifth. She was also no show on July 2, 3, 15, and 22. At the end, Officer Jefferson, who had also been witnessing both children's nonappearances, took my supplemental reports and included them to the main report. Officer P. Ramirez asked me to addition to it a written note, testifying Sheebah's absences. She added it to her written report. I took both written reports downstairs to the records division mail stop 04-0100 to be added to the monitor reports 1100 36 614 and 1100 38 282. I had at that point enough reports to take to the court.

Despite June 1, 2011, court decision, and we knew this was going to happen, Sheebah authorized Oscar D. Washington, not only to be close to my daughters, but also to be in the same room of the same apartment with both of them. It did not take long; he hit Tabô in front of her mother. I knew this from CPS Kirsten Jackson. She was the new case worker. I complained enough, and Tracy Burkhart was removed. Tabô had Tracy Burkhart's business card. It was given to her by her so she can snitch on me. Tabô called the number to report the beating, and Kirsten Jackson ended up answering. Tabô told her that she got hurt by Oscar.

"He repeatedly hit me on my head, with a closed fist. Now I am having heavy headaches."

"Where was your mother when this was happening?" Kirsten Jackson asked.

"She was there. She did not do a thing to stop the beating. What happened was that I was arguing with Oscar's son. He is a ten-year-old boy. I am a twelve-year-old girl. Instead of separating us, Oscar, a fifty-two-year-old man, took his son's side. He attacked me, cursed me, and beat me badly. I tried to call Papa, my mother intimidated me. That is why I called you."

Tabô explained that she had bruises all over her body, on her legs, her back and her chest. After taking grievances from a crying little girl, CPS Kirsten Jackson went by the book one more time. She clearly saw things through Tabô's eyes and decided to change the current of the old investigation. She called me. We talked again. She said that what Tabô said was exactly what her little sister said too. She requested from Susan Giles, their supervisor, that three CPS agents: Marlen Glen, Kristen Onumpsun, and herself be sent on the field to yet investigate Oscar Washington. Their conclusion was strict. With reason to believe, Sheebah was found neglectful. All five kids: Tabô, Loylla, Boney, Kattaya, and Baby J. were found in Oscar's filthy one-bedroom, sleeping on the floor. They all had traces of abuse on their bodies. There was no food in her refrigerator. The only drink in there was beer.

Kirsten Jackson made her report, not to the state auditor's office. They did not have jurisdiction over this issue, she said. She referred her complaints to the Health and Human Services Commission Office of Inspector General for another review and action they would deem appropriate. They have a purview over these types of complaint. She also sent a copy of the matter to Hurst law enforcement and to Health and Human Services Commission office of Inspector General. She did so because she said "there is a preponderance of evidences supporting that abuse and neglect did also occur in Hurst."

"Is there any difference between the Inspector General and the Office of Consumer Affairs? I have been sending my complaints to Consumer Affairs, they never answer me," I said.

"The Office for Consumer Affairs serves as a neutral party in reviewing and investigating complaints regarding case-specific activities of DFPS programs. Complaints regarding fraud and abuse in health and human services programs should be reported to the Office of the Inspector General," she answered.

This was how, and from there that Oscar was found, with reason to believe, abusing all five children, beating them with open fists and slashing their bodies with sticks. The decision was rendered by Susan Giles. To avoid bodily injury and substantial risk of immediate harm to them, to avoid substantial risk of sexual conduct harmful to them from Oscar D. Washington, Susan Giles then concluded that "kids must be removed, for the second time, and placed. Loylla will temporarily be with Aqueela, Sheebah's cousin in Fort Worth and Tabô with Belinda, her big sister. Their little sisters will be with their godmothers. I will bring this to Terresha D. Stevens, the kids' attorney's, attention and have a hearing set. They must be placed till Violet, your lawyer, also set a new hearing or continues with what Terresha will set. We all will bring this matter to the attention of the judge. While waiting for the decision of the judge and because the family law is preventive, I don't have to wait for something to happen to the children, so I can start doing something to really protect them. To avoid not only a physical injury coming to them, but also the use of controlled substance as defined by the chapter 481, I have to place them. We only have to pray."

"I just got a call from Susan Giles, the new case manager," Violet Nwokoye said over the phone.

"Oh yeah, that is the lady who investigated and physically removed the kids from their mother," I answered.

"It is a good thing that the kids are removed from where they temporarily were. They are placed with the Fort Worth Baptist church Boarding School," she said.

"I know, I went to visit them, this Friday, August 12, in the afternoon," I answered.

"You did well because Sheebah cannot visit them until further court decision. Oscar Washington is arrested. The temporary order hearing is still set for this Thursday, August 25, 2011, at 8:30 with the associate judge. Kirsten Jackson will be testifying. Kids will be represented by amicus attorney Terresha Stevens. We also will have a family court services conference for social study status that was set to be done on this August 25, 2011, with Amy Candler," she explained.

"Tabô called, she told me that she misses the smell of marijuana. Her mother and Oscar always gave her some to smoke," I said to Nwokoye.

When Loylla and Tabô are deeply asleep in their mother's bed, Tabô said their mother wakes them up in the middle of the night. She asks them to leave the room. Oscar rents it to people who come over there to do sex. Sheebah told her that this is how they make money to buy marijuana with. While talking, she would give her some puffs of smoke from her marijuana stick. She said she posted lot of things on her Facebook page. There are pictures of her mother and her smoking marijuana and partying with Saint, Chico, Sebastian, Sandy, Amanda, and Seth. Sebastian was a Latino boyfriend.

"When Chico was shot in the head and killed, we went in his apartment to drop beer on his dry blood and smoke in his memory," she said.

"If needed, I will be filing another motion in court on the same August 25. I have already read what you previously wrote about both children: about Loylla who had her nose busted by Oscar, about him kicking Tabô out of the apartment in the middle of the night, without shoes on her feet and wearing only pajamas, and about Ty, their mother's new boyfriend who sold Tabô's glasses to buy drugs. I will be looking into that, but I just cannot interview them, only the judge can do it. I will talk to Specialist Kirsten Jackson. CPS has a way to break into kids' Facebook. She will print out her Facebook pages and pictures you are talking about. I will get them into evidence. I will let you know the next date for hearing after I file the motion," Nwokoye said.

"I know, ma'am, you are professional and I appreciate that you go by the book, but sometimes you have to play dirty, they do it. Sheebah's lawyer interviews both girls all the time. She does that without any permission. She tells them how to lie, what to say in the court, and when to defend their mother. She even brings them in court to have Judge Wells interview them."

"I saw them the last time we were in court. They were kept in the judge's chambers. See, Bourland cannot collect evidence from them, the reason she is coaching them. She takes them to the judge for that. Loylla did not say a thing, she was timidly smiling, but Tabô was incoherent while testifying for her mother. Something was not clicking. It was only after the interview that I understood the game."

"She was playing crazy so she can be ordered to take medicine. I forced her out of it," I said.

"Or maybe she wants to stay with her mother for marijuana. Now why did you stop her from taking medicine? Never mind."

"You will have your children very soon. The uppercut is on their jaws. Don't you see how agitated Bourland is? First, she said Sheebah won't sign the retro forgiveness because you are harassing her, now she wants it to be done. Karma is a bitch. She is sure all tables are turned upside down and her client is about to pay back every penny she took from you. One more setup and they will be on the canvas. Kas, do you use drugs?" she asked.

"No, ma'am, I do not."

"Are you sure? Sure-sure?" she asked again.

"A hundred percent sure-sure."

"Okay, that is all for now, I'll talk to you later." She hung up the phone.

On August 25, 2011, the court was packed. This was the first time to see so many CPS specialists present at one place. They were all there: Jackson, Edwardo Fe, Marlen Glen, Kristella Onumpsun, and Kirsten Jackson. Some CPS students came also along, they came to practice. Each one of everyday court members was present. That courtroom was packed with different parents. They all were there to state their cases. After all legal introductions were done, the investigator from the attorney general, state of Texas, reminded every one of us why we were in there. He talked about the case from the day we left it off, by citing numbers and dates, to that current time. Mr. Susa Giles introduced her team. At the first onset, Kirsten Jackson attacked Sheebah. She said that Sheebah was abusing her own kids. She was letting her boyfriend beat them using the trash can. CPS Jackson completed her speech by saying that Sheebah's place was dirty, full of bed bugs, and did not have food in the refrigerator for her children. She didn't even have the electricity at that time she visited them.

"Before we proceed in the right direction, is the new social study I ordered done yet?" Judge Terri White asked.

"It would have been done if Mr. Kasalobi had paid. The last I know of it, he did not. He said he won't pay. So the social study is not ready, Your Honor," answered Bourland.

"The only part of the social study that is completed is my client's part. The opposite party is still finding excuses despite the fact that lot of their fees were dismissed. As ordered by the court, not only my client paid for him, he also paid Sheebah's fee, Your Honor," Nwokoye answered.

"I confirm, Your Honor. Mr. Kasalobi's social study is completed. The counselor is wrong. Up to CPS observation, it was not a matter of payment but a matter of residence. Sheebah did not give me a physical address. It looks like she did not want me to visit where she lives," Amy Candler confirmed.

"That is not true, Your Honor. Mr. Kasalobi specifically told my client that he had already paid $600 the last time around for both of them and lost the case. He won't pay anymore," Bourland said.

"And yet he did. He paid. I have a copy of the receipt. He participated. Sheebah did not. I asked for her physical address, she gave me the 9160 E. Walter Street in Bedford. Suzy Dale, the owner, said she doesn't live there, she never lived there. I asked her for another physical address. She basically refused to show me where she lives. So I did not conduct her social study," said Amy Candler.

It was here when Nwokoye entered in the fight. She started by saying, "Regarding this case and concerning her kind, Sheebah is the only person I know of who does whatever she wants. She never followed any judge's orders and nothing worries her. I wonder why, is it because she is protected? Maybe it is because she never had been punished for her mischief?" Asked Nwokoye. "This present court ordered that my client should have both children during the summer time. She just failed, one more time, to bring the kids to Arlington Police Department for the summer exchange for both June and July. My client went the whole summer without seeing his daughters," Nwokoye dryly explained. "If it was any other person, she would have been accused of contempt of the court and put in jail by now."

"I object, Your Honor. My client was always there to drop her children, but the father showed his irresponsibility one more time. He did not show up. For the entire month of June, he said he was in the hospital in Buffalo, Texas. I understand that he is diabetic, but he didn't even bother to call on time to let the mother know. He let her drive all the way from Fort Worth and spend her gas money for nothing. In July, the man found different excuses not to do his duty as a father. He refused to come and visit with his kids. He refused to spend just a little time in Arlington with his children. It started the first day, Your Honor. He was so late the police had to call him to come and visit with his kids," Bourland explained.

"Is that so, Mr. Kasalobi?" Terri White, the 325 Family District Court judge, asked.

I approached the bench a step further and stood near Nwokoye.

"Actually, it was the other way around, Your Honor. On the first day, it was in fact Sheebah who was late. It is true that the police called, but it was not I who was called. It was her who was called. She did show up, but it was after 1530 instead of 1400 as ordered. She was nowhere to be seen at 1800, the time she was supposed to come and get them. It was at this moment that Officer Rodriguez called her. She did not answer, but she showed up around 2030. Officer Rodriguez ran her names. She suspected that the reason she was not showing was because she had so many warrants for her arrest. Actually, Your Honor, she did not show up for the rest of summer," I explained.

"Mr. Kasalobi is a liar, Your Honor," Bourland attacked. She didn't even finish when Nwokoye interfered.

"My client is not a liar. I have here, in my suitcase, legal documents, written and signed by Arlington police officers. They are notarized by the city of Arlington. It is written in them that Mr. Kasalobi, here present, went to Arlington from June to July and waited for his daughters, sitting on the municipal bench every single court-ordered day. Sheebah never showed up," Nwokoye explained.

She then reached her suitcase-files, took documents out of it, and handed them to the judge. She gave a copy to Bourland and to CPS. Meda Bourland was so confused to read what was reported in it. The master of plays and setups was played. She looked at Sheebah and understood that they both fell, head first, into a very sophisticated setup. Then the judge said, "Counsel, I am very tired of Sheebah's lies. Unless you show me something else, I will bring the kids in and switch custody."

It was at this moment that Sheebah went bananas. She started screaming at me, cursing my name, and yelling that I have to go back to Africa where I belong. The judge reminded Bourland that we were still in the court of the law and she had to control her client. Sheebah did not stop screaming all kind of insanities. She stood up and left the courtroom on her own authority. The judge asked Bourland to go and get her client. She wanted her back inside. When they came back, Sheebah surprised even her lawyer. She said, "I don't want the father to be with my daughters. Instead of having him take custody of my little girls, I rather give them to CPS. I am giving my parental rights to CPS right now."

Her lawyer tried to stop her, but she was getting wilder and wilder.

"I don't think you have a power to dictate who will have your kids in my court. You have to reconsider that decision because it is you and yourself to blame. You are not feeding your children, you are selling their food stamps. You are putting the roof on their head, you're spending tandiff money and child support payment on drugs and sex. You are exposing them to all kinds of danger, your boyfriend has your approval to hit them using a weapon. Yes, ma'am, a trash can is a weapon. Therefore, reconsider your decision before I make mine," the judge said.

CHAPTER 47

SHE GAVE Y'ALL AWAY

Then, Nwokoye pleaded for both girls "to be given back to the father instead of giving them to the CPS. This is strange, in fact, no mother in the good state of mind would authorize CPS to have her children." She said.

"Your client has also a history with CPS too. He is not better than Sheebah. I don't see how he deserves to be given custody of children," the judge replied.

"Your Honor, there is no one in this court who proved that my client had ever hurt his children, none. There is no one present here who came forward and said that my client have ever beaten, slapped, or simply abused his daughters, none. My client has never ever been arrested by any police department in this country for being violent to his children or for any reason whatsoever ever. CPS will never prove otherwise. He had been accused of by Sheebah and her lawyer, investigated from, and cleared of because there never was any case in which he was involved in not feeding or mistreating his own children. I dare this court. I dare the police department, any one of them in this United States. I dare the Child Protective Services to give me just a beginning of proof of the abuse. I dare anyone in here present to do so. What you read, anything you heard, is coming from Sheebah's and Bourland's imaginations, and because these things where coming from a woman, a woman who was crying while lying, just like now, this court believed it. Children should go, not with CPS, and this is not even an issue in this court, but with their father who real cares about them. They have to be with him today because their mother didn't even do her ordered classes. My client just achieved them all. He doesn't smoke, he doesn't drink either. For the past ten years, he had been having one job and one address. He is a stable and responsible person. You just said you are transferring custody of children to my client. I insist, Your Honor, you have to do so and you will be doing justice. Let's not be biased and continue protecting Sheebah. Why does this court protect Sheebah anyway? Is it because she is a woman? Look at these pictures. This is Sheebah, with a group of boyfriends, giving alcohol and marijuana to Tabô in her apartment. May I approach the bench and hand them to you, Your Honor?" Stated Nwokoye.

She came forward and handed copies of Facebook pages and pictures to the judge. She also gave same copies to Meda Bourland and to CPS. Bourland looked at them with deception in her eyes. Her client did not look back.

"Where did you get these pictures, Counsel?" the judge asked.

"In Sheebah and Tabô's Facebook. They are everywhere in the internet, Your Honor."

"This changes everything. I cannot place a child where she or he is exposed to drugs," the judge said.

Nwokoye looked at me, as if to say that we just played everything the way it should have been.

"That is why I need a drug test to be done on Sheebah today, right at this present time, Your Honor."

"My client passed her drug screening already, there is no need for that anymore," Bourland said.

"Mrs. Susan Giles, is CPS aware of Sheebah passing her drug test?" the judge asked.

"Your Honor, Sheebah played a game of not having saliva secretion when the laboratory technician wanted a sample. She refused the cotton swab also, pretending to have open lacerations and sores in her mouth. I did verify. She was right. She did have lizard-like wounds in her mouth. And you know something else, ma'am? These kinds of dry-cut wounds can be easily explained. They are coming from the use of cocaine and marijuana smoke at the same time."

"My client passed her urine test. That is enough," Bourland said.

"Strange enough, she passed the urine test indeed. For heaven's sake, what did the woman do to pass her drug test? I know she smokes marijuana at least. One can see cocaine written all over her eyes," Susan Giles stated.

"I cannot explain how she passed her urine test either, Your Honor. But Ms Sheebah went there with her lawyer, which by itself is very strange. What was she doing inside the lab when her client was taking her court-ordered drug test? It is a question that even a good lawyer won't be able to answer right now. Is it legal for a lawyer to do so? I really do not know. This counsel, Your Honor, had been doing things…I mean, not Catholic at all. She lies a lot inside this court and had been authorizing herself to coach both children to lie. She even had been interviewing them without the presence of their father. That, Your Honor, is illegal. Frankly, I too, just like Mrs. Susan, doubt about Sheebah passing that test. Did she found a way to influence the result? I cannot answer that because I am not here to accuse, I am here to defend. On the other hand, having said that, it is a known fact that all crack addicts buy piss to take to the lab for their drug test. Your Honor, I think we need a second screening," requested Nwokoye.

"That is impossible, Counsel. Urine needs to have a certain body temperature to be accepted," Judge Terri intervened and said.

"Yes, ma'am, we all know that. Drug addicts know that too. CVS sells a medical belt to collect piss for those who cannot normally go to the bathroom. Some drug addicts do afford it and wear it around their body to keep the temperature at the normal level. Lot of them use condoms. They buy piss for about $20 and fill it up. In this case, a woman would insert it inside her vagina and a man directly between the cracks of both legs, directly behind his balls. That is how they pass their tests," Nwokoye explained.

"You are not saying, Counsel, that…"

"And that is how some men are called back to be told that they are pregnant, it is because in their case, they used pregnant woman's urine."

"Are you insinuating that Sheebah's counsel gave her the urine for the test?" the judge asked.

"No, ma'am. I am not saying that. I said her presence in that laboratory, when Sheebah was taking the urine test, was very odd, outlandish, and eccentric. Lawyers don't do that."

"Mrs. Bourland, where you in the lab with your client?" Judge Terri asked.

"Yes, ma'am. She did not have a ride, so I had to wait for her," Bourland answered.

"Okay, I heard almost everything. I am going to suspend this trial till a new drug test is done."

Judge White then ordered both of us to be escorted by one of her deputies at the county Forensic DNA & Drug Testing Services of Fort Worth. She interrupted the hearing in the middle because she did not want body fluid tests anymore. She was looking for traces of four specific drugs; therefore, she needed hair samples to be analyzed. The result was asked to be given, in copies, to Melisha Paschal for the Texas attorney general, Meda Bourland for the opposite defense, Susan Giles for CPS, and to Violet.

Representing the attorney general, Melisha Paschal suggested that CPS keeps both kids while the drug test was performed. We stepped out and started waiting for the deputy to join us. Jackson, the CPS lady come forward and said that she will be accompanying us to the drug test. Violet approached me and asked me one more time if I do drugs. I said, "Nope, I do not do drugs, ma'am. The only drugs I do take are the ones legally prescribed for my diabetes."

As we all were there, waiting for the deputy to take us over there, Sheebah come toward me, crying and cursing.

"You set me up, you son-of-a-bitch. You thought you will win by doing that? You and your lawyer can go back to motherfucka Africa where y'all are coming from. Y'all belong there, not here."

"Do not give into her provocations. We are winning. She got knocked down, very soon, she will be out. We are going to the twelfth round now. Just like a cockroach, she will have all her legs in the air. Either way, this woman shouldn't be called Mother. Do you remember the story of two widows who went in front of King Solomon for the custody battle of a lost child? Do you remember how the king knew who was the mother?" Nwokoye said.

"Yes. The woman who did not give the children to CPS," I answered.

"Almost. No parent in their right mind would have done what Sheebah did in there. It is like 'if I can't have them, you can't have them' sort of thinking. Sheebah doesn't deserve both children. Well, do not exchange a word with her from now on," Nwokoye said.

"I do not intend to. Thanks for being there for me, and thank you for today's fight. Thank you," I said.

A police officer came and took us a half mile down Weatherford Street. The technician took the hair sample. As I was leaving the clinic, CPS Jackson approached. She told me that Susan Giles wanted to know if I have the time to visit with children around 1600 hours. She wanted to observe me intermingling with both girls. A report will be sent to the judge. I drove down on 35 E going south to the seminary exit and directed myself, as instructed, inside the Catholic Charity Building. I met Giles on the parking lot. She interviewed me intensively. She then said CPS never had my current address.

"We never knew your phone number either. The only address and number we have in the main record are those given to us by Sheebah."

"You don't say. And you call yourself child protective people. Well, she made sure to play you just the way she had been playing the system, a wrong number here and a wrong address there."

Then we entered the Catholic Charity Building III. By CPS discretion, Tabô and Loylla were hidden inside. I did not get to see them that day because they were not settled yet. On August 8, I had my first visitation with Tabô and Loylla. It was supervised by Susan Giles. Both girls were well and dandy. They both had good means. Tabô asked me to take her to court so she can tell the judge that she didn't want to live with her mother anymore. Giles said it was possible to go to court, but to leave the building, we needed a written authorization from and by the judge. Nevertheless, she called Melisha Paschal to be advised. Melisha answered and said that there was no way to do so. Both girls were in CPS custody. Loylla interrupted and said, "That is not what my mother's lawyer just said."

"This woman never rests. Mr. Meda Bourland came over to coach you again? When was that?" asked Giles.

"She just left. She told us what to do. She said that she will ask the judge to bring us in tomorrow. Once in the court, we will have to cry hard. We will tell the judge that we need to go with our mother. And my mother will get us back tomorrow. But I don't want to go back with my mom," Loylla explained.

CHAPTER 48

TEMPORARY POSSESSOR CONSERVATOR

I asked the permission to freely speak to my daughters.

"Speak freely," said Giles.

I explained to both girls that it is not up to CPS, to me, or to her mother. The judge will decide where they will be and who they will be living with according to evidence introduced in court.

"Seriously, I don't see how your mother will get both of you tomorrow. She gave y'all away. Just the way your grandmother, Katrine Shahan, gave your mother away to the State of Texas when she was nine years old, your mom gave her parental right this morning to CPS. She did it to both of you inside the same Fort Worth court where her mother did it to her. Your mom spent her childhood and all her teenager life inside Leana Pope because she was given away by Katrine Shahan, her own mother. And just like her mother, she did it in front of the whole courtroom full of witnesses. I don't want to see both of you spend the rest of your lives in foster homes. I am here, and I will fight to bring you back home," I said.

"Your father is right. I saw, with my own eyes, your mother giving both of you away. That is what we all saw. I just did not understand why Terri White changed her decision. She was about to switch custody to your father when we were inside the court, but for some reasons, she backed off," Susan Giles confirmed.

At the end of the visit, once we stepped out, I explained to Susan Giles things about Suzy Dale and everything I had been going through with CPS Tracy Burkhart. She said that as CPS, her job was to save children from harm, to take care of them, and to guarantee their welfare. Her job was not to take complaints.

"There is a proper channel for that. I have a confession to say though. I have been working hard to see Sheebah keep and live with her children. Sheebah never cooperated. She numerously put them, all five, in danger. We all knew that. But the CPS hope is that kids, especially girls, are better off with their mother."

"Is it true that their mother will get them tomorrow in court?" I asked.

"Hein…I really do not know. I don't trust Judge Terri White. Say what! Ask your lawyer to change the judge. It will help," advised Susan Giles.

When we showed up there the next day to let CPS talk about the result of the drug test we took, I approached Nwokoye and asked her if she could request the change of judges, she said, "Why, this is your moment. It is your day to shine. I have been telling you to have a little faith in me and you did, I will give your kids back today. I will take them from CPS and from the court and hand them to you today."

That speech brought smile to my face. August 9, 2011, was also a day people showed up in the court to adopt abused and abandoned children. Room 5, on the fifth floor, was packed to its maximum capacity. It did not have an empty seat. People stood along the walls. When the marechal announced the judge, it was not Judge Terri White or Judge Judith Wells, two judges I got used to very much and with whom I spent quite a lot of my times in the court. It was a black lady I never seen before.

"Judge Wells is under the weather. She is sick and very packed. My humble person is filling in. She left me all her twelve selected cases. I have to finish them today. I don't know which one will make me tired before proceeding to adoption cases. So, people, I am honored, please bear with me here. For those who brought their cameras, you can take pictures. Today is a big day for parents and their children. Just to be part of this, I am blessed. May I remind those who get easily tired, like me, that we won't take a break. If you feel like going, all restrooms are on the other side of elevators and vending machines are just next door," she said.

From eight in the morning, she turned about nine cases. It was eleven on the top of the hour when the judge introduced the hearing. She said that "a full adversary meeting pursuant to chap 262.201 and 262.205 Texas Family Code is now held by the demand of Violet Nwokoye, the attorney in record, regarding the case number 325-428760-07."

After that opening, Melissa Paschall presented a petition to the court for the emergency protestation of Tabô and Loylla.

Susan Giles explained to the judge that all reasonable efforts, consistent with time and circumstances and pursuant to 42 USC Chapter 671(a)(15) and 672(a)(1), have been made to prevent or eliminate the need for removal of the children from their mother's home. But continuing leaving them home with their mother would be contrary to the children's welfare. She explained her last visit to the children. She told the court about my visit also. Questioning both children, she said, she realized that Tabô wants to live with the father. She is tired of being beaten up by her mother's numerous boyfriends. Her father never laid a hand on her. Up to Tabô herself, her father calls her "mama de moi, Muisangie Lumpungu, Tabo nginami," and all kind of little names that means "princess" in his African language. She knew about her mother's usage of drugs, but her mother always told them to stick together no matter what, she said. She is tired of protecting her because she never protected them from all beatings they received. On the other hand, the father always defended them, she said. Loylla, the youngest, did not want to live in the Catholic Charity Building anymore. In there, she said, they have been telling her what to touch and where to sit. She is not free of her movements. She misses her room at her father's place and wants to go back home. She was tired of what her mother was doing too. She wants to live with the father. Therefore, said Susan Giles, these two children should be removed pursuant to Chapt 262.104 of Texas Family Code. There is a continuing danger to the physical health and to the safety of both of them remaining in their mother's house. They could have been the victim of even sexual abuse in the future caused by their mother's style of life, having too many boyfriends around.

"It is therefore impossible to let them continue living with their mother. I am also presenting a petition, to this court, for the emergency protestation of both children," Susan Giles concluded.

Bourland claimed that Sheebah was fit to get her kids back. She explained things that did not make sense. She also gave ridiculous details that made mockery of the university she attended to learn the law. She didn't even finish stating her case, Nwokoye barged in and said, "Your Honor, on her own authority, the mother did not want the father to have both children, as it was suggested yesterday by the court. She gave the kids away to CPS, in the court of the law with her counsel as her witness. Doing so, she gave away her right as a mother. She never loved them anyway. She had been using them to obtain child support, food stamps, and other government advantages. Kids belong to CPS as yesterday, and as today CPS is their legal guardians. I am not asking Mrs. Bourland to give both children back to the father, I am asking the Child Protective Services to give custody back to the father on the basis of the fact that they cannot possibly be around their mother anymore. Sheebah is a drug addict, she is a crack head. On this last random drug test that the court ordered yesterday, she is active on a bunch of them. The most dangerous are cocaine, methamphetamine, marijuana, bath salts, heroin, opium, and ice."

"She has all that in her system?" asked the judge.

"She is full of them all. This is the result directly from the lab, printed on the federal drug testing custody and control form. Yes, ma'am, she has all that in her," Nwokoye answered.

"That piece of paper doesn't include everything. My client is taking legal and over-the-counter prescriptions," Bourland said.

"I am listening," the judge said.

She suddenly tried to change the topic. Instead of telling the judge about the over-the-counter prescriptions her client was taking, she started explaining what my daughters told her personally about who the best parent was between Sheebah and me. Nwokoye intervened directly. She accused her of "interviewing children without the consent of both parents. This conflicting counsel was yesterday at the undisclosed place, where children are hidden, to put ideas in their heads. This is not the first time she did this, Your Honor, and I don't want go through everything here. But let it be known that she always coaches them. She tells them how to lie in the court and how to behave when they are in front of the judge. She spent her precious time manipulating them again. Can you believe, Your Honor, she promised to buy for them things she won't even be able to deliver? This counsel has her priorities mixed. What is her weakness toward the kids' mother is a question I cannot answer. I know she is not the one on trial, but can she tell us why she keeps putting both kids' lives in danger? Kasalobi here is a caring father. He is a stable man with a stable job. He is appreciated by his employer. Let me repeat this, her client, on the other end, is a drug addict. Mr. Kasalobi doesn't do drugs."

"My client doesn't do drugs, Your Honor. She was taking hydrocodone mixed with Tylenol for pain. She took these products before the drug test. Any pharmacist will tell this court that these two medications, when taken at same exact time, they react. And when they do, they show cocaine symptoms like—"

"Ma'am, do you know that...ma'am...is your pharmacist in here at this moment?" the judge asked.

Instead of answering, Bourland continued explaining things using confusing chemical terms. She named different elements in the physique chart that did this and that could do that. The judge let her give diverse types of similar sorts of phenomenon that react without their body types. She concluded her argument by saying that "the physiological combination of those items and their over-the-counter medicines taken with hydrocodone at same time creates a doubt in the mind of the lab technicians. It produces a complicated chemical reaction for those who are not initiated. For them, it comes out as if the person had been taking illegal drugs. This reaction was demonstrated to me by the CVS specialist who—"

"Ma'am, is your CVS specialist present in this courtroom today?" asked the judge.

"No, Your Honor, but I can—"

"Because I want to talk to him too. We all went to school, Counsel. We know what a drug is. Are you trying to confuse this court with chemistry names?"

"No, Your Honor, but I am only explaining the physics of things."

"By his medical record, it is proven to me that Mr. Kasalobi is diabetic. Just like I am. Like me, he takes a bunch of chemical products, including hydrocodone for extreme pain. If what you are saying is scientifically correct, he should also have the same reaction with your client. The drug test should also have shown ten illegal drugs in his system. But he is 100 percent negative. Explain that, Counsel," the judge asked

"My client had flu-like fever. With the prescribed medicine she had been taking, traces of cocaine in her body are perfectly legal."

"Legal? Counsel, tell me the name of the doctor who legally prescribed cocaine to your client. I would like to hear from him explain which way a legal drug as hydrocodone, taken in the morning or in the afternoon, with or without food, with water or with liquor, can turn into a cocaine product or marijuana smoke. How long had your client been having flu-like fever?" the judge asked.

"About five days before the drug test," Bourland answered.

"You seemed to be the most educated among the rest of us. Then I'll give it to you. You know what else, Counsel, what we did was not a body fluid drug test, it was hair samples. What we found in your client was not taken six days ago. It had been there. It had been indulged in her system for more than six months. The fact of the matter is that the mother is taking drugs. We all have to agree about that because it is certified by the test she herself took yesterday. I am even amazed to see her standing up and functioning with all that in her body. We also need to agree that she should seek for help, and help she will get. Where are both kids?" the judge asked, looking at Bourland, Sheebah's lawyer.

"With the state of Texas, Your Honor," answered the district attorney.

"Your Honor, we are here to take physical possession of both girls from the custody of the state. We want them out from the system. We want them with the father starting immediately."

"There is no other way. I cannot put kids back in the house where adults are using drugs. I will order the removal of all her children, including Tabô and Loylla. It will be also ordered that both children, Tabô and Loylla, be temporary removed from CPS custody. A full adversary hearing under chapt 154.001(b) would be held. A temporary order to appoint sole managing conservator of both children will be ordered. The mother will be paying child support, pending the final disposition of the suit," the judge said.

Sheebah screamed loudly this time. She hysterically cried while saying, "He will hurt them, he will hurt them. Judge, you do not know him, he never loved them. I want my kids back. He will mistreat them. He had been sexually molesting them."

"Lady, you need to cool down. Did anyone, in this court, ever hear about this new allegation? Mrs. Susan, have you ever heard about Mr. Kasalobi sexually molesting his children? " the judge asked.

"The mother just said that, Your Honor. She just said that because you are giving the kids back to the father. She never claimed such thing and I have been investigating her for the past five years. She has excessive history with CPS, therefore, a lot of experience with the way CPS conduct investigations, if there was such case, if there is such case, she would have already told that to the system," Susan Giles said.

"Mrs. Jackson?"

"This is also my first time ever, Your Honor. I never ever heard this accusation, Your Honor. None of their children ever claimed being molested either. In my entire time I have been investigating this case, I never found anything to create even a beginning of a doubt in my mind about it, and I have been on this case for the past two years," Jackson said.

I put my hand behind my back to hide it from the judge. I lifted my middle finger and showed it to Sheebah. The whole room saw it, and I heard some reactions. The judge asked what the CPS lawyer was thinking about it.

"There was no report of any sexual abuse since this case started in 2003. That is a last move of a mother in a desperate situation."

"Mrs. Bourland?"

"Well, I heard about it. We will bring forward concrete support about it."

"Let me remind everyone that after hearing each party in here, I still have jurisdiction of this case. I won't order a new decision. I won't put kids back in the house where they are neglected and where the mother shows drugs in her system, where her boyfriend hits them with trash cans and leave bruises all over their bodies. I won't give children back to a mother who uses drugs. I won't expose children back where they have been neglected, where they are in danger. Now please stand up and hear my decision," the judge said.

We all stood up, except the clerk and the scripter.

"Mr. Kasalobi, the father, is appointed the temporary possessor conservator of the children Tabô and Loylla."

She ordered that the Department of Protective Services is appointed temporary managing conservator of said children. The temporary managing conservator shall have all the rights and duties set forth in Chapter 153.371 of Texas Family Code.

She ordered that the mother, Sheebah, shall have limited access to and possession of the children as arranged and supervised by the temporary managing conservator as it is found in the court application of the guidelines for possession of and access to the children, as set out in Subchapter F, Chapter 153, Texas Family Code. Limited access is in the best interests of Tabô and Loylla.

She ordered that the child support that I pay to Sheebah is temporary suspended from September 9, 2011, forward. She said that all said temporary orders shall continue in force during the pendency of this suit or until further order of the court.

"Kids will now go with the father," she said. "This is the court's decision. It is my decision taken with the safety of the children in mind."

The whole courtroom applauded. I thought, for a moment there, that I was in a movie theater watching a play. I did not have an idea why they put their hands together, but I liked it.

"You did it. You just won the case," I said and jumped on Violet's neck.

"I broke it open. I busted it wide open," Nwokoye Violet said, tears in her eyes.

"You are crying, Nwokoye, you are crying. Are you crying?"

"My dad said to me…when I told him that I am going to be a lawyer, my dad said to me, 'Daughter, you don't become a lawyer after your university studies. You are a lawyer on your first day of your elementary school, so start fighting,' and I started right there. I believed in what he said since, I believed in him and he made me who I am. This is my first time to cry in the court because this is the first case I won since he departed from us. I won your case with my dad's advice in my mind. I won it because I am good. I am damn good." She smiled wildly to show how proud of herself she was.

Long minutes passed by and my arms were still on Nwokoye's neck. I held her so hard and I forgot for a moment where we were. I did not feel like letting her go. I hugged the woman as if there was not tomorrow.

"I am in dust, on my knees, thanking you. You should be arrogant for an accomplishment like this one. It was not an easy fight, not easy at all. Be blessed, Nwokoye Violet, be blessed for this one extra mile you just put in my life. I will always remember this. Thank you a lot," I said to her.

Terresha Stevens, the guardian ad litem of both Tabô and Loylla, approached Melissa R. Paschal, the assistant district attorney. She asked her how to proceed on the return of children. Paschal called Susan Giles, the CPS supervisor. They went to meet inside the small preparation room that was located, at the left side of the exit door. I left the court, holding in tears of joy. I did not want to wet my face. I stepped outside. Sheebah followed me behind. She had her phone on her ears. Suzy Dale was at the other end, I overheard her voice. I sat on the bench to think about my long journey to getting my girls and the way it just ended in that court of the law and I smiled. I directed my joy to the man who was sitting on the same bench and said, "I just won the custody battle."

"Did I ask you to tell me that?" he meanly responded.

I knew there that he was not happy; he was having a very long day. I sat there anyway, waiting for Terresha Stevens's decision about my girls.

Suddenly, I heard Sheebah's voice.

"I will kill you. I will kill them. You won't have them. Go back to Africa, you moddafucka," she said to me.

"Did she just threaten to kill her children?" the man on the bench asked me.

"She just did."

"Do not respond. The woman is making a scene. She is visibly hysterical. Do not give her the pleasure of yelling at you to make you lose control," the man said.

"The judge has already decided. I am going home with my children. I think Suzy Dale just told her to play that game. I need to stay in control. I am going to report her to Melissa Paschall. Would you testify for me, sir? You heard everything, sir," I said as Sheebah continued her attacks.

"I did not hear a thing. I am sitting here because I am already in trouble myself, I don't want any more."

One more time, I closed my right fist, extended my middle finger, and flipped the bird. At that exact time, Melisha Paschall called my name. I entered inside the preparation room where they were sitting talking about my daughters' arrangement. Melisha asked me to follow the district attorney and two case workers driving to Fort Worth.

"They will release both girls to you once there," she said.

"I don't think it is safe for me to drive them from Fort Worth to Hurst. I just got threatened. Sheebah just said if she doesn't get both kids, she will kill me before I get them," I explained.

"We heard everything and saw the waving of the finger. We have seen worse, not to say that we are not taking that threat seriously. People do say these things after losing their cases in court. We will talk to her counsel about it."

"Can CPS bring the children to my house?" I asked.

"Are you going to be there at 1600 hours?" Melisha asked.

"Yes, ma'am."

PART X

YOU ARE MY FATHER FIGURE, GOD IS MY REAL FATHER

CHAPTER 49

UNDER THE BRIDGE

With high feelings in my heart, on August 10, 2011, I left both girls in their beds. They seemed peacefully dreaming when I closed their rooms behind me. I took 183 E and headed to work to Dallas. Under George Bush Bridge, just before passing Esters exit, my friend Eight's headlights started to hesitate. It was three in the morning. My engine misfired seconds later and my car died. I opened the hood to see if there was anything unplugged. Everything was at its designed place. I cranked the engine, it did not fire anymore. I tried many times to see if I can make it run. I just found myself draining the battery power. I stopped turning the key.

The first call I made was to my boss. I won't be able to make it today, my car just broke down on me, I said to him. Give him a call once it is fixed, he said to me. I tried one last time to crank the engine to see if it would start after cooling off. It didn't. I called three towing companies one by one. Their answer service came on and said that they will be open at eight. I realized at that moment that my car broke down under the bridge. Bridges are places, under which people without people and people without homes live. I had people, but they all abandoned me a long time ago. My children abandoned me. I had a home, but I did not have anyone to call from in there. I didn't even have anybody to call out there for help or for a simple ride. For someone with grown-up children, I was at that moment a people without people. Tears dropped from my eyes because I was alone, and it was night. They spent their times away from me, saying heavy things against me, things I did not do and things that did not make sense to me. They physically hit me, leaving me bruised, leaving me with broken bones and bumps all over my body. I tried to resist their assaults and ended up with a broken heart and slashed mind. My children hurt me. I did not want to cry, but I was under the bridge, a place where homeless cry, remembering the life they had and the life they left behind. I started to remember mine.

For his children, anyone can be a father, but it takes a lot to be a dad. Without any doubt, a dad will take care of his children. He will do so because he is a giving friend to his children. The man will, without hesitation, stop the time for them. That is a fact. The American appearance of a dad is easily broken and weak in significance. Even if Dad does good things for his child, sometimes something goes missing in their relationship. The same child, who calls him Dad, takes him to court in revolting manners and the child with the Mendes brothers' syndrome will kill his dad in a horrible way.

I made sure that my children do not find in me their dad but their best friend. My kids call me Papa, I made that possible. They all called me Papa because Papa is bigger than Dad. An African Papa is even bigger because he asks only respect, not all a lot in return. The respect is the diamond in the golden ring and the mother of all love. The respect creates the importance of an immense life in children back to their parents. Lots of American kids lack respect for their dads in general. That is where the problem is in today's society. Papa deserves more than respect since he can challenge a sorcerer of the night for his kids by unswervingly looking into this cold eye. Papa will find a way to catch by hand the Australian waglay regardless of its virulent spit to feed his kid and regardless of the fact that the hospital doesn't even have a vaccine against its deadly venom. When his kids are calling for help, inside a burning house, Papa will get in. He will get in the burning fire, challenge flame and smoke, and get out victoriously, his children in his arms. He will get in because this shows the love he carries inside for them, the one love that has been there since the time when they were not even born. The one love that will be there unused with the passing time, to when children would be able to stand on their own and to when they won't be able to feed themselves no more. That is what my Pa called the love that will never stop, a love that will give and keep on giving.

My kids called me Papa, they still do, because for them, I emptied my whole heart and poured it on them, like the rain on the ground, to grow rings of greatness around them. In a clear picture, I did not want to see them ending up on the streets. So I made myself their situated best friend, at least I thought so, till they begun disrespecting me. That disrespect was not from what is now called a culture clash; it was just disrespect because they knew better.

The last child to disrespect me was Belinda. Months before her graduation, we talked about what to do. I asked her to tell me the exact date of their commencement thirty days before. She answered and said that it is not fixed yet, but she will verify and let me know. The next day, I found a note on the refrigerator. It said, "Graduation March 13." I wrote it down. Days went by. Then Grace and Nira, her cousins, came down from Maryland. Grace said they were in town for Belinda's graduation. It did not hit me at that moment till I looked at the sticky note on the refrigerator. I called my daughter Belinda and asked her, one more time to remind me when she is going to have her graduation. She said, "I don't remember exactly when, but I put a sticky note on the refrigerator."

I took a picture of that sticky note and sent it to her.

"Are you sure, Belinda, this is your graduation date?" I asked her.

"Yes, graduation on March 13," she answered via text message.

I called Grace and asked her what was going on, why Belinda was telling me that her graduation will be in March.

"Uncle, we are here because Belinda is graduating in five days. Think about it, Uncle, March 13 was so yesterday. It was two months ago. We are in May. Why don't you look at your invitation?" she asked.

"Yes indeed, March 13 is so yesterday. Okay, I know the game Belinda is trying to pull on me again. She had been doing this openly and for so long. This is not the first time she is showing me her disrespect. Let me give her a call."

I dialed her number.

"Do you know that Grace and Nira are in town for your graduation? Do you also know that your graduation is in five days from today, this May, not in March as you wrote it?" I asked.

"Oh yes, about that, I meant to tell you, but I forgot. Actually, it was a mistake."

"How come I still do not have an invitation when people coming far away already have theirs, if it was a mistake?"

"I will bring it to you, Papa. I will bring it the very next day I will be home," she said.

The very next day was May 9. Including Crystal, my granddaughter, my children came down home for a dinner. Belinda did not want to sit down and eat with us. She was in a hurry. She was a participant in the day activities at her campus. I reminded her about my invitation.

"You know without it, there is no way that I would get in."

"I did not forget, I will give it to Grace. She will bring it to you in the morning of the graduation day."

Nira and her little sister Grace were spending their nights over Linda's. Their daily activities were done in my apartment. When Grace showed up in the morning that Saturday, I asked her for my invitation before saying hello.

"Belinda did not give it to me, Uncle, call her," she said.

I did.

She answered and said, "I gave it to Grace this morning."

"Grace, she just says she gave it to you," I said.

"What kind of game is Belinda playing with you, Uncle? She never gave me your invitation. I will give you mine if you want me to."

"I know she did not. That is the reason she gave March as her graduation month. She just doesn't want me to be seen with her at her campus. I bet anything the other black and rich man she always introduces as her father will be there. I will be there too. I will be there without any invitation. I need to see how far she will take her graduation game and how her story would end. I will be there."

I showed up and sent the UTA security guard to let Belinda know that I was at the main entrance door.

"Tell her also that she never gave any invitation to Grace, so she needs to come out and let me in."

The man left and come back up. "I gave her your message. She said she will be here very soon."

Belinda never came out to let me in. She was embarrassed of my presence around her. I confirmed once more that as true. I waited outside the gate till everyone with invitations got in. I waited not because the security officer asked me to, but because there was in her something that no one could ever taken away. She was my blood. With all her malignance combined, even she herself couldn't have taken that away. So I decided to wait at the entrance of the college hall. I was the only parent waiting outside, the only parent who was not invited. They all were in, enjoying different formal procedures, ritual services, and ceremonies that always come before the main event. I also missed the UT jazz band playing all kinds of music and their cheerleaders doing their thing. Then the hall opened for students who did not buy tickets. That was the time I entered. We got in when everyone was already seated, when they were calling graduates' names. I stood up against the wall, behind the last row, because every single seat was already taken. I was not pleased to see the man who had been taking my place. He was there sitting with honor in a reserved seat at front row, and I was standing invisible in the back of the third row. I had a given right to see her that close graduating instead of what could be the father of my daughter. I missed a bunch of good activities every respected parent saw, but I was happy to see her throw her hat in the air. I was happy nevertheless that my daughter graduated inside that UTA College park center. That was a good day despite the way it started.

I forgot all about being humiliated and took everybody to dinner at a new steak place, behind 360 South, on 30 E. A lot of UTA graduated students were there with their parents. We had a good time. Nira Nsanga was the most hilarious. She spent that moment doing African stuff. She was dancing around and, at same time, breaking silence with mermaid screeches. Using nothing but both her hands on the mouth, she also was making some kind of a night bird squeal. I accompanied her on that musical that only African aunties knew how to play back there when a child was born. All eyes were fixed on our table. Belinda did not like that, maybe because I was sitting next to her. To bother her more, I stood up to dance with Nira, the woman of the moment. She asked Nira to stop.

"You cannot make her stop. This is the reason she is down here for. She came down to enjoy your graduation," Linda said to her, and we played it cool.

Two weeks later, Belinda came home. As she was entering, she asked me why I used her soap scrub to clean the bathtub with and then trash it.

"Come on, Belinda. Why don't you start by saying hello, how have you been?" I asked.

"I am serious. Loylla said you were cleaning the fish tank. You made the tub dirty while doing so, and then you used my scrub to clean it. I do use that scrub on my body. What did you do that for?" she madly asked.

"I understand you are compressed with all these final exams you were taking. Please do not pick up a fight with me for 99c scrub. Find another way to decompress yourself. Get you a boyfriend or something. Your scrub is still under the cabinet. I used mine," I said to her.

"No, you did not. You used mine."

"The one I used has the same color than yours, that doesn't mean it is yours. Check it out," I said to her

"I lost all respect for you. I used to respect you, I don't respect you anymore," she suddenly said.

I did not feel her words at that moment. They were fast. Even if they were quickly said, they were sharp and they cut my heart as if they were a Gillette shaving razor blade on a brick of butter. I closed my eyes. I saw an immense pain taking place inside my head. I saw flames and I saw shooting stars. It was only after I saw my own blood rush behind my eyelids that I felt Belinda's words, very slowly first and then deeper. Her words were blows to my left ear. I kept my eyes closed to avoid losing my equilibrium. I did not want to consume that attack naively, but it took me a very long time to start digesting what she said. And what she said was an offense without a cause. It was a beginning of a fight for absolutely nothing as my pa would have said to me at that moment. When I woke up from that sudden nightmare, I asked, "Why would you say such thing? What did I do to you?"

"I don't respect you the way I used to, not anymore."

"Just like that or because of the 99c scrub? Well, it is okay with me. You are not the only child of mine who doesn't respect me. I just don't know why you guys always do disrespect me. Muntumpe has done doing a good job of destroying what I have been building for y'all. It is okay," I answered.

"It is okay that way because if you did not know, Papa, you are my father figure. God is my real father. I am opening to you to tell you that…"

"No, you are not opening. You are disrespecting me. Your father figure…Just for a reminder, my pa said once that a lack of respect for your parents is the equivalent of insulting the crocodile before crossing the river. Do you know what I mean?"

She ignored my remarks and went on and on. She talked and said nothing but stupidities. I implored her lack of respect. What she said, not a single Catholic preacher would ever let it repeated in confession; it would have scared Jesus out of Jesus himself. She continued and said, "You never have done anything for me. I raised myself. For instance, you used to give me $20 every time I had a game. It was nothing when it came to travelling with my team. My friend had more. They laughed at me because I couldn't even buy a drink." She said.

She said that she had to drive a used Mitsubishi and a used Ford Taurus at UTA when her friends were driving Mercedes and BMW. This was the reason she always denied me as her father and the reason she spent her life hiding from me every time I showed up at her game.

"It is okay, it is okay with me. You are not the only child of mine who, without any obvious and perceptible reason whatsoever, hates me. Since you are thinking you arrived given that you just graduated, let me tell you a story I was told way back when I was in elementary school. Listen carefully because they are still and so many rivers to cross ahead of you. This is the version I still remember," I said to her.

There was this French man called Mr. Seguin. He had lot of goats. He was not happy with what these goats were doing to him. He lost them to prairie wolves, one by one, all the same way. These goats started by ignoring Mr. Seguin's advice and then forgetting how good he was to them. The only thing that was in their mind was to go to the mountain. Each one of them broke the leash and went up there seeking for freedom. The last one was called Blankette; she was the youngest. She was so bearded she looked like a marine admiral officer. With her soft eyes, her two long and beautiful horns, a long white fur she wore all around her body as if it was a warm great coat, Blankette was pretty and she was not satisfied with the food that was given to her by Mr. Seguin.

Mr. Seguin had a big enclosure in his pasture he let Blankette live in. And time to time, he went to check on her to see if she had everything she needed. Not only she was okay in there, she also was happy. Mr. Seguin thought then that his new goat won't be bored in his pasture. The only thing he wanted in return from Blankette was respect. That was not a big task to ask.

One day, Blankette looked up to the mountain. She said to herself that the grass must be greener up there, on the other side of the pasture. From that very moment, Mr. Seguin's grass did not taste the same. Then just like that, without further formalities, the goat opened her mouth and talked to a dumbfounded Mr. Seguin about it. She said she was tired of living at his place. She wanted to go in the mountain where she would eat greener grass. Mr. Seguin was stupefied of that lack of respect. You don't insult the hand that fed you, the hand that still feeds you. He answered and said, "Blanky, you want to leave me? Don't you have the whole land to jump on around here? Is there not enough water you can possibly need? Don't you know that there is a big wolf up there in the mountain?"

"Yes, when he will show up, I will hit him with my horns," Blankette answered.

"I had Renauld last year. Just like a he-goat, she was stronger, repulsive, and mean. The wolf made mockery of her horns. Even if she fought bravely and stoutly all night long, the wolf made breakfast out of her without more ado. By morning break, she was eaten like a taco."

"I don't care. I want to go. I hate your grass. It was not even green, it was faded and yellow. I am not suicidal I will fight your wolf. I still want to go in the mountain," replied Blankette.

"You know, even without any form of trial, what you just said is huge disrespect. It is a breach of confidence. I thought that when you feed a mouse, using nothing but the manioc, that mouse will follow you to the mill. Apparently, that is not what you are doing after everything I have done for you. What you are about to do is to run with the hare and hunt with the hounds, which is a mission impossible. I will save you against yourself. I will lock you in."

When Mr. Seguin went to sleep after locking her in, Blankette jumped through the window and went in the mountain. When she arrived there, she felt the air of self-governance. She did not have a leash around her neck anymore or a pious to be attached to. The grass in the mountain was very delicious and tasty at that moment. Up to her, that grass was a natural mix-max that was raised out of so many plants. She ate the blue, the red, and the digital flowers that were growing right there on the mountain land that had long purple flourished and aromatic church-like chalices. She thought of these chalices as communion cups. Blankette felt herself in heaven. She jumped there and browsed them. She leaped again and grazed them. She dove under every grass that seemed to be taller than her horns. She chattered them all. After eating every kind and played every-where, Blankette thought that she was better there than over Mr. Seguin's. Suddenly, the fresh air combed her fur. It was getting night. This was the moment she heard the howling of the wolf. At that same time, Mr. Seguin started calling her on the top of the sound of his trumpet made out of an elephant trunk. It was late already.

Blankette turned around. She saw two short and straight ears under which were two gleaming and glittering eyes. That was the wolf. By his sitting position, Blankette realized that he was big and strong. The monster was motionless on his butt; he was unshaken. He started moving his long tongue in his mouth because he was not in hurry. He knew he will eat her. Blankette remembered the story of Renauld, the old goat. She put herself in a position of no return, got ready, and threw the first punch. She pulled up a big fight and held her own. The fight went on all night long. She used nothing but her moves and horns till when the rooster started to wake people up. Her bluffs were not enough, at the break of the day, she collapsed. Just like the old Renauld, she succumbed down at dawn and bled to death. To begin with, that was a lost fight. Goats don't fight with wolves. Goats don't kill wolves. Then the wolf tore her in pieces and ate her.

Now, why are you telling me that story?" Belinda asked.

"Didn't you situate yourself in that story yet? Pick what may concern you and leave the rest to other members of this family. Each one of you guys is Blankette. Each one of you disrespected me. The story ended up with a death, the death of Blankette. That doesn't necessary reflect what will happen to y'all at the end, but dying is not always physical. Look at Dimassa and Makaya, if they are not spending their nights in jails, their heads are under police officers' boots and knees. They both did not listen to me when I asked them to, like you, they spent their times disrespecting me. Like I said, dying is not always physical, just look at them. Since they don't even have a place where they can sleep, they are now blaming their failures on me. They forgot that they followed what Muntumpe offered, and that is who you are following now. Blankette said, 'I hate your grass. It was not even green, it was faded and yellow.' You said I never done anything for you. You raised yourself because I used to give you only $20 every time you had a game. You don't disrespect me that way and hope that tomorrow we will sit down around a cup of coffee, talk about it, and be forgiven. An egg broke when you called me father figure. It is impossible to pick up its yellow and shell from the floor to make it whole again. What a parent expects from the child is not necessary a material thing, it is respect. You said, from your own lips, that you do not have respect for me anymore. That means there is no way back from that. The only one thing remaining between you and me is that from now on, we grow apart. I don't even see how you guys go to church to praise something that you cannot see, if you are unable to pay respect to the person who really brought you in this word by daring to call me a father figure."

CHAPTER 50

MEDA BOURLAND IS A JOKE FOR A LAWYER

"Yeah, you are a father figure only. You never did anything for me. You—"

"Really? Do you speak English?

"Yes, I do, but—"

"I did that. I brought you here, and because of me, you are speaking the language of the land. Are you in the United States of America, the best country ever?"

"Yes but—"

"Give me credit for that too. If I did not bring you here in this great country, you wouldn't even have been able to graduate today. So respect me for that if you cannot respect me as a father. Do not show your ingratitude by saying that I used to give you $20 because $20 was all I had. I would have given you more if at that time my rent was not running late. See, that was one thing you felt to realize. I gave you more, giving you that $20, because I sacrificed my rent for you," I said to her.

"You are my foster father. God is my real father. He brought you in this world to feed me. For Him, you are the soil that provided food for me," she answered.

"See what I mean, disrespect on disrespect. My pa said to me once that each one of us makes his bed the way he wants to sleep on it. You, my friend, you really have decided to disrespect me, directly on my face. Disrespect and disrespect. I hope you do not understand what you are saying because you are telling me exactly how to treat you. I am nothing but soil…God is your real father you said. Really? I did not see God when you used to shit yellow and I used to change your diapers. I am not talking here about your American diapers or what you call Pampers. My diaper, the one I used on you, was called couche. In , it is called a couche. It was a white piece of washing cloth, similar to the one you find in kitchen. I wrapped that piece of a white cloth on you as if it was underwear. After you have done your business in it, I took it from your butt and put it in the soapy bucket. Your shit was still hanging in it as I was doing that. I rinsed it using nothing but my hands and washed it. Then I hung it to dry. Once dried, I put it back on your butt for your protection. And you took shit in it again. Despite the change of its color, I repeated the same cycle till that piece of white cloth tore apart. I touched your shit literally to help you be who you are becoming. Calling me your father figure, your foster parent, and your soil is insolently disrespectful. I did not see God touching your shit, I did not see God cleaning your butt and changing your diapers. I don't even think He would have stood up to different colors of what came out of you. I don't think He would have supported the smell of what came out from your butt. I supported it and I did it out of love I carried for you. I deserve nothing but admiration, high opinion, and reverence from you and from each one of y'all," I replied.

"The Bible says God is my real father."

"That could have been true only if your mom cheated on me with Him, which was impossible, which is impossible. God did not have a put in what I did to have you. That is the truth, the real truth. What you believe is what you were told by people who were told the same thing way back and so on. Whoever wrote these stories wrote them principally to control people and then to have money from them. He never ever sat down with God to talk with Him. Nobody has ever. God never sat on the same table with the person who wrote the Bible to dictate His will or what He was thinking about anything. Look around you and you will realize that people who keep telling God's stories are richer, filthy richer than those who are listening to them. They are richer because they receive money from stupid people and from those who are brainwashed. In fact, if there is a god, for you, it would be me. I created you. I am your god."

"You cannot say things like that. God will never forgive you," she threatened.

"That is not news to me. He never forgave Lucifer, His angel, and yet He asks everybody to forgive each other. I won't have a guilty feeling if the next time you talk to Him, you tell Him that I won't be the victim of people who are making Him a liar. I am a fighter."

Under that George Bush Turnpike Bridge, I stood desperate. I did not have anyone to call for help. No child of mine would have come anyway. They hated me. They lied about me and ended up by physically hitting me. They followed Muntumpe's orders and acceded to hurt me. I laid the car seat back all the way down, and I closed my eyes, waiting for the sun to rise. Tears wet my face. I cried choking my voice in. When I woke up, the Cardinal Towing Company was hooked up already to my friend Eight. I asked him to take it home. It was eight in the morning when I caught a ride with the Cardinal driver going back home. I did not go to work. I spent that day in bed. Tabô woke me up. She wanted to have her hair done. She asked money for it. I gave it to her. Loylla and she went to the store next door to buy all necessary gears. It took them two hours. Tabô came back in first. She wanted to know if I would tell the judge if her mom brings her money for hair.

"Yes, I would. She is not supposed to be around you or Loylla anymore. I gave you money already. What happened to it? Was not that enough?"

"Why?"

"Why what?"

"Why don't you let my mom give me money?"

"Your mom tried to sell you for sex, to Sebastian, her twenty-one-year-old Mexican boyfriend."

"It was not Sebastian, it was Saint," Loylla answered.

"To protect you against all that and more, the judge ordered her to stay away from both of you," I explained.

Tabô got mad. She ran outside. Loylla followed her. She came back in at five with two $20 bills. She was at the park and found it on the playground, she said. I advised her to go back and try to find who lost that kind of money.

"Do not mention to whoever would come forward the size of the bill, where you found it, and how much it is. We need to give the money back," I said to her.

Thirty minutes later, she came in. "I did not find anyone. Can I spend it immediately?"

"No, you cannot. Give it to me. I will keep it in case someone arrives looking for it. What happened to the money I gave you for your hair?" I said.

Just like that, with a foamed giant crayon, she hit Chrystal on her head. I told her to stop. She hit Muntumpe with it. I took it away from her and put it behind the living room cabinet. She pushed Belinda, lost the control of her feet, and knocked herself down. We all ignored her. She stood up and locked herself in her room. About five minutes later, she came out, clearly looking for trouble.

"Muntumpe, why are you looking at me?" she asked. Muntumpe ignored her. She hit her with another giant crayon again. I took that one away too.

"Why are you suddenly attacking everybody and where is the money I gave you for your hair?" I asked her

She did not answer. She went outside again. Then Muntumpe heard the noise from the other room. She said, "Papa, Tabô is out there banging on my widow. I think Sheebah sent her to create trouble with me, just the way she did when CPS got involved and took them away. Remember when we were eating rice and she hit my plate? That is exactly what she was trying to achieve today. She is out there cursing at me. I have to go to work tonight, so I need to sleep. Can you tell her to stop?"

"Of course. I think her mother has something to do with her changing of behavior suddenly."

I brought Tabô inside. I told her to sit still. She sat for about thirty minutes without moving a muscle. Muntumpe came out from the room and said, "Since I cannot sleep, sit on the high chair and I will do your hair. Where are the materials you went to buy, Tabô, and why are you suddenly attacking everybody? Did your mom send you to do so?" Muntumpe asked.

"I lost the $20 Papa gave me. I did not buy anything," Tabô said.

"That is odd. You lose $20 and you find $40 on the floor," I said.

"She did not lose anything. She spent it. The $40 is coming from her mother. Tabô said it all when she asked you if you would tell the judge about the money her mom would be bringing her for hair. It is obvious, Papa. I know the game," Muntumpe said.

"Is that true, Tabô, your mom gave you this $40?" I asked.

She did not have a time to answer. Someone banged at the door with intensity. It was exactly six in the afternoon. When I opened, J. Ceja with the Hurst Police Department was standing on my doorstep. He said that someone had called the police. Kids are been beaten up, in this very apartment. I opened my door wide and invited him inside.

"As you can see, Officer, I do have at this moment three little girls and their big sisters. Tabô is having her hair done. Loylla is playing a video game. Chrystal, my granddaughter, is talking to Bob the turtle on the balcony. No child is crying here. Who called you, Officer?"

"It doesn't matter who called."

"Must be a female called Sheebah. She called you...oh...I got it now. Tabô and the game of hitting her family...she was playing us. Her mother planned everything, one more time. It was a setup. Hoping someone would retaliate her sudden behavior...she timed it and called the police. She thought that by the time you will arrive, you would find her crying. She has gone crazy."

"May I see any order from the judge authorizing you to have both kids back because it has been brought to our attention that you don't have anything?" Officer J. Ceja asked.

I handed them to him. After reading, he said, "It seems your children are talking to their mother. This situation will create problems down the road. It is not specifically said in these orders that kids cannot talk to their mother, but I deal with this all day long. What you need to do is to take the phone away."

Both girls wanted to go back out. I let them know they have to be in at 8:00 before the sun set. When Muntumpe finished doing Tabô's hair, they stepped out. At 8:30, I started looking for them. I panicked at 9:00 and called 911. An investigator will contact me, said the dispatcher. D. Smith, a Hurst police officer, called back. He said, "The kids are with their mother. They crossed the street and went to call their mother on the public phone. It is established that you spent two days with them, you did not feed them and did not show love to them at all. You spent that time threatening to beat them. They ran from your long history of abusing them."

"None of that happened," I explained.

"Well, they ran from you. It is not kidnapping, it is parenting. The mother took them."

"That doesn't make sense. I have clear orders from the court, orders written by the judge that exclusively and particularly oblige her to stay away from both girls. By saying it is not a kidnapping, you are helping her break the law. I have custody papers, it is kidnapping and you know that. If it was me, a man, being black and everything, who had taken them without been authorized, by now I would have had handcuffs all around me and taken to jail."

"Sir, police do not take sides, they are here to help."

"Exactly, you are helping her. I have a long and much activated relationship with Hurst Police Department. I have a funny feeling about that. They do take sides. You are taking sides now."

"You need to hang up, sir. I won't let you make mockeries of Hurst Police."

"That is exactly what Sergeant Tabo said to me once when I told him the same exact thing."

I hung up. Since Sheebah was living in Arlington at that time, I went there to press kidnapping charges. The police told me that they did not have any jurisdiction on what was happening in Hurst. They asked me to go back to Hurst, present all custody documents, and ask them to arrest Sheebah for interference with child custody. I went back, and as usual, Hurt Police refused to do so. I did not respond. I turned around and left. Around 11:00 p.m., I was short of ideas. I did not know where to go. Nwokoye was out of the town; she was in Houston. I did not want to bother her from over there. I called CPS Susan Giles and told her what was going on. She said that Sheebah's lawyer wrote her an e-mail. She said, "You have been abusing the kids. They did not have food, warm clothes, and you have been yelling at them. She even accused you of not putting them in school."

"Man oh man, I did all that in barely two days? When did she want me to put them in school?"

"That is why I am taking over. Mrs. Meda and her client should have taken it to court. Orders are orders. Let's sleep on it and wait for when the office will be open," Susan Giles advised me.

I did not wait in my bed. I called off from work and went back to Arlington. I spent that night in the parking lot, sitting in my Ford Taurus in front of Nwokoye's office. I called her business phone at 7:00 and left a message, hoping she will call back. She did. She said she was just getting off from the plane. She will be in around 9:00. When her office opened, I talked to her paralegal. She said that Violet knows already; she received an e-mail from Meda, Sheebah's lawyer. She will be here in ten minutes.

She was hot when she entered her office. Her hair was unsurprisingly well done; no makeup and no nail polish on her body. She was original as one would expect from her. She greeted me more politely than before and said, "I know what happened. Meda Bourland informed me. What kind of lawyer advises her client to go against the judge's court orders? That crazy woman is putting, in writing please, that she advised Sheebah to go and get the kids because they are starving, are not put in school, are abused, they do not have clothes. She is crazy."

Nwokoye picked the phone up, dialed the clerk court number, and requested an emergency court setting. When she hung up, she called CPS Jackson, who told her, "I just gave a piece of talk to Meda

Bourland. Sheebah needs to go and drop the kids at their father's before she gets some jail time."

I saw Violette clicking the phone over; it was Susan Giles.

"Let's not forget that the mother gave both children away to CPS. She gave up her right in the court of the law. She did that in front of the judge, and it was witnessed by her peers. She doesn't have any right whatsoever to come and get them where we are housing them, no matter what. I told her lawyer that she as the only practicing woman of the law, I know of, crazy enough to give such counseling."

"The father had custody two days ago, if there was a problem, the legal procedure was to report the abuse. CPS would have taken it from there instead of sending her client to take physical possession of children. For a lawyer, she is a joke," Violette said to Susan.

"I told her the exact same thing, well, not the joke part. I said to Bourland that since their mother enrolled them in Arlington, Mr. Kasalobi was supposed to have legal papers from me on Friday, August 12. He doesn't have the letter yet. I signed it and put it in the mail. That letter would have authorized him to legally withdraw both girls from one school and lawfully put them in another. That is the reason they are not in school yet. Anyway, school is not open Saturday and Sunday. The earlier they can be enrolled is Monday. I am going to get the kids. I will be bringing them to the father after 4:00," Susan Giles said.

"And I am going to court to make sure this situation doesn't happen again," Nwokoye answered.

"CPS will set another date for a status review hearing. Sheebah needs to stay away from the children. She was unable to take care of them the first time around, she won't be able to do it this time around," Susan said.

I thanked Violet and left the office. The same day, CPS Attorney Melissa Pashall sent a confirmation of the setting to Cheryl Lopez, the court coordinator. She confirmed the setting of the styled and numbered cause for a status review hearing set for October 20, 2011, at 9:00 a.m. in the 325 district court on the fifth floor. This confirmation was made in good faith in the belief that the petitioner will be ready for hearing at the time requested, she said.

"All of the petitioner's pleading are now in order or will be at least seven days prior to the hearing date. There is no special exception or pre-trial matter, which should be presented to the court in advance of the hearing. All parties to the suit are being mailed a copy of this confirmation of setting by the US certified mail and by e-mail," she wrote.

It was hard to find an empty slot to park. Each parking lot around the court was full to its capacity on that Thursday, October 20. I drove around a couple of times, I did not see any empty parking lot. I then decided to wait for someone to pull out. I entered in and used his leftover meter time.

"This is the first time to see the metal checkpoint line this long, what is going on?" the lady behind me asked.

"I don't know. I have never seen so many people inside here, not as many as today."

"It is another adoption day today. Kids will be having new parents," an intern officer answered.

As we were waiting for the judge, Violet approached me. She said that CPS is complaining. I have been bugging Adrian Watters, the new case worker, regarding the stoppage of child support.

"You shouldn't be calling them, call me instead."

"I did not call CPS per se. I called Swift transportation pay and garnishment department. I was wondering why they still did not stop the child support as it was ordered on August 9, 2011. The Swift transportation lady I talked to said that she called the district attorney because the document was scratched and handwritten by the judge. The district attorney did not answer. She then gave me that same number to see if I would be lucky. I called. James Teel answered. He told me that the lady in his payroll did what she was supposed to do. She was protecting herself. It did not matter if the document was scratched or handwritten, it was legal and certified. She should have used it as it is. It was a document from the court of the law, James Teel said. He also said that Melissa, his supervisor, will handle the problem. It was at this moment that I called the number again to see if I would talk to Melissa Paschal. I did talk to her and told her that Swift Company wanted to speak to the district attorney or to the lady who signs documents to confirm the legality of the court order. Otherwise, they won't stop the child support. Melissa said she will look at it. That was what happened."

"Okay, I understand."

CHAPTER 51

JUST LIKE A BROKEN DOOR, YOU WILL NEVER HAVE THEM

One hour later, we approached the bench for CPS review. Melissa, the district attorney, introduced her case to Judge White. She said that on August 9, kids were removed from CPS custody and were given back to Kasalobi, their father.

"Sheebah, the mother, by the advice given to her by her counsel, went and removed both children where we were housing them. She did so without any authorization and with an open disrespect to this court. We need to end this problem before kids get hurt. This is what we have at this time, Your Honor," she pleaded.

"I am aware of that. I will give my decision at the end of the hearing. Adrian, how are the kids doing in the hands of Mr. Kasalobi?"

"They were in a good mood when I went there. For the first time ever, they were smiling and they looked dundy. As matter of fact, they were at the best they have ever been. In the hands of their mother, these two kids were not in that frame of mind. The mother is spending her spare time threatening Mr. Kasalobi. She already said on August 9, she will kill both children and then kill the father, and it was not even recorded. We need to make sure that she is more than five hundred feet from them. I have two problems nevertheless: kids do not like the food they eat, they also lack money for lunch in school," Adrian said.

"Mr. Kasalobi, what kind of food are you giving to the children?" Judge asked.

"These kids were fed on candies and burgers. That is showing in their body mass. I don't give them junkies. I feed them regular food, on African food mainly."

"What is African food?"

"The best that a person can eat. African food is regular food cooked differently. You know Chinese food, Your Honor. It is not really coming from China. It is American food cooked the Chinese way. That is how African food is. We cook it our own ways, depending of which part of Africa each one of us is coming from. In my part of town, including Pondu, we have different vegetables and greens. Pondu is the main green most Africans are fond of. It is a collected of pounded leaves from different manioc plants. We eat it mixed with almost anything: meat, fish, rice, beans, potatoes, you name it. But we like eating it with fufu or cassava bread. Fufu is not baked as regular bread, it is not steamed as a taco either, it is cooked in hot water dough. We mixed boiled water with flour and let it cook slowly by turning the dough with a mixer. Fufu is mainly made out of manioc tubercle or cassava tuber plants. One can make it from different type of flours: from grains like rice, corn, wheat, or from tubercle roots like potato, banana, and yam. We make it also with finished products like Semulina or Massa Trico. Here in America, we do fufu mostly with tortilla flour, the same flour that Latinos make tacos and fajitas out of it. Now Sheebah here is the one who is complaining. She is trying to make a fuss out of nothing as if African food is lesser than hamburgers. Actually, African foods are healthier than hamburgers. They do not contain chemicals, they are natural. No one has ever gotten fat on African foods. Burgers are okay now and then, but I will never feed my kids on them, not anymore. They will eat safe and healthy food."

"Well, it is reported to us that you give them termites, I mean insects for food, is that true?"

"With all due respect, Your Honor, I would have asked you to define what you are calling insects because you make it sound as if insects are a calamity for human health. I will tell you right now that only 8.2 percent of the world population does not eat insects. I was raised eating insects, big or small. Some you don't eat, but those we do are all sources of protein. I eat, as today, all kinds of bugs. I eat cicadas as small as leafhoppers and as bigger as the palm of your hand. I eat them all, the underground cicadas, the underwater cicadas, and the tree cicadas also called cigales. I eat all kind of beetles. I eat wing beetles, water beetles, sheathed beetles, shell beetles, and big coleopterans. Those are as big as twice your thumb. Did you know, Your Honor, that 40 percent of all insects are beetles? I still eat caterpillars, grasshoppers, palm worms, sand larvas, yellow crickets, caterpillars, and you name it. Yes, I eat ants too. Those are red in color and sour in taste. We mixed them in anything to have the lemon season flavor. The termites you heard of, Your Honor, are not your Orkin or Terminix house termites. Those are wild, about five to ten times bigger and stronger. They live in mount buildings they themselves build. The biggest recorded termite house is 98.4 in diameter and 196.8 feet tall. That is about three stories of a human being's house. Yes, I cook insects in my house. Yes, I eat bugs in my house. Sheebah here is the one making trouble about it because I am African and she doesn't like my food. Tabô and Loylla never touched any of my bugs, but grown-up kids do eat them," I explained.

"In United States, we only eat FDA-approved food," Judge White said.

"Your Honor, if the Federal Department of Agriculture did not approve of it, we wouldn't have been able to buy them in stores, in a Korean store for instance, and Americans wouldn't have been drinking liquor that contain insects. *Fear Factor* and *Parts Unknown* are two American shows that show people like Joe Rogan and Antony Bourdain going around and testing bugs. Insects are good protein food, not nuisance, Your Honor."

Then my lawyer explained to the judge that the reason kids do not get lunch money is because they are qualified for government food program.

"Where are the children at this moment?" Judge White asked.

"They are in school at this moment," Nwokoye answered.

"That is where they should be going undisturbed," the judge said.

Judge White then explained her decision to the court. She said that I, Mr. Kasalobi, have to be aware of where Tabô and Loylla are at all times. When busy, I have to name a responsible adult person by his name who must assist with watching the children while I have to sleep during the day. This person would help supervise them. He would have his background checked by the case worker. Both the person and me will be aware of the children's whereabouts all the times. I will not let children have an unsupervised contact or make contact whatsoever with Ms. Sheebah. They will do so only on the scheduled visitation times and in the presence of the case worker. The will not leave the house premises without my verbal permission or that person's consent. I will inform the case worker immediately when they are in contact with their mother and when they leave the apartment premises without my permission. This order must be respected from that moment on to the next evaluation or to the end of case. Watters, the case worker, will monitor my home. She will make unannounced visits and frequent checks of the home to verify that children have adequate food and to ensure that they are being cared for. She will ensure that I will be respecting these orders all the times.

For a total evaluation, the judge said, the case worker will monitor these tasks anytime she feels like. Despite the school food program, I will be providing lunch money or a lunch box for both children. Adrian Watters will contact the school to determine if the girls have received lunch money or if they were bringing a lunch from home. The food from home should include fresh fruits and vegetables. This safety plan is designed to ensure the safety and well-being of the children. If the case is closed and I do not follow the safety plan after that, the department may have to take serious action which may include removal of both girls from my home.

Beginning and ending the date of October 26, 2011, to the end of case, I will be picking Tabô up from school every day, and CPS will monitor that Tabô is being picked up on time at 3:15 p.m. Tabô will contact me to inform me if her daily basis has changed or if she will stay late at school.

"They will be appropriate and possible consequences if you do not carry out this plan successfully as described, Mr. Kasalobi. I am ordering you to apply for title IV-A emergency assistance to help cover the cost of the CPS services if it does not conflict with any existing court order. Mrs. Bourland, you need to control your client. Otherwise, I will slap you with contempt to the court and you will spend some time in jail. Your client should be at least five hundred feet from children till the court decides otherwise. This session is adjourned," the judge said.

My main concern was for the attorney general to stop the child support. Even if it was legally decided so in the court of the law, Sheebah was still getting paid despite the fact that I had both girls with me. Days went by and Sheebah was still not respecting the judge's orders so far. Her big fight was to destroy both girls first and me after that.

"If I cannot have them, none of us will have them. I will destroy them like a broken door," she said to me again.

I told CPS Watters about it; she took Sheebah's threats seriously and cancelled her next visitation.

"You did well. Do you remember that man, Yaser Saïd, who killed both his girls in horrific honor killing? Do you know why that happened?" I asked her.

"Yes, no one took him seriously when he was threatening both girls. Now he is a fugitive. He is one of the FBI's most wanted criminals," Adrian Watters answered.

"Wanted but still alive. Fugitive doesn't count for me. He is alive and both kids are dead. I just don't understand what kind of proof the judge wants to order Sheebah's arrest for threat to a child," I suggested.

"You need to start recording all conversations. I will tell Sheebah to have her visitation next week, same day," she explained.

Fortunately, on that next week visitation day, Loylla refused to go. She did not want to visit with her mother. She stepped out to her friend Kimberly before the arrival of Watters. She was about to take both girls to her place for her weekly visitation.

"Let's go over Kimberly's to verify if Loylla is there. Sheebah did not agree to only take Tabô there and leave Loylla behind," suggested Watters after calling her.

We left Tabô home and crossed Bellaire Street. Arriving there, Kimberly's uncle told us that Sheebah and her boyfriend were with Loylla and Kimberly at the park a minute ago.

"So she has Loylla at the park, despite all court strict instructions, and she is playing the game of hurt mother by refusing to have one child for her visitation, saying that she wants both children together at same time," Watters said.

"She always plays a hurt mother, and you guys always believe her," I answered.

Watters took note. She cancelled that day's visitation also. She later on reported everything to her superiors. Nwokoye got wind of that report and called me. She was mad. She said, "That issue will be cleared up and concluded on the twentieth hearing. But I am not happy with the way these children seem to go and come as they please. You don't even know exactly where they are most of the time, especially at night. These are things that will hurt you at trial. Please remember this case is not yet concluded."

"I understand that, ma'am. These things are happening because of Sheebah. Besides her threats, she is coaching both girls how to make me look bad."

"What she doesn't realize is that she also is losing them at the same time. Once they are bad, because that is how she is training them to be, they will be bad to the bone. Down the road, she won't be able to control them. I know this for a fact, I am a family lawyer."

Nwokoye was right. I was taking a nap the very next day when I heard my neighbor. Her voice sounded around the bend. She was mad, pretty much. After complaining about Tabô, she handed a $10 bill to Muntumpe.

"What is this for?"

"This is the lunch money your father gave to Tabô. She gave it to Juan Duran, my nephew. He is on probation for smoking marijuana. I don't want him to go back to jail, most definitely not for rape. He is twenty-one years old. I want Tabô to leave him alone. She wants Juan to buy marijuana so she can burn it inside your father's apartment. She said her mother sent her to it. Her intention is to strike you after that, expecting you to hit her back, so she can call the police and accuse your father of using drugs. Then, she will go to her mother's."

"Are you serious? I will tell Papa," Muntumpe answered.

Tabô overheard the whole conversation. She got mad. She started by throwing candies at them and then physically attacking Muntumpe. I intervened and yelled at her. She yelled back, closed her fists as if she was about to do a boxing match with me. I took my belt from the hanger and threatened to rearrange her behind. She ran and went out. I heard her banging on the next-door lady. She was ready to fight with the young man. Up to what she was saying, Juan Duran betrayed her. From that moment on, Tabô went completely crazy. I forced her to stop making scenes and forced her back inside the apartment. From foolishness to foolishness, she took her big sister's shoes, ran outside with them, and plunged them in the muddy water. We all ignored her. When she cooled down, she yet told me that her mother coached her to do so. She wanted her to be beaten up, so she can be taken away by CPS.

Two hours later, she decided to go to the mall. She wanted me to take her and her friends there. I said to her that taking to the mall was not her right, but an extra she did not deserve.

"You yelled at me, you closed your little hands on me. You were ready to strike me, and now you want me to remunerate that disrespect by giving you a ride?"

"Yes."

"You stay inside the house. There is no way I pay will you for misbehaving."

"If you don't give me a ride, I will walk," she threatened.

"Keep on doing what your mother is telling you to do, and you will end up in jail. Continue being disobedient in school and they will send you to Key's. Continue fighting, you will go to juvenile. Mark my words because you will remember them. At the end of the day, you will be in jail," I said.

"My mother said that I am too young to be sent to juvenile," she answered.

"It won't be your mom who will be locked up in juvee. It will be you. Keep it up, and you will testify. Why don't you ask your school counselor? Your mother is the only person who is not telling you the truth. She is boldly using you."

Tabô stepped out. Around eight thirty, a woman came looking for her daughter. She said, "Your wife took her to North East Mall with them. She was supposed to drop her back at seven."

"My wife? I do not have a wife. So Sheebah is with the children again. Nwokoye won't be happy with this one either. She accused me of not knowing where both girls were already."

"Tabô's mother is not your wife? She told me she was," the lady insisted.

"Welcome to my world, and thank you anyway for informing me."

Sheebah was still messing up with my daughters' brain. It was hard for me to stop her. It seemed equally hard for CPS to stop her interfering with kids' custody. Tabô misbehaved that day because she wanted the police to intervene for use of marijuana in the apartment. And because it did not work, she took both kids to the mall to make me still look bad. Her centered fight was also complicating my financial situation. It was becoming impossible to pay child support and to pay my lawyer on time while I was trying to keep up with children. Sometimes, I had to miss days from work. Sheebah knew I was running dry. She also knew I was falling behind making payments of my other bills too. Her centered fight was to make me fail, and she was succeeding at doing it. The only person who stood by me was Adriane Watters. As my daughters Unit F-2 caseworker, she did not give up on me. She knew Tabô was taking Loylla down with her. She knew I was losing control, and she promised she will have a frank talk with both girls. At same time, she gave me a copy of the safety plan she created following the Texas Department of Family Form 2604-B. The reason she gave me that copy was to see if together, we could improve kids' behaviors. What she gave me was in fact a Plan for Immediate and Short-Term Child Safety. I had to apply without delay all tasks and services in it first and then follow every term as written. These terms consisted of me listing all tasks and services needed to provide, for both children, an immediate short-term safety. She nevertheless told me that Tabô's reaction was not due only to her mother's bad advice. It was also coming from the DivalProex Sod DR 500 mg and Risperidone 2 mg she has been giving her.

"Both medications need to stop. We have to do another evaluation. I want you to go and ask Dr. Radamaki why Tabô was still taking these two chemicals."

The very next very day was Thursday. I stopped at Cook Hospital in Bedford. As I was instructed by Adriane, I asked to talk to Radamaki. Since I did not have any appointment and because he was busy, I talked to his nurse. She asked me to leave my number. He called me later. He explained things I did not know. Contrary to Sheebah explanations to CPS, Radamaki was not a psychiatrist. He was a children pediatrician. About the reason Tabô was taking these two products, he was in a cloud. He said he never prescribed any Divalproex or any Risperidone to Tabô or to anyone else. He checked with Cook Hospital records and did not find that kids have been seeing a psychiatrist. He advised me to momentarily stop giving these two medicines to Tabô. I have to go to Forth Worth Cook Hospital, at emergency room, with both children to have a second opinion.

"Someone knows what is going on. Ask them to call the name of the prescriber. It is written on both CVS bottles. He is the person to talk to," he advised me.

Before going to Cook Children Hospital, I took both kids to counseling at Merit Family Services as I have been doing it every Saturday morning. When we arrived there, Tabô jumped out of the car. Loylla followed her. Bessie Anne, the head counselor, welcomed them. They ignored her and went straight to the bull dog that was behind the main building, fenced as guard of the property. They started to provoke that big animal. I saw Tabô throw stones as I was shutting the car doors off. At the same time, Loylla was yelling at the animal, and the dog was getting very meanly excited. He was hitting the fence, running from left to right and from right to left, trying to climb up. The beast was drooling, showing his teeth, and ready to rip anything around. I held both girls by their ears, forcefully took them upstairs by pulling their arms. Five minutes later, as we were waiting for our counseling time, they said they were going to the bathroom. I let them climb the stairs down.

It did not take long, the dog starting barking again. I heard a man yelling and threatening to call the police. I went downstairs. Tabô and Loylla were at the fence attacking the dog again. The man was telling them to stop. They were screaming back at him, threatening to call CPS. Bessie Anne came down. She talked to her son, the man who was asking my daughters to stop. She told him that those two where special girls, meaning they were crazy. That hurt my feelings because till this point, I was the only one who was not seeing what my children were becoming. The man moved the dog from the front fence to the backyard. He locked him inside a dog house. One more time, I took both girls upstairs.

It was impossible for Bessie Anne to effectively do her job. As a professional, she was instructed to handle the worse of situations. She was well-known for keeping her calm when doing so. That day, with Tabô and Loylla, she was not able to. She called me in the room. When I entered, I saw Tabô standing straight on the main table. She was kicking things. Lots of office supplies were on the floor. With her feet on the table, Loylla was yelling and laughing. She was encouraging her sister to keep destroying things. Both girls were so loud to a point that even people sitting in the waiting area were bothered. Bessie was painfully holding it in. She was visibly frustrated.

"I am a children's counselor. I work with special kids, with or without ordinary needs. I was told that your daughters are special, they are not. They are behind special. Tabô is the most affected. The worse of it is the fact that she is taking Loylla in with her. As a parent, I shouldn't tell you this in a moment like this. I give up. I can't do it. I hopped I could hold the ground just a little bit, Tabô is impossible. I have to cancel this CPS-ordered counseling visitation. I will call once I have an opening," she said.

Bessie Anne never called after that. I instead called her the very week. She said she was not able to handle both children anymore. I had to find some other places skilled enough to handle my children's behavior. Tabô and Loylla were too much even for me. That answer gave me a headache. Just thinking of what tomorrow will bring to them, my blood sugar went up twice the regular limit. I took two Glyburide-Metformin pills to lower it down. Tabô and Loylla were scaring me. We were on those days I spent my time warning their mother of who they will became if she did not stop putting ideas in their heads. Tabô and Loylla were bad children. I lay down and slept, sick with dizziness. We did not have a visitation that week or the week after that. Bessie Anne refused any visitation with them.

At 2200, the television noise woke me up. Since I had to go to work that early morning, I shut it off. I asked them to go to sleep. Tabô got mad. She took the can of the black finish paint and ran outside with it. By the time I caught up with her, she sprayed it on top of the hood of my Mitsubishi. I was this close to using my belt on her, but I did not. I was so crazy mad that I thought if I did, I would have badly hurt her. Ma always said that it was not wise to punish a child when mad. I did not punish her. I took her inside instead, cut off all lights, and laid down to sleep. One hour after that incident, Tabô rewinded her alarm clock. She brought it in the living room where I was sleeping in the couch. She let it run. Loylla cut all house lights back on when Tabô's alarm clock was ringing. I ignored them and continued to try to sleep. We reached midnight, and Loylla began hitting her door as if it was an African drum. She insisted annoying me by opening and closing the bathroom door. I continued ignoring them. I knew it was not coming from them. The twisted mind of their mother was to blame.

At 1:00 in the morning, Tabô unlocked the front door. She said she was going to catch a breeze outside.

"You guys have been knocking on the devil's door. At a certain time, he might as well open it. And you will get what you are begging for. If you do not lock that door back, I will shorten my belt on your behind," I warned her.

"He said he is the devil. Papa is the devil," claimed Tabô.

"And the devil does not need food," Loylla added.

"Yeah, let's trash everything. If he uses force on us, we will call the police. If he touches us, we call CPS on his ass," Tabô said.

She then went in the kitchen, opened the refrigerator door, and hit it back in forcefully to shut it off. Boxes of cereals that were put on top got dropped down. They broke open. She smashed the rest up, wasted every grain, and spread the contents on the floor. Then, she got hold of a can of soda pop drink and held it toward the couch where I was still lying motionless. She shook it up to build the pressure. I watched her do it. She opened it. The jet of that black liquid came out spraying everywhere as if it was a party champagne. I saw myself under the downpour of that sugary drink after it popped out. That was the last stroke. I held both girls by their pants and forced them in one room. One by one, I lifted them from the ground and threw them on the top of the bed, like a bag of rotten potatoes in the trash bin. They both got hurt when they hit the wall literally. Without yelling or raising my voice, I said to them, "This is the phone. Call whoever you want to call, but the first one who will move another muscle to try to stop me from sleeping will be the first dead child of this family."

They did not move. They did not talk back. They took me seriously. Maybe it was the way I lifted them, with extreme violence, from the ground and tossed them on the bed. Maybe it was because of the four-by-four piece of wood I momentarily held while calmly talking to them. Whatever they saw in me at that time and what they thought I was capable of that day, worked perfectly in my favor. They stopped their insanity and came to their senses. Again, with my parental voice, I said, "Your mother is wrong. What you are coached to do to me will not defeat the purpose of me being your father, a good papa, and a good parent. Doing what you are doing now is simply taking away the reason of me being there for both of you. At a given time, I will give up and stop trying to help. It will be at that moment in time that you will need me the most. It will be late because I won't be there anymore. I will remember these hard moments you are giving me and my heart will be cold. You will be doing what Muntumpe, Makaya, and Dimassa have been doing, telling whoever is willing to listen that 'my father never was there for me. He never did anything for me. My father doesn't like me' and so on. They are still saying these things today, forgetting that they put themselves in that situation, the same situation you are putting in today and the same situation in which you will be tomorrow. As I said, a little noise from you in this room and you will be talking to me six feet under the ground."

It was 3:00 in the morning when I finished talking to them. I was this close to passing out. The pressure in me was so intense to a point that even if I have tried, I couldn't have gone back to sleep. My entire body was aching the way it never did before; it was refusing to normally function. My mind, if I had one at that point, was just a mess. I had only had one option remaining, to call in from work.

Around eleven that day, I received a call from Bell Elementary. The assistant principal told me that Loylla was having a serious problem with school-established authority and that was not her first time. She also had been interrupting the entire class.

"Today, the teacher told her, three times already, to cool down, she did not. For bothering other students, she was sent to the principal's office. Not only did she refuse to go, she also refused to step out and come back in after getting her senses together. She just can't stop misbehaving, and I was this close to calling the campus police. Because of her disobedience, there is not one teacher here who wants to deal with her anymore. Today was her last stroke. She is contemplating the AEP this Thursday. The principal will decide which one she will be sent to," the assistant principal said.

CHAPTER 52

BEING CALLED NIGGER DERAILS A CHILD

I had a long talk with both girls when they came back in from school. I said to them again that I will always remember what they are repeatedly doing to themselves and to me if they do not stop. As a parent, I said to them, "The intense thing about remembering a wrong your own child has done to you is the fact that even if your best intention is to put everything in the past, your inner will always refuse to forget after forgiving. Since you have a full belly and a refrigerator full of food today, you are in agreement with your mom as she is telling you that you can live without me. Maybe you can, but what would happen when your belly is empty and when you won't be able to live without me? The only thing for sure is that once I am out of the picture, which is now being caused by your unstoppable bad manners and terrible character. Very soon after that, it will be you who won't be able to live, period. Once I am out, you won't have a full refrigerator anymore. You won't have anything on your back to properly shield your body from the winter cold and to protect yourself against the summer heat. Your mom will be there still, but she will not be able to buy you anything as usual. She never did to start with. She will continue using your support money on drugs and on her numerous boyfriends. Once I am out, you will have empty plates on your mom's table. That time is on its way, and it will be the exact time you will remember me. It will be a moment you will need something from me, but I won't be around anymore. That moment is coming. You will feel it, and you will miss me. That is the uncomfortable truth. What do you thing would happen then? Will you be able to say the truth to those asking or will you simply be saying what Muntumpe has been saying that 'you were children back then, you are sorry today, and as a parent, I cannot hold anything of that past against you.' This here is the time to listen, a time to remove yourself from your mother's handmade web and to do away with her venom she is slowly bringing and engorging in you. You have to change now. You must stop destroying your life," I said to them.

They listened carefully. At least, that was my impression. Tabô pledged to change. Loylla asked for a day to think about it. At seven in the afternoon, I asked them to help me clean their clothes. They refused. I took all their dirty clothes to a public washetaria. When I came back, Tabô accepted to help ironing. Not only Loylla refused, she suddenly attacked Tabô physically. She dangerously pushed her and threw her on the floor. It was a cheap move and inexplicable violence. I intervened and removed her from her sister. She did not stop. She took Tabô's glasses from her face and threw them on the floor. She would have broken them if I did not pick them up first. She said that Tabô betrayed her; she was not following their mother's advices. She was not helping her get an extra check from the government. She opened the front door and stepped out. I asked her to stay there till she cools down.

"I won't come back in. I am going to call CPS and tell them that you kicked me out."

"Please do. You have their number already," I challenged her.

Not only Loylla had a problem with school-established authority, she also started to stop recognizing the God-given authority in me. How could I punish a child who, when I say you are grounded, accuses me of abusing her emotionally, threatened to call CPS on me, opens the door, and leaves the house without my permission?

I posed that question to myself and it did not take long, I got a call from Adriane Watters. She said Sheebah just called her. She told her stories about what happened. Adriane then asked her where Loylla was. Sheebah answered and said she did not know where she was after being kicked out. She then asked her if she talked to Petra and to her grandmother because she, Adriane, just talked to them. They told her that Loylla was talking to her mother a moment ago.

"How could you not know where is your daughter if you just talked to Petra?" Adriane Watters asked her.

"So Loylla is over Petra's?" I asked.

"She is. Please go and get her. I will be there tomorrow at your place. We need to do something about this. I just have a serious talk with Loylla. She broke down and told me the truth. I am sick and tired of this woman. I never have seen a mother doing this kind of things to her own children," Adriane said.

"Only a crazy mother can do that."

Three days later, as I was asked by Dr. Radamaki, I stopped at Cook Hospital. I had to have a medical official call the phone number that was written on CVS prescription bottles. The nurse psychiatry said it was Dr. Rupinder Singh Bhatia who prescribed Divalproex and Risperidone to Tabô. She asked me to continue giving these two medical products to my daughter. Only the doctor has the right to order a discontinuation.

At ten that night, as it was ordered, I obliged Tabô to take two pills, one out of each bottle. She said no. I said why. She explained and said that she never took them.

"My mother never let me take any of these medicines because I am not sick. She always told me not to tell CPS."

"Do not say that. You will put Mom in trouble," Loylla intervened.

"These two bottles of medicines are half empty," I remarked.

"Mom respects the time and the exact quantity I am supposed to take daily and throws them away in the sink. She does so to show to Susan Giles, in the case she ever asked, that I have been taking them, but I don't. I am not under any medication," Tabô said.

"Then why in the name of all Africans is your mom making all these fuss in the court that I don't want to give you medicines and why are you acting crazy to satisfy her stupidity? Maybe you should be put on," I said.

It was here that I decided to follow Radamaki's advice. I decided to take both girls back to Fort Worth Cook Hospital for a new evaluation. I first called Adriane Watters. I talked to her about what I discovered. Dr. Rupinder Singh Bhatia, who prescribed the Divalproex Sod DR 500 mg and the Risperidone 2 mg that Tabô was supposed to be taking, never worked at Cook Hospital. Sheebah lied about that. Cook Hospital said that he works at Excel Center Hospital. I drove up there.

"Dr. Rupinder Singh Bhatia did indeed work here. It was long time ago. He now works at Millwood Hospital," the front desk told me.

I went looking for him up there, just to be told again that he is no longer an employee of theirs. I left my number in case he ever showed up there.

On November 15, a man called back. He introduced himself as Dr. Rupinder Singh Bhatia. I talked to him about the medicines. I needed him to revaluate both medicines he prescribed to my daughter.

"Why do you want me do that?" he asked

"Tabô is zombieing out every time I oblige her to take them. She sleeps for about half of the day and fights everyone the rest of that time. I also want you to evaluate her one more time."

"I prescribed these two medicines by her mother's recommendation. You have to contact a physician if you are in need of any evaluation," he said.

"So you prescribed dangerous chemicals to poison a child simply because her mother asked you to? How much did you get paid for? I will give your number to CPS," I threatened him.

On November 30, 2011, around 10:00 in the morning, I finished the court-ordered eight weeks FACT parenting classes I was taking at NewDay Services. I gave all certifications to Watters when we met at the parent-child visitation. She made copies and displaced another plan copy for the welfare of children to her supervisor. She asked me to apply everything I learned on both girls. Girls had been doing well by this time. I saw some changes since I started applying my pa's great patience on them. They have been talking back less and cleaned after themselves more. They also were doing well in school. Loylla stopped acting up. Her teachers said she was showing some respect toward them.

At 2:00 in the afternoon, we showed up at Hurst municipal court for Tabô's misbehavior in school. Tabô accepted to go to community services for the three tickets she received for class disruption, disrespect, and cursing her teacher. For class disruption, the judge ordered her to do sixty hours' community services, five hours every Saturday.

For disrespect to her teachers, she was ordered to do three classes: a Making Better Choices class on January, a Drugs and Alcohol class on February and a Smoking class on March. Those classes were to be taken nights only from 2100 to 2300.

For cursing, she had to do three months of jury duty, once every thirty days, and three service days of help at Boys Ranch activities. She had to be there on Saturdays from 1730 to 2230. All these things needed to be started before her Teen Court scheduled for January 23, 2012.

We told the judge that these sentences will complicate her counseling weekly program.

"None of these orders will interfere with other orders. I had a talk with Bell Elementary School. The assistant principal recommended Tabô to be sent back to the AEP. Your daughter should consider herself lucky that I put every order together. She needs to be occupied so she can stay out of streets and out of trouble," the judge explained.

We took the deal and stepped out. In all that, I said to Tabô, "It is I who had been punished. I have to waste my time driving you around and stay there till you finish your punishment. Therefore, if you keep giving me troubles, if you don't change your behavior, I will take away the possibility of you directly communicating with your mother. I will take your phone away. You heard the judge, he asked me to."

Days went by, and overall, both girls started to improve their characters. Tabô stopped bringing trouble in; she also stopped going out. When she wanted to, she asked. I dropped her and picked her up most of the time when she went to the mall. I knew where she was all the time. If she was not with Kimberly or Rashay, she was with Petra or Cassandra. Adriane Watters was glad to see her implement these changes. She took both girls out to eat pizza just to thank them.

Officer Arnold D' Israel was also impressed. He changed Loylla's name to Double-Mint, Tabô became Inside-Out. But Officer Broom had a different story. He knocked on my door and told me that Alexius's mother filed a complaint. Tabô broke her apartment window. He claimed that even if they were a group of children around, it was Tabô who was throwing stones. I apologized. I said to him that I will go and meet with Alexius's mother. I will fix her window. He told me that Tabô and Loylla are both banned to enter Whispering Run Apartments. The property manager doesn't want them over there anymore.

"The police will be called on them if they do," he warned me.

Before talking to her, I went to see the Whispering Run manager. She told me a completely different story than the one Officer Broom related me. She said that Tabô was hitting the office wall with her head because she was mad. Officer Broom did not believe, even once, that Alexius's mother called both girls niggers as they were passing by her apartment to go to school. The lady manager added that she has black grandchildren; she will never let anyone call them the N word or other degrading names.

"I know Alexius's mother. She is a mean woman. Even if I was not there, I think she called them these names. Tabô became violently mad and broke the window. That is what happened. I do not blame her because I know that being called nigger does derail people, even if they are children. I did not ban them from entering here. I advised them to stay away from Alexius's mother's apartment. I also recommended them to never answer back if Alexius's mother ever attacked them again," she explained.

It did not take long, Alexius's mother attacked Loylla at the school curbside. She accused her of stepping on her daughter's leg.

Loylla's teacher intervened. She told Alexius's mother, "Loylla was not even in the same school hall at the time and moment her daughter is claiming been attacked. Alexius is visibly small, twice smaller than Loylla's size. But you won't believe this, ma'am, she is the one doing the bullying. She is attacking Loylla. It seems to me that you are pushing her forward. Loylla is not fighting back." The teacher said to Alexius's mother.

From that moment on, because they were called niggers, everything started to go down mostly. It was a roller coaster again. Tabô refused to come out from school. She said she won't go home because she had to pass by Whispering Run. Alexius's mother will call her a nigger again. She will go home only after stretching her legs up so she can run across Whispering Run. The principal reminded her that it was after 3:15 in the afternoon, "No student can be inside the property building after the hours."

"Well, I am not inside the property. I am in the hall," Tabô answered.

"Young lady, don't be smart with me. Your father is waiting for you in the parking lot. You need to go home now. If you don't get out so we can lock the main entrance, you will be escorted outside by the campus police and you will be suspended thereafter."

"If I go home, she will call me a nigger. Good luck to my dad. I am going upstairs," she said.

The principal had enough of her. Tabô was escorted out and suspended for five days. She had to go to AEP for the rest of that week.

CHAPTER 53

SHE STOLE THESE PICTURES

On one day of December 2011, as both girls and I were washing clothes at LP, a man called Garcia started yelling at them. He did not want them inside the LP. He was ordering them to leave the store. I asked why. He said that he was the manager. Tabô and Loylla were caught on tape stealing cadies. I took both girls outside of the washetaria room to talk to them. Loylla said, "This guy grabbed me by my shirt and pushed me out of the store."

I called Tsuno, the owner. I called him to complain about Garcia's attitude toward my daughter than to try to know the truth. I knew by then what they were able to do in any store. Tsuno said, "There is no tape showing your children stealing inside the store. Garcia is not the manager. He is the cooler helper. For me, he doesn't work there anymore. I fired him already because the man is mentally sick. My son hired him back, and I don't know why. Sorry to hear that he grabbed your daughter's shirt. The truth of the matter is that your daughters were indeed stealing candies. I was there when they were caught, and I banned them from entering the store."

As I was on the phone with Tsuno, I saw the police cruiser with lights on. Garcia just called them. I got scared thinking that they will write tickets, my daughters will have a record for stealing. They started by asking questions. Then they called Mr. Tsuno, the owner, to investigate. Garcia was told to never touch Loylla or another young girl for that matter again. They also told both girls to avoid the store for the time being.

"You need to talk to your daughters. They have been accused of doing bad things in this neighborhood. They have been breaking windows, staying late in Sutton Square apartment washetaria to do sex, fighting at the park, drinking, and smoking. One of these days, they will be arrested and sent to juvenile," one of the officers said.

At the beginning of December, I got a visit from Alexius's mother.

"Loylla stabbed my daughter with a pencil in her left ear. It happened inside Bell Elementary while they were in class."

"Man, oh man. I am sorry to hear that," I said.

"I will be taking my daughter to the hospital now. You will pay the hospital bills," she said.

I did not argue with her. I inspected Alexius's ear. It did not have any trace of any kind of violence whatsoever. I talked to Loylla after they left. She said the girl attacked her first. She reacted and defended herself by throwing the pencil at her. I had it at that time. I took the internet away from her as punishment. She also was obliged to dust clean her room. She refused to clean. She wanted the internet back first.

"You just lost your room privilege for talking back to me."

"Where am I going to sleep now?" she asked.

"If Tabô lets you, you can sleep in her bedroom, otherwise, you will be in the living room," I answered

After picking up Tabô from school the very next day, we directly went to the hospital to have her teeth filed. She refused to go inside. She was hungry, she said. She opened the car door while I was driving, jumped out, and ran. I canceled the appointment and drove home. When I arrived there, she was breaking drinking glasses from the cabinet. I stopped her. I asked her to go to her room so I can broom up. I did not want anyone getting a cut on the foot. She refused, went berserk, and told me that her sister and she wanted to go to the foster home.

"The best way to do that is to call Watters. She will take you there," I said to her.

"No, she will take us to the shelter."

"Same difference. Call Adriane Watters. She knows where to take both of you. From there, you will learn that shelters or foster homes are not made for children. They are not places for y'all. Ask your mother, she grew up in the system. She knows what it is."

"We are not going to call my mom," Tabô said.

"Then you guys are stuck with me till you are eighteen" I said to her.

Tabô called me a stupid asshole because I told her that her sister and she will be stuck with me till they are eighteen. Loylla intervened and insulted me too. She said that I was a dick sucker and fart fucker. I told them that if they insult me one more time, police will take care of them.

"Police won't do a thing. They will keep us for twenty-four hours only, and they will call Mother to come and get us," Tabô said.

"If Mother doesn't come, they will oblige you to come and get us. But once we are at the police station, we will tell them that you keep following Mom all the way to Dallas shelter where she lives," Loylla added.

"Yeah, stalker, leave my mother alone," Tabô added.

Both girls thought they were well trained by their mother about how the law works and equipped to just throw insults at me. This was not the first time that I was been set up by her, but it was the first time that my daughters insulted me spontaneously.

"Well, I never followed her. I don't even care about where she had been all these days. She is making you grow up with bad attitudes because she wants me to lose control. Can we spend twenty-four hours in peace without having to deal with any of these?" I replied.

As a response, Loylla hopped on the bed. She started jumping on it. Tabô went toward the couch. She began hitting it with a piece of wood. Both were challenging me and calling me names. I picked up the phone and called Officer D' Israel Arnold. He showed up quicker than I expected. From eight to ten, he spent his valuable time counseling both girls. I liked his approach. He told them the same things Adriane Watters has been telling them. He also wanted both girls to have their physical completed and to be evaluated and also to determine if the medication Tabô has been taking or lack therefore was the cause of her behavior. At the end, he asked both girls to apologize to me.

I followed Officer D' Israel Arnold and Adriane Watters' advices. On December 18, 2011, both girls were mentally evaluated by Dr. Carl Shaw of Cook Children's Medical Center for five hours in row. They were observed behind a video camera and given mental tests. They were verbally interviewed; they also were evaluated by way of medical instruments. Both girls were found only with disruptive behavior disorder which is far different from attention deficit hyperactivity disorder.

"I am not saying that this is good, but it does not justify Divalproex Sod and the Risperidone your daughter is taking. These two are strong drugs prescribed only to children with mental health conditions. Your daughters do not have mental deficit. Including myself, a team of specialist doctors spent hours observing them from the time they entered the waiting area. We studied their behaviors. We did not see them fidgeting even once. They did not have an extreme disability, any emotion struggle, or poor listening skills. We saw them eat, which told us that they did not lose their appetite. They did have a constant zoning out, rowdy behavior, inability to focus, or impaired ability to rationalize situations after eating. With these observations, we arrived to the conclusion that these two children were not bipolar. What you need to realize is that ADHD can have a far-reaching impact on a child who is not treated. We did not find anything extremely wrong with them. What this group of specialists saw is what we call the children normal behavior," explained Carl Shaw, one of the doctors.

He then recommended that because they have been participating in a lot of counseling and they did not show a concrete change, I should separate them from what was disrupting their regular way of life. He asked me to schedule them for outdoor physical education at Orexell Center Activities for the next two weeks if their behavior continues. He then gave me a medical report that showed that both children took another physical even if they were current. The note said that they were in good shape and did not need any medicine. What they needed, he said, was a place like Sundance and lot of Christmas break like activities.

Doctor Jagadegja fixed the cavity on Loylla's tooth. Tabô got braces prescribed. She had to have it done at Jefferson Dental Clinics because it was near Glenn Rose, where we lived.

There, I was asked to pay $3,524 at front. I did not have that kind of money anymore. I gave them her Medicare card. Moment later, the Jefferson Dental Clinic specialist came out and told me that Medicare refused to pay for Tabô's braces. It was not an emergency or a necessity to have the position of her teeth modified. This was the CPS Medicare. My Etna insurance accepted to pay only $1,000. I called Sheebah and asked her to pay $1,262, half of the unpaid bill. She cursed me. I reminded her that "it was ordered on January 25, 2010, by Judge Judith that you have to pay 50 percent of all non-covered medical, dental, orthodontia, ophthalmic, psychiatric, psychological, and prescription drug expenses incurred on behalf of the children within ten days of notice of the bill." She cursed me again. I found myself facing the whole amount. I asked to sign a deal for monthly payment with Jefferson Dental Clinic. They accepted. They then fixed Tabô's upper jaw first. I called Sheebah again. I insisted that she, at least, pay for her daughter's lower jaw, in the next two weeks. She asked me to report her to CPS Adriane Watters So I called her. I needed her to intervene. Adriane Watters told her that "this is a thing to do, instead of taking kids to Dr. Rupinder Sigh Bhatia to have him declare them mentally unstable so you can get paid. Help your daughters."

"I don't care anymore," she answered.

"You don't care anymore for your daughters? You cared a lot when, for money, you called Rupinder Sigh Bhatia who, with his diagnostics and complicity to you, did not hesitate to play the kind of therapist that killed Michael Jackson. He forcefully put Tabô and Loylla in Millwood Hospital for weeks. They were never sick. You sacrificed your own daughters in there to generate money for yourself through the hospital. Tabô never was bipolar. She never was crazy. She never needed any of Divalproex Sod DR 500 mg and the Risperidone 2 mg medicine she was obliged to swallow every day. That, my dear, is abuse and endangerment of children because down the road, she won't be able to think right anymore. She will take everything in front of her as if it was a game, and in the end, she won't think right, she will destroy her life by spending her days in jail or in the hospital. We are investigating you and your doctor, my dear. You need to pay your share of your daughter's bill or I will make sure you spend some time in jail."

Instead of paying, following her lawyer's advices, Sheebah counter-attacked. She called CPS the next day. She complained that Muntumpe was not respecting the filed Temporary Exparte Protection Order as it was ordered. She said that she was not supposed to be around both girls. She nevertheless took them to the fair park in Dallas. She reminded CPS that on January 25, 2010, final hearing, on miscellaneous provision # 5, it was ordered that Kasalobi is enjoined from allowing the children to be alone in the presence of their sister Muntumpe, and Kasalobi is enjoined from allowing her to strike the children. Kasalobi is helping her daughter to strike both children.

Adriane Watters was the first to answer since she was already on the case. She said to her that she will see into it, but "you have to help your daughter get her braces first. Tabô and Loylla are Muntumpe's sisters. They will be always together. I am telling you this because on miscellaneous provision # 5 you are talking about, it has been proven that Muntumpe is not the problem, you are. You are the cause she disciplined her sister. You sent Tabô, not one time but numerously, to create problems. We know this for a fact. That day, she was ill-advised by you, she went ahead and hit her food plate during the diner. She was disciplined. You cried wolf about it. You called CPS on her and lied about things. We now know the truth. There is not a judge in this world who will separate families just because they are disciplined. Your daughters are family to Chrystal Perry, Muntumpe's daughter. She has been babysat by your ex while Muntumpe was doing her military services to help this great country. So you want Chrystal to be withdrawn from school, separated from Tabô and

Loylla, her aunties, and returned to her mother for your pleasure? You want Muntumpe to stop going to school and come back because Chrystal doesn't have anyone to babysit her to satisfy you? You want your kids to stop seeing Muntumpe and stop her from coming over her father just to make you happy? Please, girl, put a cork on it. From new testimonies we received, Muntumpe has been nothing but good for your daughters. She took them to the fair park, so what? When was the last time you took them over there? Actually, Muntumpe has been acting like the mother they do not have. She brings them gifts, clothes at every occasion, and does their hair. When was the last time you did their hair? So stop this nonsense."

When I arrived home around two in the afternoon from work, on February 7, 2012, I realized that my front door was unlocked. I was not worried. Kids do leave it wide open most of the time anyway, I thought. I went to the kitchen and cooked me some fish. The smoke activated the fire alarm. I slid the balcony window and reopened my front door to air it up. After sitting on the dinner table, I saw three white lines on the opened door lock. They looked like the three nail scratches from the Monster energy drink. They were located near the safety lock. The knob was damaged; it was also seriously loosened.

I knew at that point that a forced entry happened when I was at work because my door was chipped out from inside. I looked around and inspected the house. Everything seemed there, each one at its place. I called the apartment office; they advised me to call the police even if apparently nothing was taken. In the meantime, the apartment maintenance guy, who came to estimate the damage for repair purposes, realized that my pictures were on the floor in Tabô's room. I found empty spots in the album. Some of my kids' childhood pictures were gone, mostly those when they were babies and growing up. I did not see the ones they were on potty training, swimming in bathtubs, crawling, and falling down trying to walk. As the maintenance guy and I were talking, the police came in, picked the rest of pictures, and fingerprinted the place up.

I called Adriane Watters and told her about the break-in. She said, "That is odd. I just received a call from Sheebah. She claimed that she has pictures on which Tabô and Loylla are both naked, pictures to prove that you have been sexually abusing your daughters. You have been obliging them to expose themselves, by taking their clothes off, to have explicit pictures of them taken. She is now threatening to take you to court on these pictures."

"That was her then. She forced my door open and took pictures and video tapes," I answered.

"She said she has a naked picture of Tabô when she was two years old. The picture shows her running around after taking a shower. She has another one when she is naked inside the entertainment center. She also has two of both girls naked in the bathtub. Loylla is visibly a year old on it. I told her that legally, these pictures don't worth a penny in the suing business. She should have secured them as her evidence with a warrant before collecting them," remarked Adriane."

"Yes, who doesn't have pictures of his children growing up and doing silly things?" I asked.

Sheebah is known for breaking in people's houses. In the Fort Worth police report # 04135486 or Hurst police report 04-10446 for instance, it shows that she had been arrested many times around for theft and burglary. Her method of work is well known. She uses a screwdriver and forces it between the frame and the edge to minimize damages. That is Sheebah's way. That was how she worked on November 10, 2004, to burglarize the Village Creek Towne Homes, at 5716 Fitzhugh Court, Forth Worth, Texas. But doing so, she still leaves behind distinctive traces, visibly marked, enough to start an investigation. That was the signature that led the police straight to her.

"I think she stole these pictures because of this February 21, 2012, CPS review coming up," Adriane said.

"Maybe so but she did this simply because she knows she will get away with it. Sheebah should be arrested even once to teach her a lesson. I need her to bring back my pictures. Those two are her children despite the fact that she gave them away to CPS. Why is she trying so hard to hurt her own children?"

"Why is she always after them, not after Boney, Kattaya, and Baby J.?"

"She is after child support as I have been claiming it all along. With all due respect, these three are not money worthy to her."

"You know Sheebah's lawyer will be talking about these pictures at the next meeting in court," Adriane said.

"Let her. She will look stupid when the judge asks her how and where she got them. These pictures are already reported stolen. I have the police report. What we really should be talking about right now is why Sheebah keeps showing up at my place, at any time she wants to, without the law doing anything. Who is giving her the power of defying and yet the CPS and the court rulings? What happened to her one-hour supervised visit every other week inside CPS hospice? Whatever happened to the court order that clearly says that 'the mother Sheebah shall have limited access to and possession of the children as arranged and supervised by the temporary managing conservator'? We should be talking about who is there to reinforce these decisions. I will otherwise be taking the matter on my own hands," I suggested.

"You need to send your concerns about this matter to Becky Haskin, the la CASA lady. She is there for the placement and the well-being of children."

"I will do that for sure."

March 21, 2012
From: Kasalobi
Subject: Stop telling lies about my children
To: Kjohnsonlawfw@aol.com
Ma'am,
On March 19, 2012, you testified four things in court and said that:

I. Tabô missed the STAAR test.
II. Kids do not attend counseling.
III. You visited Sheebah at her "residence."
IV. Tabô was seriously acting up.

You testified in court in the front of the judge. You said that the principal told you Tabô missed the STAAR test. Since I knew she was in class when the exam happened, I went to Hurst Junior

High and met with Mr. Weatherspoon, the assistant principal you said you met. He said you never talked to him personally. He saw you talking to Tabô couple of weeks ago, that all it was to it. Tabô never missed any school work or any test for that matter. Her grades are excellent. Mrs. Watters, her case worker, has a copy of her report card she received from Mr. Weatherspoon. The other test you talked about in court, saying that she also missed, is the state writing test. You told the judge that Tabô won't pass because she did not take it. The first part of that test is scheduled on Tuesday, March 27, and on Wednesday, March 28, students will do the second part. So when did Tabô miss it? I went to AEP, where Tabô is actually attending. There, I talked to Jodi James, the principal, who you confirmed have been talking to about Tabô. She said she never seen you there, and you never talked to Mr. Iles, the assistant principal either. Which principal did you talk to?

You testified that the kids do not go to counseling. I hoped that at the end of your speech, Nwokoye Violet, my lawyer, will stop that lie. This was the reason I did not interfere, but she did not. I still don't know what sent you to say such thing. Both girls and I, we do go to the Lancaster office, on every Tuesday of every week, from five to eight in the afternoon for counseling. Mrs. Carol, the head-master, makes weekly reports to Mrs. Watters, and regularly, Mrs. Watters updates their attendances in CPS files. As my children's lawyer, you should be talking to Mrs. Carol very often. You also need to be checking all facts before reporting anything to the court. The only time we did not go to the counseling was when Mrs. Betsy got married and went to Germany for her honeymoon. Were you talking about when Tabô and Loylla misbehaved in Mrs. Bessie Anne's session? If so, as a lawyer, you are out of actuality and should never say anything to the judge anymore.

You said that you visited Sheebah at her residence. The court heard you say that loudly and clearly. You probably did visit a woman at her residence. That woman you visited is not Sheebah, the mother of my kids. This Sheebah we are talking about today doesn't have a residence. To the best of my knowledge, she is homeless and her lawyer knows that she sleeps under the Lancaster Bridge, just after

Riverside Road. She did not deny it when Nwokoye confronted her in the last hearing in front of the judge. You heard her tell her that she was living under bridges, near and around downtown Fort Worth. If she did not deny it, even if it happened that you are new on this case, and that was the first time you were representing my children, you shouldn't ever say that you know where she lives. You are desperately trying to help a lost cause at any cost. Lot before you tried, just to found out that Sheebah is indeed a homeless mother. Please stop giving her a circumstantial home.

You said Tabô has a serious discipline problem and she is acting up. Ma'am, the first time you met Tabô was at Hurst Junior High. You introduced yourself; she did not say a word to you. You then gave her your business card. The second time was at the house. I was there. When she saw you, she jumped the fence and ran from you. Again, you guys did not talk. When she came back home, she said that it was not about you, it was about everything. She said that she did not want to talk to you at school and she did not see the reason to talk to you when you arrived home. She said she was tired of talking to CPS and she was tired of talking to the police. She is just tired talking to anybody talking about this case. She wanted to be left alone. The only person she said she likes to talk to was Betsy, her counselor. The question here is, if you did not talk to her at all, from whom do you know all these things you said against her in court?

One of the things I learned in these family classes the court obliged me to take is that "you do not make your case worker mad. She is the bridge between you and the judge." You are one of these bridges. In this case, I don't give a crap. I have to take care of my own. I was careless to break that bridge. I am defending my children against a bad lawyer that you are. I don't want to be politically correct when it comes to my children's lives. They went through a lot already. This court business started from the time they were one and two years old. I told Tabô what you said in court about her. She did not like it. She asked me why you would lie against her that way. She replied to her own question and said, "That is the reason I did not want to talk and ran from her when she came home."

She said she will never ever talk to you anymore. Now she wants the court to fire you. Those are the words of a twelve-year-old girl. Visibly, you did not investigate before reporting yourself to the judge. You lied against the children you were assigned to defend. Tabô is right. You deserved to be fired because you let yourself wide open to Sheebah and her lawyer's manipulations. For instance, in that court of the law and justice, you were given a copy of Sheebah's drug test. You read it and didn't even mention anything about it. Sheebah is a bad mother. This is not news to any one in that court, she is not defendable. She even went far and gave her parental right to CPS. As a court-appointed lawyer, you should have known that instead of lying against your clients. I am now telling you how you should have proceeded with this case; you should have defended them against a drug addict mother. You saw that she failed every single test she was asked to take. Was not that enough to see her through?

Sincerely,

Kasalobi

I sent that letter with a copy to Violette Nwokoye, Becky Haskin, and Adriane Watters. Violette did not like my approaches. She called me a day later and slapped me on the wrist about it. She said that she had spoken to me previously about these information-long e-mails I have been sending to everyone involved in this case without clearing it with her. What I have been doing, she said, is telling them my position in this matter. I should stop doing so. She said as a caution that with all these incidents happening in my neighborhood, I should consider moving out to somewhere else. I am still where I am open to Sheebah's low blows. I should move where I can start the process of looking for a new place to leave peacefully with my children. From there, I could start gathering information for a good school to start them out for next year, she said.

At the end of that conversation, she said that I was making her job very impossible. She preferred me not to send her a copy of anything I would write furthermore because I have chosen to go against her advices. If this continues, she said, she will have no other choice but to withdraw from the case.

CHAPTER 54

AMERICA, NOT A PLACE TO RAISE AN AFRICAN CHILD

I apologized for what she thought was an inconvenience. I then thanked her one more time for what she was doing. She promised when she took this case that she will give my children back. She did that. Since then, nothing was moving forward anymore. I had legal custody of both children, they were with me, and I was still paying child support. That was my main concern. I participated and completed all needed classes as ordered by CPS and by the family court, but she was not making changes to any further extent. Sheebah was still spending that money on drugs, changing her children into monsters, and coaching them how to destroy their own lives. Instead of finding a final solution to all that, Nwokoye was still letting me go to court almost once every two months without a concrete result. She also was letting the state add more people to my case. I had Becky Haskin; she was the court-appointed special advocate. I did not know exactly her job and what she was doing in this case. I had K. Johnson, another court-appointed court lawyer. She was not representing both girls as it should have been. She was there to complicate things; she was telling lies on my girls and getting paid on their expenses.

None of these people was stopping the hell Sheebah was bringing to me. So I turned to writing. The more I wrote to everyone involved in my children's case, the additional noise I made for them. The extra noise I made, the better chance I had to be heard. And it was happening. I was touching everyone and they all were reading me. Nwokoye did like what I was doing. I, for instance, complained to her, two days earlier, before sending the last letter, that Tabô did not come home after been dropped by Adriane Watters. Her answer was "Thank you for informing me." I called her again and told her that she was with five girls, including Petra. They were seen shoplifting in the dollar store. There, a lady hit her on her mouth because she was cursing on her. After a long argument, the lady sent her to come and tell me that she will be waiting for me at the apartment mail box; once I am there, she will kick my butt too. The only thing Nwokoye said about that was "Do not go over there" and hung up. These two short answers showed me that she was tired of telling me not to write. From that moment on, I decided to continue writing because nothing else was coming from her anymore.

I went to the apartment mail box anyway. There, I met with the lady's son first. He was wearing makeup, funny shoes, and long earrings. The man had female clothes on. He was exaggerating the use of both his hands and was speaking with a woman's intonation and accent in his voice. As a man, he was funny. As he was speaking to me, his mother showed up. She was ready to fight me because Tabô called her a midget. She was not a midget. Barely four feet tall, she was very small for a sixty-year-old mother.

"Your daughter insulted me. She called me a midget. She also said that you will beat me like a baby because I am less than hundred pounds. I am ready," she said.

"Where I am from, there is nothing wrong with midgets. They are great people just like me and you. You, ma'am, you are not a midget."

"Yeah? Why then she called me an American midget?" she replied.

"We are parents above all. We don't pick children fights. Without discrimination, we sit down and talk about why children have been fighting."

"Your daughter disrespected my mom. She was seen stealing in the store. My mom reported her to the manager. Then your daughter became violent. She said you will kick my mom's ass. Here I am, kick my ass instead of my mom's."

"I went to see Yolanda Jackson, the dollar store manager. She confirmed your side of story. Indira Ghandi, a great human being of this era, said once that an 'eye for eye' would accomplish nothing but making the whole world blind. How about this let's sit down, drink a beer, and talk. There are great things we can fight for, this here is not the one. Today is not the butt-kicking day. Let's talk instead," I said to him.

"I don't drink beer. I came here to fight," the lady answered.

"Well, I have three bottles of old charcoal-filtered bourbon in my car. Let's get drunk first and fight later," I suggested.

Right there, under the mail boxes, I opened my trunk and brought out the Kentucky Straight Bourbon Whisky. We sat on the curbside. With the foam solo cups I gathered from my Tonga neighbor barbeque, we appreciated Sir Evan Williams' extra smooth sour mash. The lady got drunk first, she started to talk. Her son started to misbehave with a young man who joined us. It was the beginning of a parking lot party. We forgot all about arguing. Petra's grandmother happened to pass by. The lady told her to keep her granddaughter away from her friends.

"They are bad influences to Petra herself and to Mr. Kasalobi's children."

"I will be obliged. I have been talking to their parents. Her friends don't come near me when I am around. Tabô is not a saint either. I saw her kicking and breaking the washetaria door at Sutton Square apartment. May I have some of that whisky?" she asked.

We party more and reviewed everything. We approved of the lady smacking Tabô at her mouth.

"In America, the child should belong to the village, just the way it is in Africa. What you did was good and necessary. She was cursing and you smacked her mouth. She was lucky, my mom would have washed her mouth with a soap," I told them.

"It should be an imposing punishment in America now. Spanking children is not abusing them, it is another way of getting them back on tracks. The first parent to see one child misbehave should whoop him without waiting the approval of his parents. It is the best way to make these kids behave again. We should not be scared of the intervention of the law when it comes to our children," the lady said.

"You are right. CPS is doing nothing but making them grow big mouths and bad characters," I said.

"And the government is locking them for nothing. They should lock themselves in. They are creating the situation our children are getting into," Petra's grandma said.

"Somebody must do something concrete about this new generation of children. Otherwise, they will grow up thinking everything is permitted," the lady said.

By the time we peacefully left the curbside party, we all were drunk. We made a decision not to fight among ourselves because of lies from children. We also decided not to let these girls gather together again. It did not take long, they packed and came back to bother me. It was here that I came to realized that Tabô was in fact the leader of the group. When I asked them to leave, Tabô ordered them to stay. And they did. I threatened to call the police on them if they did not go. Petra said that they were not scared of the motherfucker police. Then she called me African. Because that did not bother me because I am African, she then asked me to go back to Africa. That intentional ignorance hurt me. I said to her that even if she was born in United States, she was still from Africa.

"Just the way Obama does it, you need to respect your roots. If you don't know where you are coming from, you won't know where you are going. My pa said that to me," I said to her.

"Fuck your pa. You don't want my friends because you want me to be like you, living alone and shit. See, me, I can have a woman or a man, any kind I want at any time. But you, you can only beat yourself," she answered and said to me.

That answer hurt me more. She said that in front of all her friends. Then, she murmured something to Petra who picked a stone and threw it toward where I was standing. She missed me this close. They all started throwing stones at me. None hit me, but I felt wounded. I called Nwokoye. I wanted her to sue Petra and her friends, if necessary.

"It doesn't have a legal sense in it. Because then, you will be suing Tabô too. They all are her guests."

They left after the police showed up and distributed tickets. Tabô did not get one. Her friends said that she did not throw anything. These girls were scared of her.

Around seven in the afternoon, two days after these girls went on their stealing spree between the dollar and Kroger store, Tabô asked $10 to go to the movie. I said it was late to go anywhere. She disappeared, Loylla disappeared too. I first went at Petra's since she was with them at the moment they asked for money. Petra seemed to not know where they were. I visited a couple of other of their old friends. They did not know either. I called Nwokoye before calling the Hurst Police.

Around 1:00 in the morning, Kimberly remembered seeing Petra with them. She also remembered where they were. She said Petra told her that she left them inside a black truck at Rickel Park with their mother.

"They will spend the night inside the truck with their mother. She doesn't have a place to sleep. She also doesn't have money for food. That was the reason Tabô came back and asked you $10," Petra said to Kimberly.

I reported everything by text message to Nwokoye. I told her that Sheebah had both kids again. They were inside Rickel Park.

"Call her and ask her to bring them back. If she doesn't…"

"I just called her. She said she won't bring them back. Police and CPS won't do a thing before twenty-four hours from the time they are reported missing. Please do something," I said to Nwokoye.

I waited all night long. Nwokoye did not do a thing about it. It seemed to me that she was getting tired too. I called Adriane Watters in the morning to see if she would move a muscle that early. She did.

She said she knew about it from the Bell Elementary counselor who saw them together and called her. She had already made a new report with the child abuse hotline.

"When I contacted Ms. Sheebah, she states that she did not have the girls and did not even know where they were. Please note she did not seem to be alarmed when I told her that the girls did not go home last night. I will attempt to get new locating information for Ms. Sheebah because I am not sure where she currently is living," Adriane said.

Instead of Nwokoye being doing something, it was Adriane Watters who started talking to witnesses. She was trying to confirm where Sheebah spent that night with both kids. Patty, the lady next door, told her exactly where they were. She said, "They are, as now, in Sutton Square Apartment. I saw them yesterday after school with their mother. They were inside a parked black truck. Loylla was very upset when I approached them. She was telling her mother that she was tired of sleeping outside. She said she did not like what her mother was doing. She was asking her to let her go sleep in her father's house. If not, she will kill herself."

This threat to her own life was also reported to me, the same day, by the Bell Elementary social worker. She showed up uninvited after school at my place.

"Loylla was seen shocking herself. She had a blanket around her neck at the park. Do you know why your little girl would want to take her life?"

"She wants to kill herself?" I emotionally asked.

"I am concerned. She had been doing very strange things lately. Her teacher is also complaining about her. Loylla was interrupting her classes by constantly asking why, why, why to anything she was saying. Now, explain me why she would kill herself."

"I don't have any idea. The last time her teacher told me that Loylla was disruptive was yesterday. I reminded Loylla that she goes to school for one and one reason only: to learn. I said to her that in school, her teacher is God and she is nobody. If her teacher asks her to jump, she has to ask her how high and then jump without asking another question. She got mad. She said I called her nobody. Since that time and because I also refused to give Tabô $10, they did not come back home. Her friends said that they spent the night inside a black truck with their mother."

"They attended school today. I saw Adriane interview them," the school counselor said.

"Then Loylla must have been at Bellaire Park after school. Up to Patty, the lady next door, it was yesterday when she said to her mother that she was tired, and she will kill herself. And today she tried to hung herself?" I asked.

"Yes, at the park. A boy saw her with the blanket around her neck."

"You mean she wants to kill herself because of her mother is acting irresponsibly?"

"She is upset of seeing her mother using drugs, not holding a job, sleeping under bridges, changing boyfriends, and so on. It will be better if, for the next five days, you keep her inside after school," the counselor said.

As we were talking, Loylla showed up and saw the school social worker with me. She turned around and started to run. We asked her to stop. She did not and we ran after her. She then crossed Bellaire Drive without looking. A car squealed the tires. It swung around her and hit the curbside. Loylla was missed by an inch. We stopped following her. It was here when the Bell Elementary councilor called CPS Adrian Watters again. It did not take long, she came down and told me that Loylla was in Bedford, Texas, at the swimming pool.

"How did you find that out so quickly?"

"I call the police. Kim is with her. They want you to be there when they are taking her to the hospital."

Loylla was taken to Millwood Hospital. On her way in, she explained that the school exaggerated. She did not want to kill herself and did not mean any harm to anyone else. It was all about her mother who was wasting her life on streets.

"You threatened to kill yourself. You put a blanket around your neck and crossed the street without looking. We won't take a chance. I just talked to the doctor. He will keep you in for more than seven days," Adriane Watters said.

I told Nwokoye everything. She asked when Loylla will be released from the hospital and how was she doing.

"She seems okay. Doctor put her on Prozac. They are still trying to find what prompted that reaction," I answered.

"That is fine. As a parent though, I would have a discussion with the doctor before any Prozac is given. They did not see a need for it for all these days. Unless they feel it will help her behavior problems. I am wondering why there is a need for it now after several days without medication. Anyway, she will be getting better. I believe her doctor will make the best decision for her. Secondly, I am not sure you ever brought me the children's school records when Sheebah had them. Please bring them in today or tomorrow and drop them off at my office," she insisted.

She also wanted me to write down how many times Sheebah violated her supervised visitations, how often she took both girls without any prior agreement and the exact date she broke in the apartment to take pictures. I e-mailed her everything she wanted. Besides that, Nwokoye threatened again to withdraw from the case. I was still making her job very impossible since I was sending letters to active officials involved in my children's case, including her, she said. I was not making her job impossible; I just did not care anymore. As a matter of fact, I was about to miss her dearly at this point. But something needed to be done first. I learned from Adriane Watters that Sheebah had been preparing both girls for a possible interview with the judge. This was why they have been creating all kind of troubles. They wanted to be beaten to have police take them away, so CPS can shelter them directly in a foster home instead of living with me.

"Mrs. Meda Bourland will request them to choose between living with the mother or staying in a foster home in front of Judge White. Their answer will be a foster home evidently and the judge will let them go to a foster home," Adriane concluded.

"Sheebah had been in different foster homes since she was eight years old herself. She knows a foster home is not a place to raise her children. Why is she doing this to her own children?"

"Remember what she said in court, if she can't get them, no one would. She gave them to CPS already, why not giving them to the foster home now. You need to have a serious talk with your lawyer," Adriane answered.

My brother told me that America was not a place to raise an African child. He said that when you are ready to come to America, leave your children behind for the time being, they will follow later. Otherwise, they will break your last nerve before you even finish what you came in for. I was living that life without any doubt. My girls were potentially being sent on the streets due to their mother's lack of common sense. It was not the shelter that was about to take them over but the street. That was where their mother was sending them. Both girls were already in trouble with almost every educational institution, which was a sign that they were opening the door toward breaking the law. Actually, they were already there; they were out of control. Nothing was working anymore. What they were doing was not even equal to what kids of their age would be doing. Nothing was fitting in a small cup anymore. They were burglarizing stores, shoplifting, breaking windows, fighting in school, smoking marijuana, and so much more. Those were not petty crimes. Things were just adding up against them. They had already active and pending police reports. Not a thing seemed to work in order to subtract them from their insanity, which was in reality, their mother's doing.

I understood why most of the time, Nigerians do not raise their teenagers in America. They sent them back home to be raised the African way and bring them back only after they graduated from high school. I should have done the same because this is often the time most of kids reach the manhood. They start to understand how life rolls at this age. They would have learnt more if I have done so. Loylla was eleven years old, still in the fourth grade. She lost two years. She couldn't keep up with what her mother was putting in her head and ended up, for the second time, in Millwood Hospital. That was the strangest deed a child of her age can cope with. Millwood was a hospital for crazy children. Tabô was also losing a lot. She was also forced to be admitted in same hospital when she was in her mother custody. This happened after she got kept under lock and key into Kimbo Juvenile Center. She went there for twenty-four hours for assault and bodily injury. All these troubles were not a dilemma for me, but they were difficulties and too much for me to handle. Mostly when she disappeared that Saturday, May 16, 2012.

We spent the all day looking for her. In early morning, around 0028, Officer D'Israeli saw her with a man at the Hurst Park. By the time he turned his cruiser around, they both disappeared. He then called. He wanted me to go and find her first. Tabô was known of challenging the police. It was very late and dark outside. In a normal situation, I would have been up in hurry after been woken up with that kind of a phone call, but I was used to what Tabô was doing to me. I was so tired of what she was doing in general. I knew then that because she was spotted by Officer D'Israeli, she was still alive. That was what that counted for me at that time. So I peacefully went back to sleep. D' Israeli called me again. She said that he did not want Tabô to confront the police and disregard their authority the way she did last time, when she was at the same park. With Tabô, anything could happen, he said. She almost fought with the police before tearing up both tickets she was written to. She also threw pieces of it on the roadway. She was asked to pick every single piece off from the ground. She refused and got written one more ticket up for littering. He insisted that I go and find her first before the police got to her because if it was not for him who made her come back to her senses that night, something violent could have happened to her.

Loylla and I went at the park to try to find them. I heard movements inside the playground hut. It was dark in there. I used my flashlight just to see her kissing a visibly grown-up man. He was seventeen years old, at least that was what the boy said to me. I told her to follow me at that instant. She refused to follow me, yelled at me, and said that I was embarrassing them. She then ran behind the electrical poll as if she was trying to hide from me. I focused my attention on the young man.

"Tabô is twelve years old, and you don't look seventeen at all. Do you know what this means?"

"Don't talk to him. You said you will kick my dad's ass, fuck'm up now. You promised me to," Tabô ordered the young man.

"Who wants that young man to hit me? Is that what you are asking him to?" I wondered.

Just like that, she came out from behind the poll and started swinging blows on me. She hit me twice, burst both my lips open. I swallowed my blood. Trying to make her stop hitting me, I held her right hand with my left. I still had a flashlight on my right hand. She fought hard, twisted my arm, and released herself from my grip.

"You said you will kick his ass if he comes here, break the motherfucker's neck for me. Burst his head."

CHAPTER 55

BOOKED IN KIMBO JUVEE

At that order, the young man stood up. He kicked me, judo like, on my right leg. His desire was to drop me, but he was unable to lift my weight up from the ground. He obliquely used his right leg on my ribs and hit me on an angle known only by fighters to try to hurt my kidney. It didn't work. He used his leg on my side again. This time, I felt my breath cut in half. Actually, that was what that kick was intended for. I bent just a little bit and he advanced for the kill with another kick. His leg met with my flashlight halfway. His kick was so strong, it ended up dropping my light on the paved concrete. I was defenseless at this point. I closed my fists and threw them in a disorderly manner. I touched him two or three times. He dropped his phone. I picked it up and directly dialed the police. Tabô jumped toward me just when I finished dialing 911. She tried to take the phone away from me. I resisted. She hit my thigh. I ignored her small blow at that instant. She then pulled my glasses from my face and broke them by intentionally stepping on them. Despite blows from her and kicks from the young man, I moved her around. I did not want to hit her per accident.

"Don't touch me, hoe, I will call the police on your ass," Tabô said, reacting to the fact that I was moving her toward my safe side.

She jumped backward, removed her own glasses from her face, and broke them to pieces before stepping on them. I believed at that instant that the girls had gone crazy.

As she was breaking her glasses, I held the young man phone to my ear, hoping to hear it ring so I can talk to the police. It did not. It was blocked. I needed a code, a password, or something like that to reach 911. In order for her to take the phone from my hands, Tabô came back and bit my left arm so hard. It hurt so badly, and yet I let her sink her teeth in my skin; I did not want to brutally pull my arm off her mouth and risk breaking her teeth. She cut open an inch out of my skin. The pain made me drop the phone. The young man picked it up. He put it back in his pocket. I closed my fist and aimed for his head. He saw it coming. I missed. My second punch hit his jaw. He got hurt and temporarily lost the control of his legs. I hit him again at the same place. He backed off and went down. It was visible by the way he tried to stand up. Even so, he charged me again.

By three minutes into the fight, I was short of breath. Actually, I had to back off because I couldn't breathe anymore. I was fighting in the dark, alone, against two strong young persons. For them, I was in their way and I was the problem that needed to be eliminated, maybe without hesitation. I realized that when Tabô gave the order and both kids attacked me. This was how lot of parents got killed by their own children. I called Loylla for help. She approached. I asked her to call the police. She said I had the phone in my pocket. I forgot all about me having the phone in my pocket. I dialed 911. The young man kicked the call from my hands and ran. That did not disconnect me from the police. At this point, blows were still raining from Tabô and they were hearing the fight taking place. To stop her from continuously hitting me and because I was bleeding through my mouth and my nose, I wrapped both my arms around her. I was behind her at this moment. I squeezed her against me so hard I felt her short breathing and puffing for air.

"You are choking me," she claimed.

Loylla came to her rescue. She tried to undo my lock around her sister's body.

"What are you doing, Loylla? Are you also fighting against me?" I asked her.

"Apparently!" she answered.

"So you are okay with the way Tabô is acting up and the way she is making me bleed?"

"No, but your arms are suffocating her, you need to let her go."

I felt the weight of being a parent when she said I was suffocating her sister. From my perspective point, I was holding her sister with love as if she was leaving and I did not want her to say goodbye. I was holding her to stop her from making a bad decision. I was holding her near me, against the whole me so she can feel my pain through my beating heart. From her point of view, I was hurting her by stopping her to normally breathe. I was so tired at this point. I did not have enough strength to start another fight, even with an eleven-year-old girl, when the first was still going on.

"Back off!" I yelled.

Loylla heard my voice and backed off. I pulled Tabô with me, sat down with her on the concrete, still holding her in my arms. I was trying to stop her from constantly hitting me. Then, from nowhere, another young man came around. He said, "Tabô, stop hitting your father, you need to respect your father, young lady."

He then asked me to let her go, slowly opened my lock, and freed her as two police cruisers were pulling in. Tabô ran from the police. Loylla ran after her. My left arm was still bleeding from Tabô's teeth. Officer Jiminez talked to the young man who released Tabô from my grip first. The young man explained what happened. He then came toward me and cut his police light on me.

"Man, you are bruised. You also are badly bleeding. You mean your daughter did this to you? Never mind. Both your daughters are with Officer K. Broome. They found them walking inside the Sutton Square. They are calm and composed. We are looking for the young man. Did you take a close look at his face?"

"No, sir, we were fighting in a pitch-black park."

"Yea, all lights go off at ten. Up to your daughter Loylla, the young man you saw is not seventeen, he is twenty-one. But she said she does not know his name."

"She knows, she doesn't want to tell you," I answered.

"Mr. Kasalobi, you need to watch your back. Tabô mounted all this. We have all details. She and the young man planned to whoop you. Tabô stole $20 from your wallet when you were asleep. She gave it to him as a fee to attack you. If they have gone one step forward, we would have been dealing with a dramatic situation here. Now, by the advice of Officer D'Israeli, we have to take her to Kimbo Juvenile Center for the night. It is your decision, but we have to do this so she can learn something. We want you to talk to her before driving her there to see if it is something that needs to be done," Jiminez said.

Tabô went berserk when she saw me. Even if she was cuffed, she tried to kick me. Officer Jiminez asked her to ask for forgiveness. She said no.

"In that case, you need to choose between going back home with your father or going to juvenile."

"I'll go to juvenile. I don't like his ass," Tabô answered.

"This is not a game, Tabô," advised Officer D'Israeli.

"I will go to juvenile. Can you adjust these handcuffs, they are hurting me," Tabô answered.

"Well, it is your choice," Officer D'Israeli answered while adjusting these pieces of metal on Tabô's hands.

I agreed with them. She was taken again to twenty-four hours juvenile center at Kimbo. This was not the first time that Tabô physically hit me. I overheard Officer Jiminez asking her why she slapped her mother that same night. She answered and said, "I slapped that bitch today because she was getting on my nerves. I also slapped her also last week."

"Do you see why she needs to spend the rest of the night in Kimbo? She doesn't have any respect remaining even for her mother. She has six police tickets already: three of them for disrupting classes. Suspended from Hurst Junior High, she is again in SOS where she is still having serious disciplinary problems with her teachers. Nothing is scaring Tabô anymore, she has to be punished this way," Jiminez said.

"Not only she is failing and has difficulties in math, she also has been skipping classes. Two days before the park event, Bedford Police found her in a company of a runaway girl. And between them was a sachet of marijuana. None of them was cited because the marijuana sachet was on the floor. Mr. Kasalobi, you are losing Tabô. Kimbo is not the solution. You need to do something, like taking her back to Africa as you said it before it is very late. If not, why not send her to a boot camp or to a Catholic convent, anything positive instead of standing there and blaming her mother, not like she doesn't have any input in it. This is your daughter we are talking about," Officer D'Israeli confirmed and added to what Jiminez was telling me.

He knew what he was talking about. Hurst Police had a special program for hard-headed children. Instead of sending them to jail, they closely followed their activities up, counseled them, and made sure they occupied their time properly to avoid putting themselves in trouble. Authorized by the city of Hurst to watch over them, D'Israeli was one of the officers who was helping children in his city. He had also reports of both my girls on his desk. He was acting not as police officer but as a big brother for a lot kids living in Hurst, Texas. He said that he was ready to help reinforce all court orders in place.

"I want my two protégés to succeed. I want Tabô to become normal again. I know what had been happening and how everything started. Sheebah is tearing them apart. Lately, she was seen around both of them a lot. This is the reason they are acting the way they are," he said.

At the other hand, Tabô did not go with it easily. With things she herself was saying, her cursings, and her insults, she put me in direct situation that obliged me to agree to the temporary decision of sending her to Kimbo Juvenile for the second time. It was a way to try to save her from herself. I gave my consent because every single fight I was doing battle for was for Tabô to change. She was my responsibility, not Officer Arnold D'Israeli's. It was primarily my job to make sure she fits back in and takes her place in this American dream. It was my duty to step up and hold her upright to have her accomplish what was good for her, what still good for her, but she herself chose Kimbo Juvenile over me. For the purpose of decent corrections coming to her, Kimbo was just right at that moment. It was what we had. Tabô went in.

"She is smart, she will learn. Kimbo is capable of making her reach the appointment of giving and receiving. It has been doing the same to just anyone. It was a good decision," answered Nwokoye after I called her the same morning and told her what was going on.

"I thought the same thing too," I answered.

"Mr. Kasalobi, I know your decision about this. I know that you are thinking of you and your ex getting along for the purpose of supporting Tabô. That is good. Let me insist for the sake of both your daughters that we have already won in the court. We have been winning but for every fight I know of, opponents, adversaries, enemies, or foes sit down around the table to have at least a start of an amicable solution. We call that a negotiation. You and Sheebah don't even have a beginning of an agreeable solution for your children. She had been fighting a proxy fight against you. She had been using your own daughters against you. Only you and she have to have a solution for your differences. This fight will not be stopped by any court of the law, only by you both in agreement. That was what you were told the first time you went to the family court orientation, if you still remember. Now, it is time to talk to Sheebah for the sake of Tabô and Loylla. Don't wait till it is late."

"Correction: we are not getting together as man and woman. We were talking about getting along in order to be taking one decision together for Tabô's sake. That is what we have been thinking about," I answered.

"In that case, I have drawn a scratch for that purpose. When you approve it, I will set an appointment with the court through Laurie D. Robison. We will be meeting in Arlington form."

Decision to Mutually Raise Both Children

We, Kasalobi, father, and Sheebah, mother, decided to mutually raise, out of the court, both children together. Kasalobi is abandoning the idea of seeking to receive child support from Sheebah starting July 2012. He is also asking the court to pardon altogether back child support and fees, including garnishments, as asked in the last court hearing. Sheebah is asking the court to stop collecting back child support, including fees and garnishments pertaining to this action from

Kasalobi. As to this day, both parents decide to raise their children as follow; Tabô and Loylla will stay with the father during school year, they will be with their mother during their school breaks.

This declaration is signed by both parents and shall be notarized and certified by Ruben Ygnanzo, notary public for the state of Texas on June 29, 2012.

A day after she got released from Kimbo, on May 17, Tabô got suspended from school for disruption of class and for cursing her teacher. She was written two tickets and sent home for the rest of the day. She was told that if this situation happens again, she will be sent back to Kimbo for three days. That situation the school warned her about happened the very next day. The first thing she did on the eighteenth was to curse after entering the school haul. When asked to stop, she challenged the school authorities. She wanted to be sent back to Kimbo she yelled.

"I won't send you to Kimbo. Go to your class," the assistant principal told her. She started calling him vulgar names. She was suspended for three days but given a chance to come back on Tuesday 22, 2012, to take the rest of her final exams.

She went back to take her exams. But when I received her report card in the mail, not only she failed on average, she also failed all her main five classes. The SOS counselor said that Tabô needed to go to summer school on June 11. She will need to take only Texas History 7, English 7, Math 7, and Science 7. The registration fee for summer school was $35. Each course cost $125. June 7 was the only registration day.

We were now two days into the summer school. I still did not have a non-reimbursable sum of $535. It was hard for me to bring up that amount and to pay on time. I also had feeling that Tabô wouldn't attend the whole session without creating problems. I asked Adriane Watters to call Sheebah about the payment, if she can pay the half of the fees. Politely and with bunch of excuses in her mouth, Sheebah refused to pay. Watters then decided that CPS will take over the charges of the entire summer school fees.

Days were getting very dumpy and very short for Tabô. She was wasting her life. It was becoming hard to getting her back on rails. To keep up with what she was doing, naively but offensively was occupying all my life. It was a full-time job. The ticket she received on May 8 for skipping school was set for hearing on June 10, 2012, at 10:30 in the morning. I have to get off from work to take her to court. She refused to go after I did take off. She wanted to be there alone.

"You are not eighteen yet. It is a must that I show up there with you," I explained.

"In that case, I won't go to court," she answered.

The City of Euless constable who delivered the summons said to me that Euless does thing differently, if she is not yet eighteen, she must be accompanied by an adult. If she doesn't willingly come in, the city will send a deputy who will drag her in. They will keep her in isolation till the time she will voluntarily accept to be heard by the judge.

I reminded Tabô what the constable said. She insisted and said that she doesn't care. She won't go. At 11:00 in the morning, the judge sent three officers to get her. Before they forcefully drag her in the cruiser, with handcuffs on both her hands, they realized that she was one of Officer D' Israeli's children. He was called by Euless Police. When he arrived because he trusted Tabô that much, he asked to have handcuffs taken off from her hands. They did. And because Tabô trusted him likewise, she peacefully entered in his police cruiser. She was taken to Euless municipal court. Arrived there, she refused to speak to the judge. She was kept in jury room for three hours. It was around four in the afternoon when she finally gave in. The judge heard her. At the end of the session, he decided to keep her in for the rest of the night because of the curse word she pronounced inside the courtroom. I called Watters and talked to her about the outcome of the hearing.

"When will she be released?"

"She will be released tomorrow at 10:00," I said.

"Which means she will show up at least three hours after the summer school has started. When a student is that late and or doesn't show up at first period of her class, it is considered as an absence for that day. The summer school policy says one absence and you are out. They won't let her attend this time."

"I did not know that," she explained.

"Yup. Only one student absence puts her so much behind. It is summer school. Its pace is so fast. She's probably gonna have to wait to for the second session of this summer," I answered.

CHAPTER 56

THE RIVER HAS MEANDERS BECAUSE IT RUNS WITHOUT HELP

As expected, everything that I was scared of and that was supposed to go wrong for Tabô were going wrong. Once released from Euless Detention Center, I asked her to sit in the waiting area as I was at the clerk window, signing her release papers. She needed to go and use the restroom, she said. The restroom area was located in the hall that connected the city municipal court and the Euless police station. I let her get in. Once I finished signing her release, I did not see her. Tabô disappeared. The station cameras showed her getting off from the west side of the building. Instead of coming back where I was waiting for her, she exited on her own authority from the police entrance, took the parking lot, and walked out, taking Hurst direction. Loylla and I went looking for her all night long and were unable to locate her. She finally showed up home after 1:30 in the morning. When I opened the door, she was in the company of a boy and three girls, Petra was the fourth. She entered and invited them in.

"It is almost two in the morning, Tabô," I said.

"So they are my friends. They will spend the rest of that night in my room," Tabô insisted.

"These are not your friends, especially Petra. She is a lost cause, you are not supposed to be around her. She is continuously a bad influence to you. She is twelve years old living with her grandmother who let her have a twenty-seven-year-old boyfriend. Her mother knows that and CPS just got informed. These kids are members of this gang called Hurst Children. They are making you believe that you are licensed to do anything you want without any consequence. It is late, I don't want any of them in," I explained.

"If my friends leave, I leave with them," she threatened and tried to force them in.

"If you dare to step out, I will whoop your little behind and rearrange it in the way you won't be able to sit down for a week."

Petra laughed at that warning. She showed me her middle finger. I moved forward to do harm to her. The boy get involved; he cut my way off, cursed me, and called me a dick head. I went back in and filled a bucket with water. He thought I was kidding. Without another warning, I threw it on them. Petra and he got completely wet. He got mad and called the police. When they showed up, I saw my neighbor explain what was going on. They didn't even ask me the usual questions. Those kids were out, way past the city curfew time, and they were known as out-of-control kids. The police cuffed all of them, Tabô included. After ascertaining who was who, they distributed tickets and put them in their cruisers. Tabô was obliged to stay home.

June 9, she woke up around 1400 hours. She ate and stepped out. She didn't even take a shower. Six of her friends showed up just after she left, Petra included. I did not open the door. They started hitting on the door and on the window looking for Tabô. I asked them to leave. They did not.

"We will draw graffiti on your door if you do not open," Petra threatened.

I opened the door and saw explicit and unambiguous male sexual parts on it.

"These are your 'small parts,'" Petra said clearly.

I went back in the apartment, poured ice cubes in two buckets, filled them up with water, and used my water technique on all of them. That was more than enough to wet them all and their clothes too.

"Now, that is funny. You can call the police on me again if you want to," I said.

It was at this moment that I saw Tabô among them. She did not like it when I threw the ice water on her friends. She got mad, entered the apartment, and locked herself in the restroom. I called D' Israeli on his cell phone. I told him what happened. I also said to him that this time, I will use force if Tabô dare to step out with this squad of bad children.

"What are you trying to do, what kind of force are you talking about?"

Just when Officer Arnold asked that, Loylla convinced her sister to open the bathroom door. There, on the floor, was a pool of blood. I was looking at the blood, Tabô's blood. My daughter's blood was all over that floor. I got very scared, but I played the hard-hearted man. The girl cut open the inner part of her wrist, just below the pliable part of the palm. She did it intentionally. She barely missed the two main arteries but severely sectioned veins and nerves of the carpal ligament of her thumb muscles. Even if she missed the two blood conductors, she also reddened the whole water sink. The blood on the sink and the one still rushing out continuously on the rhythm of her heart beat made her panicked. She got frightened more when she saw me getting in. She then tried to get out from the restroom. I stood firm and occupied the entrance to impeach her from getting out of the house. I flipped the phone over, let Officer D'Israeli on, and switched lines. I dialed 911.

"Well, Tabô, you want to die, you cut your own hand. Now you are bleeding," I said, hopping that the police will get the hidden message.

Tabô hated CPS at this point. She did not like the police either. I did not want her to know I was with them on the line, and I was talking about her. She may have rushed outside and run from them as usual. With that kind of cut, there was no way of knowing what would have happened if the blood was not stopped and she did go out there.

Maybe it was the restroom lights, Tabô's skin started to look pale. She was getting weaker and weaker. She begged me to stop the flow of the blood. At that, with tears on her eyes, Loylla screamed so hard that the lady next door entered. She saw the blood, asked what happened, stepped out, and called the police.

"Keep talking to her. We are listing. Do not let her step out. The ambulance is on your way," the police dispatch said.

Three minutes into the bleeding, Tabô sat on the floor; she was getting weaker. Loylla lost her self-control; she continued shouting with tears on her eyes. That prompted Tabô to also cry. Officer Arnold arrived, he took over. He was shortly followed by the ambulance. In their investigation, they wanted to know what really happened. They also wanted to know what kind of weapon she used. Tabô refused to say. At this point, she was incoherent and illogical. She remembered her name, but did not recall her address. She remembered cutting herself but said it was in her room when that happened. She remembered breaking her bedroom door with a foot kick but did not remember cutting the couch with a knife.

"She broke a BIC shaver, extracted both razor blades, and used one to cut herself," Loylla said.

Something was definitely wrong with Tabô. She was acting as if she was high on something. With the help of Hurst Police Department, Officer Arnold decided to take her at Springwood Hospital for evaluation, after receiving by six stitches and a shot to stop the bleeding. This man had good ideas generally. He always had good ideas regarding my children. This was the reason I had great consideration and lot of esteem for him. He knew what to do, when to do it, and he was all the time there to help me do good things for them. He was the reason I never lost control. That was how much I needed him in my children's life. I valued Jiminez, his partner, also but I respected Officer D' Israeli the most. For me, he was the greatest of the entire Hurst Police Department and the best of them all.

I did not know how Sheebah knew about the Springwood. She showed up at the hospital as Nurse Jacquie was interviewing Tabô.

"Will they be a problem or a concern if Sheebah talks to her daughter?" Officer Arnold asked me.

"Not at all, actually now, I want them to have an open conversation. I need her to talk her out from hurting herself. I don't know what to do anymore. At this time and moment, I will use any principality to help my daughter."

Once Tabô saw her mother, she started cursing her.

"Mother, what are you doing here, you drug-addicted motherfucker?" she asked.

"I came to see you Tabô."

"I don't want to see a hoe. I don't want a crackhead like you around me. Fuck off."

"If you continue to be verbally abusive toward your mother, young lady, I will give you a shot on your butt. While you are asleep, I will cut all your hair," the nurse threatened her.

"You heard that, Officer Arnold. This lady just threatened me," Tabô accused.

"Actually, you are threatening your life yourself, young lady. Where did you get WET from? Explain that to the officer instead of accusing me," Jacquie said.

"What is WET?" I asked.

"I did not smoke WET," Tabô answered.

"Who said anything about smoking? Anyway, it is all over in your system. It is in your bloodstream and in your pee too. Who gave it to you?" Nurse Jacquie insisted.

"What is WET?" I asked.

"WET is a regular cigarette put in an embalming fluid first and then mixed with some other poisons. Just by looking at the pupils of her eyes and the way they are diluted, you know what will happen to your daughter. She is killing herself on a chemical liquid used to mummify dead people. It is a dangerous drug when left to dry, for about twenty four hours, on a tobacco stick. You can also guess when she will die by the color of her skin and I am not kidding," Nurse Jacquie explained.

"Don't change the subject. She threatened to cut my hair, give her a ticket, Officer," Tabô said.

"You started it. Why are you so disrespectful to your mother?" Officer D' Israeli asked.

"She is the reason police and CPS are always on my back," she answered.

"You are the reason, Tabô. You are your only reason and the reason people around you are getting hurt. When you will stop exaggerating and playing these games, you won't see any of us. Behave yourself. Stop the use of drugs. Stop fighting at the park. Respect your teachers. Stay in school, and everything will be okay. Nurse Jacquie, don't worry about the cigarette. We know where they are getting these liquid acid they are smoking. We also know who is selling these cigarettes," D' Israeli responded.

Because she was not supposed to be in the emergency for long, the nurse waited for Tabô to have the smoke dissipate in her body before giving her medicine. That night, she was given the following:

1. Equetro 200 mg / one capsule a day
2. Fluoxetine hcl 20 mg / one capsule to be taken every morning
3. Guanfacine 2 mg / one pill to be given twice a day
4. Trazodone 50 mg / one pill every night as needed to sleep

After the emergency part, Tabô was given a bed. D'Israeli and I left the hospital. Sheebah stayed behind with Tabô. Then, in the early morning, Tabô called me. In the current of that conversation, she told me she won't be coming back home. She wanted me to bring her clothes in. Her mother was authorized by Mrs. Harper to go with her once she is out from the hospital, she said.

"It will be before July 27."

"What is special on July 27?" I asked.

"Mediation," she answered.

"Mediation? What kind of mediation?"

"Oh Nwokoye did not tell you about the mediation? I have a copy from Meda Bourland. She gave it to my mom and my mom gave it to me. Following the conversation they had with Mrs. Watters's supervisor, she was told that once I feel good, and I am doing well now, I have to go and leave with her," she confirmed.

"No supervisor or Mrs. Harper or Mrs. Watters said that. The judge already stated on this case. None of them has the authority to decide singularly. Your mother lied to you about that. She is repeatedly messing up with your mind even now when you are in the hospital. You see why the court doesn't want you to be around her? In the meantime, use your cell phone, make a copy of the letter, and send it to me."

May 2, 2012
From Laurie D. Robison RN
Mediation
Dear Counselors, Meda Bourland, Violet Nwokoye, Melissa Paschall, Karmen Johnson,

This letter will serve you as confirmation that mediation of above-referenced case is scheduled for Friday July 27, 2012, at 9:00 am at the office of Laurie D. Robinson, RN. Please plan to arrive at 8:45 a.m. so that mediation may start promptly at 9:00.

Please send me a copy of the order referring the matter to mediation, the enclosed disputed issues checklist, a summary of any settlement offers as a copy of applicable active pleadings. For your info. I have enclosed the following:

A disputed issues checklist to be completed and returned.

Rules for Family law mediation.

Thank you for your cooperation and the appointment as your mediator.

I will do everything possible to facilitate the settlement of this case on terms acceptable to all concerned.

Laurie D. Robinson
RN and Attorney at Law

As I was reading the mail, Springwood Hospital called. Nurse Jacquie wanted to know why I changed my mind and decided to send Tabô to Lena Pope instead of the MHMR for closer psychiatric follow-up.

"I did not decide a thing. Who said I decided anything about Lena Pope?"

"The hospital called the provided telephone number. We talked to your wife. She said you travelled and wouldn't be able to attend.

She showed up here and told us that you okayed the transfer before travelling. We then had a meeting with the staff about it. At the end of the meeting, she gave us her authorization."

"Sheebah is not my wife. I did not talk to her about anything. She just played you too. By the court order, she is supposed to be near her daughters only on scheduled days and on supervised visitations. She was not supposed to be at the hospital in the first place, I let in by the advice of Officer Arnold D'Israeli. This was the reason we put a code in place. It was to stop her reaching Tabô or to call you guys. She switched my number to hers. That it is all," I said.

"Well, we knew she was the problem, but she exhibited a court order. She said she was authorized by Mrs. Haper, the CPS supervisor on duty, to be with Tabô unsupervised and to go to participate in that therapeutic meeting with the psychiatric. We called Mrs. Harper to verify. Nobody answered. Because the meeting itself was a time sensitive, and it was getting late. So we let her in."

"That court order is old like dirt. New orders are in place. I will provide you guys with a new copy. The only time the front desk would let Sheebah in to see or to talk to her daughter is when she is accompanied by CPS. We are trying to stop her to continuously putting things into her daughter's head. She is the main reason Tabô is in there. She cannot continue confusing her," I said.

When Tabô learned that I talked to the hospital, that I told them that Mrs. Tracie L. Harper did not authorize any of things her mother said, and did not give permission to her mother to take her to Lena Pope, she got mad. She called my cell phone and insulted me without hesitation. One of the things she said and that marked me was "You African motherfucker. You need to go back to Africa to eat monkey or to just be a cannibal like you were doing when you were there."

From the Springwood Hospital, Tabô was directly sent to Dallas Bright Star on July 12, 2012. Even if it was a different environment and they wanted them to feel home, Dallas Bright Star was nothing but an old house full of troubled children. The front door was always open. It did not have a security lock. These kids were doing what they wanted to do. They were going out and coming back late as they wanted. They didn't even respect the house curfew which was fixed at 8:00. Tabô liked that.

Dallas Bright Start did not believe in prescription first. For them, medication was prescribed as their last resort. By counseling only, they were able to provide necessary tools to reduce symptoms from whatever a child had, they said. So they took all medicines away from Tabô. She even stopped taking every single medication and pills bought over the counter. They situated on Oacklawn Avenue, around Cedar Spring areas. This was the neighborhood full of gay clubs; it still is. Tabô was initially sent in there for treatment and assessment. She was supposed to spend three months in that house. In time, she met a gathering of young ladies. These young ladies were worse than she was. I met each one of them also, some with tattoos even on their teeth, literally. Others with bad hair do that would have made the maker of *Mad Max* jealous. The rest of them had bad attitudes written all over their faces. Most of them were teenagers, few were young girls. They were free of their movements, which was strange to me because we all knew the consequences of giving that kind of free space to a young lady. Because of its habit of running alone and per the force of the nature, an unassisted river ends up having meanders says African elders.

In one way or the other, the growing into the future of preteens should be restrained. All movements of teenagers for that matter should also be unemotional and controlled despite what one think about their experiences. Their life should be brought under control, not as a hold back, but because they just cannot be released out there with that much power and freedom. They just cannot be out there running free like air as I saw them doing it at the Dallas Bright Start house. The minimum of control should have been applied on each one of them, from inside the Bright Start house to outside, with the direct discretion of a caregiver because it is good like that and that is a thing to do. It is good for their hope and it is good for their prospect. These girls were not supposed to be acting the way I saw them acting inside that house. They were getting away with lot of things. As matter of fact, it was clear to me that they didn't even have a caregiver at all. They didn't have people around them I could have called caregivers. The one they had were letting them do things I couldn't imagine. They were doing these things on the watch of the authorities of the facility. And these authorities forgot all about the reason these girls were there for.

Since what these leaders were doing defeated the purpose of children being there at first place, and because of the negative approaches from these already bad kids she met in the house of help, Tabô who was sent in there to improve her character and her inability to control her emotions became worse only in few days. Instead of learning, she who was already struggling with her restlessness, her overwhelmed feeling, her low self-worth, became more disruptive. Instead of being treated mentally and medically as it was initiated, she was being cuddled and led into irresponsibility. She was not there to be damaged furthermore as they were doing to her. Instead of being soft and tamed by their passivity, Bright Start's so-called caregivers would have worked hard on her as if there was no tomorrow. They should have curved a way in a stone just for her by using all tools they had in their tool box, if that was what it was needed to change that solid character and that bad behavior she was cultivating. That was what a real caregiver would have done and it would have made the difference. Her situation was a present and tense situation; she needed to be taken care of differently. They did not have to wait whatever they were waiting for. They should have treated her as the child she was and start teaching her how to walk from the first day she was admitted in there. I still did not understand what they were waiting for. A child doesn't walk because he is twelve months old. A child walks because there is a well-intent adult near him. He walks because he first holds that adult' legs and helps himself to stand up. He then uses a tree if he is outside and a couch if he is inside. Because he observes his surrounding, he walks because a good teacher assists him, as my pa said once. And that is what Bright Start was missing. That was the difference between a parent and an institution. These children were not learning from these adults. The facility was not helping them do that, it was exposing them to abuse. They were neglected in there.

For me, even if they were paid through CPS, the Dallas Bright Start was there to financially bleed parents who were morally suffering already. They were not helping children walk on their own. The entire facility was teaching them how to stand lose on a tall rock and then how to jump all the way down without restrictive ropes and fall protection requirements because, they seemed to say, it is a sport and it feels good to jump down. They were not telling them so far that when they do jump, their broken into pieces bodies will be collected using small spoons after reaching the rocky ground, before being disposed of, six feet under the ground. My daughter was worse than when Dallas Bright opened the front door for her. She was more damaged than when she first was admitted in there. It showed.

Because of that let-go of her teachers and because of these girls around her, nothing was improving the way it was planned to. Off from one, Tabô started going to these Cedar Spring homosexual clubs every night with them. She was still twelve. Doing so, she was coming back in late again, just the way she was doing before. She was seen smoking in open and reported doing so by the police. The mental program in Bright Start was not working for her. If there was one thing they were giving to the parents of their clients, it was a strong sense of what was not real. So if you didn't know that, look them in the eye and say to them that I told you so.

I decided to take Tabô out from there. I first called CPS for advice, I asked them to go and found what I was saying out by themselves. They concurred with me about what was going on. Bright Start was not as good as their words and slogans. They were offering bad advice to these girls and we smelled it on time. Together, Adriane Watters, her mother, and I went there and withdrew Tabô. Instead of coming back home in Hurst, she went to spend the rest of the summer with her mother in Arlington. The very next day after getting off from Bright Start, the manager of the apartment complex where Sheebah was living, complained against Tabô. She called her mother and told her that her daughter was drinking alcohol at the pool, which was strictly forbidden.

"It is against the city of Arlington ordinance to drink at public place. It is also against the apartment complex policy," she said.

CHAPTER 57

WITH HER, I STARTED WITH NOTHING, I HAD MOST OF IT REMAINING

The complex management also accused Tabô of breaking empty bottles of whisky around the swimming pool area where people walk without shoes. That is what the law calls action and intent; she wanted to see people bleed, she said. Tabô was also accused of giving liquor to her young sisters she was babysitting.

As the manager was talking to Sheebah about all this, Tabô, who was already drunk, assaulted Mrs. Shackelford, the assistant manager, by throwing a book at her. That action was strange because the lady was a mute participant; she did not say a word to her or to anyone else. It looked like Tabô had a beef against her. When Arlington police arrived, they assigned Tabô to District Alternative Education Program for a week. That did not help because Tabô spent that time attacking anyone around her. When she came out, she became aggressive and very violent toward her mother. At the end of the day, Sheebah was given two options: to get rid of her daughter or to receive thirty days' notice to vacate the Collin Park apartment premises. Her choice was clear: she sided with her daughter and she was kicked out.

At this point, Sheebah was living the real version of the law of karma. She trained Tabô to hurt me. She trained her to do bad things so I can look as if I was a bad parent. Instead of receiving what she was planning for, everything started to blow out on her own face. At any price, she wanted to win in the court of the law. She did not want to stop and look forward to see what would happen past those moments. And it happened. As it is known, what was supposed to go wrong went wrong: Tabô became bad. She was so bad she was not ashamed of what she was doing. She didn't even hesitate to be doing it in the public. There was not a stop to anything she was saying. She was pronouncing it and promising to do it, action and intent all the time, which made it hard to defend her. This was the time I declared the time of harvest for Sheebah. She was receiving nothing but what she had been wishing me for, not the change from her own money but karma, the Indian way.

With her, I started with nothing on November 11, 1993. I had most of it remaining when Tabô and Loylla were both arrested on September 16, 2012, as would have said the old wise African man. They were severely warned not to enter the Whispering Run property. They just did not listen; they were executing their mother plan: to be wild and make me look bad. Every time they could, they went in Whispering Run to insult Alexius's mother. When she ignored them, they broke something: her glass window for instance by throwing stones. The management was tired of repairing and spending money. She contacted the Hurst Police who put the restraining order on both of them.

There was a registered sex offender living on the complex. Kids knew about him as a child rapist. They stayed away from him. Tabô did not. She attacked him every time she could see him. The man never responded; he was on probation and had strict orders to follow. "Not being near a child" was one of them. He would have had his parole revoked if he was seen violent toward Tabô or arguing with any child for that matter. So he steered clear from Tabô and her sister.

That day after school, Tabô did not take his silence for someone avoiding trouble. She threw a stone at him. The man ran from her and entered his apartment. It was not clear who broke his window, but when the police arrived, they found both girls holding stones. Tabô was on probation at that time. She also was trespassing. She had about twelve unpaid police tickets on her name and more warrants than any girl of her age: three for skipping court hearings in Bedford, two for failures to appear at Hurst Municipal Court, and two for missing teen court hearing in Euless, Texas. Loylla and she were arrested, handcuffed, and booked in Kimbo Juvenile Center on September 16, 2012. This was Tabô's third time to be in Kimbo and the first time for Loylla. It was here when I remembered my brother's voice. He said, "It is hard to raise children in America. Send them back home to me and Africa will teach them the good way of life." I did not get the meaning behind his advice at that time when he concluded and said they would join you past their turbulent age. It all came back to me when both my girls got arrested. I was the one to blame in my daughters' growing difficulties, at least this was how I felt. It was not hard to comprehend and execute recommendations from a distance, mostly from back in Africa, a place of rich cultures, loaded customs, and affluent morality. I kept them in America because I thought their manners will change with the time. It did not. I kept them in this great country because American way of life is the only system that works. It is copied from, as a model. It is followed with interest by different individuals. Just the sound of it, the name America is the symbol of greatness in the entire world. Its system works for everyone else here, inside this United States and out there, around the world. But it doesn't work for our children living here with us. We have been losing them due to their lack of respect for their parents, the unconstraint from the system, and the nonchalance of different services of protection. It is not easy to raise a child in this country, mostly if he is coming from outside, from Africa for instance. Some people will talk about culture clashes, some other about the streets, but the truth is somewhere else. The entire American system of protection of children is to blame. It was probably made with them in mind, but not in fact made for them. It must be changed, restructured, reorganized, and modernized from the ground up because it is using our children as their pot of honey. CPS and police are filling them in the juveniles system to over the capacity of these facilities to enrich the greedier. The child doesn't belong in juvenile. It is not a place for those with difficulties to easily listen either or those who cannot follow advices. What this present system is calling protection of child through CPS or by the police is actually not working for those with uncontrolled emotions. Basically, juvenile is not an accommodation for troubled children. Juveniles are prisons. They are arranged houses where they send our babies, not to correct them, but for them to waste their lives in there. These houses are webs made to shamefully entangle them in and meanly keep them entrapped to wash up their minds. They then break their adolescent bodies, so they can keep their jails system filled. Our children are feeding private jail institutions. These institutions are making lot of money on parents' expenses, and that is the reason they are always creating elaborated circumstances for them to fail. And when they do fail, they attack them with force under the cover of controlling the situation or arresting them. When they resist the injustice, officials turn around and claim that their officers were assaulted first. They do so to make lots of money off our children's backs. That is why they keep on creating complicated situations so that they do not let them go. Putting a child in jail, for something we can find a remedy for, is not the life we seek in the America of tomorrow. A child is a child, he is not an adult in miniature. He makes mistakes. That is just what a child does. It is not as children cannot correctly follow orders, they are children, they do what possible to them. The job of an adult is not to punish a child, it is to instruct, educate, and protect him. We need to stop discerning and discriminating each one of them. The American system should stop been judicious about the way our children behave and right their behaviors. It should be that way. Sending them to juvenile is not protecting them. Something must be done to fit our future generation in a place they should belong into.

I say this because I had two young girls. I had them, and this very system took them away from me. My brother did not want to be philosophizing about it. I blamed him for not helping his own children to come over anyway. He said they are still in school. I said, "Well, they will learn in America."

He said, "Of course, they will, but there is nothing for them here from the moment, they will come when they are ready. For now, if I do bring them, I will lose them."

I said, "That is not fair, there is no way possible to lose a child in America."

He said, "When you will be here, you will discover these things by yourself and you will say with me that my brother was right when he said, 'America, come and get it.'"

He knew this would happen. I only understood what he meant then when I saw both of my daughters cuffed inside a police cruiser. I knew I lost them to the juvenile house system. As someone would have said it otherwise, I came to America beating my chest, I saw but did not conquer a thing. One won't criticize and find a fault about the way the education of a child is done in America when one is still outside. It takes a lot to educate a child anywhere else, and it takes more to do the same in this United States of America. It is not an easy task to keep a child safe, it doesn't work for everyone anywhere and in this country, it is definitely a hard work for lot of us who had been trying to make our children fit and raise them in a normal way possible.

Tabô and Loylla spent forty-eight hours in Kimbo Detention Center for trespassing in Whispering Run apartment. They were released to me by order of juvenile court pursuant to Chapter 54.01 of Texas Family Code after ordering them to the community-based detention as punishment. They both knowledge that and agreed that violation of any of the foregoing conditions will be grounds for and to be taken back into custody, detained and brought again before the juvenile court for further proceedings. They both were given strong conditions and were told to refrain from participating in unlawful behaviors. They accepted to observe an 8 p.m. and 6 a.m. curfew. To attend school was one of requirements demanded from them as a condition of their release, and they had to be there on time.

Loylla understood and stayed away from troubles, but Tabô continued listening to her mother. On October 14, 2012, she was arrested by Hurst Police and taken to South Surgical Hospital of

Hurst for intoxication evaluation. She was later taken to Texas Youth Commission, the Ron Jackson Correctional Complex in Brownwood, Texas.

That day, Tabô was at Hurst Park. It was crowded with young people. Lots of recreation activities were going on at same time. Boys, as well as girls, were playing basketball and volleyball. At the west side of the park were two blue electronic boxes. This was the place where drugs were exchanged by Pei-Wei. For some reasons, Tabô was fed up seeing these young men smoking and selling drugs there. She confronted three of them. The fight broke out. These young men were Pei-Wei gang members. They were not about to be challenged that way by a twelve-year-old girl. The first to show an open aggression was a twenty-one-year-old man. He started cursing all kind of words, showing gang fingers and languages at same time. Tabô attacked him first. She administered about six successful blows to his head and knocked him out cold. Without waiting, she took the seventeen-year-old to the ground and punched him numerously. The third ran away when he saw the police pulling in.

Tabô followed him and knocked him down too. She was ordered to stop. She refused to be separated. She continued kicking the young man using her feet. She was ordered again to stop, but instead of complying, she turned her anger toward the police.

She was warned, pepper sprayed, taken down, and handcuffed. Later on, after Officers D' Israeli and Jiminez arrived, Tabô developed signs of drunkenness and intoxication. They decided to take her to Hurst South Surgical Hospital. From there, Officer D' Israeli approached me and said, "Look here, Tabô is my protégé and my little sister. She is out of control and you know that. This is the third time she is spitting on police officers. She even spit on me and on Jiminez. When you spit on an officer of the law, the charge is assault with deadly weapon. You saw her resisting the police. That is a bad sign. It is time to protect her against herself. As high as she is, she may just advance toward a police officer with a pen in her hands, not like the police will intentionally shoot at her, but an accident may quickly happen. It would be called accident, but at the end of the day, you will still have a dead daughter unfortunately. Even if this is the fourth time, it is the best time to get her off the street. She will be protected that way. You also saw her attacking the gang members. She could have been killed by anyone of them. She needs to be sent to Kimbo Juvenile Center and they will decide."

"If that is what it takes, that is what it takes," I answered.

Tabô did not come back home to Hurst, Texas. After Kimbo Juvenile Center, she was taken, the same night, to Brownwood, Texas, and booked in the Texas Youth Commission Ron Jackson Correctional Complex. She had been in juvenile since October 14, 2012.

Lawyers, members of the court, Sheebah, and I met a week later on Monday, October 22, 2012, for the Mediated Settlement Agreement in Arlington. Nwokoye was tired of the marathon trials. She did not want to make this case to be her permanent case as Meda Bourland was trying to do. She was already complaining that I was running behind payments. The difference was in fact that I was struggling to pay her. Sheebah's lawyer, Meda Bourland, was taken care of by the system; the court was paying her fees. Nwokoye was also upset that the initial mediation that was scheduled on July 27, 2012, was cancelled due to Laurie D. Robinson's activities. Laurie, the mediator, was also a registered nurse. She had some classes to take and training to do. So she rescheduled. When we finally met in her office, on Matlock Avenue, Sheebah and her lawyer occupied the front office. Nwokoye and I found ourselves at the end of the hall, in Laurie's husband law office. The Department of Family and Protective Services, represented by Adriane Watters, was also present. They were in the conference room. They actually were the petitioner. With Melissa R. Paschall and Karmen Johnson as legal witnesses, CPS started the debate by phone conference. They were in the meeting room. They said that we all were there to try to agree to compromise and to settle all claims and controversies related to both children between the Sheebah's group and my group. Why we had to drive all the way to Arlington and do so by phone conference was a mystery for me. We were there already, and nobody was threatening anybody. Laurie D. Robinson was the massager going from office to office to connect all three groups, despite the video conference.

When she entered where Nwokoye and I were, she explained how she will facilitate the mediation. She actually explained that to me, Nwokoye knew how lawyers proceed in this case. Through her, I consented to try to resolve the dispute in accordance with Texas Family Law.

After a long meeting and many back and forth walks in the hall, Laurie D. Robinson made us reach an agreement. It was not constructive for me. DFPS was appointed as joint managing conservators, which means they had the exclusive right to participate in any activity regarding Tabô and Loylla while we, Sheebah and I, as parents, had all rights listed in TFC Chap 153.073 and 153.074. Since Tabô was now in juvenile, my child support payment was reduced to $600 a month. I had to pay that amount for her well-being, not to Sheebah this time but to Department of Family and Protective Services by wage withholding order. That was decided to be continuing through September 1, 2012. I also had to pay $85 a week to continue providing health, dental, eye insurance for both children. It was settled from that that Sheebah pays only $150 a month to CPS because she was still without job and homeless. But she had the duty to participate in hospital bills. She also had to continue her therapy for drug related as ordered by Dr Farmer. On that, Laurie D. Robinson decided that she should attend a NA group and obtain a NA sponsor. All groups in that mediation came to a decision that Loylla should continue with Dr Radamaki as primary care doctor. The only good thing I heard in that meeting was that once Tabô is out, both children will continue living with me at Pecan Street and Sheebah will be enjoined from corporal punishment of all her children. She also won't expose all her children to her numerous boyfriends. She will forgive the remaining of back child support of $12,749.62 from July 30, 2012, and so forth.

We freely and without duress settled this thing with the advice of Meda Bourland and Violet Nwokoye. It was a must that the agreement reached by the negotiating team stayed binding and not subject of and to revocation. Laurie said that it shall be enforceable as any other contract. Both lawyers advised us to appear in court after that. They wanted us to be there when presenting evidences to the judge to secure the rendition. When we stepped out, I approached Sheebah. I asked her to tell me what she received at the end of the day.

"What do you mean?" she asked back.

"After fighting the wrong fight for more than ten years, trying to get custody of children you abandoned. What did you get in return?" I asked again.

"What did I get?"

"Yes, what you got besides destroying your children's lives and obliterating mine. I asked you in the beginning to stop your foolishness. You did not listen. I said to you, no judge in right mind will give you my children. You did not listen. I did not want to be in this mediation meeting because I knew the outcome, but I did it for Tabô and Loylla. I did not want to meet you in the middle, but I learned a couple of reasonable tools during this fight. I accepted to mediate for both my girls. They were going wild, they are going wild. They are wild. I did it for them, hopping that something good will come out of it, but alas, it is too late. Tabô is in Juvee already and Loylla is in her way in. And you did that," I said.

"You were asked to negotiate when we went to the orientation meeting, you refused. You were asked to make a deal with me when the trial started. You preferred to fight in court. I personally begged you to get back together and live at same place, trying to raise them together, you talked about whooping God. Please be responsible, share the blame," she answered.

"I said it already. I did not want to negotiate with you. You abandoned them. You only come back to destroy them and to make them go wild. Kids don't just go wild like that. My daughters were not born to be wild, and they did not become what they became by themselves, you did that. I categorically refused to even hear anyone talking about you and me getting together. I refused because there was nothing in it for my children, you abandoned and then come back to annihilate by tearing them slowly down. What kind of man would I have been if I lived with a woman who spent her times sleeping with anything that was moving? Do not blame anything on me. My question remains: what did you get? "

"You were always sick. Even now, I don't think you will be able to take care of them. You are still sick," she said.

"Since when does a sick person not take care of his own children? Was I not sick when I was paying child support to you? You did not complain then, did you?"

"That money was used to feed my daughters. I carried them in me for nine months each. They came out from my tummy. I fed them with my breast, not yours. They are my children."

"No doubt about it. But a wise man from Ghana said that when you put a quarter in a vending machine and a can of soda pops out, that can doesn't belong to the machine, not anymore," I answered.

"What?"

"You heard me. When did you feed my children when they were with me?"

"It was a good idea to take these deals when they were offered to you. If you have taken them, we wouldn't have been bitterly fighting the way we did. We wouldn't have arrived here," she answered.

"These deals you said? Any deal, even negligible, concerning you was not a good idea. I refused all of them, even the one my lawyer made for me. I refused them all not because they were coming from y'all, but because those were not the fight I was fighting for. The kind of deal you just saw me signing for, in there, is the mother of all worse ideas that I shouldn't even be talking about right now. The mediation lady asked me to let you be a participant in my kids' activities. I let myself agree only because I am trying to save Tabô from where you put her and where she may go after that. I did it for her. She is my hope of influence. She shouldn't even ever go through things you made her go through, but you did just that. What you were doing, what you did, what you have been doing, what you have done was nothing but plain cruel to both Tabô and Loylla. See, Ma said once that feed your child so he can grow teeth, for he will feed you when you will lose yours. I fought each yard to keep both girls safe for that reason, for you first. I fought hard for them to have nothing but moments of joy and triumph. You derailed them every time I set them back on. And we both lost them. You derailed them again every moment I made them stand up. My only prayer to you, as you continue having children, is that when they reach the age of turbulence, they don't make you suffer the way you made mine make me suffer. The day you will done losing them because of what you are doing to them, you will also lose every included smile that came wrapped, not outside as a Christmas gift, but in them as a God-given presence. When that happens, you will finally open your eyes and see, with your heart, how much you made me lose. But it will be late. You will also see that you made me lose the hope I have been, with a great patience, cultivating in them through a dosed and real edification. That day will be the day you will know what I have been feeling through the fight you forced upon me and what I am feeling right at this very moment. As Muisangie Lumpungu, my mother, would have said it to you, and I paraphrase it, with you, Sheebah, I started with nothing and I still have most of it left."